The Call to Hawai'i

A Wellness Vacation Guidebook

Laura and Betsy Crites

Aloha Wellness Publishers
Honolulu, HI
808.223.2533
www.alohawellnesstravel.com

The Call to Hawai'i: A Wellness Vacation Guidebook

Published by:

Aloha Wellness Publishers
2333 Kapi'olani Blvd. #2108
Honolulu, HI 96826-4444
808.223.2533
www.alohawellnesstravel.com

First Edition

Visit our Website at www.alohawellnesstravel.com for additional information on wellness opportunities in Hawai'i.

ISBN 0-9727548-0-6

9 780972 754804 51500>

Cover picture: Nohoanu; Hinahina, *Geranium arboreum*

The extraordinary photograph on the cover of this book is by David Liittschwager and Susan Middleton from *Remains of a Rainbow: Rare Plants and Animals of Hawai'i* produced in association with Environmental Defense (National Geographic Books; 2001). Susan and David have published three books about endangered species and give slide lectures. Prints of their work are also available for sale. They can be contacted about new photography, slide presentations or prints by e-mail at esp2@mindspring.com or by phone in San Francisco at 415-543-7311.

Cover Design by Kunio Hayashi

Book Design by Joan Ryan of Plum Media Productions

Production Coordination by Valenti Print Group

The listings and information in this guidebook are based on information provided Aloha Wellness Travel and experienced by its authors. The authors are not responsible for the products and services offered by the listed and reviewed wellness providers and shall have no liability whatsoever for the direct or indirect, special or consequential damages relating in any way to the use of information provided by *The Call to Hawai'i: A Wellness Vacation Guidebook* or any of its sponsors resulting from any failure of statements or information implied or otherwise.

~ Table of Contents ~

~ Acknowledgements ~

In creating this book we have held the vision that Hawai'i could play a role in healing a wounded planet. Throughout the process, it was clear to us that many forces supported that vision. The many meaningful coincidences, the obstacles that became opportunities, and the sometimes painful path that led both of us to this work made it clear that a higher dimension was involved. To the spiritual realm, within and around us, and to the angels, seen and unseen, we give thanks.

We were supported by the enthusiasm of so many who responded to our vision and we were inspired by those who had held the vision much longer than we had.

We are grateful to **David Liittschwager and Susan Middleton** for their marvelous work that led to our cover. Their photographs of the endangered species of Hawai'i created a deeply moving exhibit at the Honolulu Art Academy and a book, *Remains of a Rainbow,* that has touched many lives. We've taken our cover picture from that exhibit. These endangered species are not only precious but serve as a symbol for the endangered planet, Earth.

We especially want to thank those who reviewed various stages of the manuscript, **Eve Hogan, Debra Greene, Virginia Beck, Zara Jean Christine, Kay Snow-Davis, Sharman O'Shea, Valerie Myles, Gerrie Morisky, Gary Berman and Pati Wilson**. **Carol Perry and Lynn Eklund** were particularly helpful in reviewing the Hawaiian information.

Our thanks also to **Zara**, on Maui, and **Aiko Aiyana**, on the Island of Hawai'i, for their diligent work in letting wellness providers know about the opportunity to be involved in the Guidebook. A special thanks to **Joan Levy** for informing her network on Kaua'i about the Guidebook as well as for the many years she put into promoting wellness tourism, building the foundation for the work we are now doing. Several of the wellness categories were inspired by a speech that **Dr. Pauline Sheldon** of the **University of Hawaii School of Travel Industry Management** gave on wellness tourism. She is one of the early visionaries in this field. We're especially grateful to **Joan Ryan** who did the design and much of the production on the book. Her commitment to using her considerable skills in crafting a visually appealing book and the long hours she spent in the production and lay out of the book were indispensable. **Jennifer Lum** of **Valenti Print Group** continued the production process with broken foot propped up to ease the pain. **Kuni Hayashi** was not only the designer of the cover but a friend throughout the process.

Special thanks to **Judy Yorimoto** with **www.wallstreetwebpages.com** for her help in creating a website, *www.alohawellnesstravel.com*, that will continue to supplement and expand on the information provided in this guidebook. Finally, thanks to **Tim Keck**, Laura's husband, for his continuing support and encouragement in all that she does.

This book was made possible, in part, by a grant from the **Hawai'i Tourism Authority**. We are deeply grateful for all of the people with the Hawai'i Tourism Authority and the **Hawai'i Visitors and Convention Bureau** who share our vision of Hawai'i as a spiritual place with a natural healing energy that transcends the individual healing and wellness resources listed in our directory.

"The ancient ones believed that all time is now and that we are each creators of our life's conditions. We create ourselves and everything that becomes a part of our lives. Any situation we might find ourselves in is brought about by us – in learning the many pathways of life."

Kaili'ohe Kame'ekua
Tales from the Night Rainbow

Introduction

The events that followed 9/11, combined with the severe problems our world already faced, have called us, individually and collectively, to take stock. How are we to heal our broken world? How can we begin to address the pain and suffering of the people, animals, and ecosystems that are striving to co-exist on this small planet? The voices of the sages, past and present, have repeatedly told us that we must begin with ourselves, with our own lives. Jesus told us to remove the beam from our own eye before attempting to remove the splinter from another's. Buddha focused his entire Eight-Fold Path on the need to perfect our own thought, conduct, and way of relating to others. They understood that our outer world reflects our collective inner worlds. Until we reach the critical mass that shifts our consciousness to a higher level, the compelling urges of fight or flight will keep us mired in isolation or conflict. If we are ever to choose love over fear on a grand global scale, we will first have to face the demons in our own hearts and minds.

When understood from this view, advancing our personal journey toward wellness of the mind, heart, body, and, spirit, and seeking greater love and understanding in our relationships becomes the highest contribution we can make toward healing the world. This may require retreating from the everyday world for awhile. A wellness vacation offers a quiet time away from the persistent media messages of fear, and gives us a time to reassess and reorder our lives. Taking time to deepen the daily practices that transform and enrich our world are large steps forward on our journey to wholeness.

There are many places with an environment conducive to healing and filled with gifted people. In our opinion there are none that equal Hawai'i. A magical convergence has occurred on these islands. Hawai'i is blessed with a year-round ideal climate, a rare and precious natural environment evolved from eons of isolation, an ancient culture full of wisdom for our times, and many modern healers and sages. For reasons we will discuss in this book, we believe Hawai'i has great power to contribute to the transformational shift needed in our world. But for this to occur, visitors need to view their vacations as more than a chance to get a good tan and see the sights.

From our outpost in the middle of the Pacific, Hawai'i offers the tools and the supportive culture and environment to launch an exciting voyage of personal discovery. These idyllic islands can be profoundly restorative to the intentional seeker who views the wellness journey as a movement toward balance and harmony on all levels of our being—the mind, heart, body and spirit. For those who open their heart and mind to new ways of viewing the world, Hawai'i will take you deep. For all of us, Hawai'i has issued a call—not just to a destination, but to our own healing journey.

Recognizing that there are many paths to achieving balance and harmony, our approach to wellness vacations is broadly defined. It may take some people down the path of lifestyle change or on an inner pilgrimage to explore the spiritual realms. It may take some to the path of service. Still others may need to address physical issues more directly through relaxation or fitness or therapeutic attention. We believe that connecting with the healing power of nature is a key element of everyone's vacation in Hawai'i.

We hope you will explore the cultural traditions of the Hawaiians as part of your vacation, for they have much to offer the world. Their voyage of rediscovery as a people in search of their true values and culture is an inspiration for the process we can all undertake. The first stage of the voyage is an honest assessment of our current location. Where are we in our life journey? Where are we stuck, unwell, anxious, disheartened, or in need of clarity or change? Stage two is taking the voyage, and for this we suggest seven categories of wellness vacations, which may help you focus on the type of healing journey that meets your deepest needs.

The Call to Hawai'i supports your journey in several ways. We invited some of the most respected alternative wellness practitioners in the state to write about the history, science, and technique of the healing methods or path of service they practice. You will also learn about their own personal healing journey. Due to limited space many of the excellent articles submitted could not be included in the book, but will be featured on the Aloha Wellness Travel website: www.alohawellnesstravel.com.

In addition, we have provided a resource section at the end of each island chapter listing providers by category of wellness vacation. Free listings were available to any who wanted to be included. This project could not have been completed, however, without a partial grant from the Hawai'i Tourism Authority and the financial support for matching funds provided by those wellness providers who purchased space. Their confidence and support for us to manifest a vision we all share has been essential.

Finally, *The Call to Hawai'i* provides some navigation for your journey by reviewing wellness providers. They are only a sample of the hundreds of very fine practitioners who are available to residents and visitors alike. Please note that we include the phone number with our review but additional contact information, including websites, is listed in the Resources section at the back of each island chapter.

Some treatments we describe may seem outside the box from a traditional standpoint, but the testimonials are mounting of people who have found improved health and sometimes remarkable healing through alternative/complementary therapies. So we have kept an open mind. We reviewed those who we personally experienced, or who came highly recommended through several sources. We considered it important that they work from a holistic perspective. We also looked at training, credibility, and professionalism. As we became more aware of the many roads to health, we began to feel more positive about the overall direction our society is taking with the help of these pioneers.

Having said that, we caution you that there are no guarantees. Our experience is just that: our experience. The therapies we sampled are gentle and non invasive. It is hard to imagine that any of them could be harmful, but we must disclaim any responsibility for the outcomes. It will help not to expect dramatic results. Gentle therapies usually work slowly, which is why they are so safe.

The question may arise as to whether it makes sense to start a therapy that cannot be continued, at least not with the same provider. Many of the therapists we visited offer tools for on-going practice or exercise. They may prescribe nutritional or herbal remedies that can be continued, and many can also be available for phone consultation. Some travelers discover a helpful treatment while on vacation and then seek out a similar practitioner in their area, or come back to Hawai'i for the therapies that are not available where they live.

For these and all the wellness experiences you try while in Hawai'i, we invite your feedback. You will find a place to give us your comments and stories on our website, www.alohawellnesstravel.com, which we envision as an ever-expanding network of providers and wellness vacationers. Let us know how this book helped you and what you would like to see in a second edition.

We hope you will respond to the call of Hawai'i and will find your way to her healing shores. Regardless, we wish you wellness in the fullest sense of the word. We trust that as each of you comes more in to the fullness of life you will make your contribution to the healing of the world.

Aloha

Aloha is being a part of all
And all being a part of me.
When there is pain—it is my pain.
When there is joy—it is mine also.
I respect all that is
As part of the Creator and part of me.
I will not willfully harm anyone or anything.
When food is needed I will take only my need
And explain why it is being taken.
The earth, the sky, the sea are mine
To care for, to cherish and to protect.
This is Hawaiian—This is Aloha!

Tales of the Night Rainbow

~ Chapter One ~

The Call to Hawai'i: A Voyage of Rediscovery

There is a mystical quality about Hawai'i that we believe can contribute to the healing and well being of all who visit here. We experience it as soon as we arrive. Gentle trade winds cool our skin, the fragrance of plumeria blossoms welcomes us, the moist air caresses us, and the grandeur of the mountains and clear blue waters fill us with awe and joy. As one newly-arrived friend exclaimed—"How can you stand such beauty!" While this is part of the magic of Hawai'i, there is something more which calls to us in a deep way. In this book we attempt to identify this quality and guide you to find and consciously experience it in a way that will transform your life.

People come here longing for something that is missing in their lives. Whether they consume their time shopping, eating, swimming and golfing or lying on the beach and allowing themselves to just "be", few people return home without having been deeply affected by their time in Hawai'i. As Garrison Keillor said when he aired one of his *Prairie Home Companion* radio shows from Honolulu, "When you return home from a vacation in Hawai'i, you just want to be a better person." Mark Twain described Hawai'i as a place where you can get drunk without drinking.

One of the first astronauts to circle the planet Earth recalled seeing two things that deeply moved him. First was the smoke from the burning of the Amazon jungle which filled him with despair. The other he described as "exquisite emerald jewels" in the middle of the Pacific which filled him with hope...Hawai'i.

What is it about Hawai'i? We believe it is a combination of three things—***aloha*** (the generosity and loving spirit of the Hawaiian people), ***'āina*** (the beauty and energy of the land and environment), and ***mana*** (the spiritual energy present in this most isolated land in the world). All of these qualities are intertwined and deeply influenced by the native Hawaiian culture.

A*loha* ~ Foremost among those qualities is the aloha spirit. It is more than a friendly greeting reserved for tourists—it's a way of life. It reflects those values identified at the beginning of this chapter. Jack London wrote ***"In what land save this one is the commonest form of greeting not "Good day," nor "How d'ye do," but "love"? That greeting is Aloha—love, I love you, my love to you."***

This spirit of aloha, of generosity, forgiveness and love, comes from the native Hawaiian people. Remarkably it has survived in spite of over 200 years of oppression. Hawaiians struggle with self-esteem issues, experience severe health problems and have their share of social dysfunction. But the soul of the Hawaiian people has prevailed and they often offer us a model of peace and understanding.

A recent situation at an international conference entitled *Building Bridges Through Traditional Knowledge* serves as a perfect example. In one of the smaller sessions being conducted by a group of native Hawaiians a very angry woman from Latin America began to dominate the group with her accusations of injustice against her people. While her anger was clearly justified, the negative energy that she sent out into the room weakened and diminished us all.

Gently, one of the Hawaiian leaders began to recite a prayer in her native language. The singsong rhythm and the deep tonality of this *pule* as well as the calm with which it was recited, filled the room with understanding and healing energy. This reflected the Hawaiian tradition of mending relationships and cooling heated arguments with prayer, followed by *ho'omalu* (a period of silence.) So often, Hawaiians model for all of us here a loving and peaceful approach to resolving conflict and healing old wounds. A foundation to their healing work is the concept of forgiveness, which they call *ho'oponopono*, an act of aloha.

Hawaiians are gentle people with a soft and flowing energy that is reflected in their music, their dance, and their language. The Hawaiian language has a lyrical quality with only five vowels and seven consonants, as opposed to English with six vowels and twenty consonants. Their consonants are soft with "k" being the hardest sound. Interestingly, Hawaiians have no swear words in their language.

The spirit of aloha of the Hawaiian people has infused itself deeply into the culture and personality of Hawai'i. It diminishes the wounding aspects of Western culture—the fierce independence, competitiveness and materialism which isolate and diminish us in ways we don't fully understand. We believe this aloha spirit is one of the enduring appeals of Hawai'i that pulls people here in response to that deep longing that has no name.

Mana ~ Accompanying the aloha spirit, but a separate and distinct concept which contributes to the magic of Hawai'i is mana (spirituality). Renowned chanter John Lake describes the concept of mana as recognition that there is an omnipotent force that is the first source. As the first source, it is embodied in all that is.

In 1982, George Kanahele, the reputed leader of the Hawaiian renaissance, engineered a series of workshops designed to clarify "***Hawaiianness***"; the goals and values of the Hawaiian people. What surfaced were the following in rank order—aloha, humility, spirituality, generosity, graciousness, keeping promises, intelligence, cleanliness and helpfulness. (Contrast this with the American values listed by John Macionis in his textbook *Sociology*: equal opportunity, achievement and success, material comfort, activity and work, practicality and efficiency, progress, science, democracy and free enterprise, freedom, racism and group superiority.) These workshops produced a general agreement that spirituality, or mana, described an awareness of the supernatural, divine power.

Early Hawaiian culture saw a vast number of things as sacred ranging from rocks to names to ancestors bones. What was sacred had power which could support or extinguish life. Abolishing the *kapu* system around 1819 did much to diminish the list of what was sacred. Among that which prevailed, however, is belief in the power and prevalence of divine energy. Hawaiian culture exhibits this belief in many ways. These include the tradition of opening and closing meetings with a *pule* (Hawaiian prayer) or chant. They also pray before beginning any healing activity. No Hawaiian healer will begin their work without invoking divine power whether they see it as a Christian God or a universal spiritual energy. Even more significant, they define their role as simply facilitating a connection between the universal spirit and the inner healer and spiritual core of the client/patient.

The long-held belief of the people of these islands that a supernatural, divine power is present in all that is, all that we say and do, contributes to the universal appeal of Hawai'i.

'Āina ~ Finally, that belief in the spirituality of all things has had its effect on the land. We consider the 'āina (the land or earth and all that sustains it) the third powerful influence drawing people to Hawai'i for healing. One of the Hawaiian creation legends described nature and humans as siblings, created simultaneously. They were to be mutually supportive and loving. Early Hawaiians were deeply dependent on nature in this most isolated chain of islands. This dependency encouraged respect, if not reverence, for the 'āina. Rather than seeing nature as an adversary to be conquered, harnessed, and forced to produce, Hawaiians viewed it as a trusted friend, a sibling to be nurtured, respected, and listened to. Most of all there was a constant extension of gratitude for all that nature offered.

Today, Hawaiian tradition maintains that relationship with the land for spiritual rather than survival reasons. They ask permission of a plant before picking it. They use flower leis to honor and celebrate. And their chants and hula often reflect that mutually supportive relationship with nature.

Thus, although there are many beautiful places around the world, the reverence and honoring of the land by the first people to live here contributes to the special energy of the 'āina of Hawai'i. Over 1500 years of the practice of this philosophy instilled such values into the culture of Hawai'i.

Aloha, mana, 'āina—all of these greet the visitor to Hawai'i. For the wellness traveler there is more. What the Hawaiians offer as a guide for our wellness journey is the process of their own voyage of rediscovery, the Hawaiian renaissance. This voyage was literally and figuratively launched with the Hōkūle'a, a double-hulled canoe modeled after the canoes that brought the first Polynesians to Hawai'i.

The destination of the Hōkūle'a, in 1976, was Tahiti. In going there, the leaders sought to return Hawaiians to their source. They looked to answer the questions, ***"Who are we?"*** and

"How did we get to where we now are?" In the words of Nainoa Thompson, the canoe's navigator, "Our goal was to recapture our traditions, to make our people feel proud of those traditions and therefore proud about themselves." *(Voices of Wisdom)* It was a voyage of healing, an emotional rebirthing. Little did they know that this voyage would deeply touch not only Hawaiians but also people through all Polynesia and Micronesia from the Cook Islands to Tahiti. The influence of this journey of rediscovery can extend to touch our lives as well.

What was most remarkable about the voyage of the Hōkūle'a was that it was conducted without compass or any technological means of navigation. Over thousands of miles, a single navigator guided the ship by means of acute observation and awareness. The motion of the waves, the direction of the wind, and the position of the stars were his guide. And there were times when even these resources disappeared. Nainoa Thompson describes the doldrums, an area near the equator where one becomes blind as a navigator—the cloudiest place on earth. At this point he was told by his mentor, *"Don't look with your eyes. Let that go. Look inside to find the answers."* What happened next is a moment of clarity for him and for all of us who are on a journey of rediscovery. *"It was getting very intense and I was extremely tired. I was so exhausted. I turned to the rail and I locked my elbows on the rail and tried to get rest standing up. In doing that, in all this rain and all this cold, I felt this really warm sensation and my mind got very clear. I could feel the moon. I knew the moon was up, but didn't know where it was because I couldn't see it. But somehow I could tell the direction." (Voices of Wisdom)*

For him, as well as for the rest of us, achieving this deep knowing was a spiritual experience, the ultimate guide when there was no other way to see.

Throughout this book we will shine a light on the Hawaiian renaissance and their voyage of rediscovery as a metaphor for our own journey. In doing so, it isn't our intention to romanticize the Hawaiian people. Nor is it our purpose to turn you into a Hawaiian. As one wise elder said, *"You can't suck up another culture with the straw of your own culture."* In our journey toward balance and harmony, toward true wellness, we need to explore who we are in the context of our own culture. The values of the native Hawaiian people and their process of rediscovering these values can illuminate our own exploration. Most of all, the nurturing and supportive culture of aloha, the spiritual power of mana, and the beauty of the 'āina provide the perfect launching point for your journey toward wellness.

Hawai'i invites you for a wellness vacation.

"Don't look with your eyes.

Let that go.

Look inside to find the answers."

Nainoa Thompson
Native Hawaiian navigator

Chapter Two

Preparing for the Voyage

As they began their cultural renaissance or voyage of rediscovery, the goal of the Hawaiians was to return to their source and to their roots as a people. From the many health, social and personal problems of the Hawaiian people, it was clear that they had become lost. Economic, religious, and political values imposed by the European-influenced missionaries did not represent their true nature. They did not expect to recreate the life they had before the arrival of the missionaries and whaling ships. Instead, they looked for a foundation that could help them rebuild their cultural identity. They knew the general direction of the voyage would be to rediscover the wisdom and culture of their ancestors, but they did not know the final destination.

Most of us could look to our own lives for the same evidence that the larger culture has taken us off course from who we are and how we want to live our lives. The pursuit of material wealth leaves us feeling empty. Our careers demand so much of us that we lose connection with those we care about and the activities that create joy in our lives. Competition forces us to feel isolated from, rather than supported by others. A heavy emphasis on right brain cognitive thinking separates us from our creative impulses.

The following stories are about people who realized they had lost something important in their lives. Through their vacation in Hawai'i they began their voyage of rediscovery.

For the past six years, Cliff and Jean have lived for their week-long vacation in Maui with their two children, now teenagers. The Mid-West couple are both high-achieving surgeons with the accompanying heavy schedule and professional demands on their time. Each year they spent their vacation in Maui visiting boutiques, getting a suntan, enjoying the fresh air and scenery and just relaxing. At the end of their week, however, they returned to their hectic lives racing to stay on top of the workload and longing at a deep level for their next trip to Maui. Nothing fundamental changed in their lives until a crisis hit. Jean was diagnosed with a chronic debilitating disease and was forced to quit her practice altogether.

The next year the family took two weeks in Maui and this time tried something different. From the time she was a small child, Jean had a passion about horses. "I chose my friends based on whether they had horses, so I could go riding." she told us. Cliff had grown up on a farm and also felt a strong affinity for horses. After Jean's illness, a shift occurred at some level and she felt drawn to reconnect with this source of passion and wonder. We met the family at the Maui Horsewhisper Experience in Makawao. Franklin Levinson was showing them how to establish trust and rapport so the horse would follow without a bridle. The entire family was experiencing a form of animal therapy.

Six years of vacations on Maui had been fun and relaxing, but they had not led to lasting changes in their lives. Finally, pushed by adverse circumstances to take more time and try new healing activities, the family was having a wellness vacation. They were reconnecting with something they had lost, something that gave them joy and satisfied a deep unspoken longing. The story of Cliff and Jean is reminiscent of the native Hawaiians who had lost touch with their source of wisdom and identity.

Chris came to Hawai'i from Seattle to get a break from her stressful job in emergency management and to try to learn from her experiences with breast cancer. She came to join Suzan Starr, founder and facilitator of the Art of the Dove a retreat experience for women recovering from cancer. "I had been under tremendous stress about my work, my health, and my partner's health." Chris told us. She had met Suzan in her art shop, **Dreams of Paradise,** in Hilo, on a previous visit and at that time discovered they were both breast cancer survivors and sailors, as well as artists. The sailing portion of the Art of Dove program was especially appealing.

When she launched out on the sailing retreat, Chris was transported to another world. "You can read a thousand books," she said, "but this takes you up and out of your daily life." While sailing, they listened to the whales with a hydrophone, did drumming, had deep talks, reflected on Hawaiian life philosophies, and absorbed the beauty. "The retreat was great. It wasn't that easy. The insights were hard, but good. I was able to look myself in the face and deal with it. It was more than a vacation".

When she got home, the positive feedback from her partner was immediate. What changed for Chris was her perspective. She gained clarity on what was important in her life. Chris continued with her job, but took more time off to be with her partner who was dying of cancer and started doing art therapy.

Both examples illustrate possibilities for a wellness vacation in Hawai'i. The critical difference is that Chris came with intention, having planned and prepared for the voyage. She left home prepared to make significant changes in her life, though she wasn't sure what they would be. After her wellness vacation she was inspired to make those changes.

We believe that everyone who comes to Hawai'i can have a relaxing and restorative vacation, just as Cliff and Jean did each year. But for them, as with most people, the effects of the vacation soon disappear. The more profound impact of a wellness vacation is only likely to occur if launched with the kind of intention that Chris took.

One goal of this book is to encourage you to come to Hawai'i with a wellness intention. This can be a two-stage process. First, establish your current location, that is, assess where you are at the levels of mind, heart, body and spirit. Second, decide what kind of experiences could best move you toward your wellness goals.

STAGE ONE: ESTABLISHING YOUR CURRENT LOCATION

The starting point, or first stage, for the voyage of rediscovery is knowing where you are now. This means asking the hard questions about where you experience imbalance and disharmony in your life. The following questionnaire is designed to help you assess your current level of wellness, your "location".

WELLNESS ASSESSMENT INSTRUMENT

Mark each statement with a number using the following scale: 1 strongly disagree; 2 disagree; 3 agree; 4 strongly agree.

___ 1. I am experiencing higher than normal levels of stress in my life.
___ 2. I would like to have more meaning and purpose in my life.
___ 3. My life feels limited by a chronic physical condition.
___ 4. I'm having trouble getting over an experience of grief or loss.
___ 5. I feel I am at a turning point or transition in my life.
___ 6. I've been diagnosed with an illness which I believe, or have been told, is life- threatening.
___ 7. I would like to improve my ability to have intimate relationships generally and/or with my current partner.
___ 8. I'm feeling bored or unfulfilled in my life.
___ 9. I would like to be in better shape physically.
___ 10. I wish I had more peace, joy and harmony in my life.
___ 11. My life often seems to be out of control.
___ 12. I know that my nutritional habits are not the best.
___ 13. My work is often dissatisfying.
___ 14. I would like to work on habits and behaviors which I know undermine my health and well-being.
___ 15. I work more hours than is probably healthy.
___ 16. I know I need a change but I just don't know where or how to begin.
___ 17. I need more relaxation and pleasure in my life.
___ 18. I often feel like I'm not good enough or smart enough.
___ 19. I long to do something fun outdoors in nature.
___ 20. I'm tired a lot.

Score Total __________

WELLNESS ASSESSMENT SCORES

20-34 I am leading a fairly balanced life, have developed healthy habits and am relatively free from illness. I might consider a wellness vacation to Hawai'i for preventive purposes and to further advance my wellness journey.

35-49 Something seems to be blocking my wellness goals. Where am I "stuck"? What aspects of my life are holding me back? What prevents me from realizing my full potential? A wellness vacation focusing on areas needing attention could give me the boost I need to move forward on my dreams.

50-64 My wellness journey seems seriously off track. What are the core issues that keep me from achieving balance and harmony in my life? Planning a wellness vacation to Hawai'i in the next 12 months would constitute a solid step in getting back on course.

66-80 I'm experiencing serious stress and imbalance at all levels of my being. It's time to seek new levels of assistance and to begin planning a wellness vacation as soon as possible.

STAGE TWO: PLANNING THE VOYAGE

The second stage of the journey is planning your direction and what you will take with you in the way of intention and awareness. One of the most powerful aspects of the voyage of the Hōkūle'a as metaphor is the profound intuitive skills that the navigators used to guide the canoe. Without a compass or any sophisticated instruments, they successfully sailed thousands of miles using only their intuition and finely tuned skills of awareness—of the wind, waves, stars, and moon. These are the ultimate tools for all of us on our voyage of rediscovery—our intuitive wisdom and our willingness to be aware of ourselves, our surroundings, and our process.

There are many avenues of approach to your wellness journey and much depends on the assessment of where you are in your life and what you most need in order to achieve greater balance and harmony. We've identified the following seven categories of wellness vacations, each one consisting of a variety of activities which can address imbalances in the mind, heart, body, and spirit. These categories aren't meant to be mutually exclusive. You may decide to incorporate the goals of more than one of them into your wellness vacation.

As you plan your wellness vacation what do you most want to achieve?

Inner Pilgrimage

Many of us need to take the voyage within, an inner pilgrimage, to discover who we are and what aspects of ourselves we have lost touch with along life's journey. The purpose of the inner pilgrimage as with all pilgrimages is to carry us to a sacred site—that site within, sometimes called the Higher Self, Spirit, Soul, or True Self. The Hawaiians considered it their "source".

This type of wellness vacation could include meditation, spiritual retreats, sacred healing, shamanic journeys, art and art therapy, self-reflection and personal development, vision quests, astrology readings, sessions with an intuitive guide, dance therapy, visiting sacred sites, and Hawaiian spirituality. The story of Chris was an illustration of an Inner Pilgrimage.

There are unique qualities to a Hawaiian vacation that can make an Inner Pilgrimage especially powerful. The ancient culture of Hawai'i has left a legacy of sacred sites and inspiring customs and practices that can give a vacationer a context for profound reflection. Also, the extraordinary natural wonders of an active volcano, an ideal climate, beautiful beaches, pristine ocean water, clean air, and lush tropical vegetation all lovingly support your intention to go deeply into your journey of rediscovery.

Lifestyle Modification

You may decide that in order for your wellness vacation to have a lasting impact, you need to make changes in your lifestyle. To do that, you could focus on a lifestyle modification vacation.

The goal of this type of vacation is to identify what in your life is keeping you off balance and how you can change it. Vacation time is perfect for this purpose. You're away from the stresses that limit you, and you have the time to rise above your life back home to take an objective look at what isn't working.

Changes may range from stopping self-destructive behavior such as smoking and unhealthy eating to releasing yourself from a relationship that diminishes you or a job or career that deadens you. You could try hypnotherapy, visiting a life coach or nutrition and exercise coach, or staying at a wellness retreat where you can have on-going support and advice while you're here.

Nature as Healer

One critical aspect of life that many people have lost touch with is the wisdom and healing quality of nature. We have become a highly urbanized society. If you find your way to nature it will probably be through recreation. We no longer live on the land. Perhaps the loss of connection to nature is one of the primary reasons people seek out Hawai'i and its legendary beauty.

A "nature as healer" vacation involves intentional and meaningful contact with the natural world in order to promote greater levels of spiritual and emotional awareness. Nature can also provide answers to questions and issues begging for resolution. On this vacation, you may seek opportunities to quietly commune with nature and allow its healing magic to restore your heart and soul. This can include benefiting from the healing power of animals such as dolphins, whales or horses, visiting gardens, hiking, going on nature meditations or eco-tours, staying on or visiting a farm, or shopping at a farmers' market. Purchasing natural healing products made in Hawai'i can also be part of a nature as healer vacation.

Relaxation and Rejuvenation

A relaxation and rejuvenation vacation can relax you in a deeper way than just hanging out at the beach. It can bring you back to life—rejuvenate you. Spas offer many opportunities to help you unwind and relax including massage, facials, and body wraps, heat therapies, watsu, and aromatherapy. In each island-focused chapter, we also direct you to similar services offered by wellness providers. In order for it to be lasting, however, we suggest that you develop some skills and awareness to continue the process. Yoga, meditation, qigong, or tai chi may be the answer.

Complementary Treatment Therapies

As you continue to explore what direction you want to take on your wellness vacation, Hawai'i offers unparalleled opportunities to try alternative or complementary approaches to treatment for physical conditions. This could include acupuncture, chiropractic, naturopathic medicine, Hawaiian healing therapies, energy therapy, herbal therapy, homeopathy, preventative medical screening, reflexology, Traditional Chinese Medicine, craniosacral, sound and voice therapy, color therapy, intuitive healing among others.

Although using your vacation time for a therapy may not fit the traditional idea of a vacation, it may be the ideal time to explore some holistic approaches that are not available at home or that you haven't had time to explore. If you have a chronic condition that tends to flare up with travel, or that requires constant attention, getting an assessment and a treatment from an alternative practitioner may lead to a new understanding of the problem. It may also be an opportunity to get a second or alternative opinion.

Fitness and Sports

This approach to a wellness vacation emphasizes using the time to undertake a fitness program or enjoy your sport in an ideal climate and environment. This could include sessions at a fitness spa, golf, races, fitness coaches, trail biking, canoeing, hiking and backpacking, and many water sports.

The year-round warm balmy climate of Hawai'i makes it a perfect place to have a Fitness and Sports vacation. The weather practically pulls you outside and encourages you to be active and fit. It has become the headquarters for several of the world's most famous triathlons that combine ocean swimming with biking and running. The island environment offers a wide range of water sports including swimming, snorkeling, scuba diving, and surfing.

Travel to Serve Others

Volunteer vacations are increasingly popular ways to truly get away from your normal routine at the same time that you contribute your skills and time to a worthy cause. Our suggestions in the island chapters range from spending anywhere from an hour to a full three months leaving Hawai'i better than you found it.

Examples in Hawai'i include a beach cleanup day, spending a day or more with Habitat for Humanity, trail clearing or other environmental maintenance projects, volunteering with a senior center or a child care program, counting whales and tending turtles with the National Park Service, or doing preservation work with The Nature Conservancy.

This type of wellness vacation can have a profound effect especially at the spiritual and emotional levels. By opening our hearts to others, applying our energy and toil, and looking deeply at what is happening in the world and how we are all connected, huge shifts can occur within us that change our lives forever. It can also be great fun. Hawai'i is a place to come for nurturing and restoring our lives. But as with all relationships, it also needs nurturing. If Hawai'i is to continue to be a place of healing for ourselves and future generations, it will require our loving attention and service as well.

Healing Accommodations

Our environment can make the difference between feeling uplifted, energized, and content or feeling out of sorts, tired, and unmotivated. The oriental art of feng shui, which recommends special ways to arrange furniture, decor, and gardens to enhance a sense of well-being, has demonstrated how subtle changes in our environment can affect our energy and mood.

Most hospitality providers in Hawai'i know this instinctively, and go to considerable lengths to design an environment and services that delight the traveler. You can find Bed and Breakfasts (B&Bs), guesthouses, or vacation rentals with sublime peace and quiet, breathtaking views, enchanting gardens and charming decor for little more than the cost of a moderately priced hotel room in a city on the mainland. Some places may throw in a hot tub, garden trails, even a pool. Many accommodations also offer massage, yoga, tai chi, reiki, and other therapies for additional charge and by appointment. Still other hosts/hostesses will take you on excursions and adventure tours, even read your astrology chart or tarot cards.

Some vacationers prefer a convivial atmosphere where they can socialize with the hosts and fellow travelers, usually over breakfast, and learn about the local color and cuisine or just enjoy conversation. This is more likely to happen where a breakfast is served, so notice when B&B is part of the name. Otherwise assume you are on your own, although most guesthouses stock the kitchenette with basic ingredients for you to prepare your own breakfast, and the owners are usually available to answer questions.

We will draw your attention to lodgings that we have personally visited or stayed in and that we think will contribute to your wellness vacation. These are places where we felt the spirit of aloha was alive and well and where the environment inspired joy, ease, and sometimes awe. Some have special wellness features such as space for meditation and yoga, or in-house massage therapists, or organic food. Many can accommodate small groups and welcome retreats. We will provide the general location; the hosts will send maps or give directions when you call for reservations or a visit.

Since prices change, we have listed the range you can expect based on the following:

Luxury: $176 and up/night

Deluxe: $110-$175/night

Moderate: $61-$100/night

Budget: up to $60/night

Whatever your choice of wellness vacation, we hope you find the accommodations that truly support your wellness journey.

In the following pages you will discover many ideas to pursue greater balance and harmony in your life. We suggest that you select a few that appeal to you but remember, you don't have to do it all. A wellness vacation is not about collecting experiences. It's about deepening your experience.

"All people climb the same mountain.
The mountain, however,
has many pathways
and every pathway
has a different view."

Kaili'ohe Kame'ekua
Tales from the Night Rainbow

~ Chapter Three ~

Wellness Vacations • Many Pathways

Inner Pilgrimage

The purpose of the inner pilgrimage is to return the individual to themselves through the cultivation of a deeper level of physical, mental, emotional and spiritual awareness. This type of wellness vacation could include meditation coaches, spiritual retreats, yoga, sacred healing, past life regression, art and art therapy, self-reflection and personal development, vision quests, astrology readings, sessions with an intuitive guide, dance therapy and Hawaiian spirituality.

A pilgrimage is defined as a frequently long journey to a sacred site, or a search for a purpose and moral significance. As part of a wellness vacation, we invite you to such a pilgrimage to the sacred site within, to rediscover the purpose and significance of your life. This journey is increasingly important to many of us as we become aware that we have lost touch with who we truly are in the process of living our busy lives. The result is a deep longing for the time, space and opportunity to reconnect with our source, our deeper selves. An Inner Pilgrimage Vacation can take you on a voyage of reconnection. In this, the journey of the Hawaiians may guide the way.

In the 1970's, after nearly 200 years of increasing absorption into a foreign culture with accompanying loss of identity and self esteem, Hawaiians began a voyage of remembrance and rediscovery. That journey, many believe, began literally with the voyage of the Hōkūle'a, a replica of the first double hulled canoe that brought the Polynesian people to Hawai'i. The Hōkūle'a transported a group of Hawaiians across thousands of miles from Hawai'i to Tahiti and back, guided only by a sophisticated awareness of the natural elements.

The Hōkūle'a launched a rediscovery of the greatness of the early Hawaiian people—the advanced knowledge that brought them to Hawai'i, the complex understanding of the body and its ability to heal, the remarkable memory that allowed them to pass down epic historical chants, and the superior quality of their farming skills. The following two writers and Hawaiian leaders contributed enormously to the process of rediscovery: George Kanahele's ***Ku Kanaka" Stand Tall: A Search for Hawaiian Values*** and Mary Pukui's two volume set ***Nana I Ke Kumu "look to the source"***. These books provided a written account of the beliefs, lifestyle and values of Hawaiians through the ages. At the same time, Hawaiian leaders engaged groups in exploring "what is Hawaiianness."

This renaissance has brought increasing peace to the souls of many Hawaiians. They have rediscovered their true values. The question they have been asking for several decades has relevance for each of us—"Who am I really?" Their gift to all of us is the invitation to engage in our own journey of remembering—an "Inner Pilgrimage" supported by the values of *aloha*, generosity, and spirituality.

There are many resources available for you to begin such a pilgrimage while on vacation in Hawai'i. The articles that follow may open some avenues for you. "Sacred Healing" talks about the Hawaiians' sense of the sacred in their approach to health, especially with respect to the gathering of herbs and the practice of forgiveness. The PsychoSpiritual perspective "takes (the) evolution in our understanding of the human mind in health and illness one step further to include the spiritual nature of a person." Walking a Labyrinth can be another powerful raft for a quiet, introspective and solitary journey to our inner selves.

There are many paths leading to the same destination. You may be on a fulfilling spiritual path and find these articles of academic interest, or they may pique your curiosity to explore something new. Whatever your path, we wish you peace and aloha on your journey.

PSYCHO-SPIRITUAL THERAPY

Joan Levy, MSW, ACSW, LCSW, QCSW, LSW,

Our modern understanding of the frailties of the human mind has been defined by the medical model, which sees the human being as a biomechanical interplay of structure, function, and interference that can result in breakdown. Over the last twenty years this orientation has expanded to allow for mental and emotional influences. Psycho-spiritual Therapy takes this evolution in our understanding of what it is to be human in health and illness one step further by adding one's spiritual nature and purpose to the mix.

Origins • Including one's spirituality is relatively new to the domain of psychotherapy and is not yet included in any traditional university curriculum. However, it can be found in some alternative universities like John F. Kennedy University or the California School of Integral Studies. Carl Jung's work danced with the Divine as he explored the depth of the unconscious and collective conscious. Scholar and visionary Rudolf Steiner addressed this in the early 1900's. Popular new age authors like Thomas Moore, M. Scott Peck, Gary Zukov, Carolyn Myss, Mathew Fox, and Deepak Chopra as well as psychotherapists like Jack Kornfield, James Hillman, and John Welwood have helped weave spirituality into the fabric of present day psychotherapy. To find practitioners one must look to the "alternative", "complementary" or "new age" therapies easily found on the Internet or in healing arts magazines.

When we are born, we come in to life at one with our true nature, connected to our divine source, and with a specific psycho-spiritual purpose to fulfill. Our psychobiology, however, is very strong and we soon begin to understand our life and identify ourselves according to the physical and emotional experiences we have after our birth. When this happens, we lose the empowerment that came with the consciousness of our true nature and we identify ourselves instead as victims of circumstance and a product of our environment. We become what happened to us instead of who we actually are.

If you think of the child's mind as liquid consciousness, then her identification with her early experience pours that liquid self into a jello mold. Once the child becomes identified with the particular shape of her experience the mold is set. The screws are tightened down. Once the jello mold is solid, a pair of psychic lenses are created that will filter and direct her perception to maintain the shape of that mold. Psychic survival instinct will do whatever is necessary to maintain the life of this presumed and felt identity.

Practical Implications • Psycho-Spiritual Therapy helps the person comprehend that 1) they are not the mold but have rather been shaped by the mold, 2) psychic survival instinct skews their perception so that things that seem and feel true may not necessarily be true, and 3) they can dissolve the mold and re-pour themselves into the shape of who they really are by relinquishing false beliefs and updating their consciousness to fit what is real and true today.

To accomplish this, however, it is necessary to find the screws that were tightened when the mold was made. Although we are poured into and identified with the limitations of our jello mold, the spiritual aspect of Self knows otherwise and seeks the truth, which is our wholeness. The unprocessed trauma or pain is unconsciously stored and anchored in the physical body, set by the psychic screws when the identification took place. Trying to find those unconscious psychic screws would be like trying to find a needle in a haystack in our normal consciousness. But thanks to our emotions which have a vibrational frequency, the miracle of life brings us present-time situations that trigger emotional experience precisely attuned to the emotional frequency we felt when the mold was set. Psycho-Spiritual Therapy teaches the person to see the present triggering situation as a purposeful event that can help them find their unprocessed, unhealed past trauma or pain, and relinquish the limiting beliefs and falsehoods that are the inevitable legacy of such injury.

What to Expect • Treatment involves: identifying false beliefs and false identities; becoming aware of unconscious motivations and fears; learning to respond to what is true now and act from choice rather than unconsciously reacting from habit, past perceptions and automatic defensiveness; and utilizing the pain and dysfunction in one's life to attune to one's spiritual purpose.

An essential aspect of this work sees the psychological dilemma within the context of the spiritual purpose and essence of the individual. Any problems that might show up in the biology, psychology, or sociology of the person are related to the need for spiritual growth and development. The client is continually invited to see herself as a co-creator of her experience.

Attendance to emotional feelings is an important aspect to this work and some kind of breath work can be very useful to help the person relinquish outmoded defensive structures that unconsciously govern their perception and behavior. Bodywork and energy work can also be helpful to assist the person to let go of these structures.

Inherent to the Hawaiian Islands is an elemental healing energy that long ago flowered into powerful ancient Hawaiian healing traditions and the precious spirit of Aloha. One cannot behold the awesome beauty and magnificence of nature here in Hawai'i and not feel some connection to Spirit. The Hawaiian Islands provide an environment and context that facilitates connecting to one's spiritual nature and therefore potentiates the process of psycho-spiritual therapy.

Joan Levy

A childhood desire to be a doctor got me to college pre-med, but at 19, the adventures of life beckoned and I answered the call. Hitchhiking around the globe, from one diverse foreign land to another, I found that people are really very much the same. No matter how differently they might look, speak, or seem there is a language of the heart that knows no boundaries.

My path eventually led me to graduate school but my interests had switched from healing the body to the mind. I began my own therapy with a woman who sat on a pillow on the floor. Her ability to be so real with me encouraged me to step outside the box of mainstream psychology. And I've been stepping out ever since.

I studied whatever therapeutic systems helped me to: relinquish the tight reigns of my ego, explore and release my feelings, surrender the self-importance of my feelings, relinquish my self-hatred and the power of unconscious beliefs to dictate dysfunctional reactions and choices, and to reconnect mind and body with Spirit.

Whatever it takes to help me/us reclaim our inherent rightness of being, enables us to live a life that is open, loving, present, and on-purpose.

Joan Levy is a psychospirtiual therapist at the BodyMind & Breath Center on the island of Kaua'i. She can be reached at 808.822.5488 joan@joanlevy.com.

~ Hawaiian Sacred Healing ~

Rev. Alalani A. Hill

Origins and Practice • In ancient times healers would gather herbs to heal the body and soothe pain. Medicine men and women conducted ceremony in prayer and sacred ritual to cast out and remove bad spirits or curses. Today, the sacred aspects of healing still resonate at the same level, although fewer people commit themselves daily to "source" and to learning the teachings of the ages.

A Hawaiian healing practitioner looks into a forest with a very different perspective from the rest of us. He or she sees nature as a pharmacy, and is intimately familiar with the various plants and trees and their healing properties. The healing practitioner trained in *lā'au lapa'au* (Hawaiian herbal medicine and healing methods) sees their faces, bodies and spirits and knows them by name. For example, a *limu* (seaweed) can have a relative plant in the mountains that is used for the same ailment. Knowing that those in the mountains who were sick could not come down to the ocean, the Divine Creator created healing plants throughout the different areas.

Understanding the Spirit of the plants, and how they support our healing process, is a sacred art. The *Kahuna* (master) *lā'au lapa'au* and the *Haumana* (student or apprentice) of *lā'au lapa'au* can communicate with the Spirit in the plants. When they go out to gather, they first pray and ask the plant and its Spirit for what they need for healing. Only so many leaves are taken from each stem, some with the left hand and some with the right. Herbs are gathered with prayer, prepared with prayer and given with prayer.

Soul Searching • In the Hawaiian culture, *Ho'oponopono* is clearing through forgiveness. If a person holds on to anger, hurt, guilt, jealousy or resentment it can cause physical problems in the body. *Ho'oma'ema'e* is to clean oneself, usually through bathing in the ocean or fresh water and cleaning the inside with blessed *Kai* (salt) water. The earth, water, fire, air and ether can all be used in sacred healing. We who are trained in this form of healing can assist a person in this process.

Sacred healing of an individual comes from deep understanding and consciousness. Understanding universal laws and ancient principles is essential for a complete healing. This results from the body, mind and spirit being treated and from the individual's own soul searching. Connecting with the center of their being by bridging the individual mind with the greater universal mind can balance their awareness. This can then extend into the body. An understanding of connecting the small mind to the universal mind is imperative.

Believing one can be healed through faith is the first step. Healers are just vehicles for the Sacred energy that is all-forgiving and life giving. As healing vehicles they usually devote themselves to God and through that love they can pass the knowledge, wisdom, herbs and Spiritual energy through to the one who is sick.

Deep within a person's consciousness there is knowingness. In this place one can experience total health, a place within that is pain and disease free. To resonate in this centered space for periods of time, or timelessness, can help an individual to create profound changes in their body and their perspective on life. It is in this place that "self" can realize its unlimited nature instead of being blocked by perceived limitations. Breaking through limiting mindsets can help one to be more in harmony and experience greater health.

Hawaiian sacred healing has been passed down and survived through the ages. We would do well to listen to this wisdom and learn from the elders who carry it.

Kahu Alalani A. Hill

My journey into healing began when I was ten years old. For years I touched people and prayed. God had given me a great gift of healing touch, vision and knowing-ness. Then I was lead to a Taoist monk "Bin" in Singapore. He initiated me and taught me how to bring divine medicine inter-dimensionally on to talismans. This process is over 2000 years old. (A bamboo brush with red root powder is used on 'ōlena (turmeric) rice paper printed with prayers. The rice paper becomes the talisman when light and incense finish the process.) Then an Indian Swami and Yogi taught me of medicinal plants, healing and yoga. He initiated me in Malaysia. In the late 80"s I was called to Maui. Here I would find my greatest teacher, my Kupuna "Papa" Kahu Kawika Ka'alakea. Papa was a great Kahuna and humble Kahu (Minister). He took me in and taught me the protocols and Hawaiian Ministry. They included blessings, weddings, lā'au lapa'au (Hawaiian healing methods/ herbs), Ho'oponopono, Ho'oma'ema'e, spiritual counseling, ceremonies, baptisms and funerals. It was an honor to study under Papa and to be his assistant in his last years of life. I am humbled that Papa chose me to carry on his work. Over time the Hawaiian ways have gone deep into my Spirit and life. It is a divine blessing to serve Akua (God) through these Hawaiian practices, and to experience the blessings and miracles that are always occurring, praise be to God!

Rev. Alalani A. Hill is a Kahuna trained Kahu (Minister) who lives in Kīhei, Maui. She does spiritual counseling, healing sessions, and Hawaiian blessings and ceremonies and can be reached at 808.879.1499 or alalani@kuhina.com

~ Labyrinths: A Pilgrimage Within ~

Eve Hogan

Origins • The concept of taking a pilgrimage as a path of wellness goes back to the ancient concept of vision questing and journeys toward sacred destinations such as Jerusalem, Mecca, Lourdes, and Stonehenge, or to power places in nature. While coming to Hawai'i as a spiritual destination is certainly a pilgrimage in its own right, one can miss the spiritual aspects entirely by focusing only on the shopping, nightlife and resorts. For a sense of spirit and an experience beneficial to one's wellness, one must look a little deeper. In addition to the beautiful beaches, gardens, waterfalls and rainbows designed to replenish your soul, the labyrinth is available here as a walking meditation.

Most labyrinths built today are replicas of the 800-year old Chartres Cathedral labyrinth. In the 1200's, the Crusades were going on and taking a pilgrimage to a sacred destination meant risking your life. Rather than journey into danger, pilgrims of the 13th century took a metaphorical pilgrimage within the confines of the labyrinth and the safety of the church. Today, we use the labyrinth in much the same way.

Metaphorical Journey • The labyrinth looks like a maze but it is not. Rather than dead-ends and multiple paths to tease and challenge you, the labyrinth has only one path that winds its way into the center and the same path brings you back out. The labyrinth offers a three-fold path, just like a pilgrimage—the journey in, the sacred destination of the center, and the return back out.

The walk into the labyrinth provides an opportunity for us to begin self-observation, contemplation and release. The task is to walk the labyrinth cognizant of a "witness" state—being the observed and the observer at the same time. Simply pay attention to what you are feeling and thinking and then, with a deep breath, release it and let it go, freeing your awareness to be available for the next moment in time. The walk in is a time of preparation, as if you are emptying your mind of thoughts, memories, expectations, and judgments, so that you are open and ready to receive guidance when you reach the center. It is the journey from your head to your heart, from thought to feeling, from logic to intuition, from believing to knowing.

The center of the labyrinth, the heart, represents the sacred destination. Just as on a "real pilgrimage," here the pilgrims sit or stand in meditation open to receiving guidance or insight. Whether you receive an answer to a question, a valuable insight about your life or merely a sense of peace, solitude or joy, the center is a quiet space in which you get what you need, if not what you came for. You come to know the stillness of the center—your center—as a sanctuary to which you always have access and can return whenever your soul needs rejuvenation. For most of us with busy lives our brains are working overtime—creating a lot of noise. Seldom do we retreat to silence—away from TV, radio or conversation. The center of the labyrinth provides the solitude necessary for accessing your inner wisdom and hearing the whisper of your heart.

The journey out of the labyrinth represents Divine Alignment—returning home, in union with God, to apply in your daily life the insights and wisdom you've gained on your pilgrimage. Truly, this action step is critical for bringing about the transformation that extends beyond the pilgrimage—the transformation of your life toward wellness, wholeness, and health.

The labyrinth works with the magic of metaphor, mirroring back to us anything that stands between us as the pilgrim, and the Divine. If you simply observe what you experience as you walk, you will see that metaphorically that is also what you experience in your "real" world. If you find yourself impatient to reach the center, impatience undoubtedly impedes your path through life, as well. If you find yourself judgmental of others as they walk, your judgments are the very thing you need to release in order to enter the temple of your heart. If you walk worried about what others are thinking of you, releasing your need for approval will move you closer to the Divine. If you stay "in your head" throughout the journey counting the paths and trying to figure it out, this metaphor reveals to you that it is time to venture into the realm of feeling, rather than merely thinking about, the Divine.

A Laboratory • By allowing the labyrinth to be the laboratory where we practice self-observation, letting go, getting centered, aligned action and the magic of metaphor, we are then prepared to expand the boundary of the labyrinth to include our entire lives. After all, does your spiritual path—and the benefit of these skills—only exist within a 40-foot circle? Or, did your spiritual quest begin when you left your home, flew across the ocean to the sacred islands of Hawai'i and then returned back home the way you came? Or, did your three-fold path begin with birth, continue with the sacred center of this life, and the return journey of death? Or is your pilgrimage even bigger than that?

For a schedule of moonlight labyrinth walks see www.HeartPath.com. For a nationwide labyrinth locator, see www.gracecathedral.org.

Eve Hogan

I have been a labyrinth facilitator on Maui for six years, facilitating monthly moonlight walks, labyrinth weddings and workshops, in addition to serving as an inspirational speaker sharing relationship and communication skills. My passion is helping people to create healthy relationships, whether with their sweetheart, children, co-workers, their Self, or with God. This work has been a blessing in my own spiritual journey as the labyrinth has served as the perfect experiential tool for gaining self-mastery. As I've practiced and mastered the various aspects of walking the labyrinth, I have then been able to expand the boundary of the labyrinth and apply these skills in my daily life.

Providing labyrinth pilgrimages for locals and tourists alike has deepened my understanding of the many applications and benefits of walking the labyrinth as part of one's healing journey. Where I once thought there were "many paths to the same goal" I now believe there is one path, but many ways to walk it! This work led me to writing "Way of the Winding Path: A Map to the Labyrinth of Life" (released Fall, 2002). Of course, Hawai'i is a sacred pilgrimage destination in its own right, and walking the labyrinth in the midst of such beauty only amplifies the effect!

Eve Eschner Hogan is a labyrinth facilitator, wedding officiator and inspirational speaker on the island of Maui and can be reached at 808.879.8648 or EveHogan@aol.com.

Lifestyle Modification

The focus of this type of wellness vacation is to achieve a more balanced life or to resolve some aspect of one's life that is interfering with inner peace. Participants engage in self-examination and reflection, developing tools and awareness to achieve their mental, emotional, physical and spiritual goals. Opportunities include working with life coaches, developing a nutrition plan, meeting with a hypnotherapist to stop smoking.

The purpose of a wellness vacation focusing on lifestyle modification is to explore those aspects of our life that are out of harmony and balance, and to develop awareness and tools to correct them. It provides us with the time and resources to objectively assess how we are living our lives.

Here again, the journey of the Hawaiians can shed light on our process. As they examined what they had lost in the process of integrating into Western culture, they became clearer about how they wanted to live their lives. A result of the Hawaiian renaissance is a renewed commitment to a lifestyle that reflects the true values of the individual Hawaiian in the context of the larger culture. For many, this means time for music, dance, surfing, and learning the Hawaiian language. It also means time for family, "*'ohana*"—which includes siblings, aunts, uncles, cousins as well as cherished friends they have taken into their family. Although many Hawaiians work two jobs in order to make ends meet, they recognize the critical role of the *'ohana* in maintaining balance and harmony. Children who go to the mainland to college say that the love and support of their *'ohana* sustains them. They often recognize that their fellow students lack this.

Many of us have also lost our balance as we try to fit into the larger American culture. We feel compelled to consume material goods, work long hours, and compete with others for limited resources. In return, we feel fortunate if we have two weeks a year to unwind and go on vacation. Or we may have a sense of who we are and what we value but don't know how to "let go" enough to begin living those values, following our dreams or doing the work that fills us with joy. All the while, if we listen to our inner voice, we know that something is seriously wrong. Something is missing in our life that leaves us feeling wounded.

A wellness vacation in Hawai'i provides the time, distance from daily stress and supportive environment to ask the critical questions that can return you to a state of balance and harmony. There are many wellness providers available to help you gain clarity about what is missing, to develop a commitment to living the life you truly desire and to support you in following through with your commitment. The three articles in this section will give you an idea of what a lifestyle modification vacation might include. Hypnosis can aid in changing old habits that interfere with a healthy life or that hold you back from performing at your best. Relationship Enhancement offers the opportunity to improve key relationships that can undermine your health and happiness. Success Coaching teaches new skills and tools for helping you shape your life in ways that are more satisfying, whether it's your career or other personal goals.

~ Personal Life Coaching ~

Reclaim Your Energy & Redesign Your Life in Paradise

Lee Ann and Javier Del Carpio

Wellness is a lifelong journey towards harmony and balance on all levels of our Selves—mind, heart, body and spirit—and personal life coaching is one of the most effective tools to help us achieve a powerful, unique blueprint for personal wellness based on an integration of **WHO** we are, with **WHAT** we want, and **HOW** we want to live.

In the same way that professional athletes use coaches to achieve peak performance in sports, people from all walks of life use personal coaches to achieve holistic personal wellness and success that integrates all aspects of themselves and leverages their unique capabilities. A coach works with you to create a life plan that maximizes your own inner resources, and helps you grow and develop in a way that is aligned with who you truly are. Continually supportive, a coach also challenges you to get clear on what's important to you and holds you accountable to take action and begin to transform your current reality. A coach facilitates your movement forward to greater growth, effectiveness and fulfillment and helps you make it through major life transitions. Most of all, a coach works with you to reach important goals in your life, bringing **WHAT** you believe and **WHO** you are into alignment with **HOW** you live.

Redesigning Your Life with a Coach in Hawai'i • When visiting the Islands you can partner with a coach who will work with you to define what a fulfilling life looks like and feels like, and help you uncover what aspects are holding you back from creating a life that you love. You partner with your coach to clarify your deepest life vision, get clear on how you want your life, career, relationships, etc. to evolve, and uncover blocks to achieving that success. Your coach can also design a week-long series of personalized coaching sessions for you to experience during your trip to Hawai'i, incorporating tools and techniques to increase the quality of your life.

In the past, many people did a form of coaching, but did not call themselves coaches. The field as we know it started in the early 1980s, with the evolution of Thomas Leonard's work as a certified financial planer. His clients approached him not only to learn more about managing money, but also seeking support in different life areas such as career development, personal growth, and designing a life based on well-being, values and spirit. Thomas' idea of coaching evolved naturally and six years later he founded Coach University, a coach training program, to teach others how to develop coaching skills. Since the late 1980's, the coaching profession has seen explosive growth, as individuals and organizations alike seek the benefits of real-time, one-on-one support in learning, development, performance, and fulfillment.

Coaching has become popular for several reasons: 1) Many people are tired of doing what they "should" do and are ready to do something special and meaningful for the rest of their lives. The problem is, many can't see it, or if they can, they can't see a way to reorient their life around it. A coach can help them do both. 2) People are realizing how simple it can be to accomplish something that several years ago might have felt out of reach or like a pipedream. A coach is not a miracle worker but does have a large tool kit to help the Big Idea become a Reality. Fortunately, people now have time and resources to invest in themselves in this kind of growth. 3) Spirituality and Wellness have become central to many people's life journey. If you've tracked the phenomenal success of James Redfield's *Celestine Prophecy* on the NY Times best-seller list during 1994, you get a sense of just how many people are willing to look at, and consider, the notion of spirituality and holistic well-being. Many coaches are spiritually based—even the ones who coach at large corporations like Merrill Lynch, IBM and Avon Products. A coach can help the client bring more of their spiritual Selves into their work and life.

The Power of Wellness Vacations + Coaching • A coaching partnership in the context of a Hawai'i wellness vacation is truly a life-changing experience, incorporating the unique spiritual wisdom of aloha with the intention of increasing physical, mental, emotional and spiritual balance and harmony, through personal success strategies.

Lee Ann Del Carpio

My journey in personal and spiritual awareness began years ago in Japan, where I learned the deeply meditative practices of Zen, Reiki and other cultural and spiritual healing traditions. For four years, I lived and traveled in Asia soaking up the wisdom traditions of each culture, often stopping in Hawai'i to experience the rich cultural and spiritual traditions of the Hawaiian huna way. These experiences became a part of my healing path, and I began to integrate them into my coaching work.

By the late 1990s, I was back in New York City leading a hectic corporate life, outwardly successful but increasingly restless, like something was missing. I knew I had a higher purpose. To truly live an authentic life and discover my deeper purpose, I had to first "empty my cup", listen to my heart and allow myself to be a beginner. That's when the dreams about Hawai'i began. It was as if Hawai'i was calling my soul, heightening my sense of awareness of who I truly was and what was possible in life. In late 2000, I finally woke up to my dreams and made the leap from the fast track of corporate life to the rich, soulful living in Hawai'i.

Lee Ann practices Personal and Leadership Coaching at Inner Power International on O'ahu. She can be reached at 808.626.4680 or at www.innerpowerintl.com

Javier Del Carpio

Moving to Hawai'i was a life changing experience for me. I used to work as an international sales manager for a pharmaceutical company in New York City. As I looked back on my life, I realized that I was becoming successful in terms of society's standards, but with a feeling of emptiness inside. Having that realization made me look for a way in which I could create balance in my life and start living in alignment with my life purpose and core values. Hawai'i was the answer for me.

A new chapter of my life started in O'ahu. I realized that many people were experiencing the same situation that I had in my previous job, and decided to help others to live from a heart-centered approach. My purpose now is to establish a bridge between people's rational minds and their hearts so they can learn to transform their own lives from simply being externally-driven to prospering from an internally-motivated mindset. I use imagery and symbolism in my coaching practice and retreats. I enjoy immensely working with professionals and progressive individuals who want to align their personal and professional lives with their deepest dreams, values, and goals. In my spare time I run marathons and teach scuba diving.

Javier is a personal and corporate coach, retreat leader and motivational speaker. He can be reached at Inner Power International, 808.626.4690 or at www.innerpowerintl.com

~ HYPNOTHERAPY ~

Tapping in to Our Intuitive Wisdom

Lorraine Bennington, M.Ed.

Hypnosis is a naturally induced trance state, which by-passes the rational mind and opens the subconscious to receive suggestions. While in this state it is possible to hear and record messages both from the hypnotist and from the person's own intuitive wisdom.

Origins • Hypnosis, or altered state awareness, can be traced back to the earliest human cultures where shamans used dance, drumming and chanting to evoke a trance state. In 1773, Franz Anton Mesmer introduced hypnosis to the modern world using magnetic passes over the body to induce a trance state. James Esdail, a British surgeon in the late 1800's, performed 3000 operations, 300 of them major, using only hypnosis as anesthesia (documented in *Hypnosis in Medicine and Surgery*). Interestingly, because physicians in those days did not wash their hands before surgery, there was a 50% post-operative mortality rate. Using hypnosis as the only anesthesia, Esdail's mortality rate dropped to 5%! Somehow, the hypnosis appeared to also boost the patient's natural immunity.

In the 1890's, Freud was inspired by a doctor named Breuer, one of the best medical hypnotists of his time, to incorporate hypnotherapy into his practice. However, Freud himself had little or no skill with hypnosis and believed all his subjects needed to attain a deep trance. When he failed to induce this state in the majority of his patients, he decided it was not a useful tool and thus blocked the acceptance of hypnosis for fifty years.

Finally in 1955 the British Medical Association adopted a resolution approving the use of hypnosis and urging doctors to develop this skill. The American Medical Association followed suit in a similar resolution in 1958. Despite these recommendations, very few medical schools teach hypnotherapy. Since the late sixties a few schools have begun to offer these courses at a post graduate level.

Research and Misperceptions • Extensive scientific research over the years has supported the effectiveness of hypnotherapy. It can be used to stop habits such as smoking, overeating and other addictions, to eliminate fears of flying, public speaking, or other phobias, and to develop strengths such as sports performance. It is effective at reducing pain, depression, and insomnia, as well as digestive disorders, asthma, allergies, and skin problems. It has gained respect in the medical establishment even though it has not been incorporated in to the mainstream of Western medicine.

There are a number of misconceptions about hypnosis; the most common being that the person is unconscious during the session. In fact, he or she is as aware as one might be in any naturally induced trance state, such as daydreaming or losing oneself in a good book or movie. Another misunderstanding is that the client can be controlled by the hypnotist. In reality, the client maintains a parallel track awareness throughout. Part of the consciousness is deeply engrossed in the inner movie, and the other part is aware of the therapy office and the presence of the therapist. Hypnosis cannot cause someone to do something they don't want to do or that goes against their moral code.

Variations • In hypnotherapy there are two quite different approaches: programming and deprogramming. Programming works well only if there is an empty space in which to receive it. In other words, if there are deep beliefs running contrary to the input, they will prevent the new material from taking root. If, after attempts at programming, repeated affirmations or guided imagery, a person still has not succeeded in changing their behavior, it is a good indicator of the need for deprogramming or de-hypnosis. This is done in a process called age regression, where the person is guided to the root cause of the limiting belief or negative self-image that is stopping the new positives from taking hold. As every good gardener knows, seeds have a better chance to grow if you weed the garden first.

Once that experience is healed, the belief can be changed and brought into present awareness. Then the affirmations and imagery can find a permanent and welcome place in the person's psyche.

The principle behind all of this is that our beliefs directly impact our actions. Belief in limitation itself limits performance.

Simply put, if you believe you can't you can't! If you believe you can, you can!

What is less simple is that many of our beliefs are buried deep in our subconscious and therefore we are not always aware of what we believe beneath the surface of our daily thoughts. It is the job of the skilled hypnotherapist to help a person penetrate these layers to get to their deeper beliefs. Then, once those are revealed, it is much easier to transform them into a new and more positive direction.

Whether you are an Olympic swimmer, ball player, smoker, weight watcher, suffering a chronic illness, or just trying to improve your golf game, hypnosis can help you let go of worn out beliefs and replace them with new and positive directions and attitudes. Then you can truly express your talent and be all that you were meant to be.

Lorraine Bennington

I first came to Maui in 1971 and spent six months here. When I returned to Canada, it was with a clear intent to return and spend my life on this beautiful island. It took over twenty years for this to materialize, but in the meantime I studied Huna (shamanism) with Serge King on Kaua'i and visited the islands regularly. In 1993 my family and I moved full time to Kaua'i and then in 1997 to Maui.

My spiritual journey has included visiting India, following a guru, living in an ashram and years of meditating two or more hours daily. Being a mother has been the most invaluable part of my spiritual path, as my two children are my light and my greatest teachers!

I did my more formal psychology training at McGill University, in Montreal, and received an M.Ed. in Counseling in 1979. I also began my astrological training in 1969 with a medical intern (physician) and in the early 70's began my practice of hypnosis, primarily doing past life regression and re-dreaming, which is using trance to have people reenter their dream state and change dream outcomes.

I have been blessed to study hypnosis with many great teachers. Over time, I have evolved my own style, which leads people to the root cause of whatever is stopping them from living their full life potential. The angels are always invited to participate in sessions.

Lorraine Bennington M.Ed. (Counseling) has an astrology and hypnotherapy practice in Makawao, Maui. She can be reached at 808.573.3383 or at content@maui.net.

~ Relationship Enhancement in Hawai'i ~

Jeffrey Marsh

Relationships are a vital part of life everywhere, however in Hawai'i they take on particular significance. This is because people from all over the world come to Hawai'i to get engaged, to get married, to honeymoon, and to celebrate the anniversaries of these meaningful life events. Many couples are drawn to Hawai'i because they know that being on the islands, surrounded by the abundant natural beauty, benefits their relationship.

An additional bounty of these romantic islands is the availability of programs designed for the specific purpose of relationship enhancement. And you don't have to look far these days to see that relationships could use enhancement. Dual career households and the changing roles of women have left many couples without a road map. Couples know the relationship model from their parents doesn't work for them and yet don't know what to do instead. More and more people are seeking quality relationships that reflect harmony, compassion, and mutual respect and that are based on true equality.

Relational Health • The experience of love and connection is more than just a sentimental ideal. It is, as Dean Ornish, M.D. points out, necessary for our very survival. Says Dr. Ornish, "I am not aware of any other factor in medicine that has a greater impact on our survival than the healing power of love and intimacy. Not diet, not smoking, not exercise, not stress, not genetics, not drugs, not surgery." The bottom line is that even our physical health depends largely upon our emotional and relational health.

To cultivate relational health, a number of programs have been developed in recent years. Some examples are the Imago work of Harville Hendrix, Ph.D., the Venus/Mars perspective of John Gray, Ph.D., the Conscious Loving approach of Gay and Kathleen Hendricks, Ph.D., the Emotional Intelligence framework of Daniel Goleman, Ph.D., and the PAIRS (Practical Application of Intimate Relationship Skills) program developed by Lori Gordon, Ph.D.

Variations and Benefits • These programs are educationally based, often teaching couples new skills that empower them to be change agents in their own lives. The focus may include a variety of topics such as communication skills, healthy expression, empathic listening, self-awareness, conflict resolution, anger management, emotional literacy, sensuality and sex, power dynamics, and family systems. This work is available in private sessions or through courses ranging in time from a half day, to a full day or weekend, to week-long retreats.

Relationship enhancement is for anyone who wants to broaden the skills necessary to sustain a loving and healthy relationship. This includes men and women of any age, ethnicity, spiritual or sexual orientation who are single or coupled at any stage of relationship—beginning, middle, or end.

A relationship enhancement course can help you improve an unsatisfying relationship, discover the causes of disappointment, avoid the mistakes made in previous relationships, and enhance your ability to create a joyful, fulfilling future with your partner.

Participants in relationship enhancement courses typically report a renewal of love in their relationships. They often experience deeper understanding, more joy and pleasure, feelings of closeness and affection, more intimacy, and the ability to work through challenges with greater ease and trust. The beauty and romance of Hawai'i makes it an ideal environment to realize these changes.

Jeffrey Marsh

I have always been interested in how things work. From a young age I was taking things apart and putting them back together. I also endeavored to do the same with people. These tendencies led me to study engineering, then ultimately sociology, as I strove to understand (at least intellectually) the wide universe of relationships.

In 1994 I sailed to Hawai'i, fulfilling a lifelong dream. I arrived in Hilo at the commencement of the Merrie Monarch Hula Festival. Enveloped in the spirit of aloha, I felt called to make the islands my home. I lived and worked striving to embody the compassion and understanding that is aloha. However, I soon discovered that saying, "aloha" was much easier than living aloha.

It wasn't until I enrolled in a PAIRS program with my partner Debra that I really acquired a skill set that allowed me to more fully embody compassion and understanding. PAIRS stands for Practical Application of Intimate Relationship Skills. Because the material is tool-oriented, I found that I could quickly relate to its' hands-on approach. Moreover, the tools had a transformative effect in challenging situations--both personal and professional. Debra and I went on to become certified PAIRS facilitators. We now teach these tools that sustain loving relationships here on Maui and on the mainland.

Jeffrey Marsh is a certified PAIRS educator and communication specialist who lives on Maui. He is the co-Founder of HeartPath: Conscious Communication, and can be reached at 808.874.6441 or info@HeartPath.org.

Nature as Healer

Intentional, meaningful contact with nature can promote greater levels of spiritual and emotional awareness as well as provide answers to questions and issues begging for resolution. In this type of vacation the traveler seeks opportunities to quietly commune with nature and allow its healing magic to restore the heart, soul and spirit. We suggest such activities as visits to gardens, hiking, nature meditations, buying healing products from nature.

"Nature is where it all begins for the Hawaiians. In fact, they call themselves keiki o ka 'āina—'children of the land.' The 'āina is not just soil, sand or dirt. The 'āina is a heart issue for Hawaiians. The very word 'āina brings forth deep emotion evolved from ancestral times when people lived in nature as an integral part of it... the word 'āina literally means 'that which feeds' and maka 'āinana, a term for the common class of people, means 'eyes of the land.' Thus, nature feeds man and man watches over nature in return." Voices of Wisdom (p 13)

Ancient Hawaiian legend has it that man and nature were created simultaneously as siblings to support and nurture each other. The Hawaiian people have always felt a mutual responsibility in their relationship with nature. It willingly offers sustenance, healing herbs, and resources for living. In turn, they must honor and respect nature. Among other things, they acknowledge that reciprocal relationship by praying and asking permission before they pick a plant. Deep within the Hawaiian culture is recognition that nature is a dear and trusted friend, a source of wisdom and healing.

Of all the lessons we can learn from the Hawaiians, this may be one of the most important. The dominant American culture tends to see nature as an adversary to be conquered, harnessed and forced to produce. Our alienation from nature is not only causing the destruction of our environment but is also deeply wounding us. Theodore Roszak in his book *The Voice of the Earth* argues that our dysfunctional relationship with nature is more damaging to us as a people than our dysfunctional relationships with each other.

We invite you during your time in Hawai'i to reconnect with nature as friend, healer and wisdom keeper. In the island chapters we guide you to the many tropical and botanical gardens that we have found especially healing. On the Big Island, viewing Kīlauea Volcano is a moving experience that connects you with the origins of the planet. One article in this section describes the healing power of dolphins. Whale watching, snorkeling, and scuba diving are other ways to encounter the wonders of the underwater world. As described in another article, visiting or staying on a farm, is a way to be close to the land and help farmers stay on the land. Hiking, picnicking, and nature meditations will get you out in the fresh air and appreciating the Hawaiian landscape close up. Nature is the ultimate color and sound therapy. Enjoy and explore, and let her work her magic.

AG TOURISM

Helping Farmers Stay On The Land

Elizabeth Jenkins

Hawai'i's motto, ***Ua mau ke ea o ka 'āina i ka pono*, "the life of the land is preserved in righteousness"** *is* Ag-tourism at its' finest!

What IS ag-tourism? • Ag-tourism, one of the fastest growing areas of the tourist industry, is all about getting back to nature. People who want to "return to the land" and take a learning vacation that gives them hands-on experience with a plethora of farming and ranching activities in a fresh rural environment can partake in what has been traditionally called "farm stay." In most cases, this means actually living and working on a farm, ranch, or orchard, staying in the farmer's house, and perhaps even sitting down to dinner with farmers and their families. However, the modern term "ag-tourism" can encompass anything from a thirty-minute tour of a flower farm, to a month-long stay on a dude ranch, and the Hawaiian version of "farm stay" often involves a Bed and Breakfast.

Background • Ag-tourism and farm stay are as ancient perhaps as the practice of agriculture itself. The ancient Incas of Peru invited farmers from one region of their empire (perhaps coastal), to come and stay in another (e.g., high sierra) to help solve agriculture or ag-related engineering problems, or to acclimatize and move crops from one altitude to another. As recent as 50 years ago in North America, it was common courtesy for farmers to host travelers passing through town simply because in most rural communities there was no place else for them to stay. In its modern form, "farm stay" has become especially popular in Europe and New Zealand amongst vacationers who want to recapture the experience of childhood visits to grandparents' farms, or to simply relax from the rush of city life. The numbers of Europeans choosing a farm stay vacation have increased dramatically over the last thirty years, and Austria leads the way with the largest numbers of farm stay accommodations in all of Europe.

For Hawai'i the practice of ag-tourism is a more recent development—within the last five to tens years—and is particularly linked to the decline of the sugar cane industry. Cane fields were transferred back to local farmers to plant more locally saleable crops, but they soon discovered their crops were not so saleable. This has led to the search for other avenues of income, including ag-tourism and the production of value-added products (meaning the farmers themselves produce and market a retail product from their crop).

Why Ag-Tourism? • Ag-tourism and the on-farm sales that come from it can mean the difference between staying afloat and folding for Hawai'i's small farmers. Here in Hawai'i, the industry seems to be alive and well, *and* on the rise. A recent study by the Hawai'i Agricultural Statistics Service placed the value of ag-tourism related income in the state at 26 million dollars for the year 2000. Although a large percentage of farms are still without ag-tourism many reported plans for such activities in the future. About 47% of all farms in the State of Hawai'i are located on the Big Island.

Ag-tourism in Hawai'i could mean anything from a one-hour tour of a macadamia nut orchard, to a three night stay at a B&B built amidst the coffee trees of a Kona Coffee farm, or weeks of riding and roping on a cattle ranch. For a map and list of ag-tourism available in Hawai'i see the website www.hawaiiagtourism.com.

Whatever may be your farm or ag-activity of choice, you can be sure that not only is ag-tourism good for you, but it is also politically, spiritually, *and* economically correct. When you chose a farm tour or ranch or orchard stay, you are supporting local farmers, the people who are practicing Hawai'i's motto, "...preserving the life of the land..." and bringing money to the rural and generally more economically depressed areas.

Elizabeth B. Jenkins

In 1988, on break from my doctoral studies in clinical psychology, I followed a deep inner calling to go to Peru where synchronicity led me to an indigenous priesthood. My experiences of the "supernatural" permanently removed the word "impossible" from my vocabulary as I was initiated into the ancient Inca tradition of nature mysticism and learned Inca Prophecies for this time. Since 1990, I have led people to Peru to undergo an authentic 10-day initiation in the Inca tradition. I also founded Wiraqocha Foundation for the preservation of indigenous wisdom, and wrote two books on my experiences including ***INITIATION: A Woman's Spiritual Adventure in the Heart of the Andes*** *(Putnam, 1997). In January of 2000 I delivered my first baby boy and by September was pregnant with number two, who, conspiring from the womb with madame PELE, relocated family and foundation to the Big Island.*

Here in the South Point area, one mile above the ancient Hawaiian town of Waiohinu, we founded 'Ai Lani Orchards, a 10.5 acre organic orchard of tropical fruits and nuts overlooking the ocean. 'Ai Lani means "spiritual food" in Hawaiian. We supply this to the public through our retreat house and Permaculture Vacations program, our on-site fruit stand, our Organic Orchard Volunteers, and our Big Island Initiation programs.

Elizabeth Jenkins lives with her husband and two children at 'Ai Lani Orchards Retreat and Fruit Stand near Waiohinu on the Big Island. She can be reached at 808.929.8785 or www.inca-online.com.

~ The Call of the Dolphins ~

Rev. Chris Reid

Dolphins have always fascinated people. In almost every culture and age, there are stories of dolphins befriending humans, often guiding those in trouble to safety. They charm us with their indelible smile, their playful presence, and apparent intelligence. In recent years, adventure travel to places like the Bahamas, Australia, Florida and Hawai'i, where dolphins are accessible in the wild, has gained wide popularity, and the dream of swimming with dolphins is shared by children of all ages.

Ambassadors in Nature • Encounters with dolphins, particularly in their natural environment, can be a beneficial catalyst for personal healing. Some have even experienced such encounters as life transforming. We attribute many human traits to dolphins: joy, power, love, playfulness, healing, and harmony. Yet the dolphins are simply reflecting to us who WE really are. Masters of the state of simply "BEing" they serve to remind us that we have the power within ourselves to find wholeness and balance. Dolphins are ambassadors in nature, reconnecting us to our Divine Creator.

To find healing in nature requires that we become fully present, not thinking about the past or the future. As we are captured in the moment, we touch the potential for transformation. Dolphins entice us into an ocean world, which many people find unfamiliar and frightening, bringing up fear of depths, of what lies unseen beneath the surface, and symbolically even death. Once a person experiences breaking through fear, they become empowered in other areas of their lives.

Observing dolphins in the wild moves us to recognize the existence of other sentient species and a new world-view opens up in which all life is connected as one. What we do affects everything else. As our awareness of the natural world begins to shift, we understand our responsibility to care for the planet's creatures and resources in order to ensure that future generations will enjoy them as well.

Dolphins in Hawai'i • In Hawai'i, the coastal spinner dolphin pods feed in deep waters offshore by night and frequent leeward shorelines and bays to rest during the day. Exploring the coast by boat is the least invasive way of observing dolphins. The best time is early in the day when the pods are traveling and being "social". Depending on the dolphins' behavior, there may be opportunities to quietly enter the water for further observation. We can learn so much by simply watching them and soaking up their exuberant spirit of play. Local tour operators and guides are careful not to disturb, displace or harass the dolphins in any way. Although not endangered, dolphins are protected by the Marine Mammal Protection Act.

There are several protected bays in Hawai'i where dolphins are often seen from shore or encountered while snorkeling or kayaking. As these are designated resting areas which are critical to the pods' well-being, it is essential to exercise respect and restraint in initiating an encounter. Be open and patient, allowing the experience to come to you. Weather and sea conditions can change or deteriorate suddenly, so stay alert.

In West Hawai'i (on the Big Island) there is also a captive dolphin encounter program that is suitable for children, those who are physically challenged, or otherwise uncomfortable in the open ocean. This provides education and intimate contact with the dolphins in a controlled environment. Behaviors encouraged in that situation, such as touching a dolphin, would never be appropriate in the wild.

Possible Restrictions • It's important to note that in the United States, human-dolphin interaction is in jeopardy. Because of the thoughtlessness of a few, National Marine Fisheries Service has proposed legislation which would either outlaw or restrict our ability to swim with dolphins in the wild. For many years, Hawai'i's eco-tour operators and guides have worked as a community to self-regulate their activities in a way that provides for the optimal experience for the visitor and also honors and protects the dolphins and their habitat. It serves both humans and dolphins to support programs that foster this awareness.

Rev. Chris Reid

A powerful connection to nature has always blessed, nourished and comforted me. It is the foundation of my personal philosophy and the source of my strength and inspiration.

From childhood I struggled with feelings of abandonment and unworthiness. That all changed in 1989 when Atlantic bottlenose dolphins surrounded me in the waters off Key West, Florida. In a matter of moments, the shell around my heart shattered, I was reminded that I am never truly alone, and I was told to "lighten up". Thus began a journey of discovery that continues today.

It was the lure of swimming with coastal dolphins that drew me to Hawai'i initially, though once I set foot upon this island I realized a resonance deeper and richer than I could have imagined. I had come home. What started more than a decade ago as an adventure would become a profound transformation of my lifestyle and the very nature of my being.

Hawai'i continues to reveal her power places and beauty, and with each new discovery I reunite with a forgotten part of myself. Healing (the return to wholeness) happens here, as I remember and reconnect with Mother Nature in the spirit of recreation and play.

Chris Reid is an island guide, marine mammal naturalist, and minister. She lives in Kealakekua on the Big Island and she can be reached at Light Spirit, 808.328.8672 or dolphins@kona.net.

Relaxation And Rejuvenation

A relaxation and rejuvenation wellness vacation focuses primarily on nurturing and relaxing the body. Opportunities at spas range from massage to aromatherapy.

Other holistic options include hypnotherapy, yoga, meditation and tai chi. The accommodation one chooses can also be critical to whether the vacation achieves the goal of relaxing and rejuvenating.

While ancient Hawaiians were active competitors, they also recognized the benefit of relaxation and rejuvenation. They were far less driven in their lifestyle than Americans are today. In fact, the American culture's constant striving to *do* and *have* has been a major source of cultural conflict for native Hawaiians. As they have rediscovered their roots, they have recognized the value of *being*. It is during those moments of *being* that we have greatest access to Spirit and to our own deepest wisdom.

Bodywork, or the *lomilomi* massage, was important to Hawaiians as a form of relaxing and rejuvenating. They believed that it resulted in enhanced wisdom, confidence and physical health. The *ali'i* and chiefs would receive many hours of *lomilomi* massage prior to making important decisions. Before going into battle, it was said that King Kamehameha's warriors received *lomilomi* massage as a form of psychological warfare. After the massage they appeared stronger and more confident.

Bodywork and massage are increasingly popular among Americans today as we recognize the ways our stressful lifestyle diminishes our strength. A relaxation and rejuvenation wellness vacation should begin and end with massage. In Hawai'i, there are many types of massage techniques including the Hawaiian *lomilomi*. You can find them in many of the spas—along with aromatherapy and healing baths—or you can pursue them by visiting individual providers in their private studios.

During your R&R vacation, you might also explore an on-going practice that can help maintain a more peaceful balanced state. This could include Eastern centering practices such as yoga, qigong, and tai chi. But one of the main ways to restore yourself while on vacation is to resist the temptation to be constantly on the go and filling up your day with activity. This may be especially hard if you are in Hawai'i for the first time and not sure when you'll be back. However, if your intention is to reach deeper levels of rest and renewal, the best way is to enjoy the quiet times and the healing natural environment that are so abundant in Hawai'i.

~ Massage Therapy ~

Many Methods—Many Applications

Kathy Edwards, LMT MAT-5480
Liza Delin, Reiki Master

Massage is a therapeutic technique that helps the musculoskeletal, digestive, respiratory, reproductive, circulatory, lymphatic, and endocrine systems, in addition to relieving stress and enhancing overall health.

Origins • The first documented use of massage was by the Chinese over 3,000 years ago. The ancient Hindus developed Ayurveda, a system of medicine that relies heavily on massage, and Egyptian tombs reveal paintings of people performing massage. Swedish massage was developed in the 19th century by a Swedish doctor, poet, and educator named Per Henrik Ling. His system was based on a study of gymnastics and physiology, and on techniques borrowed from China, Egypt, Greece, and Rome. The father of massage therapy in the United States was Cornelius E. De Puy, MD, who published the first journal on the subject in 1817.

Although traces of the massage parlor image still exist, therapeutic massage is now widely recognized for its many health benefits. It's used for people of all ages, and in all stages of life, from infancy to pregnancy to old age, and the end of life. Also, more and more people with health-challenging conditions such as cancer, AIDS, heart attacks, or strokes are turning to massage therapy for help.

Benefits • The benefits of massage therapy have been documented in a large body of scientific research. Studies show massage reduces heart rate, lowers blood pressure, and increases endorphin levels. Massage has been shown to improve immune system function, facilitate recovery from surgery, and reduce pain. Although therapeutic massage does not increase muscle strength, it can stimulate weak, inactive muscles and, thus, partially compensate for the lack of exercise and inactivity resulting from illness or injury. It also can hasten and lead to a more complete recovery from the injury or exercise.

Massage therapy also has been shown to increase the alertness and performance of office workers, and to reduce anxiety, depression, and stress. Since 80-90% of ailments brought to family practice doctors are stress-related, it can be asserted that massage therapy is an excellent tool for disease prevention and wellness. Massage also increases mind-body awareness, and satisfies the human need for nurturing touch.

Types of Massage • There are many varieties of massage therapy, and more are being developed all the time. The most common types in the US are Swedish, sports massage and shiatsu. Swedish massage is what most Americans think of as massage. It incorporates long gliding stokes, kneading and compression motions, and other techniques to increase circulation and break down muscle adhesions. This massage is most often used to induce relaxation, and to heal injuries.

Sports massage is geared to the athlete, and used during both training and competition. It reduces muscle tension, and thereby reduces injury. It can also help in the healing process after an injury by increasing range of motion and by reducing swelling, pain, bruising, and adhesions.

Shiatsu is a Japanese therapy that has ancient oriental roots, but has evolved using both Eastern and Western techniques. Shiatsu involves the application of pressure along energy meridians, and is performed with the client fully clothed. Shiatsu practitioners apply pressure with their thumbs, knuckles, palms, and elbows to move trapped ki (or life force energy), thought to be the cause of pain and illness.

Most ancient healing practices, such as *lomilomi*, or Hawaiian healing massage, offer a holistic approach. In *lomi*, the client receives healing for the spirit, mind and body. Prayer is an integral part of the practice, and Hawaiian herbs may also be prescribed.

Many modern massage therapists are incorporating ancient and modern therapies to create a mind-body-spirit approach to healing. For example, some practitioners use aromatherapy, crystals or stones during sessions. In addition, many practitioners incorporate other types of bodywork, such as Reiki (energy work), craniosacral therapy, or acupuncture.

What's Right for You Which massage is suited for you? Perhaps the most important consideration is finding the practitioner who is right for you. Choose a therapist with integrity and whose values you espouse, as well as someone who has proper training in technique. When you and your therapist are in harmony, wonderful things can begin to happen. You may arrive at your therapist's office feeling run down, stressed out and in pain, and walk out feeling lighter, relaxed and loved. There are many approaches to massage, but most massage therapists agree that the power of touch can improve quality of life in a magical way.

Liza Delin

I began my healing path after experiencing a year and a half of constant illness, culminating in back surgery for a herniated disc in 1992. Tired of living with lingering pain, I accepted a free Reiki session at a conference in 1995, and it changed my life. I began going for Reiki treatments, and my back injury healed completely during the third session, much to my surprise and delight. I continued receiving regular Reiki treatments for six months before taking First Degree and Second Degree Reiki in 1996. The more I received Reiki, the more I saw positive changes in myself, my relationships and my spiritual practice.

I moved to Hawai'i in the Fall of 1996 to begin a Masters of Public Health program at the University of Hawai'i. During an internship for school, I met Maureen O'Shaughnessy, and knew instantly that she would be the one to initiate me as a Reiki master in the Usui System of Natural Healing. Over a year later, I began my preparation as a Reiki master, and was initiated in February of 2000. I have used many other tools for my own healing, including craniosacral therapy, lomilomi, and pure essential oils. Reiki is my greatest passion and joy, however, and will remain the center of my healing journey

Liza Delin is a partner with Kathy Edwards in Rainbow Healing Arts where she provides reiki treatments and teaches Reiki.

Kathy Edwards

I came to Hawai'i in 1983, about the same time Madame Pele started spewing lava from Kīlauea. Pele and I were both starting a new path of destruction and rebirth. Once here, I really looked at the path that I knew I must pursue. Some women taught me about the healing powers of acupuncture and Chinese medicine. Others revealed to me the magic of astrology and goddess wisdom. I learned about the spirits of Hawai'i and the respect for the 'āina (land).

When I took Reiki in 1997 my life began to change. On a personal level, I experienced deep emotional and spiritual healing, which affected all my relationships, especially the one with myself. On a professional level, I decided to attend massage school and was licensed in 1999. From there my healing journey really took off. I studied craniosacral therapy, the uses of therapeutic grade essential oils, and developed a warm stone massage session.

I had always searched for my lomilomi teacher until last year when my Kumu came to me, Auntie Keonoana Neilson. Becoming part of the Hawaiian healing culture finally allowed me to resonate with this beautiful island and the ancestors of the people who inhabit it. I feel that I have come full circle in my journey and that my spirit belongs in Hawai'i.

Kathy Edwards is a licensed massage therapist who incorporates Reiki, Craniosacral therapy, lomilomi, and pure essential oils into her sessions.

~ Aunty's Lomilomi Massage ~

Jerri Lynn Knoblich

My friend lay on a table in the shade of the coconut trees down at Keei Beach, on the Big Island of Hawai'i. Lomi Master Aunty Margaret Machado was examining her. *"Pule"*, she announces, meaning "It's time for prayer". She placed her strong, sensitive hands on the patient's back and bowed her head to connect with *Akua*, in other words to ask God to be a part of this, and to give thanks for guidance. Then slowly she began examining, feeling for the injury and treating with *lomilomi* massage. She used a combination of rubbing with oil, and percussion (anything from a light tapping to pounding), stretching, rotating, and manipulating. (Aunty would first send her patients to the steam house. When the steam house was not available, she would "cook" them with a large moist heating pad to loosen up the muscles).

Before we left, Aunty explained to us that my friend might feel sore before feeling good again. Sure enough, within the next few days she noticed relief from pain, improved motion, and better circulation.

What is lomilomi? • What is the secret healing power of Hawaiian *lomilomi* massage? *"Love and Prayer is what makes Lomi work"*, she told us, *"Be happy and have a merry heart—ho'oponopono, put things right between brother and sister before the sun goes down. When we're angry it only hurts ourselves."*

"Love the body as if it were your own. If your hands are gentle and loving, your patient will feel the sincerity of your heart. His soul will reach out to yours and the Lord's healing will flow through you both. It is our love flowing from the heart through the hands, touching soul to soul."

Aunty Margaret teaches that the definition of Hawaiian *lomilomi* is **"the loving touch"** a connection between heart, hand, and soul with the source of all life. Using the *pule* (prayer) to open the way, calling the higher spiritual power to restore harmony and balance.

Origins and Practice • There is much more than just massage involved with *lomilomi.* The written history of the practice and its proper uses are very scant. Throughout the Polynesian Islands and Hawai'i this highly revered art was kept primarily a family occupation. Because of the spiritual knowledge necessary to be a truly successful practitioner, it was believed that only a chosen few were capable of understanding the reasons behind the healings. Frequently the village priests or *kahuna* would train the successor to the family knowledge. This was done over a period of years to assure his or her abilities and sincerity in becoming a healer. There are also stories about "laying on of hands", where the *kahuna* would chant ancient prayers that would infuse the student with the ability to feel the healing energies.

To connect with *Akua* (God) is an integral part of the healing process. It opens the way for the exchange of energy. Practitioners ask for guidance to recognize the blockages in the body that need to be released. They also ask for spiritual protection for themselves, for the patient, and for the place where they are. There is a traditional Hawaiian method of placing ti plants in the four corners for protection and to cleanse the energy field.

After performing a *lomilomi* session, water is used to allow the energy to flow out of the hands of the practitioner. Also flames such as from a large candle are used to release this energy into the fire.

Lomi Master Dr. Dane Silva teaches us that in the art of *lomilomi* the principles of *Huna* (the Hawaiian science of mastery) are part of the process. The following Hawaiian terms are used frequently in *lomilomi*:

NĀNĀ (nah-nah): to look – to observe with both the physical eyes and the "third eye" or inner vision.

HO'OLOHE (ho-o-lo-hay): to listen – to listen to the body, the speech, the breath, the teeth, etc. And also to close both ears and listen with the middle ear for words or images.

NĪNAU (nee-now): to ask a question – to ask where it hurts, how it happened, if it has happened more than once, about previous treatments, and about the state of the client's personal life.

PA'A KA WAHA: close the mouth – No personal information is revealed to others without the client's permission. Also during the treatment the practitioner must not talk too much as it will lose the focus necessary for the healing. It is often said, "pa'a ka waha, hana ka lima." Keep the mouth closed and focus on the job at hand.

HANA LIMA: work with the hands – the art of palpation. The practitioner uses his hands to diagnose, to perform the massage, to put pressure on, and to mobilize the joints.

Hawaiian *lomilomi* is more than another massage technique. It is a spiritual healing art that's imbued with all the customs, language, and spirit of an ancient culture. Not every practitioner will pray out loud before starting treatment, but they will probably be doing their own spiritual practice as part of the session. To receive a *lomilomi* massage, especially in Hawai'i, is to touch and be touched by the energy of the ancient healers of this beautiful land.

Jerri Knoblich

I first came to Hawai'i in 1966 to spend the summer with my aunt and uncle. I was born pigeon-toed, so aunt Charlotte massaged my feet and showed me the healing powers of massage and prayer.

Hawai'i was magical! I tried mud sliding, surfing, and hula and Tahitian dancing. I loved the island ways with its own wildly colored clothes, its own language (Pidgin English– "howzit, eh?"), and its own manners, like taking off your shoes before entering a house. When I returned to Minnesota, I vowed that Hawai'i would some day be my home.

Years past. I became a "flower child" and started going to the Rainbow Family healing gatherings to pray for world peace and save the planet. I was an enthusiastic practitioner of yoga and wanted to be a "swami" like the ones in India. My friends called me Swami Mommy because I taught yoga to my children and anyone who would let me.

In 1980 I returned to Hawai'i forever. I had the honor of studying the ancient healing art of Lomilomi massage with Auntie Margaret Machado. Then I discovered energy medicine, touch for health, Educational Kinesiology and I studied with Dr. Dane Silva, also known as Papa Lomi.

Jerri Lynn Knoblich (Swami) combines Ancient Hawaiian Lomilomi Massage with Kinesiology and Touch for Health at her office in Kealakekua on the Big Island. She can be reached at 808.323.3344 and swamimom@ilhawaii.net.

~ Qigong ~

Moving in Harmony with Nature

Karinna Kittles

Origins • Qigong (also written Chi Kung) is defined as the cultivation of life energy through managing the breath. This ancient healing art thought to be between 3000 and 8000 years old originates from China. Qigong offers meditation, movement exercises, healing techniques and various breathing practices to balance, revitalize and harmonize ones body, emotions and spirit.

Qigong is a branch of Traditional Chinese Medicine and the number one source of preventative health care from China. Like acupuncture and herbalogy, this Taoist practice utilizes the principles of nature and the body's own innate healing wisdom to balance and restore internal processes. Qigong helps individuals to cultivate Qi (life force energy) to create greater health and longevity.

Today there are thousands of different styles of Qigong. They vary in emphasis but they share the overall purpose of relaxing and strengthening the body, transforming and balancing emotions, improving mental clarity, preventing and treating illness and developing spiritual awareness.

Benefits • Qigong works by removing internal road blocks and increasing and harmonizing the flow of energy through the body. According to Traditional Chinese medicine; sickness, and pain are caused when Qi energy is blocked. When Qi cannot flow through the body, excess energy builds up where it is not needed. Then other parts of the body do not receive enough Qi. In practicing Qigong, one learns to tap into and utilize the endless reservoirs of life force energy available in nature and the universe to enable ones own life force energy to flow more freely. Qi energy can then heal and restore the body.

The medical effects of Qigong have been scientifically studied over the past two decades. The benefits include positive effects on stress, general pain (such as neck, shoulder, lower back), arthritis, respiratory efficiency, spinal alignment, female and male organ health, hormonal function, heart and circulatory health, auto immune function, and blood pressure regulation. The Qigong Institute in California currently has over 1000 studies on the positive effects of Qigong. Qigong practice is used effectively in Chinese hospitals to heal all types of diseases and is an increasingly accepted complement to Western health care regimens.

Variations • The many schools of Qigong in the West focus on different applications such as healing, self-defense, and spiritual cultivation. One of the best known, the Universal Tao system from Master Mantak Chia, offers over 20 books on the subject and has trained and certified hundreds of instructors throughout America and Europe. Most teachings will emphasis the importance of personal practice using a combination of meditation and movement exercises. Others highlight healing techniques such as emitted qi healings and Chi Nei Tsang treatments (abdominal massage to the internal organs.)

Tai Chi has the same origins as Qigong. Rather than having a particular emphasis, Tai Chi is more of a general tonic. Whereas Qigong focuses on the breath, Tai Chi emphasizes body mechanics. The purpose, effects, and benefits are all the same. In reality, Tai Chi is Qigong and Qigong is Tai Chi.

Whatever approach you choose, the experience will provide wide-ranging benefits that positively affect all areas of life. You will gain confidence in the ability of your body, mind and spirit to serve you long and well.

Karinna Kittles

In 1989 I began my studies of Taoist Healing Arts with Master Mantak Chia. Through the profound experiences I had during my first workshop, I discovered the mind, body, spirit path for me.

In 1995 my studies and preparation of the qigong practices brought me to my first real test of mastery. Overnight I developed severe liver pain, so excruciating I could not get out of bed. Western medical blood tests and sonograms were unable to determine what the problem was. After consulting with a Chinese acupuncturist who told me I had excessive fire in my liver; I increased my Qigong meditation and exercises to a daily practice which succeeded in completely resolving my liver pain.

Through this and other empowering qigong experiences, I realized that I was in the driver's seat with my health and emotional and spiritual state. I had found the tools to transform challenging situations into personal success and victory.

My personal journey through the Taoist Healing Arts has given me the desire and commitment to teach individuals and couples the tools for personal healing, love and fulfillment.

Karinna Kittles is a Certified Universal Tao Instructor and Educator. She can be reached at pgranate8@aol.com

Complementary Treatment Therapies

This type of wellness vacation guides the visitor to new and ancient alternative or complementary approaches to treatment for physical conditions. Examples include acupuncture, chiropractic, naturopathic medicine, Hawaiian healing therapies, energy therapy, herbal therapy, homeopathy, preventative medical screening, reflexology, Traditional Chinese Medicine, pain management, and intuitive healing.

Your wellness vacation in Hawai'i offers unparalleled opportunities to explore alternative and complementary treatments for physical conditions which keep you off balance. Eastern, indigenous Hawaiian, and cutting edge Western healing philosophies and treatments available here may guide you to a solution that seemed out of reach before.

Ancient Hawaiians believed that the resolution of any sickness (mental, emotional or physical) began with spirit. Rather than search for a virus, they began by asking what had the person or even their parent or family done to cause disharmony and imbalance. Prayer and a process of forgiveness called *ho'oponopono* would often initiate the healing. If that didn't work, a medical kahuna would be called in. Medical *kahunas* were highly trained. Many were selected at an early age to begin learning their art. Training continued for decades combining tutorials under a respected healer with classroom-type training at a designated place such as a healing heiau.

The Hawaiian renaissance has brought to the surface many time-tested healing remedies using herbs and plants native to Hawai'i or Polynesia. News of the healing power of these herbs, such as *'aloe vera, noni* and *kukui*, is reaching mainstream America and Europe. Just as the use of these healing plants continues today, so does the tradition of looking to spirit. Hawaiians involved in the healing arts begin their process with prayer. Spirit is invoked as they pick the medicinal plant and throughout the ritual of preparing and administering it. *Lomilomi,* the traditional Hawaiian massage begins with invoking God or divine intervention. All Hawaiian healers agree that they are simply a conduit for the healing energy of God, however one views it. They serve to connect this energy to the inner healer within each person they treat. As you explore alternative therapies you will discover that this view is commonly accepted by many wellness providers.

Following are several themes that you are likely to find with alternative therapies. First, there is an understanding that everything consists of vital, active energy and the state of our energy is key to our health. Some say that energy medicine is the medicine of the 21st Century. It is critical to the work of acupuncturists, energy healers, and kinesiologists.

Second is the important role of balance and harmony in our overall wellness. Hawaiians would look to disharmony in relationships first before pursuing a medical treatment. The Chinese believe that human disease occurs when there is internal and external imbalance. Even Western allopathic medicine increasingly recognizes that the imbalance we call stress is a major factor in disease today.

You will also find a commitment to treating the whole person rather than the individual parts of a person. Western medicine tends to see the human body as a collection of separate parts with doctors specializing in working with the heart, brain, feet, ears, nose and throat, bones, nerves, etc. Alternative therapists see the body as a whole. It is part of and influenced by the environment in which we live.

Most of these therapists also agree with the Hawaiians regarding the ***critical role of spirit*** in the balance, harmony and wellness of their client or patient. This involves a belief in the inner healer within each of us. Their role is to honor and facilitate the work of that inner healer.

The following articles offer you more insight into the principles and approaches of these alternative therapies. Articles about holistic medicine and Hawaiian healing therapies give an overview of the holistic approach from Western and Hawaiian perspectives. Applied kinesiology and other forms of kinesiology are alternative methods of diagnosis using muscle testing. Naturopathic medicine, homeopathy, Ayurveda, and Oriental Medicine are major areas of diagnosis and treatment that have evolved out of different traditions and understandings of the body/mind function. Craniosacral, energy medicine and, music and sound therapy are examples of non-invasive complementary modalities that support the body's healing process and can accelerate healing.

Holistic Healing

Listening Deeply and Partnering with Nature

Dr. Linda Fickes, DC, CCN, NMD

From acupuncture to yoga, there are many different types of therapies used by a holistic health practitioner. What defines a holistic health practitioner is the underlying philosophy behind the therapies.

Common Ground • One aspect of common ground among holistic practitioners is their emphasis on listening. Since they are looking at the structural, chemical, emotional and spiritual state and their effects on symptoms, it's important to listen carefully to the clues given by the client as they describe the issues that have brought them into the office.

Next, a holistic practitioner believes that the body is not a mere machine, but a responsive, essential participant in the healing process. They believe that the body functions and heals due to an in-born intelligence. In holistic healing there is respectful communication with the body using many methods: pulse analysis, palpation, reflex points, spine analysis, tension patterns, heat differentials, muscle testing, and more. Holistic practitioners may also use standardized testing such as blood or urine analysis, x-rays, or MRI.

Holistic treatment therapies are nature-based therapies as opposed to drug-based therapies. In hormonal balancing, for instance, when hormonal replacement is necessary, they choose hormones identical to the body's own, not synthetic hormones with their cancer-causing side effects. Holistic practitioners are looking to help repair, not make war.

A holistic practitioner looks at the function of all the organs and systems of the body in order to find the root cause of imbalance, not just compensation for resulting breakdown. For example, fibrocystic breasts are often the result of poor liver detoxification capacity and the cause of that may be as simple as a vitamin B6 deficiency. Holistic practitioners want to strengthen, detoxify or unblock the cause of the problem, not just drug or cut out the symptoms. Disease may appear as a local symptom, but it is always related to the entire system.

Holistic healers are interested in the uniqueness of their patient. They assist the healing by helping the structure, chemistry and emotions come into balance. When obstructions are removed and balance attained, the body is free to do what it is created to do—heal!

Variations and Research • Holistic healers may incorporate techniques such as chiropractic (manual adjustments to improve nerve communication and improve joint alignment), nutrition, (finding the diet that helps the patient function optimally and identifying weakening or irritating foods and nutrient deficiencies), homeopathy (using a tiny dilution of a substance to stimulate health), acupuncture (balancing the body's meridian system and energy flow using needles, herbs and pressure by hand) myofascial therapy (a massage-like therapy that releases the adhesions in the connective tissue affecting function of muscles, ligaments, tendons and joints).

Research into holistic therapies has been stifled in general, since there is little financial motivation to study them. Due to public pressure, however, Congress has recently mandated increased funding for the National Institutes of Health in order to study holistic healing projects. One project was the alternative cancer therapies of Dr. Nick Gonzalez. His pancreatic cancer patients had long-term survival rates unheard of in traditional medicine. The Stamford Research Institute has shown that chiropractic is indisputably beneficial in relieving low back pain. Research into herbal therapies is much better funded in Europe where there is examination of the active chemical constituents of herbs, their safety and best application.

Origins • The history of holistic healing is as ancient as humankind. People have used herbs, diet and touch for healing in every culture on the planet. Chiropractic type joint manipulation was used in ancient China, Egypt, Russia and Hawai'i. Chiropractic itself was founded in Iowa in 1895 by Daniel David Palmer to remove nerve interference so that the innate intelligence of the body could carry out its role of maintaining the body's health and equilibrium without obstruction. Homeopathy was also founded in the late 18th century by German physician Samuel Hahnemann. He theorized that the more a remedy is diluted the greater its potency, and that the illness is specific to the individual. The history of nutrition was strongly influenced by Roger Williams, Ph.D. a biochemist who discovered vitamin B5 in the 1930's. His research showed that each person is genetically unique and therefore requires slight variations in nutrient intake to function optimally. Another nutrition pioneer was Westin

Price, DDS. He traveled around the world in the early 1900's documenting that those populations with natural diets had excellent health and dental structures, but those who consumed the western refined sugar and flour diet had universally poorer health.

What to Expect • When visiting a holistic practitioner a client should feel safe, comfortable, and respected. Both communication and education about health related issues will be encouraged. The goal is to move toward a sense of well-being and a quality of life, strength, and energy that can prevent imbalances caused from toxins, stresses and infections.

In Hawai'i there is aloha for the ideas and practices of holistic healing. One reason for that is familiarity. Most of the oriental cultures here grew up using herbs and acupuncture for their health problems. The native Hawaiians have always highly valued their healers. They use local herbs, massage, joint manipulation, but most importantly spiritual healing techniques. The principles of holistic healing are essentially the same principles that define the Hawaiian identity and culture. Thanks to the Hawaiian emphasis on qualities such as love, harmony and righteousness, any visitor from the mainland can tell there is a more heart-centered way of life here. With less emphasis on intellectual proof and more emphasis on feeling the results, holistic healing has been well supported in Hawai'i.

Linda Fickes

My commitment to helping heal the planet drew me to work at the United Nations, first in Geneva as a student, then in New York after college. I enthusiastically worked long hours on projects for the environment, disarmament, human rights and disaster relief. After five years, my idealism waned. There was always another million refugees, but no political will to help them. One late night I realized that what I wanted was to see change right in front of me, using my own two hands. The very next day, I met two chiropractic students. I knew immediately that that was how I could use my hands and help create positive change. So I went back to school to learn about chiropractic, nutrition and holistic healing. I have always been grateful for that decision.

In chiropractic school, I discovered that my long hours of meditation over the years had yielded a new benefit–my intuition for diagnostics and treatment was excellent. However, my intuition for relationships needed refinement. I left my abusive marriage, and my Fifth Avenue chiropractic practice, and, with my infant daughter, came to Hawai'i for refuge. I wanted the freedom to practice the way I would like to be treated. Fourteen wonderful years of spiritual, emotional and professional growth have followed. Hawai'i has truly been a nurturing home.

Dr. Linda Fickes is a chiropractor, certified clinical nutritionist, and naturopathic physician practicing in Honolulu. She also provides radiation-free, thermographic breast exams and can be reached at 808.377.1811 or fickesl001@hawaii.rr.com.

~ THE ANCIENT ART OF HAWAIIAN HEALING ~

Maria-Antonetta Filippone

Origins • Before the Hawaiian people came in contact with industrial technologies and philosophies over 200 years ago, their perception of reality was essentially different from that of their white "discoverers". They utilized their material environment in all aspects of island life, being outstanding navigators, fishermen, and farmers, to name only a few fields of expertise. To them, reality extended beyond the things the eyes can see and the hands can touch; their everyday world included the realm of forces, which work behind and create material things, a realm that is experienced only through the inner senses or intuition.

For the common people, those invisible forces took the shape of gods and spirits.

Through prayers and faith they directed their own powers to influence the desired outcome of any small and large project, be it a smooth ocean journey, a bountiful catch of fish, or a rich harvest. A small part of the community devoted their life to the training of esoteric skills, and they are reported to have accomplished miraculous feats, such as calling rain in times of draught, stirring up mighty waves to fight back an army of invaders, or healing the sick by mere touch and prayer. Their supreme task consisted in striving toward an ideal state of complete oneness and harmony called *lōkahi* that encompassed the whole of their community and environment

Like everything else in their universe, traditional Hawaiians saw life and death, and disease and healing as elements of the spiritual plane, the one source of all. Perfect health reflected a state of perfect balance on all levels of a person's being: physical in terms of food, work, and play, mental in terms of relationships with family and community, spiritual in terms of attitude towards creation and creator. Physical harmony was achieved through appropriate, constructive activity, mental harmony through acts of righteousness and service, spiritual harmony through gratitude and humility. The Hawaiian healer's task was to help the ailing individual with practical measures and counseling to alleviate health problems and to regain the lost balance.

The Training of Kahunas • A traditional healer's education began in early childhood, when he or she grew into the profession by either assisting a healer parent or being adopted by a healer and living with that person. Only after decades of practice was a trainee regarded as an expert or *kahuna*. There were several classes and subclasses of specialization; three of the main fields were healing through prayer *(kāhea)*, massage therapy *(lomilomi)*, and the application of medicinal herbs *(lā'au lapa'au)*. While *kahuna kāhea* were especially famous for instantly healing broken bones without physical manipulation, *kahuna lomilomi* worked their healing power through their hands. The *kahuna la'au lapa'au's* therapy consisted in counseling and the administration of herbs. Apart from the expert healers, there was a rich body of folk medicine; each family knew how to take care of themselves to a certain degree.

Every one of the seven main Hawaiian Islands has its distinct personality. In old times, when inter-island traffic was limited to canoe voyaging, these characteristics were even more pronounced. Consequently, the healing practices also showed an individual profile on each island. Like any professional people striving for excellence, Hawaiian healers sought constantly to improve their craft by exchanging ideas and knowledge with other healers.

Groups of specialists were organized in temple guilds, and there were conventions held, which included all islands. It was believed that the Big Island of Hawai'i, with its active volcanoes, held a special spiritual power or *mana* for healing that infused its medicinal herbs and made them superior.

The Lost Art • When the people of Hawai'i embraced Christianity in the early 1800s, traditional spiritual notions were discarded as heathenish or superstitious, and with them the foundation of a rich and complex culture, well adapted to its environment and wise in economizing the use of its resources. Their outlook on healing as well as their powers posed a threat to the new establishment. Without resistance, the *kahuna* mostly ceased to share or pass on their knowledge. In the meantime, society on the Hawaiian Islands became flooded with immigrants and "westernized", while the old Hawaiian culture faded into history and the number of native descendants dwindled. The last Hawaiian king, Kalākaua, made an attempt to reestablish some of their traditions, founding, among other things, a health care center run exclusively by Hawaiian healers in the late 1800s. It was closed soon after and the remaining *kahuna* once again quietly vanished from the scene. Since ancient Hawaiians had no writing, most of the old information is irretrievably lost

In the 1960s and 70s, a cultural revival movement arose from the small community of Hawaiian and part-Hawaiian descendants, reclaiming a virtually lost heritage. Today, this movement continues and has inspired a keen interest in Hawaiian healing. Some of the body of knowledge has been preserved through folk medicine, in later literature, and through a few individuals who received some training from a lineage of kahuna. Those who give serious time and devotion to practicing the art have developed workable techniques from the fragmented information. The traditional Hawaiian healing specialties commonly practiced today are *lomilomi, la'au lapa'au* and *ho'oponopono*, which is a counseling therapy system to restore and maintain good relationships among family members and family-and-supernatural powers, that is, the Divine.

The Therapeutic Experience • *Ho'oponopono* sessions are made available by social and health services, and it has proven to be a most valuable tool in providing culturally fitting help for descendants of native Hawaiians. Several alternative counselors have incorporated the timeless wisdom of *ho'oponopono* group therapy into their practice and there is literature on the subject. Certain outstanding *la'au lapa'au* experts have been able to successfully treat modern diseases such as cancer and heart dysfunctions with herbal formulas. In general, herbs are administered mainly within families today, but the interested visitor has access to *la'au lapa'au* practitioners at lectures or workshops which are designed to perpetuate the knowledge. *Lomilomi* experts are providing the most visible contribution to contemporary Hawaiian healing. They hold training classes and serve clients in chiropractic clinics, spas and/or health retreats.

In an ideal situation, you come with an open mind, a willingness to take responsibility for your problems, and enough time to work it through under the healer's help and direction. You will be given time to talk about your health problems and your life situation. A good healer will be able to make you feel at ease, safe and respected. You will be advised to turn to the highest power with sincerity and faith and be ready to ask for forgiveness and make amends for where you went wrong in your physical, mental, or spiritual conduct. This interpretation of your problems does not make them a punishment of a stern divine judge, but puts you in charge of the maintenance of your own well-being and the gift of life you have been entrusted with. Likewise, the healer will not impose judgment on you, but will enable you, with gentle questions, to see your situation from a different angle and recognize the steps you need to take in order to help yourself.

Beside the priority of starting a daily prayer routine and reaching out to connect with your creator in a dialogue, in most cases you will be given suggestions about how to improve your outlook on things, your diet and other lifestyle habits. All those measurements are required along with the medicine or therapy that the healer will target to your specific needs. Even though physical therapies and many herbs used in Hawaiian tradition have documented effects, it is believed that their true potency is charged through your and your healer's faith, aspiration, and prayer. If possible, the healer will accompany you until full restoration of your health is achieved and in the end congratulate you that it was mainly your faith and determination that pulled you through. Since you are an inseparable part of the whole, from the Hawaiian healer's point of view, your healing will make an important contribution to the healing of your environment, thus moving towards the ideal of lōkahi.

Maria-Antonetta Filippone

"I first came from Germany to the Big Island in 1994 to study traditional Hawaiian medicine for my PhD in Anthropology. I was privileged to become an apprentice of the late "Papa" Henry Auwae who passed away in 2001. He was known nationally and internationally as one of the most highly regarded Hawaiian herbalists. He helped numerous patients overcome some of the most severe ailments. In order to perpetuate his valuable tradition, he set aside cultural boundaries and accepted as students anyone whom he considered capable of being a healer. I graduated from his 18-months class certified as Mo'olono Lā'au Lapa'au, one of the initial stages in his hierarchy of the Hawaiian healing profession. I then returned to Germany in 1996 with the intention of preparing to move permanently to Hawai'i. Since late 1999, I had been living on the Big Island where I finally completed my thesis on the apprenticeship. It will be published soon. Along with fellow apprentices, I have followed Papa Auwae's instructions to continue to educate myself in the many aspects of Hawaiian medicine and contribute my share to upholding its legacy, that it may benefit health seekers of today and the future."

Maria-Antonetta Filippone is completing her doctoral degree in medical anthropology. She lives in Kailua-Kona and can be reached at 808.937.2993.

~ Curious About Kinesiology? ~

Debra Greene, Ph.D.

The word *kinesiology* conventionally refers to the study of the movement of muscles, which is more accurately referred to as *structural kinesiology*. We are concerned here with a particular type of kinesiology, sometimes called *applied kinesiology* or specialized kinesiology, which refers to muscle response testing, or muscle testing, for short.

Origins and Theory • Muscle testing, in some form, has likely existed in various cultures for a long time. In the United States it was established in the 1960s by a chiropractor named George Goodheart. Dr. Goodheart, also a practitioner of Chinese Medicine, studied the subtle energy systems of the body as well as the physical systems. In combining his knowledge of these systems, Dr. Goodheart discovered the interrelationship among the energy meridians, the particular organs those meridians feed into, and the specific muscles that are governed by the meridians. Dr. Goodheart, along with his colleague Dr. John Thie, also a chiropractor, developed a system called Touch For Health (TFH) that forms the foundation for an entire family of kinesiology applications.

Applied kinesiology is a system that uses muscle testing to monitor the flow of energy in the body. Muscle testing produces two important responses—an observable visual response and a felt kinesthetic response. These twin indicators are produced simultaneously through muscle testing and allow for detailed observation of the body's energy systems. This is possible because, in order for a muscle to fire, an entire bio-chemical-electrical-energetic process is involved. In muscle testing, we are concerned with the energy aspects of this process.

Muscle testing is accomplished by positioning the body to isolate a particular muscle. The kinesiologist—a person trained to manually monitor the quality of the muscle response--then tests the muscle manually by applying consistent touch pressure for about two seconds. A muscle that tests weak indicates a blockage or constriction of energy flow.

Muscle testing produces a binary code—a muscle feels either strong or weak—and this code can be used as a biofeedback indicator to gain information about any part of the body and other levels as well. Muscle testing responds to verbal "questions." Thus, muscle testing can be used to access information from a variety of levels—physical, emotional, mental, and spiritual—because energy blockages may be present on any or all of these levels. An energy constriction is released by a process called a *balance*.

Variations • A kinesiology balance can consist of a wide variety of energy-centered techniques designed to assist people in moving forward on multiple levels. Depending upon the kinesiologist, physical contact during a kinesiology balance ranges from no touch to light touch pressure, to tapping or firm massage. Kinesiology balancing may also involve movement activities and/or vibrational technologies, such as visualization, affirmation, meditation, flower remedies, color, sound, symbology, and essential oils.

There are now dozens of established systems that use muscle testing as their primary assessment tool. Some examples of kinesiology applications are: Professional Kinesiology Practitioner (PKP), an expansion of Touch for Health (TFH) with advanced physical assessments and corrections including primary emotions; Educational Kinesiology (Edu-K) to activate and integrate brain, sensory, and motor systems; Wellness Kinesiology (WK) a vast system that includes emotional repatterning along with food and environmental sensitivity clearing; Ontological Kinesiology (OK) using mudras and muscle testing to unwind the unique "story" of each individual—from nutritional deficiencies to family-ancestral patterns, and Transformational Kinesiology (TK), which combines the art of muscle testing with the science of subtle energies to reveal the life patterns of an individual and transform them via soul-infusion.

Applications and Benefits • Because of its effectiveness as an assessment method, kinesiology enjoys applications in medicine, chiropractic, dentistry, counseling, psychotherapy, energy medicine, veterinary medicine, athletics, business, education, and the performing arts. It is also used as a self-help aid, for example, for assessing nutritional or herbal remedies.

Kinesiology is most often used by health professionals

and educators to help clients improve their quality of life. It can enhance learning and performance skills, correct electromagnetic distress and allergies, eliminate physical dysfunction due to energy blockages, facilitate emotional balance, and transform limiting belief systems that are outside of conscious awareness. Clients often enjoy more freedom and peace of mind. As can be seen, kinesiology has a vast array of applications and can be an important facilitator of optimal health and vitality.

Debra Greene, Ph.D.

My first exposure to applied kinesiology was as a graduate student at Ohio State University. I greeted the kinesiology experience with all of the finely honed, critical, analytical abilities of a good academic. In a word, I was skeptical. In my personal life, I was stuck in a behavior pattern that I was fully aware of, but felt powerless to change, despite my strong will. In just one Transformational Kinesiology (TK) session I focused on that behavior pattern and transformed it, never to be repeated again. I was so taken with TK that I quickly moved from being a client to becoming a practitioner and, eventually, a certified TK Educator.

I was blessed to receive training from the developers of TK, Grethe Fremming, president of the International Kinesiology College (IKC), and her husband, Rolf Havsboel. I studied the science of subtle energies and the art of muscle testing, an endeavor that made my rigorous doctorate program seem tame by comparison. I later taught in the Graduate School for Holistic Studies at John F. Kennedy University in California. In 1989, responding to an undeniable intuitive invitation, I quit my job and moved to Maui. Today, in addition to my private TK practice, I teach at the Maui Academy of Healing Arts and at Esalen Institute in California.

Debra Greene, Ph.D., is a kinesiologist, communication specialist, and certified PAIRS educator who lives on Maui. She is co-Founder of HeartPath: Conscious Communication, and can be reached at 808.874.6441 or info@HeartPath.org.

~ Oriental Medicine and Acupuncture ~

Correcting the Imbalances

Robert E. Smith, Ph.D and Scott Miller, L. Ac.

Origin • Beginning 5,000 years ago with the insights of the Taoist sages, Oriental medicine has collected a vast body of medical experience. There are similarities between Oriental medicine, the Greek medicine of Hippocrates, and other traditional approaches, including Hawaiian. All recognize the value in restoring harmony and balance to assist nature in healing the patient's body, mind and spirit. As with the practice of the ancient Greeks under Hippocrates, Oriental doctors look for the imbalances that lead to disease. The practice is to restore that balance through the use of herbs, dietary therapy, lifestyle counseling, and other therapeutic approaches.

Research and Accreditation • Extensive research has demonstrated the efficacy of Oriental medicine. Although much of this documentation is found in Asian journals and texts, there are also many English-language professional journals that are reporting research. In the mid 1990's, the National Institutes of Health reclassified acupuncture from experimental to "safe and effective". Today, auto insurance, worker's compensation, and most health insurance companies cover acupuncture treatments.

The World Health Organization recognizes acupuncture as being effective in the treatment of a variety of conditions including but not limited to: ear, nose, and throat disorders, respiratory disorders, gastro-intestinal disorders, nervous system and muscular disorders, gynecological problems, trauma, back pain, and whiplash. It is also known to be effective on internal organ disorders, sleep disorders, stress, and skin problems. Acupuncture is so effective at pain relief it can be substituted for Western anesthesia during surgery.

All states except Hawai'i now permit MDs to be licensed to practice acupuncture. The growing pressure from the western medical profession to permit such licensing itself attests to acupuncture's efficacy as a medical treatment. To date, Hawai'i takes the position that acupuncture requires a thorough understanding of Oriental medical theory. The depth of training that the public expects of all physicians cannot be obtained by a short course in acupuncture. Therefore, to practice acupuncture in Hawai'i, the practitioner must have a Master's Degree in Oriental Medicine, and pass a rigorous examination.

Hawai'i is fortunate to have two accredited colleges of Oriental medicine, the Tai Hsuan Foundation in Honolulu and the Traditional Chinese Medical College of Hawai'i on the Big Island (TCMCH). Angela Longo, L.Ac., Ph.D founded TCMCH in 1986 to carry on the tradition of her teacher Dr. Lam Kong, who had left China at the time of the Cultural Revolution. The college is located in Waimea on the Big Island.

TCMCH provides both an outstanding educational program, leading to the degree Master of Science in Oriental Medicine, and a program of public service that offers high quality and low cost health care to the community through their Teaching Clinic. TCMCH combines an excellent Chinese pharmacology (herbal medicine) program with broad training in Oriental medical theory, acupuncture and Western medical science.

Theory and Practice • Treatments are highly individualized. Twelve different patients presenting the same symptoms may be treated in 12 different ways, depending on the practitioner's underlying diagnosis of the causes of those symptoms. This focus on cause is the reason Oriental medicine is highly effective in treating chronic disease, although it can also be effective in managing symptoms during recovery.

A variety of tools are used to treat patients. The best known is acupuncture, but acupuncture is almost always reinforced by herbal prescriptions to assist the balancing process, and patients are often counseled regarding diet, exercise, lifestyle, and perhaps bodywork. All of these approaches assist the body to heal itself.

The goal of Oriental medicine is to promote balance and harmony in the patient's body. An evaluation of the whole person is performed, based on the "Eight Principles." First it is determined whether the patient's problem has its origins outside or exterior to the body, or if the problem is stemming from an interior dysfunction, then if the problem is one of an excess condition, or a deficiency, next whether it is a hot condition or cold, and finally whether it is a dry or a damp condition.

What To Expect • A patient can expect a thorough evaluation, which includes Pulse Diagnosis, a method of feeling the pulse in twelve locations on the wrist, with up to 28 different subtle qualities in each location. Patients are frequently amazed by the amount of information a diagnostician can obtain by palpating the pulses, including the state of the organ systems, emotional balance, and digestion. Tongue Diagnosis involves examining the locations of cracks, the colors and coating of the tongue, and analyzing the patterns of symptoms such as sleep, bowel movements, and sweating. This is supplemented by a thorough medical history.

The practitioner will take all this information and combine it with a little bit of intuition, to come up with a "pattern of disharmony." This provides the map for treating the patient's individual condition most effectively.

Acupuncture involves the insertion of very fine single use, sterile needles into specific points, which have been shown effective in treating various health problems. Typically a patient can expect to be needled in 5 to 30 points in various parts of the body and ears. There is little or no discomfort. A session typically lasts about an hour and is very relaxing. In addition to the needles an acupuncturist will also use other modalities as appropriate. These may include: **Electrical Stimulation:** A slight electrical current is passed through needles or through adhesive pads to stimulate the points. **Moxibustion:** An herb called mugwort is burned to heat up various points or areas on the body. **Tui-Na Massage:** a form of oriental massage where the practitioner pushes and pulls with the hands. This is usually deep work that can correct some structural problems. **Acupressure:** the application of pressure to certain points using the fingers instead of needles. **Qi-Gong:** an energy exercise that moves and builds "Qi", or energy in the body, and builds up the immune system. It may seem too simple to be doing much, but the benefits can be striking. **Herbal Treatment:** Herbs come either in tablet, tincture, or tea form. There are herbs that make tendons and bones grow stronger, herbs that relieve pain and inflammation, herbs that improve sleep, herbs that promote dryness or moisture, herbs that boost energy or reduce tension, herbs that raise blood pressure or lower it, and on and on.

Oriental medicine addresses the causes of disease rather than the symptoms. It treats body-mind-spirit as a single entity, seeking to provide the balance and harmony within the patient that promotes healing and maintains health.

Robert E. Smith, Ph.D.

Hawai'i introduced me to healing in dramatic ways. A medical scientist and medical school faculty member, I encountered new worlds of healing when I studied traditional Hawaiian herbal medicine with its foremost practitioner, Papa Henry Auwae. I saw Papa heal patients for whom Western medicine had no answers, and I came to understand Papa's emphasis on lōkahi, harmony of mind, body and spirit, as essential to the healing process. Asked to explain Papa's ability to Western medical audiences, I explained that Papa's recognition that healing is 80% spiritual, only 20% medicine, was the secret of his success.

My second revelation was my introduction to Oriental medicine. Severe respiratory disease had left my wife dying, a mute quadriplegic. Western medicine kept her alive during her hospitalization, but it was the skill of a faculty member of the Traditional Chinese Medical College of Hawai'i (TCMCH) using acupuncture, herbal medicine and dietary therapy, that enabled her to recover and walk again. I was impressed— I welcomed the opportunity to join the College as a faculty member and was honored to become its President. Oriental medicine, like Papa Auwae, restores harmony and health. Hawai'i honors both traditional and Western medicine, making it the finest center of healing I have known.

Robert E. Smith is a medical educator who lives in Waimea (Kamuela) on the Big Island. He is the President of the TCMCH as well as a faculty member of the School of Medicine, UC Davis. He can be reached at (808) 885-9226 or at tcmch1@kona.net.

Scott Miller, LAc

I could not walk without crutches, I could not sit without holding up my weight with both hands, I could not drive to get my own food, I was in excruciating pain and after two failed back surgeries was told to prepare myself mentally to be in that kind of pain the rest of my life. Then I reluctantly tried acupuncture as a last resort, and after that first treatment never needed crutches again. While I wasn't pain free, and I did continue to get regular treatments, I experienced an unbelievable level of relief.

This inspired me to get my Masters of Oriental Medicine, obtain my Hawai'i Acupuncture and Massage licenses, and open the Healing Arts Alliance Clinic in downtown Hilo. While I deal with the whole gambit of human conditions, I most enjoy working on back pain patients.

I love my work; it is my passion. I put everything I have into every treatment that I do, and this comes through to my patients. I've found that the combination of knowledge, intuition, acupuncture, massage, and topical and internal herbal therapies can produce some amazing results.

Scott Miller is an acupuncturist, herbalist, and massage therapist who works out of his clinic, Healing Arts Alliance, in downtown Hilo on the Big Island. He can be reached at 808.934.7030 or at healer@hilo.net.

~ AYURVEDA: SCIENCE OF LIFE ~

Sharon Forsyth

Origins • Ayurveda, "science of life", is considered to be the world's oldest system of health. It is an "oral" tradition passed down from generation to generation. Only in the last 5,000 years has Ayurveda been written down. The history of Ayurveda goes back as far as the Indus Valley Civilization of religion. This is considered the Pre-Vedic Era between 3000 BC and1500 BC.

Ayurvedic physicians gathered information by observing nature and the elements. As they studied their behaviors and qualities, they began to compare and understand how they work in the body. What goes on in the outside world also goes on within the human physiology. The difference is that when the elements manifest within the body they are called doshas. They are functional, unseen intelligences within the body.

Theoretical Foundations • The three main doshas are called Vata, Pitta and Kapha and they act together to bring food, oxygen and water from the GI tract to the body tissues. They discriminate between what should be retained and what should be eliminated.

Vata governs all movement in the body and is responsible for all voluntary and involuntary impulses. It is the director of transportation, causing everything in creation to move to the right place at the right time. Because it controls all movement in nature, it actually governs the actions of the other two doshas. It is the wind element or ether and air.

Pitta manifests the properties of heat and light and facilitates all transformations in the body and the mind, such as digestion and assimilation. It is the fire element.

Kapha governs form and substance and is responsible for weight, stability and lubrication. It is the water and earth element.

One of the main causes of disease is when the relationship of the doshas is imbalanced. This is often a result of improper diet, problems with lifestyle and change of seasons.

The first phase of disease is accumulation of toxins in the GI tract. The second phase involves increased aggravation as more toxins accumulate. In the third phase the toxins overflow and migrate to other tissues (blood, muscle, fat, bone, bone marrow). In the fourth phase, toxins lodge in weak tissues, overwhelming it. In the fifth and sixth phases there is damage and loss of immunity.

Sixty percent of most diseases can be reversed by proper diet and lifestyle. Treatments and proper herbal medicines are also needed to recover health.

What to Expect • The aim of Ayurvedic therapies is to maintain the youthfulness of the body and extend life span. Pancha Karma is the practice most used in Ayurveda to achieve these results. This is the oldest scientific system for detoxifying and re-nutrifying the body.

Pancha Karma means "5 actions" which are: cleansing of the small intestines, colon, stomach, sinus cavities and the blood. These actions are performed on the body in a very specific order. When done properly, they will detoxify and rejuvenate the whole system. To prepare for pancha karma, oil massages, herbal scrubs and sweating therapies are performed to penetrate the vital tissues in order to dislodge accumulations of toxins. Treatments are usually given for 7 consecutive days as there are 7 layers of bodily tissue to be cleansed.

Much like the Hawaiian culture, Ayurveda is always striving to create a balance between the elements within the body. Daily routines, proper diet, seasonal cleansing and rejuvenation are suggested to maintain health. Both cultures trust in the body's innate healing abilities, using medicinal herbs for support and the practice of prayer, in the form of chant and dance. Both systems invite the individual to get more involved in their healing. In Hawai'i *ho'oponopono* is used to "set things right" and to clear ancestral patterns; in India it is known as Tarpana.

Currently, Ayurveda is the vogue alternative medicine. A great possibility exists that Ayurveda can be combined with other schools of thought to make all treatment methods more effective, becoming part of a global medical system.

Sharon Forsyth

Aloha, my name is Sharon Forsyth. My journey in the health field began over 20 years ago. As soon as I left home as a teenager I began my search to feel healthier and more vibrant. Studying nutrition, practicing healthy diets and fasting programs, I became healthier and knew I had found my path. Massage school and a variety of other bodywork classes followed. Something was still missing. As a child I always had a hunger to know God, to know the "Truth", and so my path brought me to my first meditation teacher. Focusing on the peace inside revealed what was not at peace with me. To help heal myself and others of old wounds, I sought out training for emotional and mental healing, inner child work, movement and breathwork.

Even after all of this, I was still seeking. It was this hunger that took me to India to find the Truth. Here I met my Spiritual Teacher and found what I was looking for, my SELF....PEACE. While in India I had the opportunity to study Ayurveda and Siddha Medicines. A new passion was fueled. A passion to share the Truth and to offer healing and cleansing modalities that have been known for thousands of years. In 1996 I left India and came to the Big Island of Hawai'i, the Healing Island. In 1999, I turned my home into a healing facility and residential retreat for cleansing and rejuvenation programs in Kailua-Kona, Akash Healing Center.

Sharon Ann Forsyth is an Ayurvedic Practitioner living on the Island of Hawai'i in Kailua-Kona. She is the founder of the Akash Healing Center and can be reached at 808.331.2276 or ayusidha@ilhawaii.net

Naturopathic Medicine

Treating the Cause Rather than the Symptom

Jacqueline Hahn, N.D.

Naturopathic medicine is a growing healthcare specialty where licensed naturopathic physicians (general and family practice primary care physicians) focus on treating the cause, rather than the symptoms, on treating the whole person rather than just their condition, and on studying mechanisms for healing and restoring wellness rather than the "fight disease" mindset. Whenever possible, naturopathic doctors (NDs) specialize in using nature-based therapies rather than concentrated or toxic pharmaceuticals. They also individualize all treatment approaches to fit the needs of each patient. NDs are the only licensed family physicians clinically trained in botanical, nutritional, and homeopathic medicines as the primary therapies for all health conditions.

Origins • As with all healing traditions, naturopathic medicine was birthed through the evolution of science, medicine and the human condition. Naturopathic medical schools have been around as long as medical schools. Naturopathic practitioners were very popular prior to the golden age of pharmaceutical and technological medicine. They were the safest and most effective alternative to the medical practices of the late 1800's and early 1900's, which were still quite barbaric and toxic. As more refined drug therapies like antibiotics and vaccinations were developed, and safer more effective medical technologies came of age through the mid 1900's, medical doctors and the pharmaceutical companies became the dominant players in the business of medicine.

What to Expect • To facilitate this kind of practice, visits to a naturopathic physician are often much longer because, in addition to routine physical exams, they include a more detailed interview and analysis of an individual's mental, emotional and physical condition. Naturopathic physicians have a commitment to become partners with patients and to work as a team toward establishing health and wellness goals. To prepare for this, Naturopathic medical school training includes active counseling and teaching skills.

Some of the treatment plans used by Naturopathic Physicians are based on several hundred years of experience and research from traditions such as homeopathy, herbal medicine, and hydrotherapy. NDs tend to use the least toxic therapies first in any condition, with the focus on 1) strengthening the body's natural healing mechanisms specific to any condition, and 2) supporting detoxifying the body so it can achieve balance and homeostasis, which the human body is designed to do. Drug therapies all too often rob the body of the chance to find its own equilibrium and true healing.

Differences from Standard Therapies • Pharmaceutical medicines continue to be the main therapies offered by medical doctors. This, despite the fact that demographic studies have shown that prescription drugs are the 4th-6th leading cause of death in this country, while preventable diseases continue to rise. As drug side effects, heart disease, diabetes and cancers climb to epidemic proportions, it is again time for a less toxic, more holistic approach to healthcare.

Natural medical therapies differ from standard drug therapies in that there is more room for individual variation of treatment protocols. Patients have a larger role in their own health decision-making when working with an ND. This means more choice about which treatment modalities are used and more responsibility for the patient in following through with lifestyle changes.

Naturopaths are trained, like all primary care physicians, at accredited medical colleges to diagnose and treat disease. They use, but are not limited to, some of the same diagnostic tools and procedures, such as lab tests and referrals and consults with other medical specialists. Treatment modalities include diet analysis, nutritional medicines, botanical medicines, physical medicines, energetic medicine, emotional support, and homeopathic remedies. Some NDs specialize in obstetrics (family physicians trained and licensed to practice safe out-of-hospital birthing for low risk mothers), minor surgery and advanced homeopathy.

More and more natural therapies are being tested around the world in clinical trials. This is helping to map some of the most effective natural strategies for treating common health disorders, as well as chronic disease and "terminal" illnesses. Studies are proving for the first time in history that some of these methods can match, and in some cases exceed, the effectiveness of modern drug therapeutic approaches. In most cases a natural therapy will also be far less risky for side effects.

Because ND's work so differently from the insurance-driven, cost cutting medical system with their time intensive and individualized approach, only high end and progressive health insurance policies tend to cover their services (except in states where insurance equality among licensed physicians is mandated). This means the average consumer seeking naturopathic services pays out of pocket. Consumers vote loudest with their pocket books, however, and as they find what works for them, the demand for naturopathic services continues to grow everywhere.

Jacqueline Hahn, N.D.

Like many coming to the Big Island, it has been a long and wandering road. Although I had visited Hilo twice in 10 years, when I moved here four years ago it was like landing in the "big city". I came here with my family after living on a tiny island in the remote Pacific for four years. It had been an intensely rich and challenging journey as a mother, barefoot doctor on an island of 2000, teacher in a six-room college, public health disease prevention coordinator, and veterinary bush doctor. Nature was big and powerful compared to human existence , yet the natural balance was very comforting somehow.

The Big Island has shouldered my landing back into civilization over the last four years in a gentle and sacred way through some dramatically challenging physical, emotional and spiritual times. I am honored to find myself feeling deeply held here as I continue to grow and serve in a high capacity through a growing integrated holistic natural healthcare center that demands I bring forth all the wisdom and tools my experience, teachings and ancestry have brought me.

Dr. Jacqueline Hahn is a holistic, eclectic naturopathic physician, and founder of Hilo Naturopathic and Acupuncture Clinic on the Big Island. She specializes in chronic disease, home health care and natural child birthing and can be reached at 808.969.7848 and at dochahn@bigisland.com.

HOMEOPATHY
Like Cures Like
Dr. Glen Swartwout

Homeopathy is a system of medicine developed more than two hundred years ago. The simple beauty of this form of medicine is in its fundamental objective and mode of operation: to stimulate the body's natural defenses and gently guide the body to a state of balanced health. All signs and symptoms associated with illness are understood as an expression of the body's attempts to restore order.

Origins • The meaning of the word homeopathy reveals its working principle: homeo = same; pathy = suffering. This basic principle is called the law of similars, "like cures like." This approach, having been thoroughly investigated and demonstrated clinically by its founder, Samuel Hahnemann, seeks the remedy that produces the same symptoms the person complains of, which then stimulates the body into the necessary and appropriate healing action.

Hahnemann studied in great detail the effects of many medicinal substances of his day on healthy people. These substances were found to predictably provoke symptoms in healthy subjects very similar to those symptoms that were cured in the sick. These symptoms became known as the disease or remedy "picture." Hahnemann would then match these pictures with the symptoms presented by a sick person and apply infinitesimal doses of the remedy whose picture was similar to the suffering of this particular patient. He found that the closer the match between the remedy picture and the symptom picture of the patient, the more likely a curative response would be evoked and the body would heal itself.

When using homeopathic remedies, keep in mind the time proven axioms of Dr. Hering who was a homeopathic doctor in America in the 19th century. Dr. Hering's Law of Cures states that the cure of the body tends to follow a specific pattern. Symptoms will improve from the top of the body downward, from the inside outward (internal vital organs to the external skin), from the most important organ to the least important. The cure takes place in the reverse order in which the symptoms had their onset. For example, a sick person will begin to feel better emotionally before the physical symptoms disappear. Thus, a symptom of long duration will not resolve until a more recent symptom has resolved.

Obstacles to Acceptance • The gentle effectiveness of this method of curing acute and chronic illness was probably the cause of its rapid spread throughout Germany in Hahnemann's time, across Europe to the Americas, and on to Asia. Today, homeopathy is highly respected and widely used in Britain, France, Germany, the Netherlands, Greece, South Africa, South America and India. In America, at the turn of the century, most medical schools and hospitals were homeopathic. During epidemics of flu and cholera, documented recovery rates were much higher in hospitals that employed homeopathy, as compared to those using patent medicines (i.e. chemical drugs). For example, in 1854, there was an outbreak of cholera in London and the mortality rates were compared between the homeopathic hospitals and the 'allopathic' drug-based hospitals: 16.4% compared to 51.8%. Unfortunately these statistics were not allowed to be published at the time.

The legal advantage of patent medicine in securing a period of monopolistic profits for each new drug invented eventually led to the demise of homeopathy as the leading field of medicine in the American republic. The rich family foundations, such as Rockefeller and Carnegie that began funding education in this country, withdrew their support from these schools because their own research found them to hold less profit potential. This is because homeopathic remedies are produced from natural substances and cannot be patented. Furthermore, only small amounts of the remedy were needed to affect a cure and most cures were simple and complete, not having an indefinite period of dependence as with many of the patent drugs.

Homeopathy Rediscovered • Homeopathy is now being rediscovered in America, with a growth rate of 30% each year. Many people are becoming increasingly frustrated at the limitations of chemical medicine in dealing with areas of prevention, individualized symptomatology and even chronic disease. Many professionals, including MD's, are seeking to bring the knowledge of homeopathy into their practices and directly to their patients. A basic knowledge of this science applied to everyday minor health problems may help us prevent more serious problems from developing, including those caused by invasive medical approaches.

Dr. Glen Swartwout

In 1982, I suspected I was suffering from mercury toxicity based on my symptoms, including memory loss, glaucoma, cataracts and slurring of speech. But standard chemistry tests of blood, urine and hair failed to find the problem. Then I attended a seminar on Oligo-Element trace mineral therapies from Europe in which the Vegatest method of German Electroacupuncture was demonstrated. Volunteering as a test subject, I learned that I was indeed mercury toxic, but a non-excreter. This explained the lack of mercury on the chemistry panels.

During the 20 years of my journey of recovery from mercury toxicity, my friends have marveled at my continual rejuvenation as I applied the testing and therapy methods I use in my practice.

Thirteen years ago a Hawaiian Kahuna brought me, sight unseen, to the Healing Island of Hawai'i where her ancestors had cared for the Heiau nearest the world's most active volcano.

At first I wondered why I came to such an isolated part of the planet, but I have long since fallen in love with this reminder of Eden and those who carry on the aloha spirit here. I marvel at how the divine works with our lives, as my latest research into alchemy shows that our volcano is one of the best sources of the m-state minerals that animate life and feed the spirit body.

Glen Swartwout is a minister and doctor of optometry who lives in Hilo in the Kingdom of Hawai'i. He is the founder of the Remission-Foundation and can be reached at 808-935-5086 and drglen@wizardofeyez.com.

CRANIOSACRAL

Unwinding Stress and Pain

Alia Hallowell, CST, LMT, RPP

Origin of the therapy • The beginnings of Craniosacral Therapy date back to the early 1900's when a teopathic physician from the midwestern United States, William G. Sutherland, became intrigued by the structure and function of the human cranium (skull). Contrary to the belief of British and American physicians who believed the skull was a rigid structure, Dr. Sutherland explored the possibility of movement in the sutures, or seams between the bones. He experimented on himself with a self-designed helmet that applied pressure against specific locations in the cranium. He carefully recorded his physical symptoms, while his wife kept a journal on his emotional behavior. Through his research on himself and his medical patients, Dr. Sutherland discovered he could ease dysfunctions by applying external pressures following the natural movements of the cranial bones. He founded Cranial Osteopathy, a therapeutic tradition that continues today.

In the 1970's Dr. John E. Upledger discovered he could feel a subtle rhythmic movement in the cranial bones that continued down the spine and into the sacrum. Deviations in the rhythm, amplitude and rate of the cerebral spinal fluid (CSF) indicated various blockages or disease in the person. By gently realigning the bones of the cranium, spine and sacrum, pressure on the brain and central nervous system was relieved; thus allowing the body's own healing mechanisms to function and reestablish health anywhere in the body or mind. Dr. Upledger called this work craniosacral therapy.

Theoretical Foundation • The craniosacral system includes the cranium, spine, sacrum, fascia, central nervous system and the cerebral spinal fluid (CSF). The CSF bathes the brain and spinal cord to nourish and cleanse. This golden fluid is also believed to be the carrier of soul energy as spiritual light and sound in the body. The CSF is manufactured in the ventricles of the brain and travels from the brain up and down the spinal column and out through the spinal nerves. As the fluid fills and empties, a subtle rhythm, or tide is created. All parts of the body connected by fascia and connective tissues respond to this very subtle fluid rhythm of internal and external rotation, which creates the cranial rhythm. If a distortion, or injury occurs at any place in the connective tissue, or the dura of the brain, spinal cord, or nerve sheath, it can show up as pain or malfunction anywhere in the body. A trauma from a head injury could affect any body function.

Testimonies as to the efficacy of this healing modality include case histories of people who were unable to be helped by other treatments. Information about craniosacral work with autism, learning disabilities, ADD, post traumatic stress, severe headaches, TMJ, fibromyalgia and a variety of other symptoms can be found on the internet.

What to Expect • What can you expect on your Hawaiian vacation during a craniosacral therapy session? You will lie fully clothed on the massage table entering into a deep state of relaxation as the therapist gently (the touch is equal to the weight of a nickel) follows the rhythmic movement of the cranial bones, spine, sacrum and limbs. Tension will unwind from the tissues releasing the cellular memory of trauma as well as the physical and emotional symptoms of stress and disease. As pressure is removed from the brain and nervous system, your innate healing wisdom is supported to naturally reorganize your Being to a state of harmony and balance. You feel deeply relaxed and at peace.

While here in beautiful Hawai'i, allow yourself the gift of deep relaxation. Let go of mainland stress and fatigue and nurture yourself in a gentle way that allows your whole Being to come back into a state of peace, clarity, and integration.

Alia Hallowell

Craniosacral therapy is the healing modality that profoundly assisted my healing from injuries suffered in a double rear end collision on the Orange County freeway. The neurologist warned that I might never walk again! Craniosacral therapy reduced the inflammation and pain of three herniated discs in the Lumbar and Cervical spine, TMJ dysfunction, and a concussion. CST allowed the gentle progressive healing of the spinal cord, discs, and surrounding tissue, relieved the pressure on my brain easing and eventually eliminating the vertigo and dizziness. With the temporary use of a splint and Craniosacral treatments followed by the dentist regularly adjusting the splint the TMJ was corrected.

Even here in this Hawaiian paradise there is stress. Oh No!, you say, what could that be? Falling out of my newly purchased yard sale hammock caused some pelvic rotation that resulted in a lot of pain in the sciatic nerve and hip. I have just returned from a deeply relaxing craniosacral treatment. Under Terry's gentle touch, I felt the tension in the muscles holding the sacrum release and my hips reorganize into a position of balance. I am now, feeling integrated back in my body, more grounded, emotionally relaxed and mentally clear. Once again, Craniosacral therapy brings me back to well-being.

Alia Hallowell practices Craniosacral, Polarity, Orthobionomy, and Aromatherapy massage. She lives in the Puna area of the Big Island and can be reached for treatments and classes at 808.965.8472 and esscents@midpac.net.

UNDERSTANDING ENERGY MEDICINE

The Medicine of the Future

by Teri Holter, LSW, LCSW

Energy Medicine has its basis in the understanding that fundamentally everything IS energy. The life force in the body is animated and directed by a network of energetic systems that interpenetrate the physical body, and health and healing are regarded as natural outcomes of energetic homeostasis, or proper balance, in the flow of one's energies.

Origin and Theory • Energy Medicine modalities draw on ancient healing practices that are imbedded with cross-cultural wisdom about the mind/body connection at the energetic level. Modern research breakthroughs in the areas of quantum physics and psychoneuroimmunology support cutting-edge applications of the electromagnetic spectrum for health purposes. These range from the use of light (visible color through infrared) through sound (audible through subliminal), and from the distinct electromagnetic frequencies of crystals, bodily organs and plants to the use of counter-frequencies to neutralize and rid the body of the harmful effects of environmental pollutants and dietary toxins.

Believed by many to be "the medicine of the future", Energy Medicine refers both to the use of techniques to restore energetic balance and to the use of a variety of vibrational tools that may be used to heal with energy through the power of resonance. Additionally, medical intuitives use psychic ability to detect disturbances in a person's energy field correlating to physical manifestations of dis-ease.

While our level of scientific advancement is still inadequate for understanding the exact nature of electricity and magnetism, we have been able to make extensive use of these forces in everyday life. Similarly, we can effectively utilize what we intuitively sense about the energetic underpinnings of our physical and mental functioning, even while the growing refinement of research tools confirms and clarifies our theories.

For example, acupuncture meridians can be detected by tracking the flow of radioactive isotopes, infrared light and ions. Acupoints and chakras have an electrical resistance different from that of surrounding tissue. We have found that brain cells contain magnetite which receives its charge from the Earth's magnetic field, and that the pineal gland is an electromagnetic sensory organ which plays a significant role in altered states of consciousness.

The body's own electromagnetic and subtle energy systems are responsive to and interact with surrounding energy fields, whether that of another person interpenetrating one's energy field or those of strong, and often disruptive, electromagnetic frequencies (EMFs) from electronic devices, magnets, and toxic substances. These effects can be observed readily with the use of energy testing, also known as manual muscle testing, or Applied Kinesiology (AK).

It is now widely known that such physical problems as high blood pressure, heart attacks, stroke and asthma are aggravated, if not triggered, by psychosomatic stress hormones. Energy Medicine modalities may take this link one step deeper into the subtle energetic level. Due to the rapid and enduring effectiveness of energy psychology, including power therapies such as Thought Field Therapy, new theories are needed to explain the causation of emotional dysfunction and apparent cures.

With use of energy balancing techniques, emotional distress seems to simply dissolve. Treatment effects are often accompanied by sudden cognitive shifts in which the person automatically sees situations in a new light, with a new perspective that seemed previously unavailable. Given this, it seems that the key to emotional/behavioral disorders is not "what happened", however horrendous, but the way in which an energetic blockage or instability occurs due to a failure to "go with the flow" of, or accept, the experience.

What to Expect • While some forms of energy healing involve the laying on of hands, neither physical touch nor even proximity seem required to sense, disperse or conduct energy from the healer. Healing Touch and reiki are common examples. Crystals and stones may be placed on key energetic points on or around the body. The crystals may be charged and programmed for particular functions. Using crystalline mineral waters to hold and convey the charge, Liquid Needle products are encoded with frequencies that signal physical and energy systems to restore proper balance and boost their working vitality. These charged formulas may be used topically on acupoints or taken orally for a more widely dispersed effect. As with a tuning fork, through the power of resonance, harmony happens.

Acupuncture may be the most studied and widely accepted form of energy medicine in the West, operating on the principle of energy meridians that flow through the body. Blocked energy, believed to be the source of symptoms, can be relieved with the application of very fine needles at precise points on the body.

When one's energies are restored to proper balance, optimal mind-body communication occurs via electro-chemical signals and one's innate healing ability can naturally extend throughout all the spiritual, mental, emotional and physical levels.

Teri Holter, LSW, LCSW

An injury brought me to Maui to heal 2 weeks after fracturing a vertebra. We'd initially planned to camp and hike on Kaua'i. At first disappointed by the forced change of plans, within 24 hours on Maui I told my partner of 9 years "Honey, I can't explain why, but I just know that I have to move to Maui. Now. This year." I didn't know why, but I could feel it in my bones—and it was a broken bone that got me here!

I felt that I was home in a way I'd never felt before. I found an energy on Maui that gently yet powerfully accelerates healing and growth: an expediting force I think of as grace.

We opened our wellness center, 2 years later. At the request of our first vacation studio guest, I provided what became my first healing intensive using Energy Psychology power therapies. In three days, his core issues were resolved, he'd created a new future vision and grounded his insights while walking a labyrinth. Afterwards he wrote that this had been "the coolest thing" he'd ever done, and I'd echo that for myself. I continue to experience Maui's healing energy supporting rapid transformation whether through creativity in the float tank or in synergistic use of energy medicine modalities.

Teri Holter is a Licensed Social Worker and the founder of Radical Balance, located at New Waves Wellness Center in Makawao on Maui. She can be reached at 808. 572.5551 or toll-free at 877.4-RADICAL (472.3422)

~ Sound Therapy ~

Healing Through Voice and Music

Alicia Bay Laurel and Judith Lynne

Fundamentals • Sound therapy is based on the theory that all of creation is vibrational in nature, and that it's possible to effect vibrational fields in a beneficial way through the conscious application of frequencies. This is called "entrainment". Musician and sound healer Jonathan Goldman, in his book *Healing Sounds*, describes entrainment as "the ability of the more powerful rhythmic vibrations of one object to change the less powerful rhythmic vibrations of another object and cause them to synchronize their rhythms with the first object." This principal provides the foundation for the sound healer's work.

Healers working with sound modalities today use a variety of instruments, including "soundscapes," music, rhythm instruments, flutes, didgeridoos, Tibetan bells, tuning forks, crystal or metal singing bowls (or bowl gongs), chimes, and even electronic oscillators to produce pure sustained tones. They choose the sound to be administered much in the same way other alternative medicines are chosen, through kinesiology (muscle testing), or dowsing with a pendulum, searching for the tone missing from the body/mind's spectrum of vibrations. Perhaps no instrument is more powerfully effective than the human voice.

Voice Therapy • The human voice conveys the vibration of who we are, what we feel and all that we have experienced. Embedded in the voice are frequencies that stimulate the electromagnetic field of the body and activate the flow of chi (life force). The voice has the ability to vibrate us not only from the outside to the inside, but also from the inside to the outside. So when we sing, chant or tone, a sound wave is produced that affects the world around us. And because of the physiological way the sound is produced, the wave also affects the world within us.

When that sound wave is combined with conscious

thought, the voice becomes an extraordinary tool for transformation and manifestation. French musician and sound healer Fabien Maman in his book, *The Role of Music in the Twenty-First Century*, uses Kirlian photography to document the effect of the voice combined with prayer. When applied to a cell of cotton, the life force in the electro-magnetic field of the cell literally "lights up". Recent studies done in Japan by Dr. Masaru Emoto and documented in his book, *The Message From Water*, examine the effects of music and word on water and demonstrate the healing power of prayer.

Music Therapy • Music as human medicine can consist of a single sound vibration that stimulates or calms a part of the body-mind, a series of sounds that inspire an emotional-physical response, or a melodic enhancement to lyrics that uplift the listener.

Using music to heal may involve listening and moving to various pieces of music, each chosen to arouse a particular emotional state, for the purpose of releasing unexpressed grief, fear, regret and anger that may be causing psychosomatic symptoms.

Practically every illness evolves with stress as one of its components; many find that soothing instrumental music or songs with uplifting lyrics evoke feelings of well-being that, in turn, allow greater wellness to manifest. What music soothes an individual varies as much as what foods please. In choosing music as medicine, one must pay attention to one's feelings in response to the music, rather than to what others say about it. In Ayurvedic medicine, each chakra (energy center) in the body responds to a sound or tone; for example, "ah" (as in father) is the sound that stimulates the heart chakra.

The ancient Hawaiians understood the power of sound, rhythm and music. The deep resonance of the wooden pahu drum and the larger ipu gourd drums used to accompany chanting and sacred dance inspire courage, wisdom and strength in performers and listeners. By chanting or hearing others chant these simple vowel sounds, one can experience a change in one's mental/physical state. The Hawaiian language is rich in these seed syllables, often barely encumbered with consonants, so that Hawaiian chanting uplifts and heals.

Hawaiian Soundscapes • Good medicine is any stimulus (vibration) that opens us to our natural state of well-being. Certainly anyone who visits Hawai'i and experiences the island's "soundscape" can attest to its healing nature. The rhythmic pulsation of the waves rolling up on the beach, the whispers of the breeze moving through the leaves of the coconut palms, the melodious songs of the tropical birds, the sighs of the humpback whales and the clicking of the spinner dolphins all form part of the Hawaiian "soundscape". It's not only Paradise to the sound healer, but also a useful healing tool. A week or two in the islands can do wonders to rejuvenate the soul and restore the joy of living. A sound healing session can help deepen the experience.

Judith Lynne

My passion is the voice. My initiation occurred in the womb of my mother, an operatic soprano, and I was born singing. Blessed with a big voice, I was guided into classical music and began performing at an early age. While loving to sing arias and musical theater works, I always felt that there was more. My quest over the years has led me to study many types of singing including North Indian classical music, harmonic throat singing, and jazz. I also studied extended vocal techniques with the Roy Hart Theatre in France. This inspired me to sing my emotional body, healing the relationship between my voice and my psyche.

When I returned from France, I began to explore the metaphysical nature of the voice, synthesizing my seemingly disparate worlds of Eastern and Western spirituality and music. My exploration seemed to be revealing that not only is it necessary to heal our voices, but that the voice can actually fuel the transformation of consciousness.

In recent years my journey has brought me to Hawai'i to work and sing with the Hawaiian humpback whales. They have been called "the frequency keepers" of our planet. Could it be that we are also? I eagerly welcome their return to the islands this winter.

Judith Lynne is a sound healer who lives in Captain Cook on the Big Island. She is the founder of Harmonic Healing and can be reached at 808.987.8099 or judithlynne@harmonichealing.com

Alicia Bay Laurel

I was drawn to Hawai'i by musical affinity. I had been playing open-tuned guitar for some years, having learned in my 'teens from John Fahey, who was married to my cousin Jan Lebow. Much as I loved the intricate and soothing qualities of this music, I was a little lonely as a musician, because I did not know anyone else who played in this style; all of the guitar players I knew in California played rock and roll.

When I came to Hawai'i the first time, in December 1969, I heard people playing open tuned guitar, and realized it was part of the national music here. They called it slack key, or ki hō'alu. I felt as if I had come home! I moved to Hana, Maui, in the spring of 1974, and devoted myself to learning this music and composing new songs in it. Since that time, I have been privileged to be part of a beautiful musical tradition, and to relax and uplift myself, and others, with this wonderful music.

Alicia Bay Laurel is an artist/author/musician living in Kea'au on the Island of Hawai'i. She can be reached at (808) 334-3314. or alicia@aliciabaylaurel.com

Fitness and Sports

This approach to a wellness vacation takes the participant to a vacation spot where they can enjoy their sport or fitness activity at leisure. They might also meet with a sports or fitness specialist to develop tools for greater fitness or higher levels of achievement with their sport. A fitness vacation could include sessions at a fitness spa, golf, races and triathlons, meeting with fitness coaches, trail biking, or hiking and backpacking.

Sports were an important part of life in ancient Hawai'i with active gambling on the outcome. Some of the sports prepared the men for warfare by building endurance and agility. Others, such as surfing and canoeing, reflected the island environment. Foot racing was popular from an early age and involved long distance running as well as sprinting.

Popular sports of today in Hawai'i reflect those of ancient times. Hawai'i is one of the world centers for both surfing and outrigger canoe racing. The Ironman endurance race of long distance running, biking and swimming was first introduced on the Big Island of Hawai'i. Shorter versions of this triathlon—often called Tinman races—are scheduled throughout the year. The Honolulu Marathon is run each December and regularly draws competitors from around the world. Rough water swim competitions which expose the swimmer to the challenge of the surf are conducted year round.

In this section we've featured hiking, which combines physical exercise and interaction with the great outdoors. In Hawai'i there are also wonderful opportunities to learn about the history and geology of the land. The ancient practice of yoga incorporates many fitness elements including mindful awareness practice and deep breathing along with stretching and exercise. Whatever your fitness choice, Hawai'i offers an ideal environment for its practice and enjoyment.

THE COMING OF YOGA

Hayward Coleman

Origins • The origins of yoga are shrouded in mystery. In India, we can find ancient stone carvings and old drawings of people in contorted positions, but there is no ancient book on physical postures. The philosophy of yoga, however, was written and formulated by the sage Patangali. He defined yoga as the ability to hold the mind focused on a single point and to hold that focus without any distractions. Because yoga is defined as sustained focus, practically anything can now be described as a form of yoga. However, traditionally there are eight branches of yoga known collectively as Ashtanga (meaning eight limbs). A few of these are: Bhati yoga or worshipping the name of God, Juana yoga, the intellectual study of the scriptures; Karma yoga or doing social work of some type to honor God, and Hatha yoga, which is the physical exercises we have come to recognize as yoga. Although there are many different franchised styles of yoga, they are all Hatha yoga.

Yoga was spread from India by wandering sages. It was the great Da Mo who left India and journeyed to China where he founded the Chinese mystical energy training system called, qigong. The monks of Thailand, who had lived with the Buddha while he was alive, did a daily practice of yoga and massage. When the Buddha died, the monks returned to Thailand and brought back their unique style called Thai massage. More recently, in the last century the sages have brought yoga to America. The two most notable were Swami Sivananda and Krishnamucharya. Two disciples of Saint Sivananda, Swami Satchitananda and Swami Vishnudevananda, came to America in the early 60's to start yoga ashrams throughout the U.S. Ultimately yoga was taught in virtually every part of the world. The Sivananda organization actually started the yoga vacation and retreats as well as the yoga certification programs.

Variations • The phenomenal explosion of yoga has produced a plethora of different styles, each one trademarked and franchised. The teachers who had the greatest impact on

American yoga were the disciples of Krishnamucharya, B.K.S. Iengar and Pattabois Jois. In the 1980's Iengar's style, with its extreme attention to detail, had become the definitive style of yoga. By the early 1990's America was ready to put aside aerobics for another form of workout---the Ashtanga yoga of Pattobois Jois. Today, the latest flavor is Bikrim yoga where the room is superheated like a sauna, inducing practitioners to sweat even more. In spite of the health drawbacks of off-gassing of formaldehyde and other chemicals in a superheated room, or the proliferation of germs exhaled from a crowd of sweaty bodies, Americans have embraced Bikrim to the beat of a new center opening every day somewhere in America.

Benefits • But what are the benefits of yoga besides getting a great workout? Not only does the practice of yoga lubricate the tendons and joints, but the deep postures massage the organs and especially the endocrine gland system. These glands secrete hormones that send healing chemicals into our blood stream. The difference between aerobic exercise and yoga is that with aerobic exercises one exhales primarily through the mouth, but with yoga exercises one breathes primarily through the nostrils. More specifically, in the throat breathing, called Udjaya, the tongue is curled up back towards the roof of the mouth, the lips are closed at all times and the breath sounds deep as if in a sound sleep. This breathing technique unites the mind with the body. The focus of the mind on the breath creates chemical changes in our body, which can cause miraculous healing.

Practicing yoga in Hawai'i can compound all these benefits. The freshest air on the planet has been recorded on the eastern most tip of the Big Island of Hawai'i. The air quality of the whole planet is judged by this standard. Direct from Alaska, the air flows pure and unpolluted direct to our nostrils. And not only is the air highly ionized, it also has a sweet humid taste. The green and lush jungle filters the air from carbon dioxide and exhales the oxygen for us to breathe, thus giving it the sweet taste from the abundance of wild tropical fruit trees. Hawai'i, the world's freshest place to do yoga!

Hayward Coleman

In 1972, while living in Paris, I decided to change my life. I had been consuming over a pound of chocolate a day and an equal amount of gourmet cheese. My father had recently died of emphysema and my mother was on insulin shots for diabetes. I was on a quest for the fountain of youth.

While studying at L'Ecole du Mime Marcel Marceau I met a beautiful Indian girl who could literally bend sideways and touch her feet. She gave me my first yoga lesson. She was right when she said that the new way of breathing would change my life. I had a paradigm shift of consciousness, which altered my diet and showed me one of the important keys to longevity--living foods. Since then, the continued practice of yoga has helped me heal from four herniated disks and two dislocated joints. After much insight meditation, I was guided to come to the healing island of Hawai'i and with my yoga partner, Star, have built a retreat facility to teach the keys to the fountain of youth. Hawai'i is the best place to drink clean water, eat organic food, breathe clean air, relax in nature, and do yoga with a feeling of Aloha!

Hayward Coleman lives on the Island of Hawai'i. He is the co-director of Yoga Oasis, a retreat center for wellness of body and mind. He can be reached at Hayward@yogaoasis.org or 1.800.274.4446 or 808.965.8460.

~ Hiking ~
Fitness for the Body and Spirit

Hugh Montgomery

Myriad forms of recreation and self-improvement are currently available to us; why should anyone elect such a low-tech, unsexy activity as putting one foot in front of the other, over and over again? Why not jump on a treadmill or a stair-master conveniently stationed in your gym or home? You could then multi-task—socialize, watch TV, stay wired, be convenient to a shower, and run no risk of getting soil on yourself. Walking is at its base, after all, a matter of shifting your center of gravity forward until, to keep yourself from a face-plant, you shift your foot to catch yourself, lean again, catch yourself with the other foot, and so on. How boring does *that* sound? It's a wonder children persist through hundreds of falls to get the coordination to walk, and impressive that the adults watching them get so excited as they master the task. There must be something more to this activity than the above analysis suggests.

Benefits • "Hiking," according to the dictionary, is, "extended walking for pleasure or exercise." As a literal matter of definition, then, it is good for us to hike. Though many people identify hiking (or walking) as an activity they enjoy or would like to do, the reasoning behind the desire to move about on foot is seldom articulated. Though we could dissect the results of walking into an analysis of the benefits it provides for our minds, bodies and spirit, it would only be a pale and unworthy shadow of our direct experience. In Hawai'i, striding upon volcanic mountains and pumping through our bodies what may be the cleanest air on Earth seems a sound baseline for positive outcomes. Add to that the neurological attunement arising from rhythmic cross-lateral movement, the free flow of creativity and understanding facilitated by right-brain engagement, and the unbiased input from the natural world with the real consequences of being aware of one's body and environs–or not–and more than "pleasure or exercise" can be invoked in advocacy of hiking.

Therapists often observe that the "map" of reality that their clients are using is problematic because it is outdated or otherwise inaccurate. "Virtual reality" is not waiting for technological developments to be prevalent: it dominates the mental life of most individuals. Walking -- as natural a thing as we can do – counters the limits of our "virtual" constructions of life, and brings us into physical realities that can connect us to dimensions of infinite extent.

The Metaphorical Path • It is nearly irresistible to make the comparison of our walking literal paths with our movement through the time of our life span. The validity of this metaphor is attested to by its appearance in numerous cultures, including that of Hawai'i. A traditional prayer for walking the path of life, shared by *kanaka maoli,* or descendants of our islands' Polynesian settlers, begins with a call to focus on that infinite point where the within and the without meet and ends with an acknowledgment of one's freedom. Its name translates as, "Concerning the path:"

No Ke Ala Hele

E pule mai kākou.	**Let us pray.**
E ke akua	**O God,**
E 'oluolu 'oe	**Please**
E wehe mai 'oe	**Open the path**
I ke ala hele a mākou e holo ai.	**On which we travel.**
Mamua 'oe o mākou,	**You go before us,**
Mahope 'oe mākou;	**You go behind us,**
Ma ka 'ao'ao 'akau,	**On the right,**
Ma ka 'ao'ao hema,	**On the left,**
Maluna a malalo o mākou.	**Above and below us.**
I na hewa mākou,	**If we should err,**
Ma ka mana'o,	**In thoughts,**
Ma ka hana,	**In deeds,**
Ai'ole ma ka hehi ana	**Or in the treading**
A ka mākou wāwae,	**Of our feet,**
E aloha mai 'oe 'ia mākou.	**Be compassionate with us.**
E alaka'i mai 'oe 'ia mākou.	**Be our guide.**
'Amama,	**It is finished,**
Ua noa	**It is free.**

Your path is unfailingly before you. Walk it well, attentive to the risks and the gifts, enjoying all.

Hugh Montgomery, Ph.D.

Images of the Kula slopes of Haleakala volcano, Island of Maui, drew me to the Islands. A friend returning from his sojourn here shared his photos with me and helped shape my desire to see Hawai'i for myself. "See the Big Island, too," he suggested, "There's an active volcano there." The Maui portion of my airline ticket eventually expired, unused and superceded by the draw exerted on me by the Island of Hawai'i. At an age and in a time when everything seemed possible, I trusted my impulses and followed the chain of circumstances presenting themselves to me. Leaving a beautiful place on the margin of California's Shasta Valley and secure and satisfying work as a psychologist, I moved to Waipi'o Valley with only tenuous possibilities for residence and employment.

Teaching for the University of Hawai'i's Continuing Education division let me get acquainted with some Island communities and the folks who enliven them. A private practice in psychotherapy eventuated, giving me an identity and a way to contribute for some years. Burnout accelerated by the omnipresence of managed care facilitated examination of my self-healing practices, chief among which has always been walking in wild places. I took a year to wind down my practice and walked out the door eight years ago with scarcely a backward glance.

I'm walking still, and feel privileged to be doing so, joined as I am by some of the finest people to be found.

Hugh Montgomery is a writer, activist, and hiking guide living near Honoka'a on the Big Island. He is the owner of Hawaiian Walkways and can be reached at 808.775.0372 or hiwalk@aloha.net.

Travel for the Purpose of Serving Others

This is a relatively new and increasingly popular type of wellness vacation where participants not only enhance their lives in a permanent way, but also enhance the lives of others through their service. Examples in Hawai'i include a beach cleanup day, spending a day or week with Habitat for Humanity building a home with the working poor, trail clearing or other environmental maintenance projects, volunteering with a senior center or a child care program, counting whales and tending turtles, or doing preservation work with the Nature Conservancy.

This relatively recent and increasingly popular form of volunteer travel finds people going all over the world to support the work and needs of others. At the core of this concept is the generosity and love of the aloha spirit. While on your wellness vacation to Hawai'i, we suggest ways that you can offer your aloha spirit to the land and people of Hawai'i.

A willingness to give has been all-important to Hawaiians throughout time. Leaders were to set the standard of generosity. *E opu ali'i*, or "Be as kind and as generous as a chief should be," reflected this value. Giving or serving others was extended not only to neighbors and strangers but also to the land.

We invite you, as a wellness traveler, to honor this Hawaiian tradition by leaving Hawai'i more beautiful and better than you found it.

You can initiate your own efforts by not littering and by picking up litter as you see it. This can be done as you simply explore Hawai'i, or you can devote an hour or so with your own beach cleanup activity. You'll find more of a need in areas away from the resorts.

You might decide to plant a tree or create a garden. One woman who comes to Hawai'i for several months each winter has taken on the beautification of the back of Hanauma Bay on Oahu as her project. She doesn't share her husband's joy for snorkeling so, while he explores the underwater beauty of Hanauma Bay, she creates beauty on land. She has single handedly leveled the land at the back of the park and created a garden. Each year she returns to nurture and replant it. You don't have to be a regular visitor or stay for weeks to make a similar contribution. Instead, you might find a place where you particularly think a tree would be welcome. There are many places to buy trees or bushes. Plant something, devote some time while you are here to caring for it and then surrender it to be nurtured by the natural elements. A caution here; please buy from the local gardeners rather than bringing your own plants to contribute to Hawai'i. Too often, people have introduced plants to Hawai'i out of an interest in contributing something new and beautiful to the landscape only to have the plant take over, spread and smother the natural habitat. Hawai'i has a delicate ecosystem that is constantly in jeopardy.

In the island chapters we also discuss opportunities to donate your services to animals or to people through the Habitat for Humanity program or the maintenance of trails and gardens.

However you choose to contribute your time and energy to making Hawai'i a better place, you will be richly rewarded. To quote the humanitarian Albert Schweitzer, *"I don't know what your destiny may be but I do know this, that the only ones among you who will be truly happy are those who have sought and learned how to serve."*

⁓ GIVING BACK ⁓

Volunteer Aloha Vacations that Heal the Spirit

Gerrie Morisky

"Why do I work here? ... How we sustain the special nature of Hawai'i...by developing mutually beneficial partnerships ...can be a model for the world." Dr. Peter Vitousek, Morrison Professor of Ecology, Stanford University, Member National Academy of Sciences, in a speech to the Nature Conservancy of Hawai'i

In a sense, we all "come home" to Hawai'i. When we touch the living spirit of the land and people, we recognize a place of true origins, a refuge that welcomes us and makes us feel refreshed and whole. After receiving so much, many of us also feel an inner call to give thanks by giving back.

Traveling to serve others—with a purpose and a receptive Aloha spirit—is coming home to Hawai'i's greatest cultural and spiritual traditions. To be *pono,* to set things right and keep our promises, is our true healing. We know it's time to *kōkua*, to do our part.

Meeting the Challenge • The Healing Islands are in potentially irreversible trouble unless we all *"kōkua"* together. Hawai'i's highly threatened social, cultural and ecological landscapes offer volunteers both a global vision and challenge: "The rest of the world's ecosystems are ...altered by [what we do in Hawai'i]...Our actions contribute to meeting one of the great challenges of our time: How can a large and growing human enterprise share Earth with the nature that we all want to conserve?" Dr. Peter Vitousek.

A volunteer aloha vacation can be our time to *"mālama Hawai'i,"* to actively care for the land, ocean, families, communities and culture in sensitive and practical ways. "Shape-shifting" from wellness traveler to vacation volunteer and from consumer to contributor, can help turn the tide. Hawaiians say, "If you doubt the power of one small person or thing, just deal with a mosquito!"

Volunteer aloha vacations are guided by intention and intuition. You can help your corporation organize a rewarding team volunteer vacation, or come as an individual, to staff an educational, nutritional or medical outreach clinic, build a home for Habitat for Humanity, enrich cultural immersion programs, clear land for a park, trail system or native housing, preserve native species and habitats, and remove alien species (Aren't you glad you're not a tourist anymore?).

Satisfying volunteer opportunities are often spontaneous. "Talking story" with a local *kupuna* (elder) can lead to a nearby community project. Respectfully listening to a youth in trouble can give the crucial validation, self-esteem and empowerment of being heard. Listening to the earth and our shared breath leads to the next here and now. Thich Nhat Hanh reminds us: "Touching the present moment is the door to everything."

Simplify and Buy Locally Produced Products • Hawai'i's loss of traditional cultural and spiritual boundaries opened the door to its greatest loss. The sacred 'āina, which feeds and sustains us, is rapidly disappearing, threatening Hawai'i's future food supply and natural green spaces. As volunteers, we collectively need to turn off the engine that drives our increasing use of roads and freeways, parking lots, luxury resorts, golf courses, suburban sprawl subdivisions, shopping centers, and quick-stop fast food strip malls.

One vital form of volunteer aloha vacation travel is to "vote" with our dollars by practicing sustainable voluntary simplicity. Every single choice directs our consumer dollars toward greater consumption OR preservation of resources, and sends a powerful economic message to politicians, planners and developers. Staying in small local B&Bs, joining wellness retreats, buying locally grown organic food and native crafts at farmers' markets, recycling, and deepening our sense of place by "staying put" all help.

Volunteer aloha vacations are also good for your health. In his book *The Healing Power of Doing Good*, Allan Luks describes a "helper's high," similar to a runner's high, giving the body's immune system a major boost. *Stone Soup for the World: Life Changing Stories of Kindness & Courageous Acts of Service*, says: "True healing happens for the giver and receiver when we slow down and really connect with each other. The smallest acts of kindness bring a sense of calm, self-esteem and joy to our lives. People who take the time to give from their hearts feel less pain, depression and disease." In offering our healing hands to the land and people of Hawai'i, we ultimately heal our selves, our families, and our communities.

David R. Brower, founder of the Sierra Club, spoke for all who volunteer their skills, talents and time to make a difference: "We have a responsibility to the... people who have not yet been born... who deserve a world at least as beautiful as ours."

Come *"Mālama Hawai'i"* and help restore and preserve this rare global healing destination. Our ailing planet urgently needs its powerful yet gentle touch of Aloha.

Gerrie Mikhaela Morisky

"You do not need money to be a philanthropist. We all have assets. You can befriend Life with your bare hands... [for] Life is fulfilling its dream of itself ... and realizing its own mysterious purposes." Rachel Naomi Remen, M.D.

These words came alive for me after a series of catastrophic events and devastating "losses," including systemic lymphoma and a severe chronic immune disorder. I learned the full meaning of "shamanic death," and discovered the greater doorways that open when all the old ones close behind us.

In 1975 I took a short sabbatical from corporate management, marriage and motherhood to spend time in Tibet "reordering my life." I had studied traditional and alternative medicine, transpersonal psychology, facilitated music-breath-movement-transformational workshops, and enjoyed "the good life." Suddenly, life as I knew it was completely dismantled, and old tools didn't work. To heal, I had to go deeper... dancing with ALL of Life's shadows at the cellular level.

Our healing journey is ultimately our own design, containing hundreds of hidden practical gifts we have chosen to give back through "greater hands"... to ourselves, our families, our lands, and greater global community. We develop the spiritual muscle to extend those truly "bare hands" ...and befriend a world that needs our healing touch.

Gerrie Morisky is co-owner of Ala Loa House By-the-Sea, a healing retreat south of Hilo on the Big Island. She can be reached at alaloahouse@hotmail.com or 808.966.7887.

~ HABITAT FOR HUMANITY ~
Building Houses With the Working Poor

Timothy Keck, PhD

One of the most appealing ways to include acts of service in a wellness vacation is to work as a volunteer on a Habitat for Humanity house.

Background • Since the establishment of Habitat for Humanity in 1976, volunteers have built more than 140,000 homes in partnership with people in need around the world. The vision for this remarkable Christian ecumenical housing ministry originated with Millard Fuller, a man increasingly familiar to people around the globe. Millard Fuller's story is a reversal of the classic American "rags to riches" story. Finding himself at the age of 30 a most unhappy millionaire, with a marriage falling apart, and a complete lack of meaning in his life, Fuller literally gave away all he had. He then launched on a journey of introspection, discovery and service that would result in the rescue of his marriage, a sense of purpose and spiritual regeneration, and the establishment of Habitat for Humanity.

Philosophy • The philosophy and operating principles of Habitat for Humanity are simple and straightforward. The work of Habitat is built upon a spiritual foundation. This "housing ministry" is openly and unapologetically Christian, and many volunteers find their work an important part of their own faith journey and witness. At the same time, Habitat for Humanity welcomes people of all faiths—or those motivated by humanistic concern—to participate in this work to provide people with at least a simple, decent place to live. Partner families apply to Habitat and are selected based on need. In Hawai'i and around the world Habitat for Humanity finds and builds with families who have no other option for home ownership and meet criteria for financial need. Each partner family provides at least 500 hours of "sweat equity" on their home (most do much more) and on the homes of other Habitat families. After construction of the home is completed, families assume a mortgage at zero percent interest. Since there are virtually no labor costs families can often assume a mortgage for $400 or less for a 3-5 bedroom home, not fancy but built with high quality and durability.

Habitat in Hawai'i • In Hawai'i the work of Habitat began in 1988 with the establishment of the first affiliate on O'ahu. Since that time the organization has grown considerably, and there are now affiliates on all the major islands except Lāna'i. In all some 140 homes have been constructed over the past twelve years, and the rate of construction has increased significantly in recent years. Increasingly as well, vacationing visitors who know of the work of Habitat for Humanity, perhaps are involved in their own communities, and want to add the dimension of service to their vacation experience, augment the work of local volunteers and Habitat families. On several of the islands what began about five years ago with a church group or two working on a Habitat project has now grown to the point that several groups visit Hawai'i each year with the express purpose of working on Habitat for Humanity projects. Many have some church affiliation but others, such as corporate or foundation-sponsored youth groups, are participating as well.

Catch the Spirit • It is also not uncommon for individuals to become involved apart from any group. Several years ago a vacationing house painter from Wisconsin heard about a Habitat project on the Wai'anae Coast and spent two weeks happily working away with the family and volunteers. Later, two young architects were vacationing here from Germany, with all intentions of enjoying three weeks of surf and sand. They accidentally heard about a Habitat project and were fascinated with the design of low-income housing that could also be attractive and highly functional. After a visit to a Habitat worksite, they caught the spirit and spent their vacation hammering nails with the crew. They remained in touch with the Honolulu affiliate for several years thereafter.

Those who might be interested in spending a few hours or a few days working with a Habitat project need only call the Habitat for Humanity office on whatever island they are visiting. Volunteers are always welcome to join in this work. In Hawai'i we make three guarantees to Habitat volunteers, and these include volunteers from the mainland or abroad as well. First, if you visit a work site and catch the spirit, you will work hard and be tired at the end of the day. Second you will eat well. All our volunteers are treated to delicious lunches provided by local churches or other organizations. And third, you will leave the site with joy in your heart. A day working in this spirit of love never fails to inspire. It also reminds us that we touch the very best in ourselves when we reach out to others in acts of service and offer the most precious gift that any of us can give—the gift of ourselves.

Timothy Keck, Ph.D.

I began volunteering with Habitat for Humanity 12 years ago. For me this work has proven to be a wonderful gift—a blessing that, as part of my Christian faith journey, has allowed me to reach a deep need, which I believe is common to all of us, a need to be of service and make a positive difference in our communities and our world. I am currently serving as the president of the O'ahu affiliate and a member of the statewide board.

In Hawai'i there is a wonderful dimension to the mission to provide simple decent housing to people in need. Whether they are long time residents, members of the military, or visitors on their vacation, those who work with us experience that magical blend of caring, love, and laughter we call the Aloha spirit. They talk with, and sweat with, and sing with some of the most beautiful and joyful people on this planet—the families with whom we build. And they experience the genuine, unvarnished culture and spirit of these magic islands in a way that they never would lying on a beach in Waikiki. There is hard work—and there is joy and love in the Habitat experience.

Tim Keck, PhD, is a military historian by profession. He is also the husband of Laura Crites, co-author of this book,. For the past twelve years he has been a construction volunteer with Habitat for Humanity in Hawai'i and has served twice as the O'ahu affiliate's board president. He currently serves on the statewide board of directors. He can be reached at 808.941.8253 or at KeckCrites@cs.com

“She rules the volcanoes of Hawai‘i,
and mankind has no power to resist her.
When Pele is heard from,
her word is the final word.”

Herb Kawainui Kane
Pele: Goddess of Hawai‘i’s Volcanoes

~ Chapter Four ~

The Island of Hawai'i • The Home of Pele

Approaching the Hawaiian archipelago by air, the largest landmass in the Pacific magnetically draws our attention. Named Hawai'i Island by its original inhabitants, in modern times it is commonly referred to as the Big Island. Writers have attempted to capture what it is about this magical land that enchants and enthralls all who visit its shores. David Yeadon, writing for *National Geographic Traveler* says, "A beguiling strangeness moves on the Big Island." Frommer's *Travel Guide* says it is "steeped in tradition and shrouded in the primal mist of creation." It has also been called the rainbow island, the orchid island, the volcano island and even the healing island, but the Big Island's full magnificence and mystery do not yield easily to simple slogans.

The Big Island comes by its nickname with ease. It is more than twice the size of all the other Hawaiian islands combined and is the largest island in the Pacific. Its magnitude reaches from the core of the earth to the heavens. Mauna Loa ("Long Mountain") volcano is the most massive mountain on earth covering an area of 19,000 cubic miles. Mauna Kea ("White Mountain" or "Snow Mountain") volcano is the tallest mountain in Polynesia and lifts the world's largest telescope above the clouds to provide astronomers with an unparalleled view of the cosmos.

It's not all about size, however. The Hawai'i Island can claim some of the most unusual phenomenon on Earth, including a green sand beach of semi-precious olivine and the newest land, laid recently by an active volcano pouring lava into the sea. It has the wettest city in the country, Hilo, and the southernmost point in the U. S.

The sheer variety of climates and terrain on the island makes it a microcosm. Twelve of the earth's 14 climates can be found in an area the size of Connecticut and Rhode Island combined. There are days when you can lie sunbathing on the beach and look up at snow-capped peaks. Within an hour's drive you can leave a temperate zone, traverse a desert, and enter a tropical rainforest. Traveling north from the town of Kailua-Kona across miles of barren lava you begin to notice occasional clumps of grass gaining a foothold on the porous rock. Then, as a demonstration of the evolution of life on Earth, the vegetation gradually grows to small bushes and trees finally arriving at the diverse tropical forests of North Kohala.

Equally extraordinary, and perhaps the key to its mysterious energy, is that the island sits atop a tectonic "hot spot" from which islands continue to be born. Through the Earth's fiery release valve atop Kīlauea Volcano, the Hawai'i Island is connected to the core of the planet; the most powerful and purified elements are bubbling to the surface and birthing land before our eyes. The other islands in the chain were formed from this same fountain of magma, but the Pacific plates have shifted them off the hot spot at the evolutionary pace of three and one-half inches a year.

Using an analogy of the seven energy charkas of Hindu tradition sometimes applied to the seven major islands of Hawai'i, the Big Island holds the distinction of forming the base chakra, the grounded foundational seat of power. It is our most basic connection to the Earth and to our "tribe"–a place where the life force flows up from the Earth and into our body to fuel the other centers. One senses that this chakra is wide open in the Big Island and its energy is flowing almost wildly.

Culturally and historically, some Hawaiians believe this island resonates with the energy of warriors. It was the home base from which, in 1795, the fiercely ambitious and visionary King Kamehameha the Great conquered and united the Hawaiian Islands. In modern times it seems that the feminine power of Pele, the Goddess of Volcanoes and Fire, has reasserted itself. Like a pied piper, the island has called many centered, independent women to its shores. Out of the cast of thousands who are here to serve the visitor our interviews for this book repeatedly led us to women who came here initially for their own healing.

They had come through "initiations" of one kind or another: a grave illness, a car accident, a broken marriage, or a complete change of careers. Their stories and reflections reveal profound insights that come only through trials of fire. This is the mystique of Madame Pele. Her red-hot flow spilling out to birth new land symbolizes the emergence of an intuitive feminine energy that is charting new territory in the way we view and care for our bodies and the Earth.

There is a magical convergence occurring on the Big Island. Evolutionary forces have brought together a magnificently beautiful and productive land, the sacred 'āina. The primal flow of Pele generates a powerful healing energy. Wise elders of the old cultures, Hawaiian, Eastern, and Western, are sharing their ancient healing arts with a new generation of gifted healers that has flocked to the island.

Island Orientation

Travel on the island is not difficult if you rent a car. There is very little public transportation. The Hawaiian Belt Road circles the island and there are only a few major branches off that. Outside the cities, the small green numbered mile markers will help you find your location. Rather than use right and left or the four directions, locals will direct you to turn mauka—toward the mountains, or makai—toward the ocean.

The leeward, or dry side, (west) is the Kona district (divided into North and South Kona). Kailua, seen on road signs as Kailua town or Kailua-Kona (to distinguish it from a Kailua in O'ahu), is the main population center and the hub of most tourist activity, particularly for water sports.

In the south are the quiet towns of Nā'ālehu and Wai'ōhinu. This is the Ka'ū district, also sometimes referred to as the South Point region. In this area is the southernmost point in the United States, and the green sand beach.

On the windward, or wet side, (east) is Hilo, the county seat and home to the University of Hawai'i-Hilo. South of Hilo is the Puna district, divided between the coastal area and the higher altitude region in and around Hawai'i Volcanoes National Park. North of Hilo, is the Hāmākua Coast, a 50-mile stretch of lush tropical ravines, abundant waterfalls, and spectacular views of the ocean.

Waimea, known by the U.S. Post Office as Kamuela to distinguish it from Waimeas on other islands, is a misty high-altitude town in the northern part of the island. It is surrounded by open ranch lands and rolling hills. The Northwest point, with the towns of Kapa'au and Hāwī, is known as North Kohala.

Twenty Ways to Pursue Balance and Harmony on the Island of Hawai'i

1. Slow Down and Discover a New World Through Awareness and Meditation

The Big Island has been one of the last islands to be "discovered" by tourists and so still maintains a slower pace of life that may resonate with some wellness vacationers. The frenetic hyper-activity that characterizes much of our mainland society has not yet taken hold here. The down-to-earth wisdom of the people is to take things as they come.

The best way to still the compulsive thinking that characterizes most of our mental activity is to be still and quiet while sitting or walking in nature. It may take a little walking and searching to find the perfect spot, but when you do, claim it for your mental health. Sit and observe all the wonders this special place offers, from the tiniest life forms to the all-encompassing land and seascapes. The longer you sit motionless, the more secrets of the natural world will be revealed to you. What looked like an inanimate black lava rock begins to wiggle with the movement of black crabs and tiny snails. Watch the shadows from the trees play on the ground, feel the breeze on your skin, listen to the surf roll in, and the wind rush through.

Meditation is a way to train the mind to stop or slow its incessant activity and it can be practiced in solitude or with a group, in silence or with the aid of guided imagery or music. It can be done while sitting or walking or, after some practice, in the midst of activity.

If you would like to learn meditation or if you enjoy meditating with the support of a group, here are a few options that are available for visitors. Basic meditation instruction is given if requested and all sessions are free.

Near Kealakekua in South Kona **Chris Reid** can provide information and directions to a weekly meditation based on guided visualizations or music. (808.328.8672)

On the Puna Coast, **Eliot Rosen** and the Science of

Spirituality group host a reading, meditation, and discussion group every Tuesday at 7:30 p.m. This non-profit international organization is "dedicated to inner and outer peace through meditation and selfless service." (808.965.1279)

A meditation group in the tradition of Thich Nhat Hahn meets in Hilo every Tuesday at 7:00 p.m. Call **Gary** (808.935.8742)

Akiko's Bed and Breakfast on the Hāmākua Coast holds Zazen, Zen meditation, at 5:00 a.m. every morning and 7:00 to 8:00 p.m. Monday, Wednesday, and Friday. **Akiko** will give instruction on meditation and the formalities if needed. (808.963.6422)

2. Connect With Your Source at a Sacred Site

Heiau are the stone temples of the ancient Hawaiians. These sacred sites served a variety of purposes. Some were dedicated to the war god Kū or to agricultural deities, while others were used exclusively by women. Certain *heiau* served as *pu'uhonua*, or special places of refuge where those who had violated the harsh laws of a certain historic period could earn forgiveness. Pu'uhonua were deliberately located in areas difficult to get to, but if the guilty party could overcome the obstacles to getting there, he would find sanctuary, do penance, and, if fortunate, escape punishment (most likely, death).

Pu'uhonua O Hōnaunau, also called the **City of Refuge**, is just such a place. It is an impressive monument even by Hawaiian standards. Set among coconut palms at the edge of the sea at Hōnaunau Bay in South Kona, its 17-foot-thick lava rock walls enclose an area the size of a basketball court. Countless pleas for absolution must have been offered up to the priests and spirits in this place. The ancient site is now a national park.

A place of forgiveness has an appeal to our modern age for different reasons. Many of us are struggling with the internal demons of shame, guilt, or abuse. Our spiritual work is about forgiving ourselves and others and, as the Hawaiians say, "setting things right," or *pono (ho'oponopono)* A visit to Pu'uhonua O Hōnaunau, with its history and natural beauty, provides an opportunity to reflect on the place of forgiveness in our lives. You can enter the sheltered area from the *mauka* side and imagine leaving your burdens to be absorbed into the porous walls or taken up by God or the spirits, then exit to look out over the expansive freedom of the open sea. The glowing light just before sunset creates an aura of quiet reverence for such an occasion.

Though the City of Refuge can have a powerful effect for anyone, to be accompanied by a guide who will lead you through it with an eye toward your personal journey can be particularly helpful for deeper levels of healing. In addition to providing information about the site, a guide might perform a simple ritual or provide a context for your meditation or reflection. **Patricia Nash** (KeMa) (808.328.0007) specializes in creating ritual specifically for the person(s) she is escorting. She knows many sites around the island where meaningful encounters with nature and the cultural-historical context can help move someone out of a stuck place and into space of higher realization. **Chris Reid** (808.328.8672) is another very knowledgeable and spiritually attuned guide who will create a meaningful experience for anyone seeking to find a deeper connection with the mana (spiritual energy, power) of the sacred sites. **Judith Lynne** (808.987.8099) guides individuals through personal journeys that include excursions to Hawaiian sacred sites and especially enjoys guiding families. All three of the above live near the City of Refuge and offer accommodations. They all have very special connections with dolphins.

Tips on visiting Hawaiian sacred sites

Though sacred sites are open to the public, be mindful that they remain sacred to many people of the host culture. Be respectful the way you would be when visiting a cathedral in Europe or the US mainland. Speak quietly, don't smoke or eat while touring. Honor with your manner what you might not be familiar with or understand.

It's traditional to ask permission before entering a place especially one known to have special significance. Whether you ask aloud or silently, consciously or unconsciously, pay attention to what you're feeling as you approach; if there's any hesitation, any sense of discomfort, don't proceed. Respect no trespassing or kapu signs or sticks crossed like an X.

Do not move or remove stones or other objects or artifacts. Pick up garbage and be sure not to contribute any of your own. Consider leaving a small offering, such as a flower or a piece of fruit, as a simple thanks. Saying "Mahalo" (thanks) is always appropriate and appreciated.

3. Practice Meditation in Motion With a Labyrinth Walk, Tai Chi, Watsu

Walking a labyrinth can take you deep into the creative source within. It can be an exercise in mindfulness to bring your mind and body together in a focused journey, or it may just be a pleasant stroll. It depends on your frame of mind and spirit at the time you walk. *(See article on the Labyrinth in Chapter Three.)*

The **'Awapuhi Labyrinth** on the Puna coast South of Hilo is a sculptured meditation garden that combines the elements of open sky and native Hawaiian plants with the twists and turns of the metaphorical life journey. The path is outlined with lava rocks, flowering bushes, and ti plants used for practical and ceremonial purposes by the native Hawaiians. At ninety feet in diameter, it is larger than most labyrinths. The original in Chartres Cathedral in France is forty feet wide. **Christie Wolf** and **John Luchau** began work on the 'Awapuhi Labyrinth in 1999 and have given a generous gift to the local and visiting community of journeying souls. There is no admission fee although donations for its maintenance are accepted. (808.982.5959)

Another unusual labyrinth is at **Dragonfly Ranch** south of Kailua-Kona near Captain Cook. The path is painted on the floor of an illuminarium (protected open-air space) overlooking Kealakekua Bay. While walking this path you can meditate on the rainbow colors under your feet or take in the spectacular view. Donations accepted. (808.328.2159)

Tai chi and qigong are practices that calm us down and bring us into the present moment. The subtle gentle movements, coordinated with the breath, center our awareness in the body. These practices, which are thousands of years old, can be both energizing and relaxing. Over the long term, they can have significant restorative effects on our health. Teachers and classes may be found all around the Island. *(See article on Qigong in Chapter Three)*

In Kea'au in the Puna district near Hilo, **Valerie Myles** teaches tai chi, qigong and acutouch. She has studied with a master for many years and her practice is well tuned to the subtleties of the art. Her casual style and individual attention make you feel comfortable and confident, even though you may have just barely scratched the surface of this practice. At the first session you can expect to learn simple techniques that have lasting benefits. Valerie teaches outdoors in natural settings or at your healing accommodation. (808.966.4893 or toll free 888.265.0005)

Watsu is a profoundly relaxing water therapy. As you are gently swirled and stretched in warm water your task is to relax your body and mind and allow the movement and mild sensations to take you to a place of healing renewal. In the Puna area, some people like to receive a watsu treatment in the warm ponds, but we recommend the specially designated watsu pool at Kalani Oceanside Retreat. It's private, quiet, and the temperature is perfectly maintained. There are two very fine watsu practitioners in this area. **Lew Schwenk** (808.965.8400) trained at Harbin Springs, California with the originator of watsu. **Jivan**, also an experienced watsu therapist, considers this a form of warm water massage that can train your consciousness. (808.965.7119) The key to watsu is for the practitioner to be invisible so that you feel free-floating and totally immersed in the experience. Both Lew and Jivan do well at achieving this effect.

4. Open to the Wisdom and Meaning of Hawai'i: Experience a Hawaiian Tradition

The Polynesians who arrived on Hawaiian shores centuries ago–the *kanaka maoli*–gave birth to a unique culture founded on *aloha, lōkahi* (harmony, unity), *mālama* (caretaking, nurturing), and other universal principles that teach the interconnectedness of all life. Alignment of body, mind, and spirit were known to be the keystone to the health of individuals, extended families, and *'ohana* (communities.) All aspects of Hawaiian healing were based on an intuitive understanding and manipulation of *mana*.

Over time, other Polynesians, Asians, Europeans, and Americans have woven their cultural threads into the tapestry that is Hawai'i. Nevertheless, the traditions, practices, and values of the host culture are still alive. They may be sampled in a variety of ways.

Beginning on Easter Day in Hilo, the **Merrie Monarch Hula Festival** is the world's premier hula event. It is televised throughout the state with excellent commentary and camera work. The competition is named after King David Kalākaua, the "Merrie Monarch," who resurrected hula for public enjoyment in the 1880s. Three successive nights of ancient and modern hula featuring men's and women's *hālau* (hula schools) from all over the state (and, usually, also California) inspire viewers and participants alike with the depth and beauty of this art. (808.935.9168 or www.Kalena.com/merriemonarch)

Kamehameha Day: This event, usually celebrated on the birthday of Kamehameha I, June 11, has special meaning for Hawai'i Island because this was Kamehameha's home turf. He was born and grew to manhood in North Kohala and there received his charge to unite the islands into one kingdom. The North Kohala communities of Hāwī and Kapa'au take special pride in the Kamehameha Day celebration of their native son with traditional ceremony and other presentations at the famous original statue of the king which include lei draping of the statue, a home-grown parade, and a *ho'olaule'a* (festival with food, entertainment, and exhibits) at Kamehameha Park in Kapa'au. All events are free of charge. Kamehameha Day also is celebrated in a bold and festive way in both Kailua-Kona and Hilo.

Annual Festival at Pu'ukohalā Heiau: This two-day event, usually held the third weekend in August at the historic Pu'ukohalā Heiau just outside Kawaihae in South Kohala, includes traditional ritual and historical re-enactment, offering viewers a glimpse into the complex warrior society of old. The festival also includes a series of workshops in which participants can learn a traditional art or craft such as lei making, lauhala weaving, kapa making, Hawaiian language or hula.

Aloha Festivals: From late August to early October on all the major islands, the Aloha Festivals celebrate Hawai'i through art, music, dance, and crafts. An Aloha Festival ribbon gains you entrance to most events. Brochures with the schedule for all islands are readily available in stores, newspapers, free handouts at the airport, and other public places beginning in August. Each year the festival is ritually opened on the Big Island through the **Royal Investiture at Halemaumau** in Hawai'i Volcanoes National Park. Traditional offerings are made at the crater's edge as a royal court, chosen anew each year, looks on. *Hula hālau* perform on the lava. This powerful ceremony transcends time and can be a transformative experience. Call 808.885.8086 for information about where to purchase Aloha Festival ribbons.

5. Plan Ahead: Enroll in a Healing Transformational Workshop or Retreat

Sometimes a skillful hand, touch, technique, teacher, or knowing smile can quickly create a quantum leap in your journey of healing and personal transformation. The Big Island has attracted some of the planet's most experienced and innovative teachers. Most appreciate that you are your own teacher and healer, and provide a safe and sensitive place for your healing process.

Aided by natural wonders and a permissive climate, retreat leaders in Hawai'i use a variety of venues to awaken the participant to self-understanding and insight. *Meditation Retreats* guide participants to quiet the chattering mind through intense concentration and focused awareness. *Personal Growth Retreats* lead people to deeper understanding by examining their feelings, motivations, relationships, and life purpose. *Yoga Retreats* incorporate the practice of yoga as a regular part of each day. Some retreats include exploration of the wonders of nature such as the underwater world of spinner dolphins and the birth of new land from active volcano flows.

Since retreats and workshops come and go throughout the year, advance planning is needed to incorporate this into your vacation schedule. The most centralized places to get information about workshops and retreats on the Big Island are:

1. ***The Hawai'i Healing Arts Network e-Newsletter.*** Send an email to Sharman O'Shea at Hawaiihealing@turquoise.net to receive a bi-weekly e-newsletter with news of upcoming workshops and educational opportunities of every variety. **Holomana 'O Hawai'i** also has an extensive website listing alternative health practitioners from around the state. Go to www.Hawaii-healing.com
2. If you're already on the island, get a copy of the ***Hawai'i Island Journal,*** published every two weeks and distributed free at newsstands. Their calendar of events, a great listing of what's happening around the island, includes retreats and workshops.

Whether you are seeking solitude or companionship, planning for an organized group, a family or just yourself, you will find a wonderful variety of retreat sites on the Big Island. You can organize a group or come join one here. Notice in the accommodations section of this chapter that many of the B&Bs and guesthouses have sufficient space for small groups. Following are larger retreat centers that can house groups of 15 or more, although most of them are happy to accommodate individuals, couples, and small groups.

Wood Valley Temple, outside the town of Pāhala off Hwy 11 in Ka'ū District, is a place for quiet reflection and meditation. The owners, **Marya and Michael Schwab**, are nonsectarian Buddhists in the Tibetan Tradition. Two Tibetan monks reside at the 100-year-old temple and lead services morning and evening. Quiet your mind in the meditation room, browse the library, stroll in the large quiet gardens, and marvel at their pet peacocks. The serene atmosphere can afford a rare opportunity to do the inner travel that can be one of life's greatest adventures. This would be a good place for a silent retreat. There is a two-night minimum for groups. (808.928.8539) (Budget)

Hāmākua Ecology Center, located past Honoka'a, just off the road to the Waipi'o Valley, is a project of Earth Voice, a non-profit membership-based organization, which supports projects in sustainable agriculture. Hāmākua hosts workshops and retreats, especially yoga, sponsors conservation and restoration projects, and guides tours to the magical Waipi'o Valley. The Ecology Center can sleep up to 40 people and serves delectable vegetarian Indian food. The main center has a beautiful bamboo floor perfect for dance or yoga. On the property you can explore the organic herb and vegetable garden, the tropical fruit and macadamia nut orchards, and a bamboo demonstration garden. (808.775.9083) (Moderate)

At **Yoga Oasis**, in the Puna coastal district, you can immerse yourself in the wonder of a tropical forest that has been gently adapted for comfortable human occupation and the pursuit of balanced healthy living. The facility includes a workshop space with two screened open walls to allow you to enjoy the sights and sounds of the jungle as you stretch and breath. **Hayward and Star** will help you focus on revitalizing your body and spirit through a combination of quiet seclusion, yoga classes and delicious vegetarian meals drawing from their organic orchard and garden. They offer customized retreats throughout the year for up to 30 people. Also available are herbal and juice detox programs, Thai massage, avocado salt glow, *lomilomi* massage, and watsu. A Chi Hatha Yoga-Panorama Intensive Week is held quarterly. A "4 Element Adventure Week in Hawai'i" for women. (808.965.8460) (Moderate)

Kalani Oceanside Retreat was the inspiration of **Richard Koob** and the late Earnest Morgan who dreamed of a creative arts center in paradise. Over the years Kalani has evolved into a cultural education and wellness retreat center that can accommodate up to

100 people. They provide three organic vegetarian meals a day with fish and chicken options. There's an ethno-botanical and culinary garden, an Olympic-size swimming pool, two hot tubs, a sauna, a watsu pool, five workshop/assembly spaces, café, and gift shop. Activities, classes, therapies, and demonstrations are scheduled day and night. Add to this an array of wellness therapists available to provide massage, watsu, craniosacral, *lomilomi*, reflexology, and acupuncture and you have a self-contained wellness vacation resort/camp. (808.965.7828) (Budget to Luxury)

There are a few individuals who offer personal growth workshops several times throughout the year. **Doug Hackett and Trish Regan's** personal journeys from a fast-paced suburban lifestyle in California to the healing shores of Hawai'i have fueled their ambitious goals for helping others find their way to greater joy and serenity. They lead personal transformation workshops for couples and individuals, dolphin seminars and guided excursions to special sites on the island. The enthusiastic name of their program gives you an idea of the exuberant energy of this couple. It's called **"Joy…It is Essential!"** They live in Captain Cook in South Kona. (808.323.2731)

Suzan Starr, of **Art of the Dove** takes women living with cancer, their significant others, and health professionals seeking a healing experience on a three-day sailing retreat with the inspiring name "Sailing Into the Soul: A Retrieval of Wellness." Her program also offers a land-based retreat in the fall. Suzan is a cancer survivor so can be an especially helpful guide for someone going through the trauma and trials of such an illness. (808.967.7196)

6. Let A Wellness Coach Help Guide You to Better Health

Most busy doctors can allow only twenty minutes for each appointment. Counselors typically provide fifty minutes and you may have only begun your story. Imagine having some knowledgeable health practitioner devote enough time and attention to really help you unravel some of the issues of your physical, emotional, and spiritual health.

Anyone would thrive on the help of a wellness coach, or even a team, who takes a special interest in helping you consider *all* your issues, the bodily aches and pains along with the heartaches, longings, and fears; someone who would focus on you and help you develop and move toward your wellness goals. A wellness vacation may be the perfect time for such an experience. On the Big Island there are highly talented and versatile wellness coaches who offer exactly that service in the setting of their idyllic accommodation settings.

Marty Dean and Tanya Miller organize intensive seven to ten day retreats at their **House of Health** for five women at a time. In their luxurious tropical retreat above Kailua-Kona they lead women through a highly individualized course that covers nutrition, fitness, skin care, meditation, yoga, music, journaling, individual counseling, group sharing, and more. This life-style modification program will fully involve you in taking control of your health. These are two very professional and knowledgeable women who any woman would want on her team. They will help you get focused on, and succeed at, your goals, whether they be weight control, fitness, detoxing, improving your eating habits, or any number of other healthful practices. If you need special services, they have a team of experts on call. Above all, they emphasize that this retreat is fun; full of activities that will lighten your heart and spirit, which in itself is therapeutic. They give you wellness tools to take home and will follow-up with you by phone for 30 days. (808.982.6463 or 808.329.7249)

Tom Sherman has a special appreciation of wellness vacations. Tom, who calls himself **ChakraMan**, went through his own miraculous healing journey, resulting in recovery from AIDS. He gives massage and energy treatments in a lovely protected gazebo at his Nature Sanctuary. Through his own unique blend of bodywork and Healing Touch with chakra-balancing energy therapy, Tom gives an unforgettable demonstration of the subtle energies that are emitting from your charkas, how they influence your emotional and physical well-being, and how to keep them clear. After a session, you may notice areas of your life that had felt constricted begin to open. With his accommodations at the Nature Sanctuary it's possible to work with Tom over an extended period. (808.889.0553)

Keoki and Heidi Staab, just outside of Waimea, offer a Wellness Package that will address your wellness goals from many angles. It includes therapeutic massage, an individual stretch class with Keoki, a day at the Spa and Fitness center at the Mauna Kea

Resort, hot paraffin wax treatments for hands or feet, a session on their Chi-machine or automatic massage chair, nutritional counseling for Body Wise products, plus an individualized itinerary for your leisure time. They will also schedule appointments with health care professionals such as acupuncturists, homeopathic doctors, and chiropractors prior to your arrival. Keoki and Heidi are so vibrant and healthy themselves and so knowledgeable about fitness and health, they instill trust and confidence as guides to an improved lifestyle. (808.885.6535)

Nature as Healer

7. Experience the Power of Pele at Hawai'i Volcanoes National Park

Kīlauea volcano, on the flank of Mauna Loa, is the sacred home of the Hawaiian Goddess of Fire, Pele. Standing at the edge of Kīlauea's Halemaumau crater evokes a sense of awe at its destructive aspects, yet unity with a pervading creative presence. You can witness planetary birthing and reflect on your own emergence, growth, and "rebirth." Kīlauea is the most active volcano in the world and is a priority destination for visitors to Hawai'i.

The Hawai'i Volcanoes National Park has made this natural wonder easily accessible through paved roads, overlooks, hiking trails, and tours of nature trails. Visitor facilities include a visitors' center, a museum, and an art center. A video at the visitors' center shows the fascinating geological history of the islands beginning with the birth of a volcano itself as it rises from the Earth's core and breaks through to the ocean floor. To stand on this land is to be closely connected to the very center of creation.

The Park is worth a full day of your time and more. Hiking some of the 150 miles of trails is one of the best ways to appreciate the unusual flora and lava formations. Or take your time–about two hours are needed–driving the Crater Rim Drive that circles the Kīlauea Caldera, stopping to see sights such as the Thurston Lava Tube and the steam vents.

The Chain of Craters Road turnoff takes you on a 23-mile safari down 3,000 feet almost to sea level ending where the May 1995 lava flow covered the road. This alone is an amazing sight.

When there is an active flow on this East Rift Zone, a walk across the hardened lava trail to see Pele show her fiery stuff is well worth the exertion especially at night. Arrive when it's still light, however, so you have some daylight while walking in. Bring a flashlight (one per person), sturdy closed-toed shoes, a bottle of water, and a jacket. To watch the flowing furnace-hot lava ooze its way down the slope is to watch creation happening before your very eyes. Take time to absorb the experience. Some people have unusual bursts of energy and strength and are able to walk the trail without tiring. There is healing power here.

Health tips
Safety Around a Volcano

The Park warns that volcanic fumes are hazardous to your health. Persons with heart disease or respiratory problems, small children, and pregnant women, should avoid Halemaumau fire pit, the Sulphur Banks, and other areas where fumes are present. Heed the warning signs and instructions of the Park rangers. Areas of newly formed lava are not always stable and can be the sites of accidents and even deaths. There are hidden dangers in "volcanoland." Dehydration will occur faster than usual hiking in the tropical sun. Take water with you. Use sun block here (you're at over 4,000 feet elevation) and on any outing that exposes you to the sun. Sunburns in the tropics can be especially fierce.

Pele is temperamental, however, and may not accommodate your visit with an active flow. Even without that, there is much to see. The enormity of the volcano's caldera, the lava tubes, the hardened waves of rippling pāhoehoe lava, and the sharp clinkers of a'ā lava, the molten trees, the rain forest, and trails will all give you reason to marvel at the extraordinary process that created these islands. Call 808.985.6017 for updated information about the flows or 808.985.6000 for the main park service. The web site www.nps.gov/havo is an excellent source of information about the Park, the latest flow activity, projects going on in the Park, and volunteer opportunities.

8. Connect with the Land: Farm or Orchard Stays are Healthy for You and the Farmers

The land, 'āina, is sacred to the Hawaiians and it doesn't take long to appreciate why this is so. The 'āina speaks to the body and soul as it offers its bounty. Visiting a farm or orchard will help you appreciate how the land is being used and protected by people concerned with sustainable agriculture and preserving small farms.

Like eco-tourism, agricultural tourism (ag-tourism) encourages socially and environmentally responsible travel.

On the Big Island, ag-tourism can be anything from a one-hour tour of a macadamia nut orchard to a stay at a Bed and Breakfast built amidst the coffee trees of a Kona coffee farm.

'Ai Lani Orchards, located near the ancient Hawaiian town of Wai'ōhinu in the Ka'ū District, offers an innovative "Permaculture Vacation," a non-profit version of an "Ecological Timeshare." Call **Barney Frazier or Elizabeth Jenkins**. (808.929.8785)

Macadamia Meadows Farm and B&B near Nā'ālehu in Ka'ū district gives tours of their macadamia nut orchard where you learn about every phase of production and can try your hand at cracking those tough nuts yourself. The buttery taste of macadamia nuts is your reward. Call **Charlene Cowan**. (808.929.8097)

Volcano Island Honey Company near Honoka'a on the Hāmākua Coast produces organic honey from wild kiawe groves. The TV program Epicurius has featured **Richard Spiegel**, the owner, for his exceptionally high quality of organic honey produced without heat to preserve the enzymes and pollen. On a tour of his farm you can see the hives and the process of extracting and bottling honey, then taste the delicious product: Rare Hawaiian Organic White Honey. (808.775.0806)

Parker Ranch, for many years the largest privately owned ranch under a single owner in the country, attracts many visitors to Waimea. Their visitor center and museum features a 26-minute video about the history of the ranch. Ownership of the ranch is now under a trust foundation created exclusively for health care, education, and charitable purposes. Open daily, 9:00 a.m. to 4:00 p.m., you can take a 45-minute covered wagon ride around the pastures, corrals and property, and see the two historic Parker

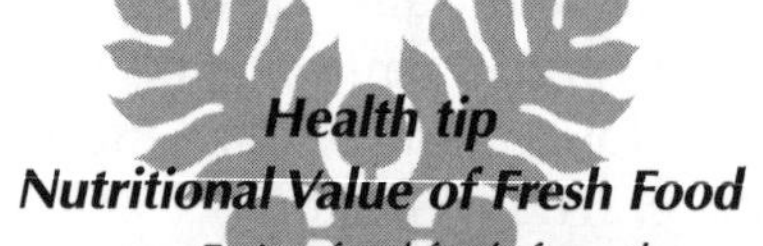

Health tip

Nutritional Value of Fresh Food

Eating food fresh from the land where its grown vastly improves the health benefits. Transporting and processing fresh produce robs its vitamins and minerals as well as the plants' energetic properties. Food that is organically grown is also generally healthier. Produce grown without chemical fertilizers and pesticides are most easily available at health food stores or at some farmers markets *(see#11)*

homes. Call for times of tours. (808.885.7311 or www.parkerranch.com)

There are 55 sites listed in the Agricultural Tourism brochure. When you stay on a farm or visit a farm operation, you are contributing to the very people that keep Hawai'i the beautiful sanctuary it is—Hawai'i's farmers. *(See article on Agricultural Tourism in Chapter Three)* For a map and list of ag-tourism sites available on the Big Island, pick up a brochure in the card rack at the airport, see the website www.Hawaiiagtourism.com or call 808.939.9023.

9. Let Nature Do Its Healing Magic: Visit a Garden

The sight of abundant shrubs, flowers and trees showcased in a well-tended landscape induces a wave of contentment. A walk in a garden is a soothing retreat from the busy world and a chance to commune with creation. Each garden has its own character and personality. Due to the isolation of the islands, the gardens in Hawai'i have plants that are found nowhere else in the world.

The **Amy B.H. Greenwell Ethnobotanical Garden**, near Captain Cook (South Kona) on the *mauka* (mountain) side of Hwy. 11, is more than a park or garden. It's a live, growing outdoor museum with displays in Hawaiian ecology, anthropology, botany, history, culinary arts, and medicine. The garden is open Monday through Friday, 8:30 – 5:30 with guided tours on Wednesday and Friday at 1:00 p.m. and on the second Saturday of each month at 10:00 a.m. (808.323.3318) (Donation requested)

On the Puna coast, **Barbara Fahs** hosts visitors at her **Hi'iaka's Healing Hawaiian Herb Garden**. This may be the most extensive herb garden open to the public in Hawai'i. Barbara has over 120 medicinal plants including 50 Hawaiian varieties, plus endangered tropical plants from Hawai'i and around the world—all of this behind her private home. This is not a meditative garden, but a place where you can see and learn about medicinal plants. Tours are on Tuesdays and Thursdays from 1:00 p.m. to 5:00 p.m. or by appointment. The small gift shop features tinctures, oils, and creams from her garden. Ask about her internships and educational retreats. (808.966.6126) (Admission Fee)

The Hawai'i Tropical Botanical Garden, seven miles north of Hilo (follow signs for 4-mile Scenic Route), is a veritable Garden of Eden. To stroll down its paths, through the more than 2,000 different species of flora, is like being a privileged visitor in a rain forest sanctuary. It calls for quiet hushed tones. The aviary, waterfalls, and crashing waves amplify the experience. Benches are conveniently located for contemplation of the beauty. The garden may uplift or it may evoke deep contemplation, but it will surely have a quieting effect on the restless spirit. (808.964.5233) (Admission Fee)

'Akaka Falls State Park, clearly marked 14 miles north of Hilo, has a comfortable walk to the tallest waterfall in the state. The path leading up to the falls wanders through lush vegetation, some familiar, some rare. Stop at the wooden bridge and watch the clear stream flowing by. Visit the secondary falls, a short detour off the path. Then, take your time climbing up the final slope to be greeted by 'Akaka. It will hold you transfixed. (808.974.6200) (Free)

At mile marker 16, **Umauma Falls and World Botanical Gardens** takes you on a quiet trail by some of the most exotic species of flowering plants you'll see anywhere. At the registration desk get a map to the beautiful Umauma Falls, a five-minute drive away. The garden owners express their aloha with some very nice touches–samples of fresh fruits in season, and flowers for the women's hair. (808.963.5427) (Admission Fee)

Health Tip • The Benefits of Sea Water

Seawater baths open the pores and help eliminate toxins. Vitamins, minerals, amino acids and trace elements are absorbed through the skin. The ocean contains all 89 known elements present in our bodies, including osmium, gold, vanadium, zinc and iodine. The magnesium content has a calming effect on the nerves. The potassium encourages good urinary flow. Even the spray is rich in iodine, which helps regulate the thyroid gland, and negative ions, which strengthen the body's immune system. Add to this the soothing effect of the movement and sound of the waves and you practically have a holistic treatment with one immersion.

10. Soak up the Healing Properties of Seawater

The ocean beckons to us from the moment we arrive in Hawai'i. Our eyes constantly scan the horizon for a view of the endless blue sea rippling with whitecaps. The connection is not incidental. Blood plasma contains nearly the same mineral content as the ocean. Understanding this helps us understand the value of Thalassotherapy, the use of seawater in restoring and maintaining health. According to **Marcel J. Hernandez**, a Naturopathic Doctor in

Honoka'a, the health benefits of bathing in seawater are both physical and psychological.

In an article in the *Hawai'i Island Journal* on the benefits of seawater, he wrote, *"The sea provides a healing magic that...forces us to become involved with it... From a metaphysical perspective, water is associated with creativity and our feelings, and is the seat of our unconscious patterns. It has to do with emotions that we have suppressed and buried. Being close to the ocean deepens our contemplation and helps us bring these patterns and feelings to the surface so we may recognize and deal with them. In color therapy, ocean blue is used to balance or enhance freedom of expression verbally and artistically..."*

The Big Island is not famous for its white sand beaches. Nevertheless, Hāpuna Beach in South Kohala district is an all around favorite and may be one of the prettiest in the state. The smaller Spencer Beach, nearby, may be even more appealing. Kauna'oa Beach is small, but beautiful, having been rated the #1 beach in America by both *Condé Nast Traveler* and *The Travel Channel.* However, Mauna Kea Resort restricts access by limiting the number of parking permits so it's best to arrive early in the day.

The local favorite on the Hilo side is Richardson Beach just south of town on Hwy. 12. In Puna, there are tide pools and warm ponds that can be accessed with help from local guides. The warm ponds are described in #5. Black sand beaches may be found in the Ka'ū and Puna Districts (closer to Kīlauea volcano)

11. Buy Fresh Food to Nurture Body and Spirit: Shop at a Farmers' Market

Eating fresh-off-the-farm organic food is one of the healthiest aspects of being in Hawai'i. If you are staying at a vacation rental and doing your own cooking, you'll find farmers markets are the best source for the freshest fruits and vegetables.

Farmers markets on the Big Island are a kind of street fair and community gathering place where local artists, crafts people, farmers, and small entrepreneurs sell their products without the middleman. These markets can be great fun for anyone who likes to mingle with the local culture and pick up bargains. Even if you're not in the market for food, the variety of vendors with flowers, crafts, home baked goods, clothes, literature, books, and homemade products will give you a taste of life on the islands. The Hilo Farmers Market is a big favorite with the greatest variety of products and people. It has become so popular, especially with tourists, it is playing a role in revitalizing the downtown area of Hilo.

The Hawai'i Island Journal has collected information on most of the Farmers' Markets around the island. They are listed here with times, days, locations and a few special features.

Kailua-Kona

Kailua Village Farmers Market •
Wednesday, Friday, Saturday and Sunday. Flowers, produce, macadamia nuts, and coffee.

Kona Farmers Market •
8:00 a.m. to 2:30 p.m. every Saturday and Sunday at Kaiwi Square, Old Industrial Park. Fresh fruits, vegetables, flowers, and breads.

Ali'i Gardens Marketplace •
9:00 a.m. to 5:00 p.m. Wednesday through Sunday on Ali'i Drive, 2 miles south of Kailua Pier. Open-air garden setting with 50 merchants displaying 500 handmade Hawaiian products. (808.334.1381)

Captain Cook •
Monday through Friday (open air every Thursday), 82-5810 Nāpo'opo'o Road (look for the Pink Donkey Sign) Orchid plants, crafts, free tours of a Macadamia nut and coffee operation—Call for times. (808.328.2412)

Ka'ū

Saturdays, 8:00 a.m. to noon in Nā'ālehu Theater. (808.929.7236)

Volcano

Volcano Farmers Market •
8:30 a.m. to 11:00 a.m. every Sunday at Cooper Center. Flowers, baked goods. Call Betsy. (808.976.7209)

Kea'au

Kea'au Village Farmers Market •
9:00 a.m. to 5:00 p.m. every Friday. Flowers, handmade Hawaiian arts and crafts, and super sweet corn. Produce available 7:00 a.m. to 5:00 p.m. daily.

Pāhoa

Caretakers of Our Land Farmers Market•
7:30 a.m. to noon every Saturday at Sacred Heart Church. Plants, flowers, fish, and small livestock. (808.965.88963)

Aloha Market •
7:30 a.m. to 2:30 p.m. Sundays on Hwy 130 near Maku'u Drive. Baked goods, crafts, books, clothes, and jewelry.

Hilo

Rainbow Falls Market Place •
8:00 a.m. to 4:00 p.m. Monday and Thursday. Across from Rainbow Falls. Hula Show, free samples, homegrown and handmade crafts. Call Mike. (808.933.7173)

Pana'ewa Homestead Farmers Market •
8:00 a.m. to 5:00 p.m. every day on the sidewalk at the Hilo Wal-Mart. Fruits and vegetables.

Mamo Street Market •
8:00 a.m. to 5:00 p.m. every day at Mamo Parking Lot

Hilo Farmers Market •
7:00 a.m. to 3:00 p.m. every Wednesday and Saturday at the corner of Kamehameha Avenue and Mamo Street. Flowers, plants, baked goods, and box lunches.

The Market Place •
7:00 a.m. to 3:00 p.m. Wednesday and Saturday. Across from Hilo Farmers Market. Local arts and crafts. Call Keith. (808.933.1000)

Honoka'a

Honoka'a Farmers Market •
Begins 8:00 a.m., Saturday. Downtown Honoka'a. Fruits, baked goods, and crafts.

Waimea

Waimea Hawaiian Homesteaders Association Farmers Market •
7:00 a.m. to 12:00 p.m. Saturday at the Kūhiō Hale Building. Produce, flowers, baked goods, potted plants, and crafts.

Hāwī

Under the Banyans Farmers Market •
7:30 a.m. to 1:00 p.m. Saturday. Fresh produce, plants, and crafts. (808.889.0615)

12. Relax With the Big Island's "Hottest Therapies"

Your wellness vacation to the Big Island offers the unique opportunity of experiencing hot therapies as a gift from the Fire Goddess, Pele. Only on this island with an active volcano will you find natural warm ponds and steam vents that are fun and therapeutic. Beyond the relaxing effect of soaking in hot water or steam, the heat dilates blood vessels, increases blood flow to the skin and relieves sore muscles. The warm ponds of **Ahalanui County Park**, are located on the coastal road 137. Ask any local for directions from Pāhoa. The ponds combine geothermal springs with ocean water to produce a large open-air swimming pond. The water temperature varies, but is usually a comfortable 90 degrees. It's hard to hang on to your troubles while soaking under the swaying palms and listening to the waves. There is minimal space to change clothes so it's easier to come dressed for bathing. There is a fresh water outdoor shower. (Free)

The natural steam vents on Hwy 130 past Pāhoa, are steamy lava tube caves of various sizes, which you can enter for a hot steam cleansing. The vents are heated by Kīlauea Volcano and can get extremely hot so stay alert and don't stay too long. There are rustic handmade doors and bench-like slats on which to recline or sit. Bring along ample water for drinking or dowsing over your body. It is hot, moist, and steamy, so everything gets wet. Be prepared with swimwear or light clothing and towels.

Hawaiian Lomi Stone massage comes out of the traditional Hawaiian medicinal arts. The therapist rests warm to hot stones on sore or painful areas of the body, then massages the surrounding skin and muscles. Ask for this therapy where massage is offered.

> ***Health tip***
> ***Heat Treatments in Moderation***
>
> *As with the sun, heat treatments are a natural therapy that carries both benefits and hazards. Persons with heart conditions, pregnant women and children are cautioned against the use of strong full body heat therapies. Too frequent bathing in hot tubs can alter the vaginal pH balance. Persons with chronic fatigue and fibromyalgia may find that more than a few minutes in a hot tub exacerbates the fatigue.*

Spas have led the way in heat treatments. Some spas use hot towels soaked in strong infusions of healing roots, like ginger, to promote cleansing and deep relaxation. The hot dry heat of saunas encourages efficient elimination of toxins through the sweat glands. A hot steam treatment has the added benefit of moisturizing the skin and clearing the sinuses. **The Lotus Center** (808.334.0445) at the **Royal Kona Resort** on Alii Drive in Kona, has a friendly caring staff and gives wonderful facials; **Spa Without Walls** (808.887.7540) at **The Orchid at Mauna Lani Resort** provides treatments in a cabana by the ocean where the sea breeze adds to the therapy; and **Paradise Spa**, at the **Hawai'i Naniloa Resort** (808.969.3333) has a hot tub and sauna and a staff trained in Hawaiian therapies.

Complementary Treatment Therapies

13. Raise Your Vibrations with Music, Dance and Voice Therapies

Tune to the Island's heartbeat through its music and dance. Big Islanders love their music. A local concert, cultural festival, or spontaneous music night at the beach or local restaurant, can connect you to the joyful spirit of its healing vibrations. *The Hawai'i Island Journal*, distributed free at health food stores and where other newspaper dispensers are found, is a good source of information about local events. Or just ask around. Consider buying a CD or cassette of Hawaiian music. They can be found in various local outlets, and Borders in Hilo and Kailua-Kona has a good selection. The modern Hawaiian interpreters and composers have created many wonderful recordings with songs in both English and the native language. *(See article on Music and Voice Therapy in Chapter Three)*

Hula, the sacred dance of Hawai'i, is experiencing a renaissance, as are numerous other Hawaiian art forms. Hula is a difficult dance to master in all its subtlety and can be a lifetime practice, but if you have a chance, give it a try. To acquire even a minimal feel for the dance can be a thrilling sense of accomplishment.

Traditionally, hula was taught in an exclusive group, known as a *hālau*, led by a teacher for whom the *hālau* was named. Here, carefully selected students were sequestered from childhood. The hālau of today have adapted to a more modern way of life, but most remain selective, admitting students by invitation. There are those rarer *hālau* that are more open, welcoming whoever walks through the door. But don't be fooled by easier entrée–the practice is just as demanding.

Hula classes are offered free or for a donation in a few places on the island. In Puna district, **Kalani Eco-Resort** (808.965.7828) has a Hula Basics class free on Tuesday nights. Elsewhere, ask your innkeeper or other locals. This information is usually passed by word of mouth.

To witness and be part of the energy of the Olympics of hula, plan your vacation around the **Merrie Monarch Festival** in Hilo, usually in April. (See #4)

At another level of vibration, a healing voice session with **Keith Amber** in North Kohala can fast-forward you out of stuck places, both physical and emotional. Keith is a "psychic soul healer" and his approach combines a remarkably resonant voice (toning on a single note), reflexology, and channeled energy, along with some healthy intuition. He has received rave reviews for his ability to relieve physical pain, gain clarity on personal issues, and even integrate past lives. He also gives tools to work with at home. Keith and his wife Sharmai also own an intriguing collection of crystals, candles, and wind chimes that are available at their **Star Light** crystal shop in Hāwī. (808.884.5429)

In North Kohala, near Pololū Valley, **Joy Gardner** offers vibrational alignment and life path counseling. Joy is the author of *Heal Yourself*, one of the pioneer books on self-care, as well as other books on crystal and color therapy, voice therapy, and pregnancy. Her wonderful philosophy that "all illness comes to us as a teaching and carries with it a gift of self-discovery" helps soften our attitudes towards our ailments. Joy uses a style of voice therapy that invites clients to express themselves through improvised vocalization. Crystals and hands-on pressure at key points on the body are also part of her therapy. You may leave her session almost in an altered state, feeling truly refreshed and with a sense of wonder about your unfolding life. (808.889.0040)

Near Kealakekua in South Kona, **Judith Lynne** introduces you to the extraordinary vibrational power of the voice. A high soprano shattering crystal is familiar, but experiencing how that level of vibration might stir the physical and emotional body is another thing. Judith projects her powerful voice up and down your charkas and you can feel those parts of your body vibrate. Judith seems to intuitively focus on trouble spots where there is pain or blocked energy. (808.987.8099)

14. "Listen" to Your Body Tell Its Story

A cultural tradition on the island is to "talk story." It comes out of the Hawaiian's oral tradition and is connected to aloha, the spirit of warmth and caring. People ask how you are and really intend to stand by listening for the full answer. In turn they share the stories of their lives at the moment, whether it's about family, health, romance, grief, car troubles, job issues, or whatever. This type of mutual sharing and listening engenders a deep connection between friends and family, and builds support and trust.

Each body has its own story. Your body "knows" how you store, integrate, and handle your daily responses to life experiences. As Dr. Deepak Chopra describes it, the body is "brimming with intelligence." Research scientists, physicians and lay people alike are exploring safe, non-invasive ways to listen to the body's wisdom, ways that may add information to standard medical tests and even to psychoanalysis. With kinesiology, also known as muscle testing, health practitioners are discovering ways to "talk" with and "listen" to the body. *(See the article on Applied Kinesiology in Chapter Three.)*

The Big Island has many alternative practitioners who use different forms of kinesiology. The Body Talk System, developed by Australian chiropractor and acupuncturist Dr. John Veltheim, operates on the theory that the brain knows how to heal the body, but the communication link between the brain and different organs or systems has become broken or obstructed. The practitioner of this system establishes "neuromuscular feedback" by touching a muscle or applying pressure as the patient lifts an arm. She then tests the strength of the "response" of the muscles as she touches different areas of the body. When she finds a blockage, she taps the top of the patient's head in order to focus the brain toward restoring the communication link so it can begin to heal in that area. Tapping the chest then stores the new balance in "the heart energy complex." This very gentle and safe therapy empowers the body's innate wisdom to heal itself. It is purported to be effective for a wide range of ailments from parasites to arthritis. Many professionals who are exposed to this have incorporated it as a primary element in their treatment. **Don Ka'imi Pilipovich and Kacey Clark** are certified in the system and offer **Body Talk** at the Orchid at Mauna Lani Spa. (808.885.2000)

Aiko Aiyana's methodology "talking story with body wisdom," helps unlock each person's healing stories. Using a well-developed system called Ontological Kinesiology, Aiko accesses an individual's unique "stories"—from nutritional deficiencies to family ancestral patterns—that may be causing psychological or physical pain and disease. During a session, the body then chooses its own safe, specific methods for release and transformation. Developed in 1986 by an osteopathic physician, the system is based on how the DNA, brain, bones, and neural pathways store and release information and trauma. Today there are many practitioners of this process worldwide. (808.982.6577)

15. Experience the Island's Ancient Healing Arts

The ancient Hawaiians had a sophisticated and enduring culture, which included a masterful command of holistic healing arts. Highly trained *kahuna*, (masters, elders) chosen from birth to study with a master teacher, learned to listen to the vast interplay of psychological, spiritual, physical, and natural forces that collided or converged in the individual and community. The wisdom and practice of *ho'oponopono*– "setting things right" with oneself, one's partner and family, with the community, and the Greater Self–were essential to the healing process. *Lomilomi* massage and *lā'au lapa'au*, the medicinal use of herbs, were also areas of high accomplishment in the Hawaiian healing arts.

The Big Island is home to Aunty Margaret Machado, one of the most beloved Hawaiian healers and a Master of Hawaiian massage (*lomilomi*). Aunty Margaret, now retired, initially received considerable criticism from other Hawaiians for sharing the secrets of her sacred art with Westerners, but she believed it would contribute to the well being of many people and should be made available. For more than fifty years, Aunty Margaret has taught hundreds of aspiring practitioners in the healing art of *lomilomi* massage. Aunty Margaret defines it as "the loving touch–a connection between heart, hand, and soul with the Source of all life." *(See article on lomilomi in Chapter Three)* Papa Henry Auwae, another highly gifted Hawaiian healer, taught and practiced well into his 90s. He has now passed away. And Sylvester Kepilino, age 75, known as Papa K, still practices and teaches in North Kohala. Like Aunty Margaret Machado, they believed that the traditional knowledge should be shared beyond the host culture.

It is not the Hawaiian way to solicit business. A potential patient must ask for help, and traditionally, healers never charged for their medicines and services, as these are believed to be gifts from God. They did accept freely given donations, and still do.

You can get a *lomilomi* massage at most of the resort spas. If you decide to venture outside of the spas, however, one very experienced *lomilomi* massage and hot stone specialist, **Jerri Lynn Knoblich**, at **Swami's Hawaiian Lomilomi Massage** in Kealakekua, studied for several years with Aunty Margaret. She has more experience than most in this field. Her skill goes beyond technique. As with all *lomilomi* practitioners, she includes the spiritual aspects, such as beginning with a prayer in Hawaiian asking the higher spiritual power to restore harmony and balance. This is what makes this a true sacred healing art. (808.323.3344)

Gyongyi Szirom "Momi" is an R.N. who practices on the Hilo side of the island. Momi has studied and practiced *lomilomi* with Aunty Margaret and other skilled teachers for the last 10 years. She also does Shiatsu and Thai massage. Massage is her spiritual practice. This is manifested through the setting of intention rather than a verbalized prayer. (808.982.9331)

Kahuna Lapa'au Kahu Ikaika T. Dombrigues (*Lā'au Lapa'au*), **Kahu Auntie Abbie Nape'ahi** (*Ho'oponopono*), and **Ke Kumu'ola Leina'ala K. Brown-Dombrigues** (Hawaiian *Lomilomi Lapa'au* (*Haha*) and Hawaiian Seawater Cleanse Therapy) are teachers and native *lapa'au* providers of these sacred Hawaiian modalities. From their clinic, **Ho'ola 'O LomiLomi Lapa'au**, at the Hawai'i Naniloa Resort in Hilo, they offer traditional *lā'au lapa'au* (herbalism), seawater cleanse, *lomilomi*, and *ho'oponopono* (setting things right) The Hawaiian seawater cleanse is offered in a one, three, five or ten-day program, which can remove years of accumulated toxins. (808.961.3118)

16. Pursue Balance and Harmony Through Energy Healing

Energy healing is an ancient concept and has also been described as the medicine of the 21st century. It is the basis for acupuncture which dates back 5000 years as well as crystal healing which was used by ancient Egyptians. Although its many variations aren't all embraced with the same enthusiasm, science has firmly established the power of energy to heal.

This section directs you to a few practitioners who specialize in various aspects of energy healing. There are many more listed at the end of the chapter and some may be closer to where you are staying.

Two talented women in Kailua-Kona combine color, music, and aromatherapies. **Sharman O'Shea and Jean Nelson** have joined forces to create **Harmonic Attunement**, a holistic approach addressing areas of physical, emotional and spiritual imbalance. Through kinesiology, Sharman and Jean discover what colors are missing, or weak, in your spectrum. They may also alert you to some food allergies. Then they tailor a treatment of colored light, improvised music and essential oils. After one session, you'll feel positive and energized. (808.324.6504 or 808.883.1410)

Carol Hannum, a medical intuitive, has a gentle charm that inspires confidence and puts you totally at ease. After 10 years of study and experimentation, particularly with energetic and spiritual healing, Carol has developed her own system, which she calls **Energy Alchemy**. She explains that she communicates with the patient's higher self. Her treatments are without medication or any physical intervention. Carol is definitely breaking new ground. She lives south of Captain Cook around mile marker 105. (808.328.7788)

In the gentle hands of **Alia Hallowell**, a Cranisacral and Polarity therapist, clients are transported to a state of deep relaxation and typically experience relief from tension and pain. Alia also offers Orthobionomy and Psychic Clearing. "Pain Relief," one of Alia's proprietary blends of aromatherapy oils, is especially popular. Alia lives in Puna off Hwy 130 south of Pāhoa. (808.965.8472)

With an open mind and some exploration, you may discover a technique, or experience a therapy, that unlocks a healing reaction in you. The process can be an adventure.

17. Get an Alternative Opinion from a Holistic Wellness Practitioner

Though no one plans to get sick or injured on a vacation, it can happen. Or, you may want to pursue a second or third opinion about a particular chronic condition or a treatment unavailable near home. The small sample of practitioners listed here are holistic in their perspective and practice integrative medicine. They are willing to see patients for short-term care and are all highly regarded by their patients and the community.

Dr. Jacqueline Hahn is a Naturopathic physician in Hilo who was voted the favorite alternative practitioner two years in a row by readers of the *Hawai'i Island Journal*. Like others in this category, Jacqueline takes on the cases that allopathic (Western) medicine has not been able to help–and with considerable success. She gives you her full focused attention---a very reassuring and skillful doctor. (808.969.7848)

Jan Ellison, is a Doctor of Oriental Medicine who did part of her training in China. She is also a Neurolink practitioner with a clinic in Kapa'au in North Kohala. Jan makes you feel welcomed and skillfully attended to. Most people who have experienced Jan's treatment describe her as "a true healer." (808.889.6900)

Scott Miller is a respected acupuncturist in Hilo. For many clients, his acupuncture treatments have been very helpful in relieving pain and restoring a sense of overall balance in the body. Scott does a unique treatment called hot ginger moxa which feels as good as a hot compress and a massage combined. (808.934.7030) *(See his article on Acupuncture in Chapter Three.)*

Dr. Yvonne Conner in Hilo was trained in allopathic medicine at Meharry Medical College in Nashville, Tennessee, and did her residency at the University of California Irvine Medical Center. She has been in practice over twenty years and has found that incorporating alternative healing modalities in her treatments has vastly improved the outcomes of most of her patients. She specializes in treating allergies, but sees herself primarily as a health educator. Her spiritual approach to illness is that health challenges contain important opportunities for personal growth. (808.961.4722)

The **North Hawai'i Community Hospital** in Waimea has been a pioneer in forging cooperative links between Western medicine and alternative complementary treatments. It is a full-service acute care hospital with an integrative approach. (808.885.4444)

18. Walk in the Footsteps of the People of Old: Hike the Ancient Trails

Hiking the ancient trails of Hawai'i is a venture through time and space. The same forces of nature that humans have always experienced impact also on contemporary travelers.

Probably nowhere are ancient Hawaiian trails more accessible on the Big Island than on the shorelines. Though the coast has seen much modern development and, in some places, the ocean has eroded the shoreline and the trail that was on it, much remains. The United States' newest national historic trail, the "Ala Kahakai," or "trail by the sea," encircles nearly 200 miles of the Island's coastal area.

The State of Hawai'i Trails and Access Program, **Na Ala Hele** "trails for walking" (808. 587.0051 or 0062), has marked and mapped some segments of coastal trails, as well as some *mauka-makai* (mountain-to-the-sea) connecting trails. On the Island of Hawai'i, a community group dedicated to the protection and enjoyment of ancient and historic trails, **E Mau Na Ala Hele** ("perpetuate the walking trails") (808. 587.0051), has been hard at work for decades. Either of these organizations can assist those seeking to connect with nature and tradition by walking in ancient footsteps. Visitors may also find usable trail segments on maps. One of the best is the University of Hawai'i Press *Map of Hawai'i: The Big Island.*

To hike with a local expert who has been active in preserving the ancient trails and is well versed in their history, as well as the natural and cultural history of the island, call **Hugh Montgomery** at **Hawaiian Walkways** (808.775.0372).

In addition, **Sierra Club** hikes go on year-round on all parts of the island. There are seven to eight overnights planned throughout the year. Call Phil Barnes at 808.965.9695 for information. **The Hawai'i Volcanoes National Park** leads regularly scheduled hikes in the Park. They will also guide customized educational hikes for groups. Call Mardie Lane at 808.985.6018.

19. Maintain or Start your Fitness Program

Using your vacation to start a fitness program may be a turning point in your overall health. If you are already aware of the joys of a regular workout, you probably won't want to let that go while you are here. The resort spas all have fitness workout rooms and pools for their guests. If you're staying at a B&B or vacation rental there are many on-going classes of yoga, aerobics, and stretching available to the traveler.

In Waimea, **Uvonne Lindsey** has ongoing classes of tai chi, qigong, karate, Cardio Step and aerobics at her **Pacific Coast Fitness Center**, which is open 6:00 a.m. to 9:00 p.m. The admission covers the use of the workout equipment, a towel and locker. Some classes have additional fees. (808.885-6270)

Also in Waimea, **Keoki Staab** leads a free stretch class for seniors on Wednesday nights. He has also produced an excellent half-hour instructional video of his **Easy Stretch** program. It concludes with a relaxing meditation to the sound of ocean waves. (808.885.6535)

There are yoga classes going on all over the island. The **Boundless Yoga Center** in Waimea, offers classes seven days a week in Hatha Yoga and Viniyoga. Beginners are welcome. Class cards are available. (808.885.9642.)

In Puna, **Yoga Oasis** has yoga classes every morning at 8:00 a.m. led by **Hayward Coleman**. He teaches various levels in the same session. (808.965.8460)

At **Akiko's B&B**, on the Hāmākua Coast, you'll find a class in Iyengar Yoga (stretching for flexibility and strength) on Sundays from 8:30 a.m. to 10:00 a.m. (808.963.6422)

In Hilo, **Yoga Centered** has classes Monday through Thursday and Saturday. This is a full-body workout that uses Ujjayi Breathing (re-opens circulation pathways and allows more oxygen to enter the body.) (808.962.0150.)

If your interest tends toward something more strenuous, aerobic and competitive, such as a race, there are many of them scheduled throughout the year. To do some advance planning, check the website www.hawaiirace.com for information about running, walking, swimming, and bicycling races. The big races on the island are the **Ironman, Ultraman, Keauhou-Kona Triathalon,** and the **Lavaman**. If you're already on the island but would like to watch a race, look for the *Hawai'i Race* magazine, free at sports shops. To join in the fun as a volunteer, race organizers are always looking for people to staff the finish line, the aid stations, and the support teams. Volunteers are also invited to the award party after the race. Call Jane Bockus at 808.322.2120.

The **Kīlauea Volcano Wilderness Runs**, held in July in Hawai'i Volcanoes National Park, include a five-mile walk/run, a ten-mile run and a 26.2-mile full day marathon. This is the only wilderness run in Hawai'i and a great way to see the scenery in the Park. (808.985.8725)

For paddlers, **the Keauhou Club** near Kailua-Kona is open to visitors to join crews of outrigger (Hawaiian style) canoes. Join the fun at 6:00 a.m. Tuesdays, Thursdays, and Saturdays. (Call Jane Bockus at 808.322.2120.)

Travel to Serve Others

20. Give Something Back to the Healing Island

The magical qualities that make the Big Island a healing island are gifts that are in jeopardy. The isolation of the Hawaiian Islands has been the key factor in preserving their beauty. Hawai'i has an open, vulnerable heart. It welcomes visitors with aloha, but like any beautiful place, it can be overwhelmed by excessive demands on the land and water, and by the unconscious energies of haste, greed, and thoughtlessness. There are many residents who understand the need to preserve the natural resources of the island, its cultural heritage, and its energetic healing *mana*. They invite visitors to join them in keeping the Big Island, and all of Hawai'i, a place that can continue to be restorative and uplifting for the rest of the world.

There are many small things you can do just in the course of your vacation to help preserve the Big Island. Pick up trash wherever you see it and properly dispose of your own. Conserve electricity and water. Buy locally produced goods.

Consider volunteering directly and concretely in an area that excites your interest. Some volunteer opportunities are described here but you are encouraged to seek out any other ways to serve and support the land and people of Hawai'i.

Animal lovers who would like to support efforts to rescue dogs and cats, and get their own dose of animal therapy, will find their venue at the **Rainbow Friends Animal Sanctuary** founded by **Mary Rose and Lanni Sinkin**. The couple has taken in 65 dogs and puppies and 100 cats and kittens. The orphaned animals are in varying degrees of healing themselves and in need of friendly human contact. The Sinkins welcome ongoing and short term volunteers to help with cleanup, grooming and exercise, or just to spend time with the animals. The 7.5 acre sanctuary has an easy path for walking and there are tours for children. They are located between Hilo and Volcano, outside of Kurtistown, on Hwy 11. (808.985.6001)

Hikers might like to serve the community of nature lovers by contributing to the construction, maintenance, and preservation of trails. The Division of Forestry and Wildlife of the Department of Land and Natural Resources sponsors the **Na Ala Hele Trail and Access Program** ("trails to go on"). Volunteers are needed to construct, rebuild or repair trails, build boardwalks and bridges, do erosion protection, and whack weeds. Tools are supplied; bring gloves and wear work clothes. This is physically strenuous, but invigorating and satisfying work. The stewardship outing may last six to eight hours. For individuals or small groups it's best to plan for a weekday involvement. Groups of ten or more can work on weekends. The projects respond to conditions and could be anywhere on the island. It's possible to camp on the trails if you bring your own equipment. Call Rodney Oshiro at 808.873.3508.

Hawai'i Volcanoes National Park has very interesting student intern and volunteer opportunities for ecologically minded travelers. Volunteers are needed for periods of eight to twelve weeks. A volunteer might monitor and protect the nesting of the rare Hawksbill turtle or monitor and work on predator control for flocks of endangered Hawaiian *nēnē* (geese). There are openings for volunteer interpreters to guide visitors in the park. The **U.S. Geological Survey** (USGS) takes volunteers to help conduct research on volcanic activity. These are highly-prized opportunities and, as such, are competitive. One must fill out an application several months in advance. There are a limited number of dorm style rooms available for volunteers. Check the website www.nps.gov/havo. Look for the "volunteer" link. For the USGS go to "In Depth" on the Volcano Park home page, to "Eruption Up-date," then "Volunteer Program" under Hawai'i Volcano Observatory. Or call 808.985.6001 and ask for Jim Quiring.

Finally, one of the simplest and most profound ways to give back is to say mahalo (thank you) frequently–to all the people you meet, to all the places you explore, and to the Island herself and all she encompasses. Gratitude is an attitude that can heal, and like any healer, can shift your life.

Healing Accommodations

Kailua-Kona and the South Kona Coast

In Kailua-Kona there are dozens of hotels but we have discovered two particularly healing accommodations away from the crowds, with sweeping coastal vistas that we want to share with you.

Lopakatu, a picture perfect tropical estate just 2.5 miles north of Kailua-Kona off Palani Boulevard has rooms that verge on luxurious, each with a private entrance. The ozone-purified swimming pool, complete with a waterfall, and the workout area look out over a stunning view of the coastline. A large modern kitchen allows you to make your own meals or you can have them catered. In addition to the big house, there is a studio and Pool House. The hosts, **Bob and Marty Dean**, are health conscious, experienced travelers who have given a lot of thought to wellness vacations. Ask about their retreats for women. Minimum rental is a week. The entire complex can accommodate up to 12 people. (808.329.7249) (Moderate – Deluxe)

Another welcome alternative to the busy streets of Kailua-Kona is **Ka'ula Farm**. This family-style lodging frequently books retreats and conferences of up to 14 people, but even if you are not with a group, call to see if they have space. Resting high above Makako Bay just north of the city, you can relax by the solar heated, salt-water pool and enjoy the unobstructed view of Hualālai sloping down to the ocean. A spacious sunlit meeting room can serve for yoga and meditation or group activities. Kaula Farm is convenient to the Keāhole-Kona airport and to activities in the Kona area should you decide to go out for shopping or dining. Bathrooms and the kitchen are shared, but you can enjoy a tranquil, modern estate for a very reasonable price. **Tom Hohler** is the friendly host who keeps Kaula Farm humming. (808.825.5268) (Budget – Moderate)

In Kealakekua, off of Route 11, the **Areca Palms Estate B&B** greets you like an oasis. Manicured lawns and gardens, a hostess with aloha plus, a AAA top rating, and close proximity to beaches, snorkeling (gear supplied), and historic sites, make this a very desirable place to stay. The rooms are modern and guests share a cozy living room and large *lānai* overlooking the garden. **Janice and Steve Glass** offer a full breakfast tailored to your health needs, and they enjoy helping guests plan their activities. They also have a recommended massage therapist who will come to you. For a retreat site or family reunion, it can hold up to 12. (808.323.2276) (Moderate – Deluxe)

Heading south, the Napo'opo'o Road winds down a steep decline to Kealakekua Bay. Just before the road's end is the **Kealakekua Bay B&B**, situated on a five-acre tropical fruit farm. Built well off the road yet within walking distance of three beaches, this is an ideal site for the traveler who likes the ocean close at hand yet wants seclusion, away from the crowds. The view from the *lānai* is a real eye pleaser, spanning a broad lawn and tropical garden with the ocean as a distant backdrop. **Shakti**, the hostess, provides an all-organic continental breakfast. For small retreats, a two-bedroom cottage with kitchen, laundry, cable TV and other amenities, sleeps 6. Add the rooms in the house and a total of 15 could be accommodated. (808.328.8150) (Moderate)

South of Captain Cook between mile markers 106 and 107 is **Affordable Hawai'i at Pōmaika'i (lucky) Farm B&B**. **Nita Isherwood** is the owner and Pōmaika'i Coulon the manager of this homey farm style B&B. It's only four acres, but it produces enough coffee, eggs, and macadamia nuts for your breakfast, as well as fresh fruit for the syrups and jams. Breakfast is family style around a big dining table. Guests also gather on the deck, overlooking the farm and the coastline. A century old coffee barn has been converted into a rustic but charming guestroom. Other rooms in the Greenhouse wing have private baths and entrances. Hawai'i is very dear to Nita so aside from hosting guests, she devotes her energies to preserving the present character of the island and to environmental work. Pōmaika'i officiates at weddings, leads guided swims, and hosts journeys to sacred sites with prayer and ceremony. (808.328.2112) (Budget)

Near Captain Cook around mile marker 108 is **KeMa Kama**, owned by **Patricia Nash**, also known as KeMa. The attraction here is a breathtaking view of Kealakekua Bay, the peaceful garden and macadamia nut grove, and KeMa herself. KeMa was a life coach before coming to Hawai'i and is highly attuned to the needs, both spiritual and material, of her guests. Whether she is taking you snorkeling (complimentary gear), or sharing her knowledge of the Big Island, you will feel accepted and supported wherever you are in your wellness journey. She also rents the upper house with a master bedroom and futon, 2 baths, kitchen, living room, large *lānai*, and deck. (808.328.0007) (Moderate)

A short drive off of Hwy 11, on Route 160, **The Dragonfly Ranch B&B** offers a rare combination of outdoor living with luxury. Laid-back owner **Barbara Moore** has created an environment that welcomes adventurous people who go with the flow. Her unique family-style jungle paradise includes a bright airy space overlooking the bay. Here you can do yoga, meditate, walk a labyrinth or just sit and absorb the awe-inspiring view. All the rooms have private outdoor showers, a treat in a climate like Hawai'i. You are supplied the ingredients, including organic fruits from her garden, for a continental breakfast at your leisure, or you're welcome to a hot breakfast with the group or to take back to your room. This up-scale Swiss Family Robinson estate rents a range of options from a honeymoon suite to a Lānai Cubby. (808.328.2159) (Moderate – Deluxe)

Ka'ū District (near South Point)

In the more traditionally Hawaiian South Point area, along Hwy 11, you will come upon **'Ai Lani Orchards**. **Barney Frazier and Elizabeth Jenkins** own a 10.5-acre organic orchard with a modern guesthouse to accommodate travelers. The image of picking fresh fruit off the trees for breakfast comes alive at 'Ai Lani where you're surrounded with lemon, macadamia nut, avocado, banana, and grapefruit trees. The owners are "cultural creatives" with visions for agricultural tourism, workshops on modern applications for traditional agriculture techniques, and more. Ask about their Permaculture Vacation and Orchards Volunteer Program. The green sand beach is only a 20-minute drive away and Hawai'i Volcanoes National Park is a 40-minute drive away, but adventure also awaits you right on your cottage porch where you can see how macadamia nuts are picked, and processed, and learn about organic farming. Their modern guest house has three bedrooms, three baths and a full kitchen. (808.929.8785) (Deluxe)

Just up the road on Hwy 11, is the **Macadamia Meadows Farm and B&B** run by **Charlene Cowan**. This is an operational farm where you can learn all about macadamia nut farming and pick, shell, roast, and eat them yourself. Charlene is an energetic hostess who will happily give you a complimentary educational and hands-on orchard tour, explaining everything from the origins of macadamia nuts to the current research and processing methods. The farm has opportunities for exercise with tennis, a swimming pool, and basketball hoops. The accommodations are luxurious by most farm standards and range from a room with a shared bath to a honeymoon suite. Ask Charlene about the Agricultural Tourism Committee; she's the Chair. (808.929.8097) (Moderate – Deluxe)

Driving along Hwy 11 toward Volcano you'll come to the old plantation town Pāhala. This is the only watering hole for about 25 miles around. The **Wood Valley Temple** provides an economical place to stay and retreat whether alone or with others. See #5. (808.928.8539) (Budget)

Volcano

Volcano Inn, owned by **Joan Prescott-Lighter**, comes with a AAA rating and is a member of the Green Hotel Association. She serves a full hot breakfast, some days with Hawaiian specialties, plus homemade yogurt and granola. Joan is a do-it-yourself multi-talented women who built her fireproof, earthquake-resistant house herself, and furnished it with Hawaiian artifacts and antiques. She is a quilter and horsewoman and takes people on trail rides with horses from her small near-by ranch. Her lovely Volcano Inn can accommodate up to 35 in the 1928 plantation-style house and five cottages. (808.967.7293) (Moderate – Deluxe)

Volcano Country Cottages is a warm and friendly place, which includes a wellness center where owner **Kathleen Porter** teaches yoga classes, and holds seminars and workshops. Breakfast fixings, including fresh fruit, baked goods, and granola are brought to your cottage the evening before. She has an outdoor Jacuzzi and bathhouse in a private area of the garden looking out on the forest. There is also a room for massage by appointment. Ask Kathleen about her teachings and practice of "Balance Work." (808.967.7960) (Moderate – Deluxe)

Puna Coast (Kea'au, Pohala)

On the Puna Coast, there are a number of fine B&Bs, guesthouses, retreats, and vacation rentals. All of these are convenient to Hawai'i Volcanoes National Park, Hilo, and the activities described in the Puna area.

Ala Loa House By-the-Sea is an ideal spot for romantic getaways or extended healing retreats. Located off Route 130 between Kea'au and Pāhoa, this bright and breezy one-bedroom cottage apartment overlooks Puna's scenic coastline with miles of nearby shoreline trails, refreshing tide pools, and whale-watching (October to May) A soothing double Jacuzzi, comfortable king-size bed, private phone line, dining-living room, and fully- equipped kitchen open to a spacious deck, surrounded with tropical gardens. **Gerrie Morisky**, the owner, is a master of the "nice touch," including fresh orchids in each room. She has an organic garden of herbs, vegetables, fruits, and fragrant flowers. Gerrie is also very knowledgeable about the island, and offers special wellness tours and packages. Optional on-site massage, ginger wraps, oxygen and other healing therapies are all available. (808.966.7887) (Moderate)

Hale Makamae B&B, in Leilani Estates off Route 130 past Pāhoa is owned by **Petra Weisenbauer and John Tucker**. These world travelers have settled in to raise a family and offer their warm hospitality. Petra is a native of Germany so her full delicious continental breakfast, served on the screened patio, has a European flavor. The atmosphere of the tranquil garden and the simple comforts of their apartments invite the traveler to slow down and enjoy the casual island lifestyle. Petra is well versed in interesting things to see and do and is available to give you guidance and directions. Hale Makamae is approved by the Hawai'i Island B&B Association. (808.965.9090) (Budget – Moderate)

Farther down Route 130, a mile past the turn off to Pāhoa, take 137 toward the ocean and wind your way to **Hawaiian Retreat**. This jungle hideaway is managed by **Eliot Rosen**, the author of *Experiencing the Soul*, a popular anthology featuring the reflections of some of the world's most renowned spiritual leaders. As it is owned and operated by practitioners of the Science of Spirituality, they ask that guests not cook or eat meat on the property. The lodging in the main house consists of an upstairs, private two-bedroom apartment with full bath, kitchen, living room, and *lānai*. Extraordinary Balinese woodcarvings of dolphins dancing in ocean waves add to the charm of this peaceful lodging.

Downstairs is a private bedroom, shared bath and kitchen. To get closer to nature, the Nature Cottage sits in a corner of the garden with half-screened walls and an outdoor shower. Ask about weekly and monthly rates. The house and cottage together could accommodate ten to twenty people. (808.965.1279 or 808.937.6867) (Moderate – Deluxe)

Kalani Oceanside Resort (800.800.6886) and **Yoga Oasis** (800.274.4446) are also great places to stay in the Puna District, as described earlier in #5.

Hilo

Fans of the **Hilo Seaside Retreat** a hideaway on Kalaniana'ole Avenue a short drive east from downtown Hilo, love its niche right on the ocean. The back lawn stretches a few yards to tidal pools where salty waves mix with a fresh water spring. These cold estuaries are only a few steps from the Jacuzzi if you're up for "contrast bathing." The hot bath expands the blood vessels and the cold causes them to contract resulting in an exhilarating rush of blood that owner **Patti Oliver** says makes "a great circulatory pump." You might also try the furo bath, a traditional Japanese bath in a redwood box where you sit up to your neck in hot water and get a good sweat. A loft overlooking the ocean serves as the massage room. Ask Barbara, the hostess, about their massage and Reiki therapists. The private downstairs Seaside Suite is simple but comfortable and opens out on to the lawn. They stock the kitchen with the basics for a cold breakfast. The upstairs house has three bedrooms, a large living room, one bath and kitchen. It can sleep six to seven. (808.961.6178) (Moderate – Deluxe)

Hale Kai Bjornen B&B enjoys an enviable perch on the Honoka'a Coast overlooking Hilo Bay. Most of us would be happy to camp on a hillside for such a view, but **Evonne and Paul Bjornen-Tallett** have created a haven with all the creature comforts so you can be at ease as you take in the healing panorama. A full gourmet breakfast, swimming pool, and Vera, the massage therapist who will come to your room, all add to your enjoyment. Hale Kai Bjornen was selected by Frommer's *Travel Guide* as "one of the 100 top B&Bs in the US and Canada," and for good reason. Evonne, who was the architect and contractor of the house, literally trains novices on how to run B&Bs. She is a "pro." We particularly liked how the decor reflected the background and interests of the owners and the warm hospitality. Evonne is Norwegian and Paul is Hawaiian. (808.935.6330) (Moderate – Deluxe)

Hāmākua Coast

Taking Hwy 19 up the Hāmākua Coast, look around mile marker 15 for signs to Wailea on the *mauka* side. Wailea's mom and pop businesses used to thrive on the traffic passing through, but after the new highway by-passed it, the town turned into a sleepy village with **Akiko's Buddhist B&B** as the main enterprise. This is one of the best economy accommodations on the Big Island. You get a simple but comfortable private room with shared bath and kitchen in the Plantation House and a full breakfast. Breakfast is served in the Monastery House where there are also rooms with futons. The meditation hall is always open. If you are so inclined, you can join the Zen meditation scheduled at 5:00 a.m. every morning and 7:00 p.m. to 8:00 p.m. Monday, Wednesday, and Friday. **Akiko** invites local talent to feature their crafts in her gift shop, perform in her garage (converted to a performance hall), and teach classes. Akiko's talents as a flower arranger and author of children's books, as well as a cook and hostess, shine through as well. The name and the occasional Buddhist statue, as well as the observance of silence in the Monastery House from 6:30 p.m. to 6:30 a.m., give it a definite flavor, but you certainly don't have to be Buddhist to enjoy your stay here. (808.963.6422) (Budget)

Just past Akiko's place is an enchanted one-mile walk or drive down to Kolekole Beach Park. There's no beach at the park but you can watch the Ka'ahakini Stream flow into the sea.

Waimea (Also known as Kamuela)

Waimea is a small city in a cool misty climate. For mainlanders it may be just right, but it is "highlands" and a sweater and umbrella may come in handy. The sweeping hills southwest of Waimea are a contrast to the lush tropical Hāmākua Coast that leads up from Hilo, but the broad sloping terrain gives a sense of space and perspective, and a breathtaking view of the coastline. The options listed here are all convenient to the beaches on the Kona Coast.

In a quiet neighborhood just south of town off Kawaihae Road, **Aloha Cottages** rents a studio and one bedroom 'Ohana

Cottage, owned by a very active and health conscious couple, **Keoki and Heidi Staab**. It is within easy drive to the coast. Reserve time for a massage in their home, or try their Qi Machine. Keoki teaches a free stretch class for seniors on Wednesday nights in the community, using a method he developed himself called "Easy Stretch." Ask about their Wellness Package. (See #7) (808.885.6535) (Moderate)

Also in this vicinity, **Mare Grace** has fashioned a combination of quiet rooms and skillfully tended gardens that will delight the traveler seeking a serene comfortable environment. She calls it **"Aaah, the Views!..." B&B**, no doubt taken from the exclamations of her guests who can enjoy their fresh, healthy breakfast to the music of a rushing stream, or from other points near-by while taking in the views of volcanoes, mountains, and the ocean. The main house has a meditation and yoga room equipped with crystal bowls, drums, and other instruments if you're inclined. This is listed with the Hawai'i Island B&B Association and is one of only two lodgings on the island that is a member of the Green Hotels Association. Ask her for details. (808.885.3455) (Moderate)

Ideally situated between Waimea and the Kona Coast, is **Ho'onanea Vacation Rental**. (*Ho'onanea* means "go with the flow of life and the wind.") **Shay Bintliff and Barbara Forman** have transformed a rocky gulch on the barren volcano slopes into an oasis including a studio cottage retreat for women. These two will warm your heart with aloha hospitality. Their house is a short drive from the beaches, hiking in Pololū Valley, and visits to Parker Ranch or the Kona Coast resorts. While there, watch their video "Surfing for Life." Among the star surfers who brought the sport into its own in Hawai'i is Shay herself, an inspiration for anyone wishing to stay fit and active into retirement. Ho'onanea may be in one of the world's prime locations for star gazing, and if you're an animal lover, stop to greet their Barbados Blackbelly sheep and Border collie, Tessa. 808.882.1177. (Moderate)

North Kohala Coast

The historic northern coast, known as North Kohala, is not heavily traveled. While this is good for preserving the mana of the area, it means there are fewer healing accommodations available.

Tom Sherman's Nature Sanctuary in Kapa'au, just one turn off Route 270, is one of the few. His expansive redwood modular home rests on a hill overlooking gardens especially designed for quiet contemplation and renewal. A secluded gazebo provides a nature spot for meditation, yoga, and healing sessions and an outdoor, ocean-view Jacuzzi offers a place to soak in silence. Tom's healing sanctuary has a large Chakra Suite with an ocean view, private bath and shared kitchen and a room inside the main house with private bath and shared kitchen. The whole house can be rented for retreats of up to eight people. (808.889.0553) (Moderate)

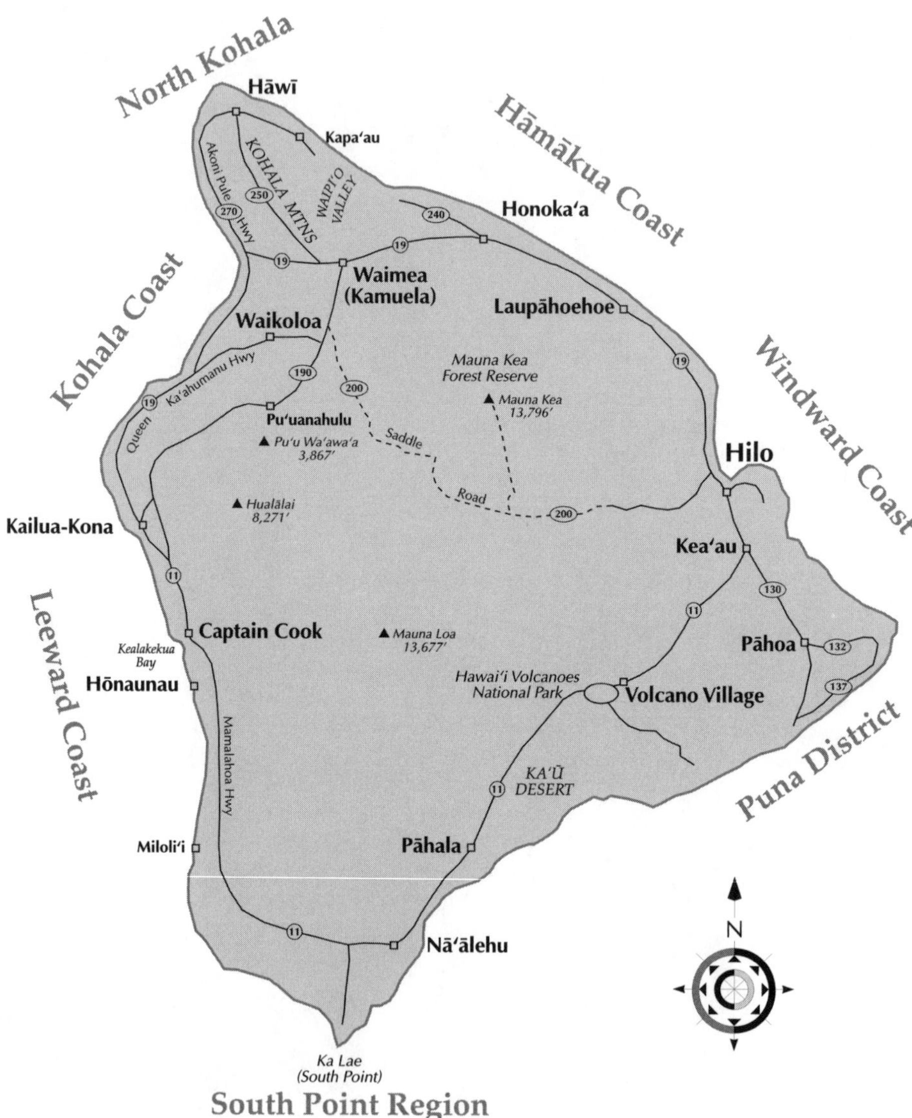
North Kohala
Hāwī
Kapa'au
Hāmākua Coast
KOHALA MTNS
WAIPI'O VALLEY
Akoni Pule Hwy
Honoka'a
Kohala Coast
Waimea
(Kamuela)
Laupāhoehoe
Waikoloa
Queen Ka'ahumanu Hwy
Mauna Kea
Forest Reserve
Mauna Kea
13,796'
Windward Coast
Pu'uanahulu
Pu'u Wa'awa'a
3,867'
Saddle Road
Hilo
Hualālai
8,271'
Kailua-Kona
Kea'au
Leeward Coast
Captain Cook
Mauna Loa
13,677'
Pāhoa
Kealakekua Bay
Hōnaunau
Hawai'i Volcanoes
National Park
Volcano Village
Mamalahoa Hwy
Puna District
KA'Ū
DESERT
Miloli'i
Pāhala
Nā'ālehu
N
Ka Lae
(South Point)
South Point Region

Resources

The Island of Hawai'i

ISLAND OF HAWAI'I - WELLNESS DIRECTORY TABLE OF CONTENTS

Art & Art Therapy

Art of the Dove
Suzan Starr, RN, BSN
PO Box 301 • Volcano, HI 96785
808.967.7196
dreamsop@bigisland • www.artofdove.com

Breath Therapy

The Experience of Breath
Gretchen Vanderslice
HCR 2, Box 9608 • Kea'au, HI 96749
808.966.5085
sadie@bigisland.net

Hawaiian Healing

Ho'ola 'O LomiLomi Lapa'au
(Hawaiian Healing)
PO Box 6202 • Hilo, HI 96720
808.961.3118
LokahiLapaauHi@webtv.net • www.LokahiOla.org

Self Identity Through Ho'oponopono
The Foundation of I, Inc.
(Freedom of the Cosmos)
PO Box 645 • Volcano, HI 96785
808.985.7211 + fax
omakaokalah@aol.com • www.hooponopono.org

Swami's Hawaiian Lomilomi Massage
contact: Jerri Knobllich LMT
Kealakekua area
808.323.3344
swamimom@ilhawaii.net

Volcano Art Center
Education Dept.
PO Box 104
Hawai'i National Park, HI 96718
www.volcanoartcenter.org

Personal Development & Psychology

Create Waves
Boost your creativity and get over creative blocks with an in-depth, individual creativity consultation as part of your next vacation or business trip to Hawai'i. In your work, can you afford to not be creative?
PO Box 556 • Hōnaunau, HI 96726
contact: Drew Ross
808.322.2400
drewross@panaceum.com

Healing in Motion
(Tai Chi, Qi Gong, Acutouch)
HC 1, Box 5240
Kea'au, HI 96749
contact: Valerie Myles
808.966.4893
acuchi2@hotmail.com

Jarnie Lee, EdD
(psychotherapy, ancient Hawaiian problem solving & stress release)
101 Aupuni St., Suite 119
Hilo, HI 96720
808.961.3616 Fax: 961.3616
homeward@hawaii.rr.com

Marriage & Family Therapist
PO Box 38377
Waikoloa, HI 96738
contact: Sherrian Witt, M.A.
808.883.9855
Sherrianwitt@hotmail.com

Sacred Movement in Sacred Sound
Box 913
Hōnaunau, HI 96726
contact: Shanawo & Renee-Wo
808.936.3294

Retreats

Akash Healing Center

Sharon Forsyth, Ayurvedic Practitioner and creator of Akash Healing Center, provides a private, sacred space for people to rejuvenate, heal and reconnect. Detoxification, rejuvenation and transformational treatments are given as a one day experience or as an intensive 3 -10 day, life changing program. Accommodations are available to create your own private retreat, allowing time to deepen into your own Self... couples are also welcome. Sharon considers and treats all aspects of a person and is here to support a deepening into Peace, Vitality and Truth. Trainings are also offered.

Sharon Forsyth • Kailua-Kona, HI • **808.331.2276**
www.akashhealingcenter.com

Kalani Oceanside Retreat

Kalani Oceanside Retreat is your safe haven in the heart of the Pacific. Kalani, "heaven on earth," is located on the lush, tropical southeast coast of Hawai'i, the Aloha State's "Big Island." Kalani uniquely celebrates nature, culture and wellness by providing a variety of eco-adventures, events and comfortable accommodations. For 27 years, Kalani has been a soulful place of refuge and renewal for worldwide guests.

RR 2, Box 4500 • Pāhoa, HI 96788
contact: Denis Fuster, Marketing Director
808.965.7828 or toll free 800.800.6886
kalani@kalani.com

Wood Valley Temple and Retreat Center

A non-profit Buddhist retreat center and lodge located in the Ka'ū district of Hawai'i, close to the Volcano and Punalu'u black sand beach. Please go to our website for information regarding activities, meditation programs and store. The center provides a peaceful garden sanctuary for rest with daily meditations led by our monks.

Nechung Dorje Drayang Ling
1 Temple Road, Wood Valley, Ka'ū
PO Box 250 • Pāhala, HI 96777
contact: Michael and Marya Schwabe
808.928.8539 fax: 928.6271
nechung@aloha.net • http://www.nechung.org

Yoga Oasis

We are a secluded and private sanctuary, off the beaten path, nestled on 26 acres of lush rainforest. We are close to the ocean, geo-thermal warm springs, tide pools, sauna steam caves, a black sand beach, snorkeling and a green lake. We offer yoga classes, Thai massage and delicious vegetarian cuisine.

PO Box 1935 • Pāhoa, HI 96778
808.965.8460 or toll free 800.274.4446
info@yogaoasis.org

Retreats

'Ai Lani Retreat House
PO Box 500 • Nā'ālehu, HI 96772
contact: Barney Frazier & Elizabeth Jenkins
808.929.8785 or 808.929.7370
elizabeth@inka-online.com
www.inka-online.com/retreat

Akiko's Buddhist Bed and Breakfast
PO Box 272 • Hakalau, HI 96710
808.963.6422
msakiki@aloha.net
www.alternative-hawaii.com/akiko

Essential Joy of Dolphin/Spirit
PO Box 171 • Captain Cook, HI 96704
contact: Doug Hackett, Trish Regan
808.323.2731 toll free 800.874.8555 or 800.874.1244
joy@essentialjoy.net

Hāmākua Ecology Center Waipi'o Garden
PO Box 1350 • Honoka'a, HI 96727
808.775.9083. Fax 808.775.9085
Waipio@ilhawaii.net
www.earthmediahawaii.com

Hawaiian Retreat
Papaya Farms Road • Pāhoa, HI 96788
contact: Eliot Rosen
808.965.1279 1.877.965.1279
info@hawaiianretreat.com
www.hawaiianretreat.com

KeMa Patricia Nash
83-5621 Mamalahoa Hwy
Captain Cook, HI 96704
808.328.07 or 808.895.3674
kemakama@aol.com
www.kemakama.com

Light Spirit
PO Box 1598 • Kealakekua, HI 96750
contact: Chris Reid
Tel/Fax 808.328.8672
dolphins@kona.net
www.revchrisreid.com

Ohana House Rural Retreat
PO Box 6351 • Ocean View, HI 96737
808.929.9139 or 1.888.999.9139
www.alternative-hawaii.com/ohana

Paleaku Gardens (Retreats)
83-5401 Painted Church Rd.
Captain Cook, HI 96704
contact: Barbara De Franco
808.328.8084
paleaku@hawaii.rr.com
www.paleaku.com

Sapphire Moon Women's Spiritual Adventures and Retreat
R2Box3898 • Pāhoa, HI 96778
808.834.8205
pelefire@gte.net
www.greenfireproductions.com

Volcano Rainforest Retreat
PO Box 957 • Volcano, HI 96785
1.800.550.8696 or 808.985.8696
volrain@bigisland.net • www.volcanoretreat.com

Spiritual Healing

Keith Amber, Psychic Soul Healer

Keith Amber has 30 years of professional experience as a Healer, Reader, and Psychic Therapist. Through Sound Healing, Clairvoyance and Clairaudience, etc. Keith can assist you in finding yourself, unraveling your life's mysteries, heal physical, emotional and spiritual issues becoming more thoroughly fulfilled. Healings are gentle, insightful, powerful and life-altering.

PO Box 400 • Kapa'au, HI, 96755
contact: Keith or Sharmai Amber,
808.884.5429
insights@lava.net • www.InsightsForYourLife.com

Eve Naia, Spirit Painter

A consultation with Eve results in your "30x22" Spiritpainting. Eve attunes with Hawai'i's Energies and Angels to create your personal "window" to healing higher dimensional energies and frequencies. "The potential for awakening, shifting, growing and healing are unlimited! Eve is a very gifted artist who creates doorways to the higher dimensions." (C. Q. England)

75-5669 Kuakini Hwy. #1-101 • Kailua-Kona, HI 96740
contact: Eve Naia
808.326-9826
www.evenaia.com • mermaideve@hotmail.com

Spirit Path: A Guide to the Higher Self

Liz works multidimensionally with the whole being—body, mind, spirit and emotions—to clear emotional and spiritual blocks and patterns imprinted in the subconscious mind. This work uses the individual's own Higher Self guidance to work in present time to create powerful transformation. The perfect work for someone who wants to effectively use their retreat time on Hawai'ito see true healing change happen in his or her life. Four sessions in a week's time are recommended.

Liz Randol (RA) • Captain Cook, HI 96704
808-328-2226
lizr@aloha.net • www.liz-randol.com/spiritpath
www.seaflow.org

A Sacred Pilgrimage with Leinala

PO Box 1171 • Pāhoa, HI 96778
contact: Leinala Gamulo
808.965.9554

Awapuhi Labyrinth Project

Hawai'i Paradise Park
Kea'au, HI 96749
contact: Christie Wolf and John Luchau
808.982.5959
awapuhil@aol.com

Spiritual Healing

Bridging the Gap Resources
PO Box 4327
Kailua-Kona, HI 96745
contact: Kikikipa Kretzer, MS, CFNP
(Certified Family Nurse Practitioner)
808.322.6161324.7316 fax

Sukie Colegrave
Lightbody Facilitator
PO Box 132 • Hāwī, HI 96719
808.889.5003
www.lightbodypath.org

Karin Cooke, RN
PO Box 1585 • Kapa'au, HI 96755
808.889.9893
kokolulu@bigisland.com

Harmonic Healing ™
(Transformational Healing
with the Voice)
PO Box 641 • Kealakekua, HI 96750
contact: Judith Lynne
808.987.8099

Hawai'i Nature Fast
PO Box 1360 • Kapa'au, HI 96755
contact: Tom Sherman, Ph.D., LMT, CHTP
808.889.0553
sherman@kona.net
www.wavesofchange.org

MoonStar's Psychic Readings
PO Box 1122 • Pāhoa, HI 96778
contact: MoonStar Rae
808.331.3154
moonstara@yahoo.com

Vibrational Therapies by Asherah
Gemstone and Crystal Healing
40 S Wiliwili Street
Hilo, HI 96720
808.935.5530
asherra_@hotmail.com

Hypnotherapy

Bernie Lustgarten, M.A.
Certified Hypnotherapist
HCR 2, Box 9608 • Kea'au, HI 96749
808.966.5085
sadie@bigisland.net

John K. Shuster, CHT
The Center for Positive Change
PO Box 2495
Kealakekua, HI 96750
808. 322.8840 • Fax 808.322.6659

Success Coach

Aiko Aiyana, Cmt
(Ontological & Clinical Kinesiology)
RR3 Box 1455 • Pāhoa, HI 96778
808.982.6577.
globalaiko@msn.com
www.angelfire.com/poetry/aiko/Aiko

Keith Amber
(Insights for Life)
P O Box 400 • Kapa'au, HI, 96755
808.884.5429
insights@lava.net
www.InsightsForYourLife.com

House of Health
74-4963 Kiwi St.
Kailua-Kona, HI 96740
contact: Bob Dean
808.329.3455
Bob@surfhawaii.net/Lopakatu

KeMa Patricia Nash
(life coach)
83-5621 Mamalahoa Hwy
Captain Cook, HI 96704
808.328.0007 or 808.895.3674
kemakama@aol.com

LightSpirit
PO Box 1598 • Kealakekua, HI 96750
contact: Chris Reid
808.328.8672
dolphins@kona.net
www.revchrisreid.com
www.kemakama.com

Raydiant Health Center
(Wellness & Cleansing)
contact: Raydiance
808.965.0100

Socially Responsible Investing

Natural Investment Services
PO Box 390595 • Keauhou, HI 96739
contact: Michael Kramer
Toll free: 888.779.1500 • 808.331.0910
Michael@naturalinvesting.com • www.naturalinvesting.com

Tai Chi

Healing in Motion
(Tai Chi, Qi Gong, Acutouch)
HC 1, Box 5240 • Kea'au, HI 96749
contact: Valerie Myles
808.966.4893
acuchi2@hotmail.com

Shanawo's Peaceful Dragon Academy
(Martial Arts, Yoga, Meditation)
Box 913 • Hōnaunau, HI 96726
contact: Burley Luvell Benford
808.936.3294

Weddings

Big Island Weddings-Where two become One
contact: Reverend Julie Paul
808.965.6281
revjuleshi@aol.com • www.alohaweddingshawaii.com

Animal Therapy

The Dancing Dolphins Retreat

A heart-opening healing experience with a unique blend of fun activities, art therapy, spiritual growth, trips to magical sites, daily bodywork, and swimming with wild dolphins. Visit our website to read about our 'Intensives' and call for a brochure:

contact: Christiane Mulkearn

1.800.856.4134

www.dolphin-dimension.com,

Essential Joy of Dolphin Spirit

Weekend trainings or week long retreats on the Big Island, including swims in the ocean where the dolphins dance. Come away to paradise to rejuvenate your spirit and learn about the essence of joy and spiritual transformation with small groups, in peaceful beautiful surroundings. Eight years safe and joyous experience.

PO Box 171 • Captain Cook, HI 96704

contact: Doug Hackett, Trish Regan

808.323.2731 toll free: 800.874.8555 or 800.874.1244

joy@essentialjoy.net

LightSpirit

Explore and experience a deep connection with the spirit of Hawai'i through it's natural beauty and wildlife. Chris is an inspiring guide, facilitator, and marine naturalist offering intimate island tours, eco-adventures, and retreats where the spirit of aloha and the healing power of nature combine to create an unforgettable vacation.

PO Box 1598 • Kealakekua, HI 96750

contact: Chris Reid

Tel/Fax 808.328.8672

dolphins@kona.net • http://www.revchrisreid.com

Ag-Tourism

'Ai Lani Orchards

contact: Barney Frazier & Elizabeth Jenkins

808.929.8785

elizabeth@inka-online.com

www.inka-online.com/hawaii

Macadamia Meadows Farm and B&B

contact: Charlene Cowan

808.929.8097

www.macadamiameadows.com

kaleen@aloha.net

Ag-Tourism

Parker Ranch Visitor Center and Museum

67-1185 Mamalahoa Hwy
Kamuela, HI
808.885.7655
http://www.parkerranch.com

Volcano Island Honey Co.

PO Box 1709 • Honoka'a, HI 96727
contact: Richard Spiegel
808.775.0806 fax: 808.775.0412
honeybee@bigisland.net

Ecotourism

Hawaiian Walkways, Inc.

Since 1984 Hawaiian Walkways has been guiding seekers of Hawai'i's essence to amazing, little-accessed places, some of which are otherwise quite unavailable. On these hiking adventures, immersion in the restorative power of nature, by turns gentle and forceful, is blended with engaging information connecting visitors to the land and its life.

contact: Dr. Hugh & Kaulana Montgomery
Island Hiking Adventures
808.775.0372
www.hawaiianwalkways.com

The Dancing Dolphin Ministry

PO Box 2945
Kailua-Kona, HI 96745-2945
contact: Rev. Pomaika'i Coulon
808.328.7421

Hawai'i Pack and Paddle

1.808.328.8911
gokayak@kona.ne
www.hawaiipackandpaddle.com

Kanoelani Naone

kanoe@palehua.org
www.palehua.org

Dan McSweeney's Whale Watching Adventures

PO Box 139 • Holualoa, HI 96725
888.942.5376 • 808.322.0028
konawhales@netscape.net
www.ilovewhales.com

Sierra Club, Makuloa Group

PO Box 1137 • Hilo, HI 96721
contact: Phil Barnes
808.965.9695

Gardens

The Amy B.H. Greenwill Ethnobotanical Garden

PO Box 1053 • Captain Cook, HI 96704
808.323.3318 Fax .808.323.2394

Hawai'i Tropical Botanical Garden

PO Box 80
27-717 Old Mamalahoa Hwy
Papaikou, HI 96781
contact: Scott Lucas.
808.964.5233
htbg@ilhawaii.net
www.hawaiigarden.com

Hi'iaka's Healing Herb Garden

HCR 2, Box 9620 • Kea'au, HI 96749
contact: Barbara J. Fahs
808.966.6126
goddess@hiiakas.com
www.hiikas.com

Hawai'i Volcanoes National Park

808.985.6017 for updates about flows
808.985.6000 for main park service
www.nps.gov/havo

Umauma Falls and World Botanical Gardens

PO Box 411 • Honomu, HI 96728
contact: Dave Adams
808.963.5427
www.wbgi.com

Health Products of Hawai'i

Easy Stretch Video

PO Box 1395 • Kamuela, HI, 96743,
808.885.6535, 877.875.1722
www.easystretch.com.

Hawai'i Holistics, LLC (Certified Organic Noni Products)

PO 1288 • Pahoa, HI 96778-1288
808.965.919 or965.1461 fax
info@hawaiinoni.com
www.hawaiinoni.com

Raw Paradise

Hawai'i Island Sanctuary
PO Box 393 • Pāhoa, HI 98778
trees@rawparadise.com

Share Wellness (ecofriendly home products)

PO Box 1026 • Pāhoa, HI 96778
808.965.7860
shareatrust@yahoo.com

Star of Roses Organic Farm

49-1169 Kumupele Rd
Honoka'a, HI 96727
contact: Judy & Peter Rosenstern
808.775.7238 or 775.1905
starrose@aloha.net

Retreats

Waves of Change

Offering personalized healing services to support individuals, groups, and organizations in their life reflections, visioning, transitions, and transformation. Tom Sherman, Ph.D, LMT, CHTP (aka CHAKRAMAN), an eco-healer/energy practitioner provides: Transition Consultation; therapeutic healing sessions; and personal growth retreats with Nature as Healer. Tom's Nature Sanctuary is available for individuals, groups, and special events

PO Box 1360 • Kapa'au, HI 96755
contact Tom Sherman
808.889.0553
sherman@kona.net
www:wavesofchange.org (overall services)
www:chakraman.com (healing services)

Healing in Motion (Tai Chi, Qi Gong, Acutouch)

HC 1, Box 5240 • Kea'au, HI 96749
contact: Valerie Myles
808.966.4893
acuchi2@hotmail.com

KeMa Patricia Nash

83-5621 Mamalahoa Hwy
Captain Cook, HI 96704
808.328.07 or 808.895.3674
kemakama@aol.com
www.kemakama.com

Acupuncture

Healing Arts Alliance

Indulge yourself with one of the ultimate healing experiences. Allow Healing Arts Alliance to pamper you with a combination of Acupuncture, an incredible Warm Ginger, Oil Treatment, and Massage; all in one session for the very reasonable rate of $45.00. Located in the heart of historic Old Downtown Hilo.

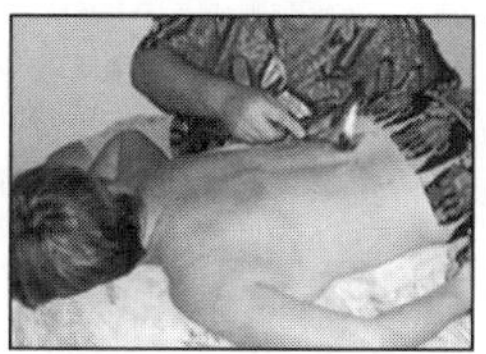

103 Kalākaua St • Hilo HI 96720
contact: Scott Miller, Licensed Acupuncturist
808.934.7030
healer@hilo.net • www.healing-arts-alliance.com

Janice Dale Ellison, Doctor of Oriental Medicine

Provides traditional Chinese Medicine, acupuncture, Chinese herbs, Dynamic Interface Subtle Energy Field in working with pain relief, stress relief, chronic fatigue, women's health, menopause, PMS, breast health. Is Beijing-trained. Diplomate, National Certification Board

54-3884 Akoni Pule Hwy. • Kapa'au, HI 96755
808.889.6900
jdaifu@email.com

Acupuncture

Lori Campbell, Lac
HCR1, Box 5655 • Kea'au, HI 96759
808.961.4410
retreat@bigisland.net

Nancy J. Fiacco, Dipl.Ac.
(NCCAOM)
PO Box 994 • Kamuela, HI 96743
808.889.5844
nancyjfiacco@aol.com

Chandra Lange
77-114 Nahale Pl.
Kailua-Kona, HI 96740
808.322.5662 Fax 808.322.9617
chandra@konacoast.com

Scott Lee, RN, Lac
159 Keawe St, Suite 5 • Hilo, HI 96720
808.969.6819
llamasii@hotmail.com

Nancy (Feather) Menier, Lac
HCR-3 Box 13022 • Kea'au, HI 96749
808.982.5463
hawaiiacupuncture@Hotmail.com

Traditional Chinese Medical College of Hawai'i
PO Box 2288 • Kamuela, HI 96743
contact: Robert E. Smith, Ph.D., President
808.885.9226
Clinic: **808.885.7886 or 808.885.9226**
mcsmith@ilhawaii.net
http://www.kona.net/~chinese/

Waimea Natural Health Ctr
65-1298 Kawaihae Rd #25
Kamuela, HI 96743
contact: Karl Toubman, Lac, LMT
808.885.9661 or 885.4228
qiman@aloha.net

Megan Yarberry, Lac
142 B Kino'ole St. • Hilo, HI 96720
808.938.2631
myarberry@tourquoise.net

Ayurvedic Practice

Akash Healing Center
Kailua-Kona, HI
contact: Sharon Forsyth
808.331.2276
ayusidha@ilhawaii.net
www.akashhealingcenter.com

Vitality Works Day Spa
(Ayurvedic Practice)
PO Box 2577 • Kailua-Kona, HI 96745
contact: Darmani Zelin, LMT
808.987.1402 or 329.1829 fax
Dharmini_z@hotmail.com

Chiropractic

Keauhoa Chiropractic Clinic
78-6831 Alii Dr., Suite K-10
Kailua-Kona, HI 96740
contact: Jeffrey Daso, DC
808.322.3344 or 322.3235 fax
jdrblues@aol.com

Carol Zimmerman, DC, Lac
Doctor of Chiropractic and Licensed Acupuncturist
PO Box 445
Nā'ālehu, HI 96772
808.929.9229
zimmermanrudy@aol.com

Craniosacral

Alia Hallowell, LMT, RPP
(craniosacral, polarity, orthobionomy, aromatherapy)
PO Box 787 • Pāhoa, HI 96778
808.965.8472
essents@midpac.net

Energy Therapies

Aloha Inspirations
Nurturing optimal health, excellence in self-expression, and inspired living. An invitation to heal and replenish your body, heart and soul on the Big Island of Hawai'i ENERGETIC MEDICINE TREATMENTS & CREATIVITY COACHING Treating the root cause of illness, blocks, and stubborn life conditions.
contact: Peri Coeurtney Enkin
PO Box 2605 • Kailua-Kona, HI 96745
808.322.4084
www.golbalhealingarts.com

Back to Balance
Discover E.F.T. (Emotional Freedom Technique) in Hawai'i with William & Kathryn Silver. E.F.T. is an easy-to-learn, amazingly effective treatment for anxiety, phobias, panic attacks & traumas (past and present). We offer private healing sessions, educational presentations and even E.F.T. over the phone!
PO Box 2083 • Kailua-Kona, HI 96745
contact: William and Kathryn Silver
808.325.1655
sterling.silver@turquoise.net • www.back2balance.com

Energy Therapies

Center for Alchemical Medicine

Expect a through body analysis, and benefits from a non-invasive wellness system, which can result in Testimonial: *Carol's work speaks for itself. After our first session I was able to decrease my heart medication from 2 to half a tablet a day. Now I don't take any heart medication at all. I live in gratitude and awe. J.B.* (D.C.)

PO Box 613 • Captain Cook, HI 96704
contact: Carol Hannum
808.328.7728 or 888.730.1631
cannum@kona.net

Harmonic Healing ™
Transformational Healing with the Voice

Ms. Lynne, an expert sound healer, is the creator of leading edge techniques including Harmonic Healing ™ and Vocal Energetics™ . Profound transformation with healing at every level is catalyzed by balancing frequencies and integrating vibrational shifts. Private sessions in person or by phone are offered, as well as international workshops.

contact: Judith Lynne,
PO Box 641 • Kealakekua, HI 96750
808.987.8099 (in Hawai'i) 503.289.6389 (in Oregon)
judithlynne@harmonichealing.com
www.harmonichealing.com

Aiko Aiyana, Cmt

(Ontological and Clinical kinesiology)
RR3 Box 1455 • Pāhoa, HI 96778
808.982.6577.
globalaiko@msn.com
www.angelfire.com/poetry/aiko/Aiko

Keith Amber

PO Box 400 • Kapa'au, HI, 96755
808.884.5429
insights@lava.net
www.InsightsForYourLife.com

Chakra Man

(Energy Therapy)
PO Box 1360 • Kapa'au, HI 96755
contact: Tom Sherman, Ph.D., LMT, CHTP
808.889.0553
sherman@kona.net
www.chakraman.com

Energy Healing Therapy

PMB 116,
65-1158 Mamalahoa Hwy, #8A
Kamuela, HI 96743
contact: Martin Davis,
808.990.9416
energyhealing@hawaii.com
www.energyhealingtherapy.com

Hale Ka'ela

(hands on healing)
PO Box 8 • Kapa'au, HI 96755
contact: Carol Perry
808.889.0317
iolani17@ilhawaii.net

Alia Hallowell, LMT, RPP

(craniosacral, polarity, orthobionomy, aromatherapy)
PO Box 787 • Pāhoa, HI 96778
808.965.8472
aliahllwll@aol.com

Energy Therapies

Susan Medeiros
(Healing Touch Ohana)
Healing Touch Treatments
by appointment.
East side of the Big Island (Hilo area)
808.968.8645
Healingtouchohana@hotmail.com

Marco Montagnini, PhD
48-5520 Waipio Rd
Honoka'a, HI 96727
808.938.3702 Fax808.775.1483
mmontagnini@juno.com

Eve Naia, Spirit Painter
Kailua-Kona, HI 96740
808.960.4116
www.evenaia.com
mermaideve@hotmail.com

Wendy Rundel, LMT
Stillpoint Center for Wellbeing
PO Box 6714/ Ironwood Center •
Kamuela, HI 96743
wendyjohn@aol.com

Sacred Hawaiian Healing
Essences, Herbs & Natural Medicine
Ala Loa House By-the-Sea
HCR 3, Box 10072 • Kea'au, HI 96749
808.966.7887
alaloahouse@hotmail.com
www.vrbo.com site 9026
cat@watersongsanctuary.com
http://www.watersongsanctuary.com

David Stebbing, D.O. (UK)
British Cranial Osteopath
PO Box 190592 • Hāwī, HI 96719
808.889.6399
oplumeria@aol.com

Vibrational Healing Programs
PO Box 730 • Kapaau, HI 96755
contact: Joy Gardner, Director
808.889.0040
vibes@aloha.net

Vibrational Therapies by Asherah
Gemstone and Crystal Healing
40 S Wiliwili Street • Hilo, HI 96720
808.935.5530
asherra_@hotmail.com • Hawaiian Healing Therapies

Hawaiian Healing Therapies

Ho'ola 'O LomiLomi Lapa'au
PO Box 6202 • Hilo, HI 96720
808.961.3118
LokahiLapaauHi@webtv.net
www.LokahiOla.org

Holistic Health Practitioners

Clif Arrington, M.D.,ABAAM
American Board Certified Anti-Aging Medicine324-7522 fax
Hohalo Business Center
79-7266 Mamalohoa Hwy Suite 3 • Kealakekua, HI 96750
808.322.9400
Clifton@aloha.net • www.anti-agingmd.com

Holistic Health Practitioners

Bridging the Gap Resources
PO Box 4327 • Kailua-Kona, HI 96745
contact: Kikikipa Kretzer, MS,CFNP (Certified Family Nurse Practioner)
808.322.6161or324.7316 fax

Yvonne Conner, MD
150 A Kino'ole St. • Hilo, HI 96720
808.961.4722
res0fuyq@verizon.net

North Hawai'i Community Hospital (Integrative Medicine)
67-1125 Mamalahoa Hwy
Kamuela, HI 96743
808.885.4444
guibejh@nhawaiipo.ah.org
http://www.planet-hawaii.com/nhch

On Site Therapeutic Bodywork
Prince Kuhio Plaza
Medical Massage Therapy
contact: Beverly Garcia, LMT
Licensed Massage Therapist
Hilo, HI 96720
808.987.6968

Remission Foundation
351 Wailuku Drive • Hilo, HI 96720
contact: Dr. Glen Martin Swartwout
(homeopathy, natural eye care)
808.935.5086 800.788.2442
drglen@aloha.net
www.wizardofeyez.com

The Body Talk System
65-1206 Mamalahoa Hwy, #2-101
Kamuela, HI 96743
contact: Don Ka'imi Pilipovich & Kacey Clark
808.887.6438
kaimiloa@msn.com
www.bodytalksystem.com

Iridiology

Karen Alvarado, (Certified Iridologist)

Specializing in Anti-Aging, Hormone Balancing and Weight Loss using Nutrition and Quality Herbal Products. Determine the body's health through an evaluation process using Iridology, Nutritional Muscle Response Testing, pH Testing and Metabolic Testing. Then a custom health program is created to support the overall body systems and nutritional requirements.

75-5955 Kuakini Hwy, Suite 802 • Kailua-Kona, HI 96740
808.987.0629
hawaiikaren@hotmail.com

Lymph Drainage Therapy

Health in Motion

presents- LYMPH DRAINAGE THERAPY sm- LYMPHATIC BREAST CARE sm. LDT is a well needed preventive therapy stimulating the immune system. Reduces swelling, improves chronic infections and inflammation such as sinusitis, acne, and allergies. Cosmetic applications to minimize scars, wrinkles and cellulite- MUSCULAR MASSAGE - Therapeutic - Scrub & Wraps.

contact: Alain Schiller, LMT (MAT#1785) and/or Sandy Schiller

PO Box 384737 • Waikoloa, HI 96738

808.987.9866

mail@healthinmotion.net • www.healthinmotion.net

Naturopathic Physicians

Michelle Suber, ND

Innovative community education and patient-centered, comprehensive healthcare for women, men and children. Licensed staff physician at North Hawai'i Community Hospital utilizing clinical nutrition, botanical medicine, homeopathy and lifestyle counseling.

PO Box 2385 • Kamuela, HI 96743

808.887.8792 • Fax: 808.887.1712

Agasthya Siddha Vaidya

PO Box 21 •Holualoa, HI 96725

contact: James Bishop, LMT, PhD Naturopathy

808.938.7059

jamzbishop@yahoo.com

www.longlifehawaii.com

Hilo Naturopathic & Accupuncture Clinic

142B Kinoole St. •Hilo, HI 96720

contact: Jaqueline Hahn, ND

808.969.7848

dochahn@bigisland.com

Pacific Naturopathic Retreat Center

47-4268 Waipi'o Road •Honoka'a, HI 96727

contact: Marcel Hernandez, N.D. and Connie Hernandez, N.D.

808.775.1505 (voice and fax)

hawaiind@ilhawaii.net •www.naturopathicretreat.com

Massage and Body Work

Lisa Aitken, LMT

Trager, tranquil fluid motion for body, mind & soul is a unique approach to bodywork & movement education. The gentle stretches, rocking & vibration work on the core nervous system to deeply relax as well as enliven at all levels

PO Box 6535 • Kamuela, HI 96743
808.885.6040 • Fax: 808.885.0903
aitken@ilhawaii.net

Angels with Hands

Offering a 90 minute luxurious massage, combining an eclectic blend of techniques (deep tissue, myofascial release, joint mobilization, reflexology, rocking, lymphatic drainage) designed specifically for your body's needs. Or experience authentic Hawaiian Lomilomi, or Lomi'ili'ili (hot stones therapy). Angela Leslee, LMT(mat # 4052) is a massage instructor with a private practice in Kona since 1995.

contact: Angela Leslee, LMT
81-6263 Piko Road • Captain Cook, HI 96704
808.323.8353 or cell 808.937.6019
angelwhand@aol.com • www.angelwithhands.com

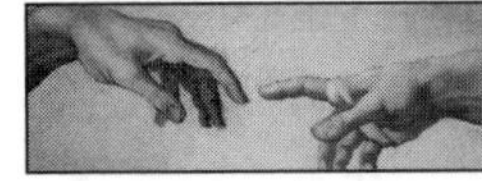

Get in Touch

A Massage and Bodywork experience combining Muscular Massage, Cranial Sacral Therapy, Reiki, and Touch for Health. Our goal is to help you achieve balance and symmetry in body, mind and spirit. Each session is designed specifically for you and your unique set of circumstances.

contact: Moku-wai C.C. Busch LMT,
PO Box 618 • Kealakekua, HI 96750
808.896.2118
konasumo@hawaii.rr.com

Helen Behrmann, LMT

PO Box 483 • Nā'ālehu, HI 96772
808.929.9275 • FAX 808. 929.9974
behrmannh@aol.com

Big Island Academy of Massage

201 Kinoole St. • Hilo, HI 96720
808.935.1405
lomilomi@bigislandmassage.com
www.bigislandmassage.com

Big Island Watsu and Massage

RR2, Box 4857 • Pāhoa, HI 96778
contact: Lew Schwenk, LMT, MAT #6688
808.965.8400
watsuLew@juno.com
www.bigislandwatsu.com

Body Therapy

82 Alae Street • Hilo, HI 9672
contact: Gosha Kowalczyk, LMT
808.935.5788
goshahawaii@hotmail.com

Massage and Body Work

Mary Brown R.N., LMT
Licensed Massage Therapist
PO Box 11288 • Hilo, HI 96721
808.987.4801
heavenlygoddess@hotmail.com

Noa Caiserman, LMT
Relaxiation, Pain Relief
and Deep Tissue
Kaalaiki Road, House #220
Nā'ālehu, HI 96772
808.928.8107

Lilia Cangemi
(Watsu and Dolphin Dance Instructor)
PO Box 1569 • Pāhoa, HI 96778
808.938.1847
liliacangemi@hotmail.com

Charlena, CMT
HCR 3 Box 11105 • Kea'au, HI 96749
808.966.6739
Islandsong3@yahoo.com

Karin Dahlgren, LMT
201 Kino'ole St. • Hilo, HI 96720
808.961.2707

Lisa Flores-Slattery, LMT
RR#2 Box 4522 • Pāhoa, HI 96778
808.965.9801

Chet Glenn, LMT
(Thai and Sports Massage)
75-233 Nanikailua Drive #129
Kailua-Kona, HI 96740
808.329.1830 +fax
chetglenn@webtv.net

Haloa (lomilomi)
PO Box 511 • Kamuela, HI 96743
contact: Mel Ward, LMT
808.855.2180
lomilomi@gte.net

Hawaiian Islands School of Body Therapies and Wellness Center
81-6587 Mamalahoa Hwy
Kealakekua, HI 96750
808.323.3800
massages@gte.net

Inner Balance by Cinder, LMT
(Massage and Spa Treatments)
94 Kamehameha Ave. Suite 4
Hilo, HI 96720
808.938-8019
touchingtiger@hawaii.rr.com

Island Skin Care Solutions
PO Box 794 • Nā'ālehu, HI 96772
contact: Tami Patton
(Licensed Paramedical Esthetician)
808.929.9944

Island Therapeutic Massage
(Lomi and Hot Stone Therapy)
140 Keawe Street • Hilo, HI 96720
contact: Kathleen Alvarez, LMT
808.935.9272 or 961.2003
kalina@bluehawaii.net

Massage and Body Work

Jeneye, CMT
Integrative Bodywork
351 Wailuku Drive • Hilo, HI 96720
808.935.5086
jeneye@ccc.ac

Jivan (watsu)
14-4324 Kapoho Rd.
Pāhoa, HI 96778
contact: Richard Zeisse
808.965.7119 or 966.7342
papayaretreat@yahoo.com
www.watsuInHawaii.com

Shar Kahumoku, LMT
201 Kino'ole St. • Hilo, HI 96720
808.961.2707

Kenko Therapeutic Massage
Japanese Speaking
56 Waianuenue Ave. Suite 213
Hilo, HI 96720
contact: Hiromi Leadbetter, LMT
800.509.2741 • 808.966.9735

Ki Mana Academy
184 Kamehameha Ave. • Hilo, HI 96720
808.935.2596

Kona Hawai'i's School of Muscular Massage
(offering student & professional massages)
75-6082 Ali'i Drive, #10
Kailua-Kona, HI 96740
808.331.2830
www.muscularmassage.com
muscularmassage@hotmail.com

Massage Therapy Center Hilo
(Spa and Lodging)
498 Laukapu Street • Hilo, HI 96720
contact: Merrie (Chrissie Ball), LMT #1124
808.935.2844
MCBII1@aol.com

Laura Moorehead, LMT
Individualized Aromatherapy and Massage
PO 190593 • Hāwī, HI 96719
808.889.0777
laurasophia@juno.com

Megan Neal, LMT
211 Kino'ole St. • Hilo, HI. 96720
808.935.1405 • 808.969.7676

Jean Olson, Cmt
(Lomi Lomi and Swedish Massage)
PO Box 1887 • Pāhoa, HI 96778
808.938.2648
spcyrngr@aol.com

South Kona Massage Therapy
PO Box 895
Captain Cook, HI 96704
contact: Natalie Sato, LMT
808.328.8422
phowa@turquoise.net

Lynne Starke (watsu)
83-5572 Middle Keei Rd
Captain Cook, HI. 96704
808.328.1600
whaleswisdom@cs.com

Massage and Body Work

Swami's Hawaiian LomiLomi Massage

PO Box 403 • Hōnaunau, HI 96726
contact: Jerri Knoblich
808.323.3344
swamimomi@kona.net

Gyongyi (Momi) Szirom, RN, LMT

(lomilomi)
CR-1, Box 5403 • Kea'au, HI 967-9530
808.982.9331
gyongyis@msn.com
www.lomilomi.org/momi.html

Transformational Bodywork

(Massage & Yoga)
Christy Welsh, LMT
808.937.9045
thepathofdevotion@yahoo.com

Vitality Works Day Spa

(Massage and Ayurvedic Practice)
PO Box 2577 • Kailua-Kona, HI 96745
contact: Darmani Zelin, LMT
808.987.1402 329.1829 fax
Dharmini_z@hotmail.com

Watsu/Wassertanzen

RR2 #48570 • Pāhoa, HI 96778-9727
contact: Dwight Stevens, CWP
808.965.8500
warmwatermassage@aol.com

Lew Whitney

PO Box 1585 • Kapa'au, HI 96755
808.889.9893
kokkkolulu@bigisland.net

Lisa Yee. LMT

68-1787 Ho'oko • Waikoloa, HI 96738
808.883.9377 or 883.8612 + fax
Lisayee07@hotmail.com

Yoga Oasis

contact: Hayward Coleman
808.965.8460 or 800.274.444
Hayward@yogaoasis.org
www.yogaoasis.org

Retreats

Green Fire Productions Present

A "magical" woman's spiritual adventure—on the warm ocean in Kapoho...in a beautiful fairy palace. Come & share with Sapphire Moon... internationally known educator and shaman—a sacred journey of the heart into the teachings of Mother Pele. Exotic adventures, telepathic trainings, individual & group retreats.
Sapphire Moon
(808) 934-9205
pelefire@gte.net • www.greenfireproductions.com

Akash Healing Center

Kailua-Kona, Hi
contact: Sharon Forsyth
808.331.2276
ayusidha@ilhawaii.net
www.akashhealingcenter.com

Ala Loa House By-the-Sea

HCR 3 Box 10072 • Kea'au, HI 96749
808.966.7887
alaloahouse@hotmail.com
www.vrbo.com Site 9026

Retreats

KeMa Patricia Nash

83-5621 Mamalahoa Hwy
Captain Cook, HI 96704
808.328.07 or 808.895.3674
kemakama@aol.com
www.kemakama.com

Kokolulu Farm &Wellness Center

55-3472 Aloni Pule HWY • Hāwī
PO Box 1585 • Kapa'au, HI 96755
contact: Karin Cooke, RN
808.889.9893
kokolulu@bigisland.com

Light Spirit

PO Box 1598 • Kealakekua, HI 96750
contact: Chris Reid
Tel/Fax 808.328.8672
dolphins@kona.net • http://www.revchrisreid.com

Spas

The Lotus Center

A spa, chiropractic and facial fitness center located in the heart of Kona at the Royal Kona Resort on Alii Drive. Our day spa services include massages, facials, chiropractice, acupuncture, micro-dermabrasion, sound therapy, permanent make-up, waxing, tinting, wraps, hot earth rock massage, steam, jacuzzi and "TLC.

contact: Lanette Abraham-Duncan, owner, manager, LMT
75-5825 Ali'i Drive, Suite 166 • Kailua-Kona, HI 96740
808.334.0445 • Fax 808.329.4117
tlcspa@kona.net

Paradise Spa

Hawai'i Naniloa Resort
93 Banyan Drive • Hilo, HI 96720
808.969.3333 • FAX: 808.969.6622

Spa Without Walls: The Orchid at Mauna Lani

One North Kaniku Drive
Kohala Coast, HI 96743
808.887.7540
info@orchind-manunalani.com

Vitality Works Day Spa

(Massage and Ayurvedic Practice)
PO Box 2577 • Kailua-Kona, HI 96745
contact: Darmani Zelin, LMT
808.987.1402 329.1829 fax
Dharmini_z@hotmail.com

Tai Chi

Healing in Motion

Tai Chi, Chi Kung(QiGong), & Acutouch
HC 1 Box 5240 • Kea'au, HI 96749
contact: Valerie Myles
808.966.4893 or 888.265.0005
acuchi2@hotmail.com • www.healinginmotion.net

Yoga

Kona Yoga

Kona Yoga holds weekly public classes in the Iyengar tradition of Hatha yoga. Instructor Barbara Uechi, a licensed massage therapist, also offers The Art of Balance: six-90 minute private lessons which will allow you to locate equilibrium through a basic series of yoga postures, breathing techniques and muscular massage.

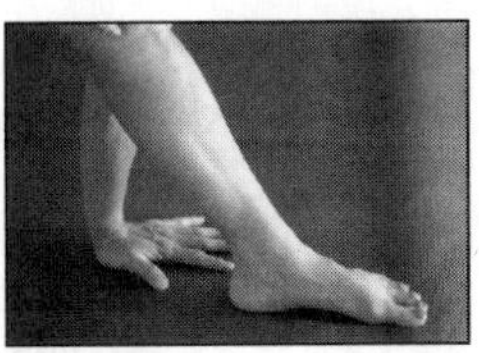

contact: Barbara Uechi, LMT, owner #MAT 6578
73-1282 O na O na Drive • Kailua-Kona, HI 96740
808.325.7089
Barbara@konayoga.com • www.konayoga.com

Boundless Yoga Center

St James Cirlce • Kamuela, HI 96743
contact: Nancy Candea
808.88.9642
candea@interpac.net

Fitness and Sports

Healing in Motion

(Tai Chi, Qi Gong, Acutouch)
HC 1, Box 5240 • Kea'au, HI 96749
contact: Valerie Myles
808.966.4893
acuchi2@hotmail.com

KeMa Patricia Nash

83-5621 Mamalahoa Hwy
Captain Cook, HI 96704
808.328.07 or 808.895.3674
kemakama@aol.com
www.kemakama.com

Yoga

Pacific Coast Fitness

65-1298 A Kawaihae
Kamuela, HI 96743
contact: Uvonne Lindsey
808.885.6270

Shanawo's Peaceful Dragon Academy

Burley L. Benford
Box 913 • Hōnaunau, HI 96726
808.936.3294

WALK, WALK, WALK

(race and power walking
PO Box 931 • Pāhoa, HI 96778
contact: Shayna Kristen, L.Ac., MAT
808.937.0973
shaynakristen@hotmail.com

Yoga Centered

330 Kamehameha Ave
Hilo, HI 96720
contact: Cori Martinez
808.962.0150
www.yogacentered.comss

Na Ala Hele Trail and Access Program

Contact: Curt Cottrell
Division of Forestry and Wildlife
Dept. of Land and Natural Resources
808.587.0062
www. hawaiitrails.org

KeMa Patricia Nash

83-5621 Mamalahoa Hwy
Captain Cook, HI 96704
808.328.07 or 808.895.3674
kemakama@aol.com
www.kemakama.com

Volunteers in Parks

Place of Refuge Volunteer Program
contact: Blossom Sapp
808.328.2288
www.nps.gov/puho

Rainbow Friends Animal Sanctuary

PO Box 944 • Hilo, HI 96721
contact: Mary Rose and Lanni Sinkin
808.985.6001 or 808.982.6160
2rainbow@ilhawaii.net

Retired and Senior Volunteer Program (RSVP)

34 Rainbow Drive #101
Hilo, HI 96720
contact: Stuart Kearns
808.961.8730 • FAX 808.961.8709
rsvp@co.hawaii.hi.us

Hawai'i Volcanoes National Park

(and U.S. Geological Survey)
Volunteer Programs
contact: Jim Quiring
808.985.6001
http://www.nps.gov/havo

Waimea Nature Park Waimea Outdoor Circle

808.885.8855
woc@aloha.net

Ala Loa House By-The-Sea

Wrap yourself in peace & quiet: Your own private home with jacuzzi, sunny deck, master suite, kitchen & tropical gardens. Enjoy miles of unspoiled coastline trails & forest preserves. Healing warm ponds, volcano viewing. Massage, oxygen & most therapies on-site. $650/week, $105/night 3 night minimum.
808.966.7887.
www.vrbo.com/vrbo/9026.htm
alaloahouse@hotmail.com

Dragonfly Ranch Healing Arts Retreat

"Where aloha abounds" An upscale Swiss Family Robinson retreat and B&B attracting fascinating, ecologically minded and spiritually aware visitors. Space for small retreats. A large yoga studio and labyrinth on the premises. Lomi lomi massage is a specialty of Dragonfly Ranch. The atmosphere is informal with invitations to visitors to participate in meal preparation and sharing from the organic garden.

Box 675, Hōnaunau • HI 96726
contact: Barbara Moore
808.328.2159 or 328.9570
dfly@dragonflyranch.com
www.dragonflyranch.com

Hale Makamae

A wonderful place, located in the Puna area of the Big Island, where you get to know a little piece of the old Hawai'i and its Aloha Spirit. The tranquility of the gardens and the peacefulness of the area create an environment of relations and healing. All our Suites have private baths and separate entrances and two offer kitchenette, dining room and living room. Rates from $55 to $85. Besides English, we also speak German.

13-3315 Makamae Street • Pāhoa, HI 96778,
contact: Petra Wiesenbauer
808.965.9090
tuckers@aloha.net
www.bnb-aloha.com

Healthy Vacations

Beautiful Big Island Vacation Rental at Kehena Beach with private Chef. New 3 story home, VERY private, ocean views. Custom vacations, choose from: weight loss menu, exercise programs, organic foods, detox-cleansing programs, private yoga, hiking, meditation, massage, gourmet dining, swimming snorkeling. Enjoy taking care of yourself while having fun.

12-7207 Maukanui St. • Pāhoa, HI 96778
contact: Jeffrey Rozzelle
808.965.7865 • cell 808.936.8705

Healing Accommodations

Hilo Seaside Retreat

Enjoy a spectacular view of a secluded tropical lagoon from your private suite of rooms, private entrance, kitchen, bath, living room, lanai, and bedroom/s...Lawns and gardens lead to freshwater tidal pools. Luxuries include: bird songs, ocean melodies, trade winds, fresh fruit, beach activities, Jacuzzi, laundry, massage therapy, telephone, catv/vcr. Private breakfast includes: coffee tea, fruit and cereal. Ten minute to town or airport.

Box 10960 • Hilo, HI 96721
contact: Patti Oliver
808.961.6178
www.hilo-inns.com • pattio@hilo-inns.com

Kema Kama

Nestled on the magical slopes of Mauna Loa, overlooking bays frequented by dolphins and whales. Feel caressed by sensual offerings of lush, tropical vegetation on eleven private, peaceful acres. An idyllic sanctuary for a couple or individual. Beautiful spacious vacation rental (full kitchen). Personal spiritual retreats. Unique Island adventures.

KeMa Patricia Nash
83-5621 Mamalahoa Hwy • Captain Cook, HI 96704
808.328.07 (H) • 808.895.3674 (cell)
kemakama@aol.com • www.kemakama.com

Ocean and Beach Front Vacation Rental Homes

All located on the ocean or at the beach. Fully-equipped houses available for nightly, weekly, and extended stay vacation rental lodging. Each of these beautiful properties is owned and managed by the same family. We take pride in providing our guests with top quality homes that are new, modern, and spotlessly clean. Chose from our selection of 1-4 bedroom houses in Hilo or Kona. Complete ocean front privacy.

contact: Karri Sakai
800.813.3306
www.hilokonabeachrentals.com • inquiries@8palms.com

Peaceful Oceanside Cottage

Stunning views of smashing waves, cliffs, swaying palms and red-gold sun rising out of the sea. Great walks: seaside, tide pools, forest... Refresh in our large oceanside swimming pool. 30 minutes to Hilo, 45 minutes to Volcano. Natural Breathwork & Hypnotherapy sessions, other services available. Intimate cottage for one or two: $95.00.

Bernie and Gretchen
HCR 2, Box 9608 • Kea'au, HI 96749
808.966.5085
sadie@bigisland.net

Healing Accommodations

"Aaah, The Views..." Bed & Breakfast

PO Box 6593 • Kamuela, HI 96743
contact: Mare Grace
808.885.3455 • Toll Free 866.885.3455
Fax 808.885.4031
tommare@aloha.net
www.beingsintouch.com

Affordable Hawai'i At Pomaika'i (Lucky) Farm B&B

83-5465 Mamalahoa Hwy
Captain Cook, HI 96704
contact: Nita Isherwood
808.328.2112 • res: 800.325.6427
nitabnb@kona.net
www.luckyfarm.com

'Ai Lani Retreat House

PO Box 500 • Nā'ālehu, HI 96772
contact: Barney Frazier
& Elizabeth Jenkins
808.929.8785 or 808.929.7370
elizabeth@inka-online.com
www.inka-online.com/retreat

Akiko's Buddhist Bed and Breakfast

PO Box 272 • Hakalau, HI 96710
808.963.6422
msakiki@aloha.net
www.alternative-hawaii.com/akiko

Aloha Spirit Oceanview Guesthouse

RR2 Box 3947 • Pāhoa, HI 96778-9754
808.965.1208
revmj@hotmail.com
www.home1.gte.net/rymark
/index.htm

Aloha Vacation Cottages

PO Box 1395 • Kamuela, HI 96743
contact: Heidi and Keoki Staab
808.885.6535 • 877.875.1722
alohastudio@hawaii.rr.com
www.easystretch.com

Areca Palms Estate B&B

PO Box 489 • Captain Cook, HI 96704
contact: Janice and Steve Glass
808.323.2276 • toll free 800.545.4390
merryman@ilhawaii.net
www.konabedandbreakfast.com

Barbara J. Fahs, M.A.

Hi'iaka's Healing Herb Garden, LLC
HCR 2, Box 9620 • Kea'au, HI 96749
808.966.6126
www.hiiakas.com

Hale Kai Bjornen B&B

111 Honolii Pali • Hilo, HI 96720
808.935.6330 • Fax 808.935.8439
bjornen@interpac.net
www.interpac.net/~halekai

Hawaiian Retreat

Papaya Farms Road • Pāhoa, HI
contact: Eliot Rosen
808.965.1279 or 1.877.965.1279
info@hawaiianretreat.com
www.hawaiianretreat.com

Healing Accommodations

Healinc
(Arranges wellness travel packages)
PO Box 504 • Kapa'au, HI
contact: Christine Calvo
808.889.1661
spirit@ilhawaii.net • www.healinc.biz

Holualoa Coffee Cottage
PO Box 188 • Holualoa HI 96725
contact: Suzanne Koan
808 322 0886
info@thecoffeecottage.com
www.thecoffeecottage.com

Kaula Farm
PO Box 2652 • Kailua-Kona, HI 86745
808.325.5268 • Fax 808.325.5268
vacation@kaulafarm.com
www.kaulafarm.com

Kai Mana Retreat & Guest House
PO Box 1297 • Kealakekua, HI 96750
contact: Sandia Siegel
808-323-3320
mapu@ilhawaii.net

Kealakekua Bay B&B
PO Box 1412 • Kealakekua, HI 96750
contact: Shakti
800.328.8150 • 808.328.8150
www.keala.com

K-Bay Vacation Home and Cottage
82-6284 Pu'uhonua Road
Captain Cook, HI 96704
808.328.9340 • toll fre 888.328.9340
pam@kbayhawaii.com
www.kbayhawaii.com

Kia'i Kai Bed & Breakfast
HCR 3 Box 10064 • Kea'au, HI 96749
contact: John & Tory Mospens, Innkeepers,
808.982.9256 or toll free1.888.KIAIKAI
kiaikai@gte.net
www.hawaii-ocean-retreat.com

Kukui Hale
PO Box 4182 • Hilo, HI 96720
16-1919 36th Ave. Auli'i / Ilima
Orchidland Estates, Kea'au, HI
contact: Stacy/Desmon Haumea
808.982.6508
Haumea@aol.com
www.HaleOla.com

Lopakatu
74-4963 Kiwi St.
Kailua-Kona, HI 96740
contact: Bob and Marty Dean
808.329.3455
bob@surfhawaii.net
www.surfhawaii.net/lopakatu

Macadamia Meadows Farm B&B
PO Box 756 • Nā'ālehu, HI 96772
contact: Charlene Cowan
808.929.8097 phone/fax
kaleena@aloha.net
wwwmacadamiameadows.com

Healing Accommodations

Ohana House Rural Retreat
PO Box 6351 • Ocean View, HI 96737
808.929.9139 or toll free 1.888.999.9139
www.alternative-hawaii.com/ohana

Pu'uhonua O Puako A Place of Refuge
alohadebbi@aol.com
www.hawaiioceanfront.com

Ho'onaunea Vacation Rentals
(a women's retreat)
Soular Farms and Wellness Center
PO Box 6450 • Kamuela, HI 96743
contact: Shay Bintliff, MD
808.882.1177

Tropical Hideaway
84-5053 Keala 'O Keawe Rd,
Captain Cook, HI 96704
contact: Kathleen Carr & Phil Monette
808.328.8672
info@tropicalhideawayhawaii.com
www.tropicalhideawayhawaii.com

Volcano Country Cottages
PO Box 545 • Volcano, HI 96785
contact: Kathleen Porter
808.967.7960
aloha@volcanocottages.com
www.volcanocottages.com

Volcano Inn
PO Box 490 • Volcano, HI 96785
contact: Joan Prescott-Lighter
808.967.7293 or 800.997.2292
volcano@volcanoinn.com
www.volcanoinn.com

Publications, Resources & Food

www.Hawaii-Healing.com
Select from our most precious natural resources to enhance your wellness experience on-line! Access Natural Health Care Providers offering a variety of health enhancing & wellness solutions that promote rejuvenation, refresh your senses, enliven your spirit, and raise your level of well-being, in the most healing place on earth.

Hawaii-Healing.Com

Holomana 'O Hawai'i
Hawai'i Healing Arts Network
Sharman O'Shea Executive Director
PO Box 1502 • Kamuela, HI 96743
808.887.0044
holomana@turquoise.net
www.hawaii-healing.com

Publications, Resources & Food

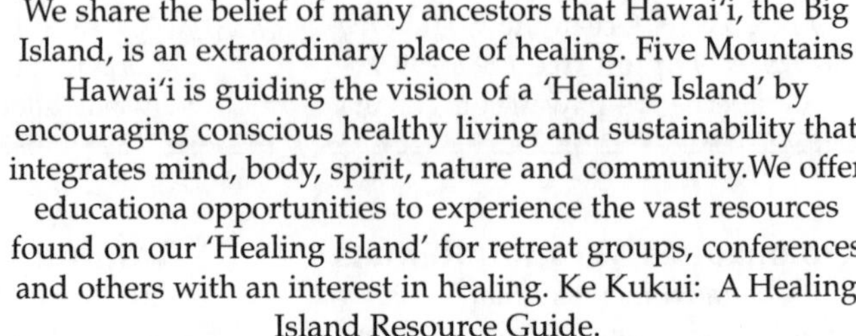

Five Mountains Hawai'i

Five Mountains Hawai'i
Nā Kuahiwi 'Elima

We share the belief of many ancestors that Hawai'i, the Big Island, is an extraordinary place of healing. Five Mountains Hawai'i is guiding the vision of a 'Healing Island' by encouraging conscious healthy living and sustainability that integrates mind, body, spirit, nature and community.We offer educationa opportunities to experience the vast resources found on our 'Healing Island' for retreat groups, conferences and others with an interest in healing. Ke Kukui: A Healing Island Resource Guide.

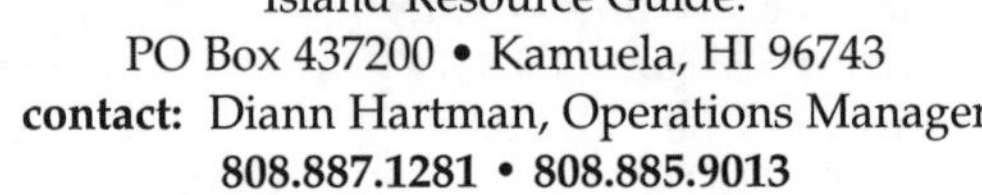

PO Box 437200 • Kamuela, HI 96743
contact: Diann Hartman, Operations Manager
808.887.1281 • 808.885.9013
request@fivemountains.org • www.fivemountains.org

Mana Cards

(Communication Consulting)
191 Ka'iulani St • Hilo, HI 96720
contact: Catherine Becker, Ph.D.
808.969.4906 + fax
kalama@manacards.com • www.manacards.com

Healthy Food Resources and Restaurants

Abundant Life Natural Foods and Café

Hilo's Bay Front Natural Living Store
292 Kamehameha Avenue
Hilo, HI 96720
808.935.7411 or 935.6154 fax
www.abundantlifenaturalfoods.com
abundantlife@livingnaturally.com

Island Naturals (Health Food Store)

303 Maka'ala St. • Hilo, HI 96720
contact: William Heideman
808.935.5533 • Fax: 808.934.8035

Raw Paradise

A Vegan Raw Foods Sanctuary Fun Park
The Gold Buddha
Papaya Farms Road • Pāhoa, HI 96778
808.938.9098 or 895.1126
www.rawparadise.com

Notes

Please visit our website for updated and new wellness resources and information.

www.alohawellnesstravel.com

“We were taught that when the mana (personal power) is strong and people accept themselves as the powerful beings that they are—all things are possible.”

Kaili‘ohe Kame‘ekua
Tales from the Night Rainbow

~ Chapter Five ~

The Island of Maui • The Magic Isle

When visiting Maui you are likely to hear, *"Maui nō ka 'oi,"* which means "Maui is the best." Many people have a passion about Maui that brings them back year after year. For them, the distinct energy, history and personality which is Maui represents Hawai'i. Geologically, Maui is the second youngest of the islands by a million years. Perhaps this youthfulness contributes to the high level of energy and creativity one finds here. People from the other islands sometimes describe Maui as "little California." From the yin/yang perspective, Maui could be seen as yang or masculine in its energy. It is progressive, active and dedicated to making things happen.

The seven islands of Hawai'i have been likened to the seven chakras or energy centers of the body. Maui corresponds to the sacral chakra the center of creativity and reproduction, sexuality, and pleasure. In support of this comparison, Maui has more counselors ready to help people with their sexuality than any other island. It also has a statewide reputation for being highly creative. People on Maui come up with innovative ideas and follow through with making them happen. Examples range from innovative prison rehabilitation programs to a hugely successful international writers conference and a world renowned film festival. There are also more artists on Maui than elsewhere in the state and many movie stars have bought homes here. In short, Maui is a "do it, can do" island. Energy doesn't get stuck here.

Maui has been described as having a dual personality. On one side are the beach-lined coastal areas of Wailea, Kīhei, and Ka'anapali. Sunshine, surf, sand, snorkeling, spas and fine resort hotels and condominiums characterize these areas. The Kīhei-Wailea area in south Maui is adjacent to Mākena beach, a vast expanse of white sand that stretches unencumbered by development. Near here you can hike the King's highway or swim where sea life abounds with exotic tropical fish, sea turtles, dolphins, and whales. Further up the coast, near Ka'anapali, is the old whaling town of Lahaina, the former capital of Hawai'i. Walking down Front Street you'll find countless specialty shops, restaurants, and the famous Banyan Tree Park.

A few miles away is Maui's other side, a pastoral world of misty mountainsides called Upcountry, which covers the slope of the dormant volcano Haleakalā. The town of Makawao is at the center. It combines the rural flavor of Upcountry with sixties style charm, specialty shops, and healing centers. Wailuku, the county seat of Maui, has the feel of old Hawai'i. It is nestled at the entrance of the stunning 'Īao Valley. Pā'ia is a former plantation town and modern day surfing mecca due to its proximity to Ho'okipa, one of the premier wind surf spots on the globe. Ho'okipa is host to international sail boarding and surfing competitions annually. At the Eastern point of the island is Hāna, about as otherworldly as you can get. At the end of a long, but dramatically beautiful, drive featuring one-lane bridges and countless waterfalls, is Hāna, a quiet, sleepy village where you will often hear Hawaiian spoken. For some, it provides a welcomed balance to the active pace found elsewhere on Maui.

The Maui coastal resorts are so self-contained that visitors can comfortably spend an entire vacation between the beach, the spa, the poolside, and the shops. This slow, relaxed pace can be a wellness experience all by itself. While the healing effects of sparkling sun and brilliant blue ocean cannot be denied, especially for those visitors fleeing frigid climes and the color-starved world of winter, we encourage you not to miss the lush green beauty of rural Maui. There you will find some of the most beautiful, soothing scenery you're likely to encounter in Hawai'i. Many people divide their vacation time between the coastal areas and the more rural part of Maui. That way they get to experience the best of all worlds that are available on the island of Maui.

Twenty Ways to Pursue Balance and Harmony in Maui

1. Ease In and Out of Your Wellness Vacation With A Silent Retreat

At the beginning and the end of your wellness vacation on Maui, consider taking a silent retreat. This experience can gently integrate you into your wellness vacation or provide a conclusion to it that allows time and space for reflection. It might be a half day, full day or several days. A silent retreat provides space to simply be with yourself and your environment. Although books may be good for reflection, if you devote your time to reading it detracts from the process and goal of such a retreat. Writing may facilitate your retreat reflections, but again, shouldn't dominate the time. If it's for a few hours, you might want to go to a garden or place in nature to walk around, observe, sit, think, and feel. If you plan to retreat for several days, we recommend one of the B&Bs with a separate cottage. Explain to your hostess that you are on a silent retreat.

2. Pursue Inner Peace in Sacred Spaces and Places on Maui

If your wellness intention is an inner pilgrimage that involves spiritual reflection, we've identified some special places you might explore for that purpose. It's hard to describe what it is about a place that invites us to a connection with the Divine. What works for us may not work for you, but our experience is that the places we recommend have a particularly powerful spiritual energy. Sometimes this is evoked from the history or beauty of a site. Most often it is found in true silence in a place surrounded by the peace and quiet of nature. In these sacred spaces and places, our quest for greater peace, understanding and compassion for others and ourselves will be rewarded.

Keawala'i Congregational Church, at the end of the road in Mākena, Hwy. 31, is a simple stone church built in 1932 to serve the area's small farmers. The church is separated from the pounding surf by a cluster of old gravestones and a moss-covered stonewall. The quiet stillness of the sanctuary and graveyard, juxtaposed with the active surf crashing against rocks just a few yards away, reminds us of our ability to achieve inner peace though surrounded by turbulence.

St. John's Episcopal Church, in Upcountry Maui, brings a different spiritual awareness. Shim Yin Chin, who was called to the islands from China in 1900 to teach and minister to the immigrant Chinese farmers, founded this church. First Shim, then his wife after he died, and later his son, each led the church. Over the past 100 years, the Shims, and Heather Mueller-Fitch, the current priest who has served for 20 years, have been the vital force behind this charming 100-seat church (that's 100 small people.) The church is a white frame building with simple stained glass windows. It sits on the Kula hillside overlooking the valley below. The simplicity of the interior reflects the truth that our greatest joy comes from the simple things in life.

As you turn to leave, the doorway frames a magnificent view of the beauty of the natural world. The few passing cars along the road to the Tedeschi Winery fail to disturb the peace and serenity of this special place. On the pavement in front of the church is a labyrinth inviting you to take a contemplative pilgrimage. Below the church, a short distance down a small road, is St. John's retreat house. The Chinese farmers are gone and the congregation consists mostly of transplanted people from the mainland. We were pleased to see the prominent role of women at the service we attended; not only the priest but also the readers were women. The church is located on Lower Kula Road, Hwy 37, halfway between the 16 and 17 mile markers on the ocean side of the road. Sunday services are at 7:30 and 9:30 a.m. (808.878.1485)

Finally, if your travels take you to Hāna, we suggest that you visit the **Charles Lindberg gravesite**. Just past the 41 mile marker beyond Hāna, turn onto a narrow road, drive through a tunnel of trees to a clearing where a church sits almost hidden among hedges. It is stark in its simplicity and badly needs repair, but the grounds filled us with a sense of the sacred. Behind the hedges, a small group of gravestones opens up to a grassy knoll overlooking the ocean at least one hundred feet below. Lindberg's grave is set apart from the others identified by a marker flat against the ground with the following engraved quote *"If I take the wings of the morning or dive to the inner most depths of the sea"* (*"even there shall thy hand lead me, and thy right hand shall hold me."* completes the quote from Psalms 139). Perhaps, what makes the experience of this place so moving, and what Lindberg might have felt, is a deep awareness that even here, on the isolated windswept coast of the most remote group of islands in the world, we are not alone.

Haleakalā Volcano is considered by Hawaiians to be one of the most sacred places on all of the islands. See #4 for a discussion of the power and beauty of Haleakalā.

Spiritual experience is guided from deep within each of us. You may discover other places that have an even stronger impact on you, but to find a place or space that speaks to you in a significant way can be the most meaningful part of your Inner Pilgrimage vacation.

3. Advance Self-Understanding With an Astrology Reading

Astrology, a tool for understanding ourselves and our world, is thousands of years old. In our current state of uncertainty and insecurity it can be a useful tool for gaining clarity about the path we are on, who we are meant to be, and the work ahead for us. On Maui, astrology has gone high tech with computer programs that can not only help illuminate past, present, and future but can also adjust for geographical relocations.

Eliza Bassett does an astrology column for the weekly Maui paper. Her individual astrology readings can be surprisingly accurate in not only validating the path you are on but also explaining how planet alignment during geographical moves you have made may have affected your life. Eliza will bring her laptop computer and cassette recorder to where you are. (808.283.7543)

Lorraine Bennington, another astrologist, has a charming office in Makawao above the Dragon's Den herbal store. She offers a comprehensive astrology reading and is prepared to combine it with hypnotherapy and conventional counseling to help you make desired shifts in your life. (808.573.3383)

Whether or not you subscribe to the theory behind astrology, you will undoubtedly leave a reading with something to think about.

4. Soak Up the Power and Beauty of Haleakalā

Haleakalā, the dormant volcano that rises to a height of 10,000 feet, has been considered by Hawaiians to be one of the most powerful sacred sites of all the islands. Here the demi-god Maui lassoed the sun to slow it down so that his mother could have time to dry the tapa cloth. The road to Haleakalā climbs rapidly offering several lookouts, each with an increasing breadth of vista. You will also find parks with picnic tables to enjoy a picnic in paradise and trail heads where you can launch out on a hike. Pu'u 'ula'ula Overlook, the final summit, provides an unparalleled view on a clear day.

A popular ritual for many visitors to Maui is watching the sunrise from the summit of Haleakalā. Many describe this as a profound spiritual experience. It can take up to 3 hours to get there by car from the Kīhei or the Ka'anapali coast, so you need to get up early. The mountain can also be cold early in the morning, so bundle up. Call ahead for a weather report, as conditions may be hazy or cloudy. (808.871.5054)

We've found it equally moving to go up during the day for a hike (there are 36 miles of trails), or at sunset to watch the closing of the day. For people who live in cities, viewing the stars from Haleakalā can be an unforgettable experience. Without the interference of city lights, they seem so bright and so close that you may feel you can reach out and touch them.

Whatever time of day you choose to experience Haleakalā, it promises you a deep connection to nature.

5. Seek the Wisdom of Your Center By Walking a Labyrinth

Pilgrimage as a spiritual journey has existed for thousands of years and involves many spiritual practices, including walking the labyrinth as a meditation. The labyrinth used on Maui as an inner pilgrimage is a replica of the one in the Chartres Cathedral in France which dates back 800 years. Walking the path is a metaphorical journey into a deeper awareness of oneself. As you move toward the destination, the center, you will seem to get further and further away. The indirect path may create frustration, impatience, and judgment of one's self and others. The gift of the path and the process comes through self-awareness and observation—seeing the journey toward the center as a reflection of your own life journey toward wholeness, balance and harmony. As part of an inner pilgrimage, a labyrinth walk on Maui has the potential to be particularly powerful. The labyrinth we recommend is at one of the sacred places mentioned earlier, **St. John's Episcopal Church** on the hillside above Kula. Eve Hogan, a labyrinth facilitator on Maui, together with **Reverend Heather Mueller-Fitch** of St. John's church, offer you guidance and an opportunity for reflection and discussion on this unique process for deepening awareness. Full moon labyrinth walks are scheduled each month. For information, call 808.878.1485 the number for St. John's Church, or 808.879.8648 for Eve Hogan. Or see the schedule on www.HeartPath.com. *(See the article on labyrinths by Eve in Chapter Three)*

6. Open to Your Spiritual Source Through Meditation

What better time and place to discover or learn to meditate than while on a vacation to Hawai'i. So much about your vacation in this extraordinary land will invite you to a deep sensitivity on many levels. Meditation can guide you to quiet the mind and experience more profoundly the beauty of the environment. Walking meditation can make your visits to the gardens an even richer experience. Silencing your mind in order to fully experience the trade winds caress your skin, the fragrances of plumeria blossoms and the symphony of our winged friends will deepen your experience of Hawai'i. Following are some suggestions on where to explore a lesson in meditation.

The **Maui Academy of Healing Arts** in Kīhei offers mediation classes. **John Sanderson**, its director, left an active counseling practice and a healing academy which he started on the mainland, planning to retire on Maui. Instead, he brought his considerable skills here and opened the Maui Academy of Healing Arts. Call him early in your visit to see what classes and lectures are scheduled. (808.879.4266) Meditation instruction is available from **Amarshareen**, owner of **Beyond Heaven** in Makawao. (808.573.8828) If you are staying at a resort with a spa, you might ask if a member of their staff can provide you with instruction. For example, the Grand Wailea Resort has been offering yoga and meditation classes for the past ten years.

7. Discover Your Creative Center Through Art

Artistic expression is increasingly recognized as a way to tap into hidden parts of oneself. It can also be a form of meditation. Focusing on what we are creating quiets our mind to all outside stimuli. Art offers a vehicle for expressing and capturing the beauty around us. In addition, visiting an art gallery can result in the acquisition of a piece of art that elicits memories long after the vacation is over.

Maui has about five hundred resident artists so art galleries can be found throughout the island, especially in the coastal resort areas. The appreciation and purchase of art require contemplation so we're featuring art galleries that have a serene environment. **Hui No'eau Visual Arts Center**, located in a lovely 1917 historic plantation mansion one mile below Makawao at 2841 Baldwin Avenue, highlights local artists in rotating exhibits. Guided tours are available on Tuesdays and Thursdays. (808.572.6560)

The **Curtis Wilson Cost Gallery** in the tranquil Upcountry Kula area is located at the Kula Lodge. It focuses only on one artist—the gallery owner. (808.878.6544) The **Hāna Coast Gallery** at the Hotel Hāna-Maui is filled with museum quality wood carvings, sculptures, oils and fine art reflecting the culture of Hawai'i. (808.248.8636)

Makawao has become a center for local artists. There you will find **Gallery Maui**, an elegant and warm gallery down a path behind Tropo Men's Store. It has a diverse but small selection of wood items, ceramics and paintings as well as affordable placemats. (808.572.8092) **Viewpoints Gallery** is located in the courtyard across from Café Del Sol. It is one of the best in the area, with a wide variety of art to interest almost anyone. (808.572.5979) While in the courtyard, stop at **Hot Island Glass** to watch the creation of museum quality blown glass art creations. (808.572.4527)

A section about art galleries on Maui would not be complete without mentioning Lahaina, which has the highest concentration of art galleries on the island. Here you'll find the full range of artistic expression, from amateur to world-renowned professional, and from abstract to fantastical realist, in painting, sculpture, glass and jewelry.

Perhaps your time on Maui will stimulate the inner artist and you'll decide to take an art class to create your own visual memory of your wellness vacation. One of the best places is the **Hui No'eau Visual Arts Center**. Call and ask for their newsletter that includes a calendar of classes. (808.572.6560)

The Art School in Kapalua also offers a rich variety of artistic classes ranging from yoga and dance to ceramics and painting. (808.665.0007)

We encourage you to take art home, either yours or a piece by a local artist, to serve as a daily reminder of your wellness experience on Maui.

8. Improve Relationship Communication With a Specialized Counselor

The 9/11 national trauma left most of us more deeply aware of the importance of friends and family in our lives. It made us seek out meaningful relationships and perhaps become more committed to doing the work necessary to improve those we have. A vacation is a perfect opportunity to do this. It gives us the space and time, free of daily stress, to focus more on what is important in our intimate relationship and how to improve where improvement is warranted.

Maui has many relationship counselors and probably more of them focusing on the sexual aspects of our relationship than any other island.

Jeffrey Marsh and Debra Greene, Ph.D. of **HeartPath** offer relationship coaching and conscious communication seminars in the Kīhei and Wailea area. They are licensed, certified PAIRS (Practical Application of Intimate Relationship Skills) facilitators who teach on Maui and the mainland. Debra is also a highly trained kinesiologist and makes this process available to couples in pursuit of their deepest truth. Jeff and Debra are an easy couple to be open with because of their own warmth and authenticity. (808.874.6411)

Joan and Tomas Heartfield offer sessions addressing couples' communication as well as their sexuality. Their counseling studio is a charming octagonal cottage at the end of a long dirt road in Upcountry Maui. Joan and Tomas offer a workshop called *Conversations that Matter* that is particularly popular with local residents. They met when she was leading an ecotour group in the jungles of Ecuador and their evident respect for each other and genuine enthusiasm for their work make them particularly effective. (808.572.1250)

Kutira and Raphael conduct tantra sexual counseling sessions and group retreats at the **Kahua Hawaiian Institute for Inner Transformation** about 20 minutes from Makawao in Upcountry. (877.524.8250) *(See our website www.alohawellnesstravel.com for an article on Tantra)*

Finally, **Eve Hogan**, the author of several books on relationships, is also an online relationship advisor. She is available to do counseling, particularly by means of the labyrinth as a route to greater awareness for couples. (808.879.8648)

Relationship counseling can be done with both partners present or you can have an individual session to explore issues and gain clarity. Working on your relationship while on Maui, one of the most romantic destinations in the world, gives you the space, time and nurturing environment to reflect deeply and make changes on all levels of your being. This could make your vacation to Maui one of the most significant events of your life.

9. Pursue Family Harmony With Intention and Awareness

Families are constantly struggling to achieve a greater level of balance and harmony. As such, they are often our best learning laboratory. On a family vacation to Maui you may want to explore activities that can heal old wounds and promote better communication and understanding. Many of the wellness suggestions throughout this chapter can be adapted to achieve this. The process begins with "intention." This means deciding as a family—however that family is constructed—on the goal of greater harmony and balance. Of course, you may not get the same level of commitment from every family member, but that can evolve if it seems more like fun than a hassle (we're especially thinking of teenagers here).

The next step toward your goal is to have each person commit (at least to some extent) to identifying what within him or her is getting in the way. What do you each need to learn about your role in the family in order to contribute to family peace and harmony? A notebook can be helpful to jot down ideas and record thoughts and experiences.

As you set out to explore ideas in this chapter, begin each one with the intention to pursue harmony within the family and to discover how each person can uniquely contribute. For example, as you go to the **Maui Ocean Center**, agree that you will each look at the way the fish live together to see if there is a lesson there for you. As you go to a garden, do a nature meditation with this intention in mind. A plant that is dying because it is overshadowed and squeezed out by a larger, dominant plant may be a metaphor for a relationship in your family.

Focusing on what you need to learn and what you can contribute, rather than on what you think is wrong with the other person, will likely achieve more awareness and peace.

The principle here is that our most difficult relationships are our greatest teachers and we often find these in our family. Think about using your vacation on Maui as a wonderful opportunity for family growth.

10. Explore Ways To Create Greater Balance in Your Life

So often, vacations leave us feeling that something important is missing from our daily lives back home. The blur of our busy routine clears away during vacation only to envelop us again within hours of our return home. A wellness vacation gives us the time and resources to rise above that fog to look objectively at what changes might create more balance and harmony in our life. It is also a time to begin to manifest those changes.

For most of us a critical question is whether we are living our life values. Meeting with a life coach while on vacation can guide us to breakthrough insights as well as provide a road map for moderate to radical change. **Laura Monaco** offers life coaching and also uses the Emotional Freedom Technique to help overcome fears of making the changes you truly want to make. (808.874.7544) **Sharon Rose,** of the **Center for Self Mastery**, has successfully provided life coaching to a number of celebrities from California and the East Coast. She came to Maui several years ago to heal from a series of traumas and began her life's work of helping others live the life they yearn for. Her cottage on the slopes of Haleakalā, above Makawao, offers the perfect nurturing environment to ask those deeper questions. (808.573.3280)

Perhaps one of the things you will discover is a need for a daily practice that can bring greater peace and focus into your life. Both yoga and tai chi are forms of eastern meditative arts that can launch you into a lifelong practice promoting the peace you seek. **Pia Sanderson** of **Health Associates** in Kīhei offers classes in kundalini yoga as well as meditation. (808.874.9172) The **Maui Academy of Healing Arts** in Kīhei (808.879.4266) also offers yoga classes as well as lifestyle and self-care counseling. Yoga classes and individual instruction are available at the **Beyond Heaven Center** in Makawao (808.573.8828) as well as with **Maui Yoga Shala** in Lahaina. (808.661.7272) If you are staying at a resort hotel, ask the spa manager what they offer. For tai chi, **Ron Perfetti** is one of the most experienced and popular coaches on Maui. (808-572-6994)

Take advantage of your time on Maui to get some clarity about what might be missing in your life and what you can do to change it.

11. Connect With Your Soul in Quiet Maui Gardens

Whoever wrote "You are closer to the heart of God in a garden than anywhere else" must have visited Maui where you will find a multitude of gardens. Marvel at the wonders of the plant kingdom and allow your soul to be fed by the beauty and gentleness of this part of Maui.

The **Ali'i Garden** and **Nanea a'o Kula** (Maui Lavender) in Upcountry Maui above Kula is a partnership between **Ali'i Chang** who owns the garden, and **Darlene Ane and Easter Martin** who create the lavender products. They conduct tours of the garden and sell products ranging from lavender eye pillows to a lavender herbal salt, which goes wonderfully on everything from meatloaf to vegetable dishes. Darlene and Easter also serve a British-style high tea as well as luncheon several times a week, centered around lavender food items. This may be your only chance in this lifetime to eat lavender scones! Call ahead for an appointment to see the garden as well as to schedule a high tea or luncheon. (808.283.3777) (Fee for tea and luncheon)

Another favorite is **Kula Botanical Garden** on Upper Kula Road, (Hwy 377). This privately owned hillside garden is great for picnics or just quiet time to commune with nature. You'll find a koi fish pond, covered bridge, gazebo, orchid garden, and strategically placed benches to encourage you to spend time in reflection there. No need for an appointment. (808.878.1715) (Admission Fee) (Open every day of the year including holidays, from 9:00 – 4:00.)

On the road through 'Īao Valley behind Wailuku are three places that we recommend. First, is the **Tropical Gardens of Maui**, a privately owned garden that is a popular site for weddings. There are four acres of plants, garden paths and a lily pond providing both beauty and serenity. Open from 9:00 – 5:00 Monday through Saturday. (808.244.3085) (Admission Fee)

On the same road, toward the end of the valley, **Kepaniwai County Park and Heritage Gardens** has a large picnic area with sheltered tables and a cultural display of houses ranging from a Polynesian thatched roof hut to a Japanese bathhouse representing the various cultures and historical periods of Hawai'i. You'll also find a beautifully maintained Japanese garden. The towering mountains surrounding the park and the stream moving through it make this public garden especially appealing. (Free)

On down the road, near the parking lot of 'Īao Valley State Monument, you'll find the **Hawai'i Nature Center**. Although the Center is designed largely as an interactive educational center, they do offer hikes Monday through Friday into the 'Īao Valley. The 1.5 – 2 hour hikes are highly recommended because of the excellent guides as well as the exquisite scenery. The hikes are scheduled at 11:30 and 1:30. Center hours are 10:00 – 4:00 Monday through Sunday. (808.244.6500) (Admission and Hike Fee)

At the end of the road you'll encounter one of the most famous and beautiful natural landmarks of Maui, the **'Īao Needle**, a single spire towering 1200 feet above the valley. The area is often misty, inviting you to almost whisper as you begin the walk up to the waterfall. In ancient times it was identified by Kakae, the ruler of Maui, as a sacred burial ground for royalty. Walk up to the lookout point, if you haven't taken the hike with the Nature Center, and feel the energy of this extraordinary place.

There are several garden opportunities on the way to Hāna. We especially liked the **Ke'anae Arboretum** at the 16-mile marker. If you've passed up other opportunities to stop at lookouts along the way, by the time you reach mile 16, your body will be begging for a stretch. The Arboretum is an easy and lovely one mile round trip in and out. (Free)

Just on the edge of Hāna, at the 31-mile marker, is **Kahana Gardens**. Here you will find one of the most sacred places in Hawai'i, the magnificent **Pi'ilanihale Heiau,** which is the largest sacred site in all of Polynesia. This National Tropical Botanical Garden is one of several throughout the state dedicated to administering gardens of extraordinary beauty and historical significance. Hours are from 10:00 – 2:00 Monday through Friday. (808.332.7324) (Admission Fee)

Let your garden visits be a time to feel deep gratitude for the beauty and healing quality of nature in Hawai'i. Perhaps you will decide to make visiting a garden, or creating a garden, a regular practice when you return home.

12. Take Hawai'i's Healing Energy Home With You: Buy Hawai'i's Healing Products

Maui makes some of the best natural products for healing and soothing the body. **Maui Medicinal**, the creation of **Mark Dunlap**, works only with certified organic farms in transforming their healing herbs into top quality medicinal products. Their *noni* product is particularly recommended because it is organically grown, hand picked at the perfect stage of ripeness, and processed to preserve the healing enzymes. Research has shown that *noni* that is grown in the volcanic soil of Hawai'i, hand picked and freeze dried, is far superior in its healing capacity. Maui Medicinal sells their products almost exclusively in food and health stores in Hawai'i. (Visit www.alohawellnesstravel.com for more information about *noni*) (1.800.936.6532)

Nanea a'o Kula is a company specializing in lavender products, one of the least allergenic of all the flowers. Lavender has been known to calm nerves, relieve stress and headaches, and lift spirits as well as ease depression and arouse passions (according to Darlene and Easter). You'll probably be as surprised as we were with the variety of ways that lavender can become part of your life. They've created lavender vinegar, lavender herb salt (definitely our favorite), lavender tea, lavender eye pillows, and lavender soap. (808.283.3777)

You'll see at the end of this chapter several skin products that are made on Maui. Somewhat of a cottage industry, these wellness products are pure and free of additives. Often they have been inspired by the pain and discomfort of skin problems. **Betty Schneider** created her own line of all natural facial products **Derma Spa Essentials** because commercial creams and oils containing artificial substances and aromas created havoc with her skin. She found she wasn't alone with this problem so she came up with a solution. Betty orders the herbs from the Far East and mixes the formulas in her home. Five-star spas and salons use them worldwide but her pure smooth complexion is sufficient testimonial. You'll find her at the Grande Wailea Spa. She is also available to do facials or sells her products out of her home. (800.772.1933)

13. Experience the Peace and Serenity of the Underwater World

Our ocean friends offer a unique healing experience and there is no better place than Maui to visit their world and experience their gifts. The tranquility of their environment, the ease with which they move, their cooperation with each other and the silence that envelopes them offer healing on many levels. Firefighters and rescue workers from the trauma of 9/11 were brought to Hawai'i as guests of the state in early January 2002. One of their visits included the **Maui Ocean Center**, where one man, observing how the fish coexisted so gracefully in a seemingly small environment, commented, "I wish we could do that." This is a world class aquarium which will not only delight and fascinate you but, when undertaken as a wellness experience, can offer metaphors for life and an experience of tranquility. It is located at Mā'alaea Harbor. (808.270.7000)

Maui is also a world destination for whale watching. Between the months of November and May, these gentle mammals return to their winter home in Hawai'i with many of them choosing the coastal areas of Maui as their favorite. The result is that Maui's waters have become famous for watching and researching the behaviors of whales. The primary research organizations are the **Whale Research Center**, (808.249.8245) which is part of the **Island Marine Institute**, and the **Pacific Whale Foundation**. (808.879.8811) Both of these organizations offer educational whale watching experiences, often conducted by the scientists who are doing the research. The size of these underwater giants is part of the fascination that draws people to Maui for whale watching but their playfulness and gentleness is what truly touches us. It is common to leave a whale-watching trip feeling both awe and reverence. Many people also find themselves feeling protective of these special underwater creatures that are both huge and vulnerable. The efforts to protect them and understand them better deserve our support.

Scuba offers a superb opportunity for delight in connecting with the natural underwater world. It can also be a powerful meditative experience. Regardless of how chaotic the surface conditions are, when you drop just a few feet below the surface, you discover tranquility and calm. You can look up and observe the chaos, without being a part of it…slow, steady breathing in the midst of turquoise tranquility, looking eye to eye with ancient turtles, listening to the whales sing, swimming with a school of fish, in forced verbal silence; this is truly one of the great spiritual experiences on the planet. A mom and pop scuba diving charter business on Maui, **Mākena Coast Charters,** takes beginners (introductory divers), certified divers and snorkelers to Molokini and the Mākena Coast on a daily basis. (808.874.1273)

Sea Fire Charters is considered by locals to be one of the best snorkeling companies on Maui. It operates an 18 passenger motorized raft out of the Kīhei Boat Ramp and provides daily snorkel trips. This owner-operated company has a high regard for sea life, safety and fun. (808.879.2201)

Finally, if you're satisfied to get or rent your own snorkel gear and explore good snorkeling beaches at your leisure, here are some suggestions. Snorkeling and diving are best done early in the morning (before 11:00) as the tradewinds typically pick up in the early afternoons making the surface conditions turbulent. **Ulua Beach** in Wailea is a popular snorkel spot for safe, easy entry snorkeling. It is located off of Wailea Alanui right between the Renaissance and Outrigger Resorts. There is a sign and a parking lot for easy access. Further south past Mākena Beach, just before La Pérouse Bay, is **Ahihi Bay Marine Reserve**. A cove just off Mākena Road is popular for snorkeling and you can park once you've reached the lava rock fields. The reserve offers pristine, remote snorkeling areas. **La Pérouse Bay** at the very end of Mākena road also has good snorkeling and quite often is a popular spot for sighting dolphins. Another favorite for shore snorkeling is **Black Rock** off of the Sheraton in Ka'anapali. Reportedly, this is the "best" shore snorkeling spot on Maui's westside.

While on vacation in Maui, give yourself a gift of at least one of the many opportunities to experience the peace and serenity of the underwater world.

14. Find Tranquility in Maui's Other World: Drive Through Upcountry Maui

Throughout this chapter, many of our suggestions take you to Upcountry Maui for a wellness experience of one sort or another. Now we're suggesting that you just go there to *be* rather than to *do*. A drive through this wonderful part of Maui will introduce you to a new level of tranquility and joy. The roads are free of traffic and the hillsides are alive with flowers and butterflies (in season). Don't let a rainy day discourage you, because they are frequent. The lush green hillsides have a distinct appeal with the rain and mist sweeping over them.

You will take Haleakalā Hwy #37 to reach this area. Known as Lower Kula Road, the route takes you through rolling green hills with broad vistas of the valley below. Along the way you'll come across one of the sacred places mentioned earlier, **St. John's Episcopal Church**. Shortly beyond the church is a good place to stop for a break and stretch—**Grandma's Coffee House**. They have good sandwiches to eat or take out and their pineapple coconut squares are a favorite. The same family has owned this shop for four generations and it's claim to fame as a coffee house is both the good coffee and the fact that it has been raised, handpicked and brewed there from the days that "Grandma" first opened her little wayside stop. On the left just past Grandma's is a turnoff to the **Kula Hospital and Clinic**. The garden with fountain, quiet serenity, views over the valley and careful landscaping make this worth a stop.

As you return to Lower Kula Road to continue your exploration of Upcountry, you will come across the **Sun Yat Sen Park** on your right. This park is a monument to the early Chinese immigrants who first came to Upcountry to work the land. Most of them are gone now but those who remain take responsibility for tending the park. The Chinese statues are arranged in a somewhat haphazard fashion in a small square of pastureland. But they were important to people who knew and cared about this land many years ago.

Your next destination on Lower Kula Road will be the **Tedeschi Winery**. Don't miss the wine testing opportunity to experience "pineapple wine". It will make a unique gift for your wine loving friends. There is much history to this oldest winery in Hawai'i. It once was a retreat for King Kalākaua, and changed hands several times as various people tried to make it a viable ranch. The Winery is now on the **Ulupalakua Ranch** property but is a separate corporation. Grounds around the Winery are lovely and well kept with magnificent trees that offer both shade and a suggestion of the history they have witnessed. Across the road from the winery is the Ulupalakua Ranch's general store. They serve tasty sandwiches, sell many products made in Hawai'i and have a limited supply of groceries. Down the road a bit from the winery is a church that still provides solace and inspiration to the small community of this upcountry ranch land. As you continue on past the winery and the church, the road takes you through wooded hillsides alternating with flowing pastureland until you come to a quiet, desolate lava field. This road ultimately leads to Hāna becoming a rather rough dirt road that you are asked not to drive on with a rental car. It can be especially troublesome after a heavy rain.

On the return drive, take the turn off to Upper Kula Road, Route 377. A favorite garden along this road is **Kula Botanical Garden**. As you drive along Upper Kula Road you will often see buckets of protea sitting by the side of the road inviting you to help yourself. They ask, of course, that you drop money in the appropriate container. There are also a number of protea farms offering tours. If this interests you, call the **Maui Flower Growers Association** in advance to get a list of those farms. (808.878.6357)

As you progress along Upper Kula Road you might want to stop at the **Kula Lodge** for a break since the intention is leisure. Their dining room looks off over the valley providing an inviting atmosphere for relaxing. Here you also will find the **Curtis Wilson Cost Gallery** described in # 7. Continuing on the road, look for the Olinda/Makawao cutoff to the right that will take you on a backroad adventure into Makawao. This narrow, winding country road is lined with eucalyptus trees and occasional horse pastures.

Finally, don't miss **Makawao**, the town center of Upcountry, and the capital of cowboy country on Maui. Western-style false storefronts and two story buildings give a feeling of the old West. You'll even find what appears to be a hitching post or two. This is a charming town with many boutiques, artists' galleries and several places to have refreshments outside in the fresh Upcountry air.

If your energy and sense of adventure are still intact, consider another jaunt straight out of Makawao up the mountain on Olinda Road. You'll go by a rather non-descript coral church, **Po'okela Church**, built in 1843, and begin to climb a winding road higher and higher, past estates tucked into the forest, through eucalyptus groves until you reach the Tree Growth Research Area run by the University of Hawai'i. On the way back down you will encounter several places to pull over and enjoy the view.

When you return to your coastal resort accommodations, if this is where you are staying, you will surely appreciate that you have been in another world. The soothing tranquility and lush greenness of your drive through Upcountry will linger in your memory.

15. Nourish Body and Soul With A Picnic In Paradise

Because the beauty and nurturing climate of Hawai'i invites you to spend as much time as possible outdoors, it's only natural that eating outdoors would be one of the options. We consider a picnic in paradise one of our favorite wellness experiences. There is something about nourishing the body in the midst of nature that also nourishes the soul. Depending on where you picnic, the tradewinds will often support you in having a picnic without bugs—a true paradise!

Returning to the drive through Upcountry, if you have "picnic" in mind, there are several places to stop in Makawao at the beginning of your trip to stock up. **Casanova's** has a good carryout as does the **Café del Sol** in the **Paniolo Courtyard**. If you are making Makawao your stop at the end of the trip, you can buy sandwiches at Grandma's Coffee Shop along Lower Kula Road, mentioned above. You can also get picnic supplies at the **Ulupalakua Country Store** across the road from the Winery.

Picnic locations will call to you throughout your drive. The gardens of the **Kula Hospital and Clinic** have picnic tables; some with a view and others near the fountain. **Tedeschi Winery** has several picnic tables on the carefully manicured grounds. On Upper Kula Road, the **Kula Botanical Gardens** welcomes picnickers. They have tables outside the garden along with cold drinks but don't object to your taking your picnic into the gardens. There are no tables there although you'll find a lovely stretch of lawn to spread out on as well as benches throughout the garden.

Consider a sunset picnic along the beachfront sidewalk stretching from the Wailea hotels to the Fairmont Kea Lani. Here you will find a breathtaking shoreline which is especially spectacular during sunset. There are also many beachside parks with picnic tables stretching along the coastline from Nāpili Bay to Lahaina to Kīhei. If you have a picnic in mind, there will be no shortage of places to discover.

Having a picnic in some of the most beautiful natural surroundings you are likely to experience will surely nurture and nourish you on all levels.

Relaxation and Rejuvenation

16. Nurture Your Body With Massage and Spa Treatments

Perhaps the first goal of a wellness vacation is to relax and let go of the stress that is part of your normal life. Relaxation is needed mentally, emotionally, and physically. As you unwind you become more open to all of the possibilities waiting to be discovered. Maui offers many opportunities to truly relax at a deep level.

A great way to begin is with a "flotation session" at the **New Waves Center** in Makawao. You will find yourself floating weightlessly in salt water at skin temperature, free from all other sensory stimuli. Benefits of Flotation R.E.S.T. (restricted environmental stimulation therapy) include deep relaxation, expanded mental awareness, enhanced creativity and accelerated learning, reduced stress hormone levels, and increased production of endorphins, the body's natural feel good pain killers. (808.572.0664)

Nearly every resort along the coast has a spa or offers massage and body work experiences. We enjoyed two in particular. **The Spa Grande** at the **Grand Wailea Resort** is the "grandmother" of Maui's spas. It was one of the first Maui resort spas and has been voted one of the top ten spas in the United States by *Condé Nast* and *Travel & Leisure* magazines. The huge bath area brings to mind images of ancient Rome replete with fruit, healthy drinks, and pampering attendants.

An attractive alternative is the **Wailea Massage and Body Work Center** at the **Renaissance Wailea Beach Resort**. The smaller scale creates a more personalized feel and they strive to make their services affordable without cutting quality. Their ocean side massage is a favorite. (808.879.8244)

If you prefer to have a massage in your room **Aloha Spa** (808.573.2323) sends individual massage therapists to you.

Many opportunities exist outside the resort area. **Candle Summers** has created a spa-type center in her home above Kula in

Upcountry. Many people who make an appointment for a massage come early to sit in her garden and drink tea, or mellow out in her massage chair or enjoy her hot tub and Jacuzzi in a homey environment. (808.878.6484)

For the price of one spa treatment, you can have a massage nearly every day of your vacation if you go to a massage school. In Makawao, the students of the **Maui School of Therapeutic Massage** offer massages as part of their training. (808.572.2277) A similar arrangement is available at the **Spa Luna** in Ha'ikū where students enrolled in the aesthetician program also offer facials. (808.575.2440) The **Maui Academy of Healing Arts** in Kīhei offers student massages using Eastern, Western, and Hawaiian massage techniques. (808.879.4266)

Still, the best deal for relaxing as you launch your vacation may well be to just "hang loose" at the beach. The ocean is a natural healer.

Complementary Treatment Therapies

17. Seek Alternative Approaches to Health and Healing

The wide variety of highly qualified wellness providers makes Maui a great place to try any treatment that may not be available where you live. For example, a couple from the Northwest who come to Maui annually schedule a rolfing session each year because the closest rolfer to their home is two hours away.

Many of the providers listed are in Upcountry Maui, in particular, Makawao. You might want to schedule a day in Makawao, have lunch at Casanovas or the Café del Sol in the Paniolo Courtyard and browse through the shops and art galleries in between meetings with wellness practitioners.

Anne Hoff is a highly experienced rolfer who found her passion through a series of coincidences while living in Japan. Rolfing is the product of 50 years of study by Ida Rolf, PhD. The ideas behind her work are simple. They include the premise that most people are significantly out of alignment with gravity, that they would function better if they were lined up with the gravitational field of the earth and that our system is sufficiently plastic that this alignment can take place at any time of our life.

Anne's friendly air of competence encourages immediate trust. Her office is in the **Grace Health Clinic** in the courtyard behind the Dragon's Den Health Store. (808.572.6699)

The Dragon's Den is part of this courtyard complex of wellness providers. It is a combination of healing center and herb shop with the longest standing herb shop on the island. Here you'll find herbs from China in a jar carefully selected for purity and freeze dried. Ask about their free weekly consultations. Across a brick path in the courtyard is the healing center with a focus on oriental medicine. **Dr. Malik Cotter** was trained in China and has a degree in Traditional Chinese Medicine. His wife **Johanna** is a partner at the healing center teaching yoga and qigong and providing massage therapy. The healing center supports and gives guidance on lifestyle change that provides a long lasting wellness experience. They also offer colonics and detoxification treatments.

Dr. David Kern, director of **Grace Health Clinic**, is also located in this courtyard. One of the most experienced and well-respected naturopaths on Maui, he works with neck and back pain, immune functions, diet & nutrition, natural hormones and anti-aging. Dr. Kern is also a licensed acupuncturist. He operates out of offices in . Makawao (808.572.6091) and Kīhei (808.874.5660).

Shelley St. John's office is one of those you'll find in this charming courtyard of wellness providers. She offers colon hydrotherapies which is a relatively painless way of clearing out accumulated toxins. Shelley is an experienced nurse and administers her therapy with professionalism and gentleness. (808.870.8168)

Before you leave Upcountry, we want you to know about **Dr. Julie Holmes** and thermology, an alternative to mammography that has a far higher success rate in identifying early stage, precancerous cells. Dr. Holmes has one of the few breast thermography machines in Hawai'i. According to an article by Dr. Linda Fickes on our website *"Breast thermology has the ability to detect the first signs that a cancer may be forming – up to ten years before any other procedure can detect it. Extensive clinical trials have shown that breast thermology augments the longterm survival rate of its recipients by 61%. Thermology is 90% accurate for early diagnosis of breast disease. There is no health risk to the use of thermology – there is no compression* *or radiation involved. Thermology is accurate for all ages, even for those with implants or mastectomies. Thermology reads the heat and activity of the cells instead of reading shapes like a mammogram does. The thermal image can find heat emitting lesions years before there is enough of a shape to show on a mammogram. It can show whether a breast lump is a risk or not and rate its level of risk."*

A quick trip to Dr. Holmes' office in Kula for a screening will allow you to return home with more information about your health than many of your women friends. We encourage you to visit Dr. Holmes and also read more about this process on our website www.alohawellnesstravel.com. (808.878.3267)

If you are interested in a chiropractic adjustment, **Aloha Family Chiropractic and Wellness Centers** is a family friendly place with game ball machines for kids to play with while you're getting a treatment. They have offices in Kīhei and Kahului. (808.874.9644 in Kīhei and 808.871.1170 in Kahului)

As you continue your exploration of alternative approaches to health and healing, **Debra Greene, Ph.D**, can introduce you to one of the most fascinating forms of diagnosis we've encountered; kinesiology. This process is increasingly popular with complementary health providers although it has yet to be embraced by the Western medical profession. Kinesiology operates similar to the lie detector test. From that process, we have known for many years that our body will tell the truth even when we may consciously choose to do otherwise. Through kinesiology, our body will reveal information about our health that isn't otherwise accessible, even with the most sophisticated medical devices. Debra, a certified kinesiologist in Kīhei uses a modality called Transformational Kinesiology (TK), which combines the art of muscle testing with the science of subtle energies. Manual muscle testing and dialogue are used to find blockages on a variety of levels—physical, emotional, mental, and spiritual. In a TK session, you identify and transform self-limiting beliefs that prevent you from achieving the balance and harmony you seek. (808.874.6441) *(See the article by Debra about kinesiology in Chapter Three.)*

Finally, there is a unique acupuncture opportunity available through **Margy Campbell** who will bring her needles to you. (808.385.1643)

18. Retrieve your spirit and joy in life: Visit a Spiritual Healer

Many people come to Hawai'i to recover from a loss, to move past grief, or to try to rediscover joy. The spiritual energy and beauty of the land as well as the friendliness of the people may help you rediscover joy while you're in Hawai'i, but when you return home the emotional or mental state that drove you here to begin with reappears. Perhaps during your Hawai'i wellness vacation you can take a larger step that will have a more lasting impact.

There are several particularly effective healers to support you in achieving a lasting process of spiritual recovery. **Robin Youngblood**, a Native American healer with years of successful experience in using her indigenous skills, understands how to help others heal at the spiritual level. She offers soul retrieval work as well as a sweat lodge experience. (808.573.2784)

Maha Conyers is originally from Germany but has studied healing arts all over the world. She has led highly successful and popular group healing experiences and has worked individually with people who have come to Maui specifically to meet with her. Maha is prepared to create an individualized spiritual healing retreat for you from start to finish. She will book you into a healing accommodation, link you with the wellness resources you most need, and offer her own considerable skills as a wellness practitioner. One highly placed executive came to her for a life makeover and left describing Maha as his savior. (808 876.0409)

Mara Gerhard, also from Germany, has trained extensively in the Hawaiian approach to spiritual healing. Recognized by her Hawaiian teachers as having the *mana* (spiritual energy) necessary to bridge cultures, Mara offers one, two, or three day Huna Intensives, individual sessions, past life regressions, hypnosis, and neurolinguistic programming. (808.874.1884)

Finally, **Alalani Hill** has trained for many years with one of the last great Hawaiian healing elders (*kahuna*) on Maui and is now offering her skills and knowledge in Hawaiian and other indigenous healing methods to people seeking a deeper level of lasting harmony and balance. (808.879.1499) *(See her article on Hawaiian Sacred Healing in Chapter Three.)*

Interestingly, many of the Hawaiian healing elders have chosen to pass their wisdom on to non-Hawaiians. For many years it was forbidden for a Hawaiian to teach the secrets of their healing wisdom. After the laws were removed, the taboo continued to be supported within the Hawaiian culture. Traditionally, only a person who was identified from an early age as having "the gift," and was tutored over many years, could practice Hawaiian healing. Unfortunately, few young Hawaiians were interested. Several years ago, a native Hawaiian healer by the name of Papa Auwae chose to break with tradition and actively seek out those who were willing to take the healing wisdom and use it for the betterment of others. Since then, others have identified gifted people to tutor and mentor. Alalani and Mara are two of the non-Hawaiians who have been trained by Hawaiian healers.

Fitness and Sports

19. Start a Fitness Program/Improve Your Game

The gentle climate, trade winds and moderate temperatures of Hawai'i invite you to be outdoors. In this environment we tend to expose more of our bodies than in less nurturing climes and this tends to make us more aware of how we look and, hopefully, how we feel physically. This climate also encourages people from all over the world to come to Hawai'i for sports activities.

On Maui, the primary sport is golf with most of the courses along the Kapalua to Mākena coast. You will also find tennis courts, both public and private, or resort owned. Resorts have tennis and golf pros available to help improve your game. An alternative approach to skill enhancement would be a session with **Lorraine Bennington,** a sports hypnotherapist in Makawao. Through subconscious programming, she can help you overcome apparent blocks to your maximum performance. (808.573.3383) *(See her article on hypnotherapy in Chapter Three.)*

If you are interested in taking advantage of Hawai'i's climate to improve your fitness or begin a fitness program, **Strong Stretched & Centered** in Kahului has an excellent, comprehensive fitness program that includes an initial assessment, personal coach, and workout facility. An interesting option is to turn your life over to them for the entire vacation, booking into one of their condo rentals, working with their nutritionist, being coached by a personal fitness trainer, and working out on a regular basis at their facility. They do allow time off for good behavior in case you want to explore other wellness options. (808.572.2125)

And then there is biking. Maui is known for the ritual of the long, early morning bike ride down Haleakalā Volcano. This bike ride is as strong a tradition as the drive up Haleakalā to see the sunrise. Since the only muscle strain on this down-the-mountain ride is the hand muscle applying the brakes, this ride doesn't qualify as a fitness exercise. There is, however, the opportunity to bike throughout Upcountry Maui, using your own strength and muscles to get around.

Aloha Bicycle Tours, the only bike company we've discovered that doesn't focus on the "downhill ride", takes their customers up a short distance on Haleakalā road. They then start down and begin wandering along the tranquil Upcountry roads to the Tedeschi Winery. Each trip is launched with a light breakfast and ends with a healthy picnic lunch at the winery. The company is family owned by **Marc and Karen Friezner**. Karen prepares breakfast and lunch and both Marc and Karen spend time with their customers over lunch to share information about other hidden Upcountry adventures. One unique aspect of their tour is that Marc will individualize the experience, sending cyclists who want more exercise up a side road for a serious workout. (808.249.0911)

To stretch and strain even more of your muscles, **The Hyatt Regency Maui** has launched what it calls **Beach Boot Camp**. Their high impact workout takes place on the beach and in the ocean—something you're unlikely to experience back home. (808.661.1234).

Finally, surfing is not only an exercise in fitness but also a spiritual experience as practiced by the traditional Hawaiians. Check with your travel host or local surf shop to see what is available in the way of surfing lessons.

Travel to Serve Others

20. Leave Maui Better Than You Found It

Once you have begun to experience the healing energy of Maui, you may want to consider how you can schedule an opportunity to give back to this beautiful island and its people. A few hours, a day, or a weekend invested in leaving Maui better than you found it will stay with you as a special memory when you return home.

Maui is known internationally as the place to whale watch. While hundreds of people come to Maui during the months of November through April to watch whales play, nurture their young, and engage in mating rituals, Maui is unique with its opportunities to give back to the whales. **The Pacific Whale Foundation** offers many volunteer opportunities to contribute to the well-being of these gentle giants. Your work with the Foundation may vary from helping with customer service mailings to doing a whale count. Regardless of what you do, you will have the good feeling of working next to people dedicated to better understanding and supporting the whales that call Maui their part-time home. (808.879.8860)

The **Maui Ocean Center** also has volunteer opportunities. This world class aquarium is healing just to be around. Their commitment is to increase sensitivity to our fellow travelers under the sea and to help us understand how we impact their world. (808.270.7000)

Finally, the **Hawai'i Nature Center** (808.244.6500 ext. 12) and **The Nature Conservancy** (808.572.7849) offer opportunities to serve the *'āina*. Work can range from trail clearing to gardening and landscaping. It's important to wear sturdy shoes and clothes for outdoor activity—your swimsuit and/or shorts and sandals won't do.

Healing Accommodations

The success of a wellness vacation will be strongly influenced by where you stay. A healing accommodation needs to give you space to breathe, an environment that nurtures and supports your wellness goals and people who genuinely care about you. We hope you will find that the following places are truly healing accommodations for you

Along the Ka'anapali coast is the **Ritz-Carlton**, at the far end of the road past Lahaina, on Hwy 30. It is positioned on a hill overlooking the ocean and blends into nature to the extent that you can see it only as you drive up to the entrance. The Ritz went through a humbling experience 10 years ago when Hawaiians, protesting their plans to build over Hawaiian sacred sites, brought its construction to a halt. Now the resort honors these ancient sacred ruins and has gone to great lengths to incorporate sensitivity to Hawaiian culture into all they do. The aloha spirit is ever present and the spa emphasizes Hawaiian healing arts. (808.669.6200) (Luxury)

The **Ka'anapali Beach Hotel**, along the same coast, is a regular winner of the state's "Keep it Hawai'i" awards. It is one of the most popular resorts on Maui, in large part because of the warmth, generosity, and aloha spirit of its staff. The hotel staff dearly love General Manager Mike White and the joy they all feel in working at this special resort is demonstrated daily. Staff members are encouraged to pull out their instruments and offer impromptu concerts for the visitors. (808.661.0011 or 800.262.8450) (Moderate to Deluxe)

Near the Kīhei/Wailea coast, the romantic **MauiHouse** with your hosts **Debra Greene and Jeffrey Marsh**, is situated on over half an acre of lush greenery and surrounded by a fifteen foot flowering hedge. MauiHouse is a charming one bedroom cottage that overlooks its own private hot tub and swimming pool; perfect for a moonlight swim. Away from the tourist bustle, yet just one mile to the beach and Kīhei town, this is ideal for people who are combining their time on Maui with a couple's retreat. The cottage has a full kitchen and bath with high-beamed ceilings and sliding glass doors. (808.874.6441) (Moderate)

Upcountry Maui offers several places to stay for a wellness retreat. **The Kula Lodge** has guest cottages with lofts and some have fireplaces for the cool evenings that are part of Upcountry life. The rooms are simple and comfortable with wooden balconies from which to enjoy the view over the valley to the ocean. The restaurant is beautifully situated with a wide expanse of windows. Anticipate enjoying the food as much as you will the view. (808.878.1535) (Moderate)

Two other accommodations in Upcountry market themselves as retreats but have places to stay for individuals and couples. **Kahua 'O Mali 'O Bamboo Farm** and **Bamboo Sanctuary Retreat** are each about fifteen minutes from Makawao. They both offer massage and body work with staff on site. The Bamboo Farm has three separate, beautifully designed and decorated houses with bamboo as the theme. Scattered throughout the attractively landscaped property with paths down to the ocean, each house has cooking facilities. (877.524.8250) (Moderate to Deluxe)

The Bamboo Sanctuary Retreat is located on a quiet, wooded hillside. It is a dormitory-like structure with bedrooms and shared baths. Guests also share the kitchen. You'll find paths and serene natural beauty as well as a yoga room to support your meditation and retreat goals. (808.572.4897) (Budget)

Among our recommendations for healing accommodations are several exquisite B&Bs only a few minutes drive down backcountry roads from Makawao. All four are in the Twin Falls area just off the Hāna Highway. Each is decorated with superb taste, exhibiting the personal touch of the owner, and is arrayed throughout with flower arrangements.

Diane Epstein, a well-known silk artist, owns **Ha'ikū Cottage Maui**. Your stay will be in a separate cottage with porch overlooking her garden. The cottage has a vaulted ceiling, natural wood floors, cooking facilities and flower arrangements throughout. Diane is an enthusiastic, friendly and generous host. More than one guest has left with the feeling they have made a new friend. You may even decide to buy one of her exquisite silk creations. (808.572.9501) (Moderate)

Maluhia Hale is perched on a hillside looking off over the ocean. It offers both a separate two bedroom cottage and a studio with private entrance at the corner of the main house. The accommodations are a symphony in white with lace trimmed pillowcases, crocheted bedspreads, luscious deep flokati rugs and the best coffee we've had accompanied by a great breakfast selection of fruit and pastry. Owner **Diane Garrett** affords you the privacy you may want at the same time she is ready to share ideas and suggestions for your stay on Maui. (808.572.2959) (Moderate)

Halfway to Hāna House is a short distance down a dirt road off the main highway to Hāna. The guest room is at the lower level of the house with a separate entrance through the garden. Just outside the room is a patio looking out over the fields to the ocean. The beautifully color coordinated room is cozy with a queen size bed and reading chair, microwave, toaster oven, and a refrigerator at the back door supplied with a variety of beverages. Flower arrangements grace the bedroom and bathroom. As part of your healing experience, you can sit in bed, enjoy the uninterrupted ocean view and soak up the quiet of this peaceful rural environment. The hostess was on the mainland for a family emergency so we weren't able to meet her. (808. 572.1176) (Moderate)

Maui Tea House is one of the most unique B&Bs we've encountered. Guests are treated to a beautifully decorated three-room cottage surrounded by rain forest. The screened-in porch is furnished with a small dining table and comfortable couch giving you open exposure to the lush, tropical vegetation. Inside is a kitchen, living room combination with a sofa perfect for curling up on during those rainy times that give the rain forest its name. And then there is the bedroom. This may be the only place in Maui where you can have your morning coffee in bed while looking out one window to Haleakalā, and the other window to the ocean with a rain forest spread out in front of you. A short walk across the deck is the outdoor shower and toilet facility. A guest book allows you to share in the healing stories visitors before you experienced in this special tropical paradise. Hostess **Ann DeWeese** prides herself on creative breakfasts that are left ready for you to enjoy on your porch table. (808.572.5610) (Moderate)

The **Silver Cloud Ranch** is most frequently mentioned by locals as their favorite B&B. It's a nine acre "ranch" in Upcountry between Kula and the Tedeschi Winery. The ranch house has six bedrooms. There is also a private cottage and a bunkhouse with 5 studios. The location with its beautiful views, the friendliness of the staff and its full breakfast make this a special place. (808. 878.6101) (Budget to Moderate)

A hidden secret in Upcountry Maui is the **Retreat House of St. John's Episcopal Church** along Lower Kula Road, down the hill from the church. The bedrooms are private whereas the kitchen, dining and living room (with a view over the valley) are shared. Guests are expected to provide their own food. (808. 876.0280) (Budget)

Finally, we encourage you to consider one or more nights in Hāna. This isolated village returns you to true Hawai'i. Hāna provides the quiet beauty and serenity many of us need in order to truly get away. It isn't for everyone, however. If you find peace and joy in the activity of the coastal resorts, you may be disappointed in Hāna. As one man said, "Yeah, I drove to Hāna and I didn't get it."

Enthusiastic, visionary owners recently purchased the **Hotel Hāna-Maui**. They feel a responsibility for the land, a commitment to the community and they share the vision of Hāna as a wellness mecca. The hotel is creating a wellness center that will draw on ancient Hawaiian, international and modern approaches to achieving balance and harmony on all levels. They particularly focus on guiding visitors into the surrounding countryside to connect with and learn about nature, Hawaiian style. The hotel consists of cottages scattered around the grounds overlooking the ocean. Most rooms have a hot tub on their deck. (808.248.8211) (Luxury)

For a somewhat more moderately priced stay, there is the **Heavenly Hāna Inn**. Guests enter through a Japanese door into a garden surrounding the inn. Rooms are outfitted in Japanese style. The graciousness and simple beauty of this place will surely enhance your wellness goals. (808.248.8442) (Moderate)

When in doubt, as you pursue a healing accommodation, contact **Donna Stafford** at **Chameleon Vacation Rentals**. Donna has scouted the island for accommodations with heart. She describes her criteria as looking for places that people have put their heart and soul into creating, that are authentic and have *mana* (spiritual energy). (866.575.9933)

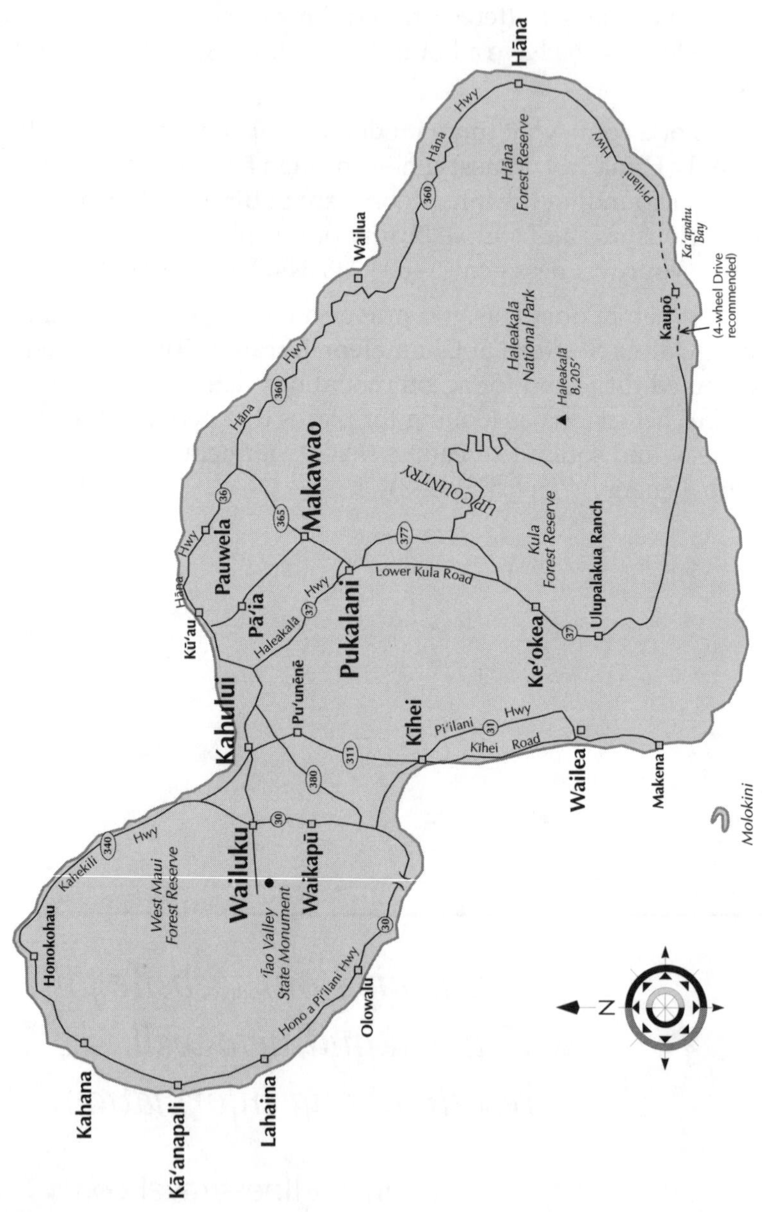

Hāna
Hāna Hwy
360
Hāna Forest Reserve
Pi'ilani Hwy
Ka'apahu Bay
Wailua
Kaupō
(4-wheel Drive recommended)
Haleakalā National Park
Haleakalā 8,205'
Makawao
UPCOUNTRY
Kula Forest Reserve
Ulupalakua Ranch
Pauwela
36
365
377
Lower Kula Road
Pā'ia
Haleakalā Hwy
37
Kū'au
Pukalani
Ke'okea
Kahului
Pu'unēnē
Kīhei
Pi'ilani Hwy
31
Kīhei Road
311
380
Wailea
Makena
Molokini
Kahekili Hwy
340
West Maui Forest Reserve
Wailuku
Waikapū
30
'Iao Valley State Monument
Honokohau
Hono a Pi'ilani Hwy
Olowalu
Kahana
Kā'anapali
Lahaina
N

Resources

The Island of Maui

MAUI - WELLNESS DIRECTORY TABLE OF CONTENTS

INNER PILGRIMAGE

Art and Art Therapy

Betty Freeland (artist)
works appear at:
Dolphin Galleries • Maui Hands
Pictures Plus • Village Galleries
contact: Jorma Palmer
808.870.7129
www.MauiArtOnline.com

Curtis Wilson Cost Gallery
Kula Lodge
Haleakala Highway, Kula
808.878.6544

Gallery Maui
3743A Baldwin Ave.
Makawao, HI 96768
808.572.8092
gallery@maui.net

Hana Coast Gallery
at Hotel Hana-Maui
808.248.8636

Hot Island Glass Studio and Gallery
The Courtyard
3720 Baldwin #101-A
Makawao, HI 96768
808.572.4517
hotglass@maui.net
www.hotislandglass.com

Maui Crafts Guild
43 Hana Highway
Paia, HI 96779
808.579.9697

Art and Art Therapy

Hui Noeau Visual Arts Center
(Offers classes. Ask for newsletter)
3841 Baldwin Avenue
Makawao, HI 96768
808.572.6560
hui@maui.net

Pacifica Island Art, Inc.
PO Box 120
Haiku, HI 96708
800.222.7327
info@islandartcards.com
www.islandartcards.com

The Art Center
2070 Vineyard
Wailuku, HI 96793
808.243.0027

The Art School
(Offers classes)
800 Office Road • Kapalua, Maui
contact: Molly McMillan
808.665.0007
info@kapaluaart.com
www.kapaluaart.com

Astrology and Numerology

The Inside Story • Hypnosis and Astrology
(hypnosis instructor & astrologer)
Hypnosis Training: (May and November) Experience dynamic self-growth and become a Certified Hypnotherapist with the National Guild of Hypnotists.
Astrological Consultation: Designed for self-knowledge and conscious life planning.
contact: Janis Mary Persons. BSW, CH, AI • Wailuku, HI
808.243.0050
janis@mysticmaui.com • www.mysticmaui.com

Helen Kritzler
Helen Kritzler is a third generation Palmist with 40 years of experience. Maui is an opening in the vortex of your life. Stop time for a moment and look into your Palm with Helen as she sees the undercurrents of your path etched in your hand while psychically answering your unspoken questions. Your fingers and hands reveal your true soul's urges.
21 Makalani Place • Makawao, HI 96768
contact: Helen Kritzler • 808.573.6343
www.mauiresources.com/helen.htm
kritzler@attglobal.net

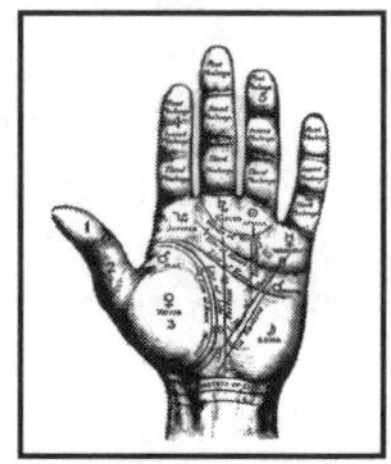

Eyes of Heaven
PO Box 951 • Lahaina, HI 96767
contact: Eliza Bassett
(Astrology/intuitive)
808.573.3039
makalani@tiki.net

Lorraine Bennington M.Ed.
(hypnotherapy and astrology, French bilingual)
PO Box 1347 • Makawao, HI 96768
808.573.3383
content@maui.net

Astrology and Numerology

Numerology
777 S. Kihei Rd. #203
Kihei, HI 96753-7508
contact: Bruce Griesman
808.875.7659
bruce224@aol.com

Anthony Piscitelli
1152 Makawao Avenue
Makawao, HI 96768
808.573.1390
anthony@ahaproductions.net
www.ahaproductions.net

Dance • Movement • Sound Therapy

Lasensua, Dance Ethnologist
Lasensua is one of the most talented and versatile dance instructors in Hawaii. Her ongoing African and Salsa dance classes draw on her years of living and traveling throughout Africa, Brazil, Cuba, Bali, India and Tahiti. African dance classes are accompanied by trained drummers and her Salsa dance class have the latest Latin music. Feel better, more fit and joyful with dance in your life. Private and group lessons.
PO Box 790161 • Paia, HI 96779
contact: Lasensua • 808.243.0550
lasensua@bigplanet.com

Brain Gym® for Memory Enhancement
"Educational Kinesiology" Explore simple techniques that sharpen and improve our memory. Learn easy, enjoyable activities that directly enhance brain function. Feel results immediately. Improve your performance —intellectual, athletic, creative, interpersonal. Private sessions and groups.
PO Box 791339 • Pā'ia, HI 96779
contact: Karen "Freesia" Peterson, M.A. • **808.573.3109**
freesia@maui.net • www.givingbackmentoring.org

Alexsandra Burt
(Feldenkrais)
124 Mahola St.
Makawao, HI 96768
808.573.8662

Movement & Sound Energetics
(and Sound Healing)
contact: Megan Don
808.573.3002
mythinmotion@yahoo.com

Ohana International Institute for Nurturing Art
PO Box 1465 • Makawao, HI 96768
808.876.0409
contact: Maha Conyers, Rev., MA, Ed.Psych
mahana@maui.net
www.maui.net/~mahana

Intuitive Guidance

Center for Self-Mastery
(intuitive guidance, personal growth)
1135 Makawao Ave. #144 • Makawao, HI 96768
contact: Sharon Rose
808.573.3280
spirit@aloha.com • www.CenterforSelfMastery.org

Hawaiian Healing

Kuhina Hawaiian Healing

Kahu Alalani is a Kahuna trained Minister. Trained in Hawaiian ministry and Lā'au lapa'au (Hawaiian healing methods and herbs). Her work includes spiritual counseling, healing sessions, Hawaiian blessings, Lā'au lapa'au, and ceremonies such as Ho'oponopono, Ho'oma'ema'e, Awa, and vow renewals. Readings on Maui or via phone are also available.

PO Box 268 • Kīhei, HI 96753
contact: Rev. Alalani Hill
808.879.1499 • ph/fax 808.875.6887
alalani@kuhina.com • www.kuhina.com

Mara Keala Gerhard

Mara is an international therapist, HUNA teacher and counselor. Huna is an ancient Hawaiian system for spiritual growth and psychology. It is sacred Hawaiian healing based on Aloha which means "let there be love between us." She offers 1, 2 or 3 day Huna Intensives, individual sessions, past life regressions, hypnosis and neurolinguistic programming.

3378-A Keha Drive • Kīhei, HI 96753
contact: Mara Keala Gerhard
808.874.1884

Hawaiian Heart Blessings

(Therapies and Heartwork)
PO Box 1036
Kula, HI 96790
contact: Maile Orme
808.573.3116
Mailemoo@juno.com

Kahuna Lā'au Lapa'au Mahi'ai

3526 Akala Drive
Kīhei, HI 96753
contact: Kaipo Kaneakua
808.226.5556

Laura Monaco

(Lomi Pohaku)
631 Kumulani Drive • Kīhei, HI 96753
808.874.7544
touch@xmail.com

Personal Development & Relationship Counseling

Avatar

Avatar is the most powerful, purest self development program available. It is experiential and enables you to rediscover yourself and align consciousness with what YOU want to achieve. Free yourself of old restraints that make you unhappy! Feel more secure about your ability to conduct life! Experience the state of consciousness traditionally described as enlightenment! Avatar can make this possible.

contact: Manuela Christener
808.877.6078
manuela@avatarmaui.com • www.avatarmaui.com

Personal Development & Relationship Counseling

Center for Self-Mastery

Life-transforming personal development programs, guided retreats and private sessions custom-designed to: release limitations; connect with your unlimited self. Access your full wisdom, love and power to create your heart's desires. Achieve harmony and success in every area of your life. Attain inner bliss with simple meditations/exercises. Find your life's purpose and live your highest dream.

1135 Makawao Ave. #144 • Makawao, HI 96768
contact: Sharon Rose
808.573.3280
spirit@aloha.com • www.CenterforSelfMastery.org

Heart and Soul Therapy

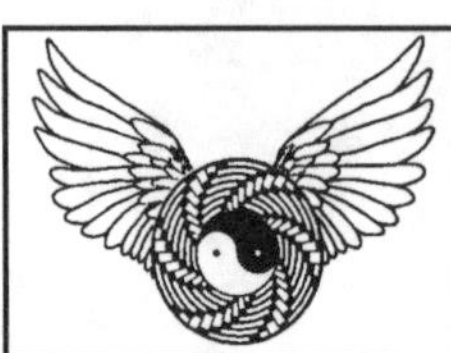

Dr. Abrams serves as an ally on the journey towards greater peace, creative self-expression and freedom from addictive behaviors and limiting beliefs. He offers tools for accessing inner wisdom and communicating from the heart. With his coaching, couples break through to new levels of intimacy by releasing resentments and renewing their soul connection.

3620 Baldwin Ave., Suite 207 • Makawao, HI 96768
contact: Dr. Lew Abrams PhD (licensed clinical psychologist)
808.572.2332 or cell: 808.283.8057
labrams@t-link.net

HeartPath

Individuals • Couples • Retreats

Specializing in PAIRS (Practical Application of Intimate Relationship Skills), user-friendly communication tools that turn conflict into connection and create deeper understanding. And Transformational Kinesiology (TK) which utilizes muscle testing to identify and transform unconscious beliefs that block your full potential. Enjoy single-session success.

Kihei/Wailea area
contact: Jeffrey Marsh & Debra Greene, PhD
808.874.6441
info@MauiHouse.net • www.HeartPath.org

Lorraine Bennington, M.Ed. (Counseling)

Metaphysical Counselor

(Astrology, Hypnotherapy, Couple Counseling)

A POTENT COMBINATION FOR CHANGE Free yourself from limitations. Be de-hypnotized and release ancient fears, false beliefs and addictions and claim all that you were born to be. Astrology can help you see your path clearly, hypnotherapy can then eliminate whatever stops you from walking it! Twenty-seven years experience.

PO Box 1347 • Makawao, HI 96768
contact: Lorraine Bennington
808.573.3383
content@maui.net

Personal Development & Relationship Counseling

The Art of Being, LLC

Art of Being vacation courses are led by Alan Lowen, its founder. Learn to celebrate your body, nature, sexuality, feelings, heart and being, and to awaken to spirit with one of the world's great teachers. Discover true community in the Art of Being circle and visit Maui's loveliest places together.

PO Box 790269 • Pā'ia, HI 96779
owner/contact: Alan Lowen/Jan Day
808.572.1435 • 1.800.871.1068
info@artofbeing.com • www.artofbeing.com

Alexsandra Burt

(Feldenkrais)
124 Mahola St
Makawao, HI 96768
808.573.8662

Destiny

307 Kaeo Place • Lahaina, HI 96761
contact: Linda J. Gilmore, CCHT
808.667.5356
gilmorel001@hawaii.rr.com

Eve Hogan, M.A.

(relationship/labyrinth)
PO Box 943 • Pu'unēnē, HI 96784
808.879.8648
EveHogan@aol.com
www.EveHogan.com
www.HeartPath.com

Moonjay

Hale Akua, Start Rt. 1, Box 161
Ha'īkū, HI 96708
808.573.7762
smoonjay@excite.com
www.WomenHeal.com

Ohana International Institute for Nurturing Art

PO Box 1465 • Makawao, HI 96768
808.876.0409
contact: Maha Conyers, Rev., MA, Ed.Psych
mahana@maui.net
www.maui.net/~mahana

Sacred Loving

contact: Niyaso Carter
1.800.688.1715 or
808.572.2234
niyaso@maui.net
www.sacredloving.net

Retreats

Adventures in Movement

Gentle Adventure Retreats for Women

Draw on gentle nature experiences, profound bodymind teachings and traditional Hawaiian culture. You'll stay in a beautiful, secluded Maui retreat center, devote time to your own health and transformation in a relaxed and magnificent environment staffed by gifted cultural artists and retreat leaders.

contact: Meriah Kruse
808.276.4962
www.gentleadventure.net

Retreats

Health Associates

Empowering Retreat Weeks for Women on Kauai, Maui and Santorini, Greece. 7 Days – 7 Chakras. Includes daily Meditation, Kundalini Yoga, Self-Healing methods and walking, hiking, swimming and sacred site journeys. Nurture your Spirit, Clear your Mind and Strengthen your Body.

contact: Pia Back Sanderson

808.874.9172

santoriniretreat@onebox.com

http://home.ix.netcom.com/~ulfi/santorini_home.html

Magic Moments on Maui

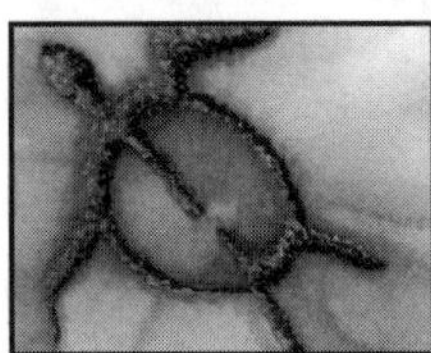

"Walk this land of Aloha and find your own Sacred Place within." Personal Retreats and Workshops re-connecting you to the land, to your Self, to Living in the Moment. Experience the Healing Power of Sound and the Freedom of Movement as we swim and sing and dance in the magic of each moment.

contact: Megan Don

808.573.3002

mythinmotion@yahoo.com

www.ishqdesign.com/momentsonmaui.html

Ohana International Institute for Nurturing Art

Maha Conyers, Rev., M.Ed. will host your retreat with the warmth of the true Aloha spirit developed by years of spiritual activity and study, world travel and international work as healer, counselor, bodyworker and intuitive. Her passion is to create an unforgettable retreat experience of aliveness, joy, rejuvenation and meditation.

PO Box 1465 • Makawao, HI 96768

contact: Maha Conyers, Rev., MA, Ed.Psych

808.876.0409

mahana@maui.net • www.maui.net/~mahana

Spiritual Retreats in Paradise

(custom-designed personal retreats)

1135 Makawao Ave. #144 • Makawao, HI 96768

contact: Sharon Rose

808.573.3280

spirit@aloha.com • www.SpiritualRetreatinParadise.com

Retreat Centers

Kahua Hawaiian Institute for Inner Transformation

Enrich your vacation with a Tantric touch. Nurture and deepen your connection to yourself and your beloved. Schedule a private session with world-renowned Tantra Teachers, Kutira and Raphael, or even stay at their sacred retreat center on Maui. For accommodations, guided retreats, workshops and private sessions visit their website.

PO Box 1747 • Makawao, HI 96768

Toll free 877.524.8250 or 808.572.6006

info@KahuaInstitute.com • www.KahuaInstitute.com

Retreat Centers

Kolealea Retreat Center

Nine Acres of Forest and Glen. Walk across a covered Footbridge to: Privacy, Serenity and Peace. Large (24x36) Meeting Room with surround sound, bamboo floor, picture windows, view of tropical foliage, waterfalls and valley, and to distant sea. Twelve charming rooms for two, shared or private bath.
PO Box 641 • Ha'īkū, HI 96708
contact: Paula and Drew Wagner
Toll free 866.720.7898 or 808.572.6239
info@kolealea.com • www.kolealea.com

Mana Lea Gardens

1055 Kaupakalua Road • Ha'īkū, HI 96708
808.572.8795 or 1.800.233.6467
mlg@maui.net • www.maui.net/~mlg/

Sacred Healing

Earthways, Inc.

(shamanic, medicine wheel, sweat lodge, etc.)
PO Box 880572
Pukalani, HI 96788
contact: Robin Youngblood
808.573.2784
earthways,inc@verizon.net

Mystical Extravaganza

(Visionary-Ethereal Art and Personalized Soul-Portraits)
PO Box 973 • Kōloa, HI, 96756
contact: Eleawani
808.573.3002
Eleawani@hotmail.com
www.Eleawani.com

Sacred Sites of Maui Tours

P.O. Box 1567 • Makawao, HI 96768
contact: Solomon
808.572.5083
joh@safe-mail.com

Tai Chi Chuan

Ron Perfetti

PO Box 1552 • Makawao, HI 96768
808.572.6994
taichi4u@maui.net • www.maui.net/~taichi4u/taichi.html

Yoga

The Yoga Path

PO Box 646
Kīhei, Hi 96753
contact: Deni Roman
808.874.5545
deniyoga@maui.net

Well Being International, Inc

(yoga, meditation)
PO Box 2300 • Kīhei, HI 96753
contact: Meenakshi Angel Honig
808.874.1887 • 808.573.1414
angel@angelyoga.com
www.angelyoga.com

Fitness

Strong, Stretched & Centered
PO Box 790758
Pā'ia, HI 96779
contact: Emily Marshall
808.572.2125 or
toll free 866.289.8539
fpi@mauifitness.com

Well Being International, Inc
(nutrition, stress management, goals clarification)
PO Box 2300 • Kīhei, HI 96753
contact: Meenakshi Angel Honig
808.874.1887 • 808.573.1414
angel@angelyoga.com

Hypnotherapy

The Inside Story
Wailuku, HI
contact: Janis Persons, BSW, CH, AI
808.243.0050
Janis@mysticmaui.com
www.mysticmaui.com

Lorraine Bennington M.Ed.
(Sports hypnosis)
PO Box 1347,
Makawao, HI 96768 USA
808.573.3383
content@maui.net

Life Coaching

Center for Self-Mastery
(intuitive guidance, personal growth)
1135 Makawao Ave. #144
Makawao, HI 96768
contact: Sharon Rose
808.573.3280
spirit@aloha.com
www.CenterforSelfMastery.org

Laura Monaco
(Lomi Pohaku)
631 Kumulani Drive
Kīhei, HI 96753
808.874.7544
touch@xmail.com

Nutrition

Changes International
A Pill to Lose Weight? Believe it!
100% Natural
Miracle Fat Loss Supplement.
Not a diet. Incredible Neutraceutical products that really work!
contact: Marleen Bauer
1.800.522.1138
www.marleenshawaii.com

Institute for Health and Happiness
141 Kuloli Place
Ha'īkū, Hawaii 96708
contact: Sabrina Werkmeister, macrobiotic cooking teacher & nutritional counselor
808.573.2917
cell: 808.283.3600
mauimacrobiotics@yahoo.com

The Traveling Gourmet
"Vegetarian Meals on the Move"
128 Peni Place • Kula, HI 96790
contact: Heidi Schopen
808.878.3170
hschopen@hotmail.com

Kahua Hawaiian Institute for Inner Transformation

Enrich your vacation with a Tantric touch. Nurture and deepen your connection to yourself and your beloved. Schedule a private session with world-renowned Tantra Teachers Kutira and Raphael, or even stay at their sacred retreat center on Maui. For accommodations, guided retreats, workshops and private sessions visit their website.

P.O. Box 1747 • Makawao, HI 96768

Toll free 877.524.8250 or 808.572.6006

info@KahuaInstitute.com • www.KahuaInstitute.com

Sacred Loving Programs

(Consultations, Classes and Retreats in the areas of intimacy, sexuality and Tantra)

Learn how to bring your relationship and your lovemaking to a higher level of fulfillment and sacredness. Our Tantra Counseling Vacation Packages combine vacation time with powerful learning experiences that will change your life and relationship. You can set the dates that work for you. Educational Tantra video available.

PO Box 790038 • Pāʻia, HI 96779

contact: Niyaso Carter

Toll free 1.800.688.1715 • ph/fax 808.572.2234

niyaso@maui.net • www.sacredloving.net

Source School of Tantra

Charles and Caroline Muir, America's foremost teachers of "Tantra: The Art of Conscious Loving," offer vacation seminars at a honeymoon setting with pool, hot tubs, jungle waterfalls on site, ocean views and gourmet meals. As seen in the movies, Bliss and The Best Ever.

PO Box 1451 • Wailuku, HI 96793

contact: Charles O. Muir

808.243.9851

For free brochure: 888.6.TANTRA

tantra@mauigateway.com • www.sourcetantra.com

Tomas, C.T.E. and Joan Heartfield, Ph.D.

help singles and couples create a strong foundation of understanding and skills for relationship. Their workshops and private sessions have inspired thousands to create a spirit based practice which provide strong foundations that empower every aspect of your life. Their communications technologies and Tantric instruction help to propel relationships to the highest levels.

contact: Joan and Tomas

808.572.1250

j&t@talkinghearts.com • www.talkinghearts.com

Tantra

Moonjay
Hale Akua, Start Rt. 1, Box 161
Ha'īkū, HI 96708
808.573.7762
smoonjay@excite.com • www.WomenHeal.com

Weddings

Kuhina Hawaiian Healing
contact: Rev. Alalani Hill
808.879.1499
alani@kuhina.com

Yoga

Beyond Heaven
3660 Baldwin Avenue
Makawao, HI 96768
808.573.8825
beyondheaven@aol.com
www.beyondheaven.com

The Yoga Path
PO Box 646 • Kīhei, HI 96753
contact: Deni Roman
808.874.5545
deniyoga@maui.net

Maui Viniyoga
PO Box 1266
Makawao, HI 96768
contact: Lahar Goldberg
808.572.3464
lahar@maui.net
www.mauiviniyoga.com

Maui Yoga Shala
120 Hana Highway • Pā'ia, HI 96779
808.579.6257 or
181 Lahainaluna Road • Lahaina, HI
808.661.7272
nadia@maui-yoga.com
www.maui-yoga.com

Nature as Healer

Animal Therapy

Island Marine Institute
808.249.8245

Maui Horse Whisperer Experience & Adventure
PO Box 1419 • Makawao, HI 96768
contact: Franklin Levinson
808.572.6211
808.572.4996
franklin@mauihorses.com

Maui Ocean Center The Hawaiian Aquarium
192 Ma'alaea Road
Wailuku, Maui, HI 96793
808.270.7000
www.mauioceancenter.com

Pacific Whale Foundation
808.879.8811
www.pacificwhale.org

Ecotours

Makena Coast Charters
(scuba, snorkel and
whale watching tours)
808.874.1273
www.MauiUnderwater.com

Sea Fire Charters
(snorkel tours)
808.879.2201
www.MolokiniSnorkeling.com

Healing Products

Derma Spa Essentials, Inc
Realizing the need for all natural, high quality products, Derma Spa Essentials was founded in 1996 by Betty Schneider. Derma Spa formulations nurture ultimate beauty through the healing essence of pure herbs and are used by professionals in award-winning five-star spa and salons worldwide.

contact: Betty Schneider
800.772.1933
dermaspa@maui.net • www.dermaspa.com

Busy as a Bee Creations
(lotions)
PO Box 665-A • Kula, HI 96790
beecreation@aol.com

Maui Excellent
(all natural body care)
mauiexcellent@aol.com

Maui Medicinal
PO Box 1840 • Makawao, HI 96768
contact: Mark Dunlop
808.572.9331
toll free 800.936.6532
mauiherbs@hotmail.com
www.mauimedicinal.com

Maui Passionflower Herbals
808.573.3669

Maui Tropical Soaps
(soap & lotion)
244 Papap Place, Bay 11
Kahului, HI 96732
808.871.7667

Namolata, Inc.
(glycerine soap)
www.namolata.com

Nanea a'o Kula
(lavender products)
1100 Waipoli Road • Kula, HI 96790
808.283.3777
www.mauilavender.com

Tropical Elements
PO Box 252
Kula, HI 96790
888.923.8377

Gardens and Parks

Alii Gardens of Maui
Alii Chang
808.878.3004

Hawaii Nature Center
875 'Īao Valley Road
808.244.6500

Island Flower Designs
Tom and Jody Jewwell
808.878.6059

Kahanu Garden
(off Route 360 at Ulaino Road)
Part of the
National Tropical Botanical Gardens
808.248.8912

Keanae Arboretum
(16 mile marker
on the way to Hā na)

Kula Botanical Garden
on Kekaulike Avenue
Highway 377
808.878.1715

Maui Tropical Garden
200 'Īao Road
808.244.3085

Nanea a'o Kula
1100 Waipoli Road • Kula, HI 96790
808.283.3777
(call for appointment)

Massage and BodyWork

Always Quality Touch

Candle Summer's Upcountry homebased massage and bodywork services offer the visitor an opportunity to relax with tea in the garden by a fountain, lounge on her massage chair, relax in a hot tub, and experience the deep healing touch of her myofacial and cranio/sacral bodywork. "One hour with Candle chased away all the stress of a Chicago lawyer's life." Douglas Uhlinger-lawyer

4536 Lower Kula Road • Kula, HI 96790
contact: Candle Summer • **808.878.6484**
candle@maui.net

Moonjay

With 20 years experience as a healer, Moonjay offers body-centered ounseling, massage therapy with Pohaku Lomi Lomi (Hawaiian massage art using hot stones) and Tantra teaching. WomenHeal is a heartfelt vision and a calling. This vision embraces women's sexual healing, intimacy coaching for men and women, healing rituals, retreats and women sacred circles.

Hale Akua, Start Rt. 1, Box 161 • Ha'īkū, HI 96708
contact: Moonjay • **808.573.7762**
smoonjay@excite.com • www.WomenHeal.com

Aloha Body Medicine

114 Waimele Place
Kula, HI 96790
808.242.3332
Hawkeye Lannis, LMT-MAT
alohabodymedicine@hotmail.com

Beyond Heaven

A Day Spa
3550 Baldwin Avenue
Makawao, HI 96768
808.573.8828
www.beyondheaven.com

BLISS

• Belief in the Sacred Self •
• Hot Stone Body Therapy •
Bamboo Mountain Sanctuary
1055 Kapakalua Rd • Ha'īkū, HI
contact: Robin Garrison
808.283.3500
charob@maui.net

Health Associates

1993 S. Kīhei Road #211
Kīhei, HI 96753
contact: John & Pia Back Sanderson
808.874.9590
Piasanderson@msn.com or
John@massageschoolmaui.com

Helen Barrow, CFP, LMT

(Feldenkreis)
PO Box 822 • Makawao, HI 96768
Helen@ahaproductions.net

Keith Ranney

(Somatic Awareness Coach)
PMB 945, POB 959 • Kīhei, HI 96753
808.875.4154
kbranney@earthlink.net
www.whollyone.org

Laura Monaco

(Lomi Pohaku)
631 Kumulani Drive
Kīhei, HI 96753
808.874.7544
touch@xmail.com

Massage by Jonathan

Island Surf Building
1993 South Kīhei Road, Suite 210A
Kīhei, HI 96753
808.874.5681
deBeer@maui.net

Maui School of Therapeutic Massage

Student Clinic
Makawao Ave, Suite 207
Makawao, HI 96768
808.572.2277
www.massagemaui.com
info@massagemaui.com

Maui Academy of the Healing Arts

(Student massage, yoga and self-care classes)
1847 Kīhei Road, #103
Kīhei, HI 96753
contact: John Sanderson
808.879.4266
info@massageschoolmaui.com

BodyWork and Massage

Ohana Health Care
PO Box 411
Pu'unēnē, HI 96784
contact: Zoee Crowley
808.242.9162
zoee@maui.net

Ohana International Institute for Nurturing Art
P.O. Box 1465 • Makawao, HI 96768
Maha Conyers, Rev., MA, Ed.Psych
808.876.0409
mahana@maui.net www.maui.net/~mahana/

Reiki and Healing Touch
(Makawao)
contact: Monique Smith
808.572.0866
chimoni@hotmail.com

Three Treasures
(Acupuncture, Herbal Medicine, Massage)
42 Baldwin Avenue
P.O. Box 790569 • Pā'ia, HI 96779
contact: Ricardo Molczadzzi & Chinta Mackinnon
808.579.6070

Well Being International Inc.
P.O. Box 2300
Kīhei, Maui, HI 96753
contact: Meenkshi Angel Honig
808.874.1887 or 808.573.1414
angel@angelyoga.com
www.angelyoga.com

Yarrow King
(MAT#531 massage • reflexology cranial sacral • lomilomi)
P.O. Box 790721
Pā'ia, HI 96779
808.281.3204
lulu143king@hotmail.com

Spas

New Waves Wellness Center
Experience the adventure of a RESTful vacation as you float your cares away. Enjoy a weeks worth of vacation in an hour's time with Xtreme REST and relaxation. Floatation Reduced Environmental Stimulation Therapy relieves jet lag, alleviates stress and releases endorphins for a natural high.
Energy balancing and bodywork also available.
1170 Makawao Avenue • Makawao, HI 96768
Toll free 877.4RADICAL (877.472.3422)
or 808.572.5551
float@HolisticTherapy.com
www.HolisticTherapy.com

Luana Spa Retreat
LUANA SPA RETREAT

On Kauiki Hill, overlooking Hana Bay, Luana Spa Retreat offers traditional lomilomi and Hawaiian therapies, as well as contemporary spa treatments and skin care. Two 16 foot diameter yurts serve as guest accommodation and spa treatment room. A traditional Hawaiian hale (thatched house) provides a special location for weddings and couples massage.
5050 Uakea Road • PO Box 399 • Hāna, HI 96713
contact: Nancy D. Plenty, Director
808.248.8855 • fax: 808.248.8553
www.luanaspa.com • info@luanaspa.com

Spas

Spa Luna European Day Spa

A full service spa dedicated to Relaxation, Health and Beauty. Feel and Know the Difference! Holistic and natural treatments for body, mind and spirit. Returning to the originals of cosmetology Spa Luna Maui. Come and revitalize your whole self!
810 Ha'īkū Road, Suite #209 • Ha'īkū, HI 96708
808.575.2440 or toll free: 1.800.347.6449
www.spaluna.com • dayspa@spaluna.com

Wailea Massage and Body Care

Wailea Massage and Body Care is located in the Renaissance Wailea Beach Resort, offers luxurious treatments in a resort setting at affordable prices. Massage, oceanside and in clinic, facials and bodywraps with an emphasis on organic products are offered 9am-9pm. "There is nothing better at the start of your stay on Maui than a visit to Wailea Massage to begin the process of stress relief, relaxation and healing."
Renaissance Wailea Beach Resort
3550 Ala Nui Drive • Wailea, HI 96753
contact: Sudha Scott or Laura Rosenthal • 808.879.8244
infoseek@waileamassage.com

Derma Spa Essentials, Inc.

(Facial Services)
62 Hiwalani Loop
Pukalani, HI 96768
contact: Betty Schneider
808.572.8929
dermaspa@maui.net
www.dermaspa.com

Spa Grande

Grand Wailea Resort
3850 Wailea Alanui
Wailea, HI 96753
808.875.1234 ext. 4949
1.800.SPA.1933
info@grandwailea.com
www.grandwailea.com

Complementary Treatment Therapies

Acupuncture

Acupuncture Center

630 Olinda Drive
Makawao, HI 96768
573.8286

Dragon's Den Healing Center

(Acupuncture, Massage, Traditional Chinese Medicine)
3681 Baldwin Ave.
Makawao, HI 96768
808.572.5267

Grace Health Clinic

contact: Dr. David Kern
Makawao, HI
808.572.6901
Kihei, HI
808.874.5660

Margy Campbell

Licensed Acupuncturist & Massage Therapist
808.385.1643
taropatch@hotmail.com

Acupuncture

Oriental Healing Arts

(acupuncture &
bio resonance therapy)
contact: Linda Wertheimer
808.573.8698

Three Treasures

(Acupuncture, Herbal Medicine, Massage)
42 Baldwin Avenue
PO Box 790569 • Pā'ia, Hi 96779
contact: Ricardo Molczadzzi & Chinta Mackinnon
808.579.6070

Cellular Rejuvenation

Ascension Into Light

Cellular rejuvenation purifies and regenerates the cells creating optimal lymph and immune function. State-of-the-art Lymph Technology assists the body to: eliminate toxic wastes and remove blockages of parasites, fungus, chronic fatigue, clots or cancer, revitalizes and nourishes each living cell in the entire body helping to achieve optimum health and well-being.
PO Box 624 • Ha'īkū, HI 96708
contact: Marie Gardner
808.572.7950
spirit@maui.net

Chiropractic

Aloha Family Chiropractic & Wellness Centers

47 Ka'ahumanu Ave. #28
(Kahului, HI 96732
808.871.1170

Lifestyle Chiropractic

"Your Healing and Learning Center"
375 Huku Li'i, #210 • Kīhei, HI 96753
contact: Dr. Jeff Parham
808.875.9993
www.lifestylechiro.com

North Shore Chiropractic & Massage

16 Baldwin Ave. • Pā'ia, HI 96779
contact: Michael Fleischer
808.579.9134

Pukalani Chiropractic

7 Aewa Place, #12
Pukalani, HI 96768
808.572.5599

Colon Hydrotherapy

Shelley St John, R.N., Certified Colon Therapist

Shelley offers a unique combination of emotional support, massage, aromatherapy and hypnotherapy along with lifestyle management skills to empower you to make healthy choices in your life. The colon is a wonderful organ, if functioning properly the overall health of the individual will be elevated. Benefits • Increased Vitality • Greater Mental Clarity • Detoxifies Your Body • Eliminates Excess Weight • Improved Digestion • Heightened Inner Peace
contact: Shelley St. John
Box 1502 • Makawao, HI 96768
808.573.0696
shelley@peace-temple.com

Colon Hydrotherapy

Vibrant Life Center

Kihei and Makawao HI

contact:

Adrianna Levinson C.H.
808.870.8168
adrianna@aloha.net

Shelley St. John, R.N., C.H.
808.573.0696
shelley@peace-temple.com

Energy Therapy

Healing Gracework

Laurel works with healing grace to release energies blocking full expression of the life force. She is a graduate of the Barbara Brennan School of Healing and practices in a cottage overlooking Wailea and the ocean.

996-A Kupulau Dr. • Kīhei, HI 96753
contact: Laurel Murphy
(808) 874-9511
halama@flex.com

Laura Monaco

(Lomi Pohaku)
631 Kumulani Drive
Kīhei, HI 96753
808.874.7544
touch@xmail.com

Dr. Shedema Goodman, EdD

(Energy Self-Healing, Psychoneurimmunology)
280 Hauoli St., A17 • Kīhei, HI 96753
808.986.8585
shedema@yahoo.com
www.healers.ws

Hawaiian Healing Therapies

Mara Keala Gerhard

Mara is an international therapist, HUNA teacher and counselor. Huna is an ancient Hawaiian system for spiritual growth and psychology. It is sacred Hawaiian healing based on Aloha—which means "let there be love between us." She offers 1, 2 or 3 day Huna Intensives, individual sessions, past life regressions, hypnosis and neurolinguistic programming.

3378-A Keha Drive • Kīhei, HI 96753
contact: Mara Keala Gerhard
808.874.1884

Kuhina Hawaiian Healing
contact: Rev. Alalani Hill

808.879.1499
alani@kuhina.com

Holistic Health Practitioner

Ohana International Institute for Nurturing Art

PO Box 1465 • Makawao, HI 96768
contact:
Maha Conyers, Rev., MA, Ed.Psych
808.876.0409
mahana@maui.net www.maui.net/~mahana/

Radical Balance

PO Box 79107
Pā'ia, HI 96779-1017
contact: Teri Holter, LSW, LCSW
toll free 877.787.4440
or 808.572.0664
RadBalance@aol.com
www.ikekala.com/Services_inclx.html

Homeopathy

Homeopathic Family Practice

offers classical homeopathy from two of the most skilled, experienced homeopaths in the entire USA. Jeff Baker, ND, DHANP, CCH is a licensed naturopathic physician, board certified in homeopathy. Susie Baker, RSHom (na), CCH is a professional homeopath board certified in classical homeopathy. Susie and Jeff not only practice in Pukalani, Maui, but also run a vibrant organization, the Maui Academy of Homeopathy in which advanced training for practitioners who are already in practice can further refine and hone their skills.

Makawao Avenue, suite 201A • Pukalani, HI 96768
contact: Jeff and Susie Baker
808.572.2220
sjbaker@t-link.net • www.mauiacademy.com81

Naturopathic Medicine

Dr. Julie Claire Holmes, N.D.

A Naturopathic Physician practicing for twenty years, offers a blend of conventional western diagnosis with natural healing methods. Specializing in women's health care, she is skilled in the use of natural hormones with menopause and hormonal imbalances. Offers Breast Thermography to detect precancerous changes 5-10 years before a tumor can be seen in a mammogram.

2846 Omaopio Road • Kula, HI 96790
contact: Julie Holmes
808.878.3267

Neurofeedback

Christman Center

PO Box 837
Puunene, HI 96784
contact: Dr. J. Randol Christman, D.Ac. L.M.T.
808.879.4341
rxman234@webtv.net

Pain Management

Alexsandra Burt

(Feldenkrais)
124 Mahola St
Makawao, HI 96768
808.573.8662

Rolfing

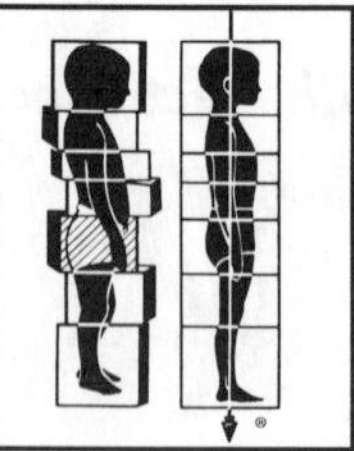

Rolfing Structural Integration

Anne is a Certified Advanced Rolfer professionally trained in Rolfing, craniosacral work and visceral manipulation — modalities that are particularly effective in releasing chronic pain (neck, back, headache, TMJ, sciatica, etc.), improving posture, enhancing flexibility and sports performance, reducing stress and healing injury. Early booking is recommended to guarantee an appointment.

Anne F. Hoff, CAR
PO Box 834 • Makawao, HI 96768
808.572.6699
AnneFHoff@aol.com

Fitness

Pat Masumoto, M.Ed.

Laugh Coach and Expressionist Painter
Pat is a professional speaker, author, and developer of "Laughter Aerobics ©," has brought joy to thousands of individuals, including visitors, by teaching the Hawaiian-Style Belly Laugh, guaranteed to promote good health and boost brainpower. Pat's art is featured at Gallerie Ha, her studio/gallery on Market Street, Wailuku.
PO Box 880415
Pukalani, HI 96788
808.572.5050
yespat@maui.net • www.gallerieha.com

Strong, Stretched & Centered

Since 1980, SS&C has offered the most comprehensive mind/body fitness programs available. Including: a 3,000 sq/ ft Personal Training Center with eight professional trainers, Two-week health and fitness vacation programs. The six-week fitness instructor certification/career school. Plus, specialty certifications in yoga, pilates, and more.
Free catalog at www.mauifitness.com
PO Box 790758 • Pā'ia, HI 96779
contact: Emily Marshall
808.572.2125 or 866.289.8539 toll free
fpi@mauifitness.com

Aloha Bicycle Tours

808.249.0911 or 800.749.1564
marc@mauibike.com • www.mauibike.com
808.579.9134

Sports Hypnotherapy

Lorraine Bennington M.Ed.

(Sports hypnosis)
PO Box 1347
Makawao, HI 96768 USA
808.573.3383
content@maui.net

Travel to Serve Others

Serving Animals

Maui Ocean Center
The Hawaiian Aquarium
192 Ma'alaea Road
Wailuku, HI 96793
808.270.7000
www.mauioceancenter.com

Pacific Whale Foundation
808.879.8811
www.pacificwhale.org

Whale Research Center
808.249.8245

Environmental Services

The Nature Conservancy
(volunteer opportunities the third Saturday of each month)
808.572.7849
www.nature.org/Hawaii

The Nature Center
975 Iao Valley Road
Wailuku, HI 96793
808.244.6500 ext.12
hinature@maui.net

Healing Accommodations

Hale Ho'okipa Inn
Makawao's Historic Bed & Breakfast
A blend of Craftsman's style elegance and Old World charm, this 1924 home is now a B&B within walking distance of Makawao. Each room is beautifully appointed with period pieces and local art.
32 Pakani Place • Makawao, HI 96768
808.572.6698 • 808.573.2580
mauibnb@maui.net • www.maui.net/~mauibnb

Kahua 'O Mali 'O Bamboo Farm
& Maui Retreat Center
A magnificent secluded ocean front sanctuary on Maui. Lush grounds, elegant/private bamboo accommodations, meditation temples, hiking trails, tropical waterfalls, sacred pools, ocean access, yoga, massage and healing sessions available. Lots of privacy, perfect for honeymoons and weddings. A sacred and magical land. This is real Hawaii!
PO Box 1747 • Makawao, HI 96768
877.524.8250
info@MauiRetreat.com • www.MauiRetreat.com

Healing Accommodations

Bamboo Mountain Sanctuary
1111 Kaupakalua Road
Hāna, HI 96708
808.572.4897
www.maui.net/~BambooMt

Chameleon Vacation Rentals
P.O. Box 350 • Ha'īku, HI 96708
contact: Donna Stafford
808.575.9933
toll free 866.575.9933
newleaf@maui.net
www.donnachameleon.com

Haiku Cottage Maui
261 S. Holokai Rd.
Ha'īku, Maui, HI 96768
contact: Diane Epstein
808.572.9501
dianee@maui.net

Halfway to Hana House B&B
PO Box 675
Ha'īku, HI 96708
contact: Gail Pickholz
808.572.1176
gailp@maui.net

Heavenly Hana Inn
PO Box 790 • Hāna, HI 96713
808.248.6442
hanainn@maui.net
www.heavenlyhanainn.com

Hotel Hana Maui
PO Box 9
Hāna, HI 96713
808.248.8211
www.hotelhanamaui.com

I Ke Kala's Hula Hale Studio
Makawao, HI
Toll free 877.787.4440
808.572.0664
www.iKeKala.com
reservations@iKeKala.com

Kā'anapali Beach Hotel
2525 Kā'anapali Parkway
Kā'anapali, HI 96761
808.661.0011 • 800.262.8450
www.kbhmaui.com
res@kbhmaui.com

KOOLAU Vacation Services
PO Box 641 • Ha'īku, HI 96708
contact: Paula and Drew Wagner
Toll free 866.720.7898
808.572.6239
info@koolauvacations.com
www.koolauvacations.com

Kula Lodge
Haleakalā Highway, Kula
808.878.1535 or
800.233.1535
www.kulalodge.com

Maluhia Hale
(Peaceful House)
PO Box 687 • Ha'īku, HI 96708
contact: Diane Garrett
808.572.2959
djg@maui.net
www.maui.net/~djg/index.html

Maui House
Kīhei/Wailea
contact: Debra Green
808.874.6441
info@MauiHouse.net
www.MauiHouse.net

Healing Accommodations

Maui Tea House
PO Box 335 • Ha'īku, HI 96708
Contact: Ann DeWeese
808.572.5610
teahouse@maui.net
www.mauiteahouse.com

Ritz-Carlton
1 Ritz-Carlton Drive
Kapalua, HI 96761
808.669.6200
www.ritzcarlton.com

Retreat House
St. John's Episcopal Church
Kula, HI 96790
808.876.0280

Silver Cloud Ranch B&B
R.R. 2, Box 201
Kula, HI 96790
808.878.6101 • 800.532.1111
www.silvercloudranch.com

Please visit our website for updated and new wellness resources information

www.alohawellnesstravel.com

"We consider the environment to be sacred. Not to be contaminated, polluted and desecrated, but to be treasured. 'Āina, our term for land, means 'that which feeds.' The 'āina feeds us. If we don't take care of it, it won't feed us. We'll perish. The land, the Earth, is our mother."

Kekuni Blaisdell, MD
Voices of Wisdom

~ Chapter Six ~

The Island of O'ahu • The Gathering Place

O'ahu is known as "the gathering place." As the most populous island and the home of the state capital, it serves as both the cultural and political center of Hawai'i. As with each of the other islands, O'ahu has its own personality. Using the Hindu concept of the seven-chakras to describe the islands, O'ahu corresponds to the throat chakra, or communication center. O'ahu is the voice of Hawai'i. The primary communication and technology centers are here. The state legislature and capital of Hawai'i are in Honolulu and they speak for the state in ways that often frustrate the other islands.

As with Maui, O'ahu is dominated with the yang, or masculine energy. According to Chinese philosophy, this energy reflects "doing" values such as analysis, planning, controlling, and shaping. O'ahu is an active, assertive force in the state. Things happen on O'ahu, or at least a lot of planning goes on here to make things happen.

For a wellness vacation, O'ahu offers almost everything. Here you'll find gifted healers ranging from native Hawaiians to naturopathic doctors and holistic health practitioners. Within Honolulu are hiking trails and botanical gardens to feed the soul. Outside of Honolulu is a rural area that rapidly transports you into a world of beaches, mountains, pineapple plantations and great vistas, all of which invite you to relax and soak up healing energy. For those who enjoy the classical arts, Honolulu has a world class symphony and three excellent art museums. And, then there is Waikīkī Beach.

Waikīkī Beach and Diamond Head are two of the most famous landmarks of Hawai'i and rank near the top worldwide. Although once criticized as too touristy and without charm, the current city and county administration has transformed Waikīkī into a justifiably famous resort. The visitor can shop at small bazaar stands or classy boutiques, walk along the patterned brick sidewalk lined by small gardens with waterfalls and wading pools, or experience a sunset picnic at one of the oceanside parks where Hawaiian musicians play. It used to be the place that residents loved to hate, but now they're returning to Waikīkī to enjoy all that it offers.

George Kanahele, the spiritual leader of the Hawaiian renaissance, invested particular energy in bringing a Hawaiian sense of place to Waikīkī. His commitment grew in part out of knowledge that Waikīkī was a healing destination for Hawaiians in ancient times. Included in the renewed sense of place are the melodic strains of Hawaiian music. After several years of catering to what they thought the Japanese wanted, hotels have returned to Hawaiian entertainers as their primary source of music

Kanahele was also the visionary behind development of a self guided tour of the Hawaiian history of Waikīkī. Ask your hotel concierge for a map of the 23 markers, which are in the form of a surfboard. On this tour you will rediscover the area where Princess Ka'iulani lived and the favorite surfing sites of the *ali'i* (royal class). Many hotels also showcase Hawaiian crafts and have Hawaiians demonstrating their work in lei making, weaving and carving. Check with the Outrigger Waikīkī Beach Hotel for information regarding their lectures on Hawaiian healing herbs, the artistic crafts of the Hawaiians, and other aspects of the native culture of Hawai'i.

Outside of Waikīkī, Honolulu distinguishes itself in the extensive historical information available about the Hawaiians. The Mission Houses Museum and 'Iolani Palace (the only palace in the United States) tell the story of early Hawai'i. At the Palace you learn that Hawaiian royalty were accepted and respected by members of royal families throughout the world. Unfortunately, their only experience of racism was in the United States. You'll learn that King Kalākaua had electricity, running water, and a telephone in the Palace even before the White House in Washington, D.C. "went modern." Members of the royal family were accomplished musicians, authors, and composers and could converse in several languages. The Mission Houses Museum tells the story of the early missionaries and their struggle to survive and thrive in Hawai'i. Just outside of Honolulu along H-1, is the highly respected Bishop Museum, which contains a sensitive and thorough coverage of ancient Hawaiian and Polynesian culture. Because we believe that the history of the Hawaiian people is an important part of the healing energy of Hawai'i, we encourage you to use some of your time on O'ahu to learn more about that history.

In addition to the above, the wellness traveler to O'ahu will find a wide variety of wellness practitioners trained in the Eastern, alternative, and indigenous healing traditions. Many of these people are doing cutting-edge work. In part because of the strong Asian influence in Hawai'i, many of those operating from the Eastern philosophy have studied with masters in India, China, Japan, and throughout Asia.

Places to stay while on O'ahu range from the luxury of a Waikīkī hotel, the intimate accommodations of a B&B in a neighborhood away from the fast paced city, to one of several resorts around the island. Regardless of where you stay, if you decide to explore the wellness suggestions we offer, you will meet people and go to places off the well beaten tourist track.

Island Orientation

Before you begin, a note about directions that you often will hear while on O'ahu.

There are four primary directions: mauka (toward the mountain); makai (toward the ocean); Diamond Head (in the direction of Diamond Head crater); and, 'Ewa (in the direction of the town of 'Ewa, which is basically west of Honolulu and Pearl Harbor). You'll hear about windward O'ahu, which is the part of the island on the other side of the Ko'olau Mountains from Honolulu. Because of the prevailing trade winds, it is windier, rainier, and greener than Honolulu. You'll also hear of the North Shore, which is at the top of your map of the island. Finally, the Leeward coast is along the western side of the island.

So, when someone tells you to get on the H-1 Freeway going Diamond Head, take the Wai'alae exit and turn makai on Kīlauea, you'll know what they're talking about.

Twenty Ways to Pursue Balance and Harmony on O'ahu

1. Have a Hawaiian Healing Experience

The ability of ancient Hawaiian *kahuna* to both heal and destroy through the apparent use of will power and thought is legendary. This lore is so prevalent that the word "*kahuna*" is often associated with sorcery. In fact, there were many kinds of *kahuna*.

They included those who guided the making of canoes, or presided over temple rituals or were respected as agricultural experts. Healing *kahuna* had subspecialties including bone setting, birthing, massage, herbalism, and healing of the spirit. Finally, there were the *kahuna* of dark magic who could destroy through the power of a death prayer. Whatever their specialty, *kahuna* were considered the guardians of esoteric knowledge and were people of great *mana* (spiritual energy). They were the "keepers of secrets." Regardless of the focus of their work, the source of their power was always seen as spiritual.

The eventual dominance of western civilization in Hawai'i along with the influence of Christianity forced Hawaiian healers underground. Only in recent years have they begun to resurface and engage publicly in their healing art. As an indication of the openness to this Hawaiian renaissance of the healing arts, the state legislature exempted the *kahuna* from certification standards for healing arts practitioners.

With this public acceptance, little by little, the keepers of the secrets have chosen to share what they know. Often those who have dedicated themselves to learning the art of Hawaiian healing from the *kahuna* are non-Hawaiian. Areas of study include the ancient art of Hawaiian massage (*lomilomi*), herbal remedies (*lā'au lapa'au*), or the spiritual process of facilitating forgiveness, (*ho'oponopono*). Whichever specialty a healing arts practitioner offers, all are centered on a belief that healing is a spiritual process, that all illnesses should be healed in the spirit first. Following are people on O'ahu who have been trained at various levels in Hawaiian healing arts. They are prepared to advise and work with you regardless of what ails you—mentally, emotionally, physically or spiritually.

Waimānalo, on the windward side of O'ahu, is one of two communities on the island with a concentration of Hawaiians. Here you will find the **Cultural Healing Center** of the **Waimānalo Health Center**. Its director, **Kawaikapu Hewett**, is a well-respected healer and teacher of hula. The center specializes in *lā'au lapa'au, ho'oponopono*, and *lomilomi*. In addition, they have an herb garden of medicinal plants tended by volunteers from the community. Although the focus of their work is providing culturally appropriate healing to Hawaiians, they welcome non-Hawaiians. You should be aware that although they, as with many Hawaiian healers, are reluctant to charge for their services, it is not appropriate to leave without paying something. (808.259.7948)

Also in Waimānalo is **Velma Dela Pena** a popular native Hawaiian practitioner of the healing arts who traces her healing lineage back to one of the initial 127 *kahuna* of ancient Hawai'i. More recently, her grandfather was a recognized *kahuna* who tried to pass his wisdom on to his son. Velma's father refused the "gift." Jumping a generation, Velma, picked up the work from her grandfather and has made it her life's mission. It was evident to Velma at the age of three that her life was to be dedicated to the Hawaiian healing tradition. In recent years she has become committed to sharing her knowledge with those who are interested and has several people studying under her. She believes deeply in the spiritual dimensions of healing and will call on her Hawaiian ancestors to support her work. As with other Hawaiian healers, Velma is prepared to work with you regardless of what issues you present. She also does not have a set fee for her services but please leave a donation comparable to what you would pay any other healing arts professional. (808.259.6805)

Another gifted spiritual wellness practitioner of the Hawaiian tradition is **Lynn Kealohaleimakamae Eklund**. Although not a native Hawaiian, she has become respected as someone who has the gift of healing and spiritual work. Her "office" is often one or more of the sacred sites around O'ahu. A popular workshop presenter, she has traveled around the country sharing information on Hawaiian healing arts. She also offers her services as a psychic and does *lomilomi* massage. As she is a paraplegic, her wellness journey has been particularly remarkable. On three occasions, her back was broken and twice she died on the operating table. Lynn now has only the use of her arms. It is clear that she is at peace with her condition. She is a living demonstration of balance and harmony through adversity. Testimonials to her healing skills come from all over the world. Lynn is humble about her abilities and unselfishly serves as a referral source to other healers if she believes they can best serve you. (808.847.7478)

One of the most familiar aspects of Hawaiian healing is the *lomilomi* massage. The **Lomi Shop Va'a** is dedicated to providing cultural health and wellness services through the healing art and practice of Hawaiian *lomilomi*. This is much more than a place to get a massage. It is a cultural experience. The two Hawaiian women who launched this business see their work as a metaphor of the voyaging canoe that connected Polynesians with their ancient roots and the wisdom of their culture. The Lomi Shop Va'a is designed to give the visitor a simulated experience of a voyage at sea—minus the potential for seasickness. The wooden floors represent the deck of the canoe, walls are painted with mountain and sky scenes, and the Lomi Shop Va'a is filled with unique, authentic Polynesian products made only in the islands. This shop, plus a smaller version at the Hyatt Regency Hotel in Waikīkī, offers something almost mystical. A big part of that essence is the *aloha* spirit which is the centerpiece of their belief system and their work. The two sisters, **Ka'auhane Lee and Maile Lee-Tolentino**, have given workshops to travel writers and travel agents regarding wellness opportunities on O'ahu and the affect they have had, through their genuine *aloha*, was deeply moving. Be sure to experience either The Lomi Shop Va'a in Waikīkī, which offers seated massage or the larger store at Windward Mall that offers the full range of services. Windward Mall (808.234.5664), or Hyatt Regency Waikīkī. (808.926.5664)

Much of what Hawaiian healers believe and do runs contrary to the beliefs and principles of Western, allopathic medicine. For Hawaiians the journey is first and foremost an inner pilgrimage, becoming "right with spirit." Although approximately 1,500 studies have shown the role of spirituality in health and wellness, this aspect is seldom addressed by the traditional medical profession. If you choose to venture into Hawaiian healing, you will experience something far different from a visit to your primary care physician. But we trust that those who embrace the concept of a wellness vacation are open to new ways of viewing wellness and the accompanying journey.

2. Heal Your Pain by Finding the Higher Meaning

There is increasing evidence that one of the greatest factors contributing to physical illness is an unhealed emotional wound. Whether it's a personal slight or a deeper trauma, we're seldom able to detach enough to rise above such an experience and see it from a higher, clearer perspective. The result is that we often are stuck in resentment, grief, uncertainty, and anger. From time to time we hear the stories of others who have found meaning in their pain and transformed it into their life's mission. We get a glimpse of the power of this possibility, but then, too often, we lose that potential as the waves of our pent up emotions sweep over us.

A book like **Viktor Frankl's** *Man's Search for Meaning* reminds us not only of the power of finding meaning but also the freedom we have to choose what something will mean to us at every moment of our day. Frankl's book grew out of his experience in a WW II concentration camp. If he could find a higher meaning there, it is possible in all circumstances.

Frankl tells of a widower who came to him in deep grief, feeling unable to go on without his wife. His life felt empty. Frankl suggested to him that the meaning of his wife's death was that she was not the one who had to suffer the loneliness that he was now suffering. When the man could see himself bearing the pain that his wife would otherwise have had to bear, his grief, and life, had meaning. The German philosopher, Friedrich Nietzsche, wrote, "He who has a *why* to live can bear with almost any *how*."

A wellness vacation is a perfect time to achieve peace and resolution by searching for the higher meaning of some issue you are working to resolve. The beauty and nurturing aspects of Hawai'i and its people will support you. On O'ahu there are several psychospiritual therapists who understand the importance of this perspective. **Silke Vogelmann-Sine** is one of the most highly respected psychologists in the state. After her own bout with cancer, she began to emphasize the importance of healing and transforming the meaning of a painful experience. Silke uses a wide variety of approaches to help her clients let go of painful experiences. Among the tools she uses are hypnotherapy, EMDR (Eye Movement Desensitization Reprogramming) metaphors, rituals, and symbols. (808.531.1232)

Gwen Williams works with the concept of the heroes journey in helping people discover how they can move past the challenges and trauma of their lives. Mythologies throughout cultures include stories of overcoming obstacles, pain, and suffering to arrive at the ultimate place of reward, which leads to enlightenment. These are the heroes' journeys that Dr. Joseph Campbell popularized with his book *Hero With a Thousand Faces*. Gwen is a highly sensitive and extremely effective counselor. (808.375.1746)

Laura Crites, co-author of this book, is available to work with you in releasing old wounds by transforming the meaning. She has several years experience as a psychospiritual therapist working with both individuals and groups, particularly those with a history of domestic abuse. Laura teaches psychology at a local university where logotherapy (the therapy of meaning) is part of her instruction. (808.941.8253)

The spiritual energy of Hawai'i and the skilled counselors who practice here, together with your intent to find and choose what a time of challenge will mean to you, can allow you to return home with a transformed and healed perspective.

3. Take an Inner Pilgrimage to Sacred Spaces and Places

There are several special, quiet, and spiritual places on O'ahu that you can visit as part of your inner pilgrimage. The energy, surroundings, and history of these places contribute to their spiritual quality. On our tour of these spaces and places, we guide you to locations representing the varied culture and history of the Hawaiian Islands.

Reflecting the Asian influence on Hawai'i is the **My-Ryang-Sa Korean Buddhist Temple** (2420 Halelā'au Place) at the back of Pālolo Valley. The setting is quiet and peaceful, ideal for a temple dedicated to world peace. Standing in the center of the courtyard you feel embraced in the arms of the mountains. The gentle green of the roof blends into the hues of the surrounding hillside while the brilliant colors and dramatic designs that decorate the cornices and interior of the various temple rooms give ample opportunity for study. (808.735.7858)

This is the first Korean Buddhist Temple complex built in Hawai'i and the largest in any country outside Korea. Stop by the small temple to the right of the driveway entrance to pick up a booklet describing the symbolism and history of what you will be seeing. Allow yourself to move about silently and just observe, feel, and be. You might want to reflect on the Buddhist Four Noble Truths and the Eightfold path and ask for guidance regarding that which offers you the greatest challenge.

Four Noble Truths

- ***Suffering exists.***
- ***All suffering has a cause.***
- ***That cause may be terminated.***
- ***The means of termination is by following the Noble Eightfold Path.***

Eightfold Path

- ***right understanding***
- ***right intention***
- ***right effort***
- ***right speech***
- ***right action***
- ***right livelihood***
- ***right mindfulness***
- ***right concentration***

> ***Directions to My-Ryang-Sa Korean Buddhist Temple***
>
> *Take Kapi'olani Boulevard mauka until it becomes Wai'alae Avenue. Proceed on Wai'alae Avenue, turning left on 10th street. Continue into the valley until you near the back of the valley. Turn right on Wai'oma'o Street and then a couple of blocks later, take a sharp uphill right on Halelā'au Place. The temple driveway is on the left)*

The next stop on the sacred spaces and places tour is **Kawaiaha'o Church** across from Honolulu City Hall at the corner of King and Punchbowl streets downtown. This was the first Christian church in Hawai'i. You'll want to explore the grounds including the fountain on the *mauka* side of the church and the little graveyard in back. Around the interior walls are portraits of Hawaiian royalty. The simplicity of the church is soothing in its contrast with so much of the world around us. This, more than any other church on O'ahu, represents the enduring influence that the early Christian missionaries have had on the Hawaiian people as well as the commitment of the Hawaiians to honor their own history and culture. The second service on Sunday is conducted primarily in the Hawaiian language. (Services are at 8:00 and 10:30. 808.522.1333)

Behind the church are the **Mission Houses Museum** and the **Winterbourne Tea Parlor** (808.537.3806). We recommend timing your visit in order to have lunch or British-style high tea in the Winterbourne. One visitor wrote, "This is so relaxing. I should do this more often. Thanks for a lovely afternoon." The scones are especially good. Nikki, the parlor's owner, offers you quiet, comfort, and relaxation in a room reminiscent of a bygone day. If you plan to do lunch, you'll need to call ahead as they only have five tables. (Teatime doesn't necessarily require reservations, but it's not a bad idea.)

A sacred site of special significance to the Hawaiians is the **Keaīwa Heiau**, an ancient healing *heiau* about 20 minutes from downtown Honolulu. You'll find it at the top of 'Aiea Heights Drive, a winding road up through a middle class hillside community. The *heiau* is on your left just as you enter the park grounds. As with all Hawaiian sacred places, enter the *heiau* with sensitivity and silence, and profound insights that your inner pilgrimage may emerge. Give yourself time and space to enjoy the serenity and energy of the place. Since this is the remains of a place of sacred healing, meditation on what within you is crying out for healing or wholeness might bear fruit. For those of us who like to write or are visual, a journal or piece of paper is recommended.

Directions to Keaīwa Heiau

To get there, get on H1 Freeway 'Ewa. When it goes off to the right, stay left to follow Hwy 78. Take Exit 1E into Ulune Street. When you come to a "T" in the road turn right and go to the next stop light which is 'Aiea Heights Drive. Turn right and continue up the hill until it terminates at Keaīwa Heiau State Recreation Area. The park is open 7:00 a.m. to 6:30 p.m.

After you finish at the *heiau*, we suggest that you drive to the top of the park. There you'll find a trailhead leading to two of our favorite trails—Aiea Loop and Aiea Ridge trails. You'll also find many picnic tables.

4. Enliven Spirit With a Day of Art

Awareness of the therapeutic and emotional effects of art goes back centuries. Early Christian art was meant not only to tell a story but also to send a message of morality and promote a connection with God. The artist was often seen as a messenger from God. The viewer was to be uplifted and inspired to live a life of devotion.

Experiencing art has other therapeutic effects. A beautiful painting can transport us into a state of peace, joy, and gratitude. That is why our Web site www.alohawellnesstravel.com is filled with the work of artists of Hawai'i that we find particularly healing and inspiring.

Having art in our environment, (office or home) can also have an effect on the energy of our surroundings, sometimes in ways we may not suspect. Using the principles of feng shui may reveal barriers created by the unconscious placement of a painting or art object. For example, having a mountain scene in front of your desk may create the effect of barriers whereas an ocean scene may support greater opportunity and openness.

Think about buying a piece of art from Hawai'i that will continue to remind you of your wellness vacation, and create positive energy in your office or home. Following are suggestions about where you can view, create, or buy art on O'ahu.

Honolulu stands apart from the other islands in the number of art museums, if your love is *viewing* art, you'll be happy you're on O'ahu. **The Honolulu Academy of Arts** (808.532.8701) is itself a treasure, aside from the treasures within. Our bias in favor of natural surroundings as part of a healing environment should be more than evident by now. The Academy is a classic example of what we mean. It abounds in courtyards with birds, trickling fountains, plant life and places to sit and *be*. The first courtyard welcomes you and you'll find a courtyard in every direction you turn. The building is a converted and expanded home of one of the wealthier families of early Hawai'i. The Academy of Arts just celebrated its 75th anniversary and, recently added a section devoted to art of the Hawaiian Islands. You could make this visit a full day experience. The courtyard café is very popular, in part because of its setting fronted with fountains and sculptures. If you're bringing your children or want to introduce a child to the healing quality of art, pick up a Keiki Packet. (808.532.8734) (Admission for the exhibit. Closed on Monday)

The Contemporary Museum (808.526.0232) is up the mountain behind the city. It is also a converted mansion with an exquisitely landscaped garden looking out over the city. The art can be more challenging than soothing and healing, but we often find ourselves powerfully moved by their exhibits. If you want to combine food with art, reserve a table at the indoor/outdoor café. The inside is air-conditioned, which some people seek out, but the real demand is for the outdoor tables so be sure to request your preference. (808.523.3362) (Admission for the exhibit. Closed on Monday)

In early November 2002, a new art gallery dedicated to artists of Hawai'i opened in the stately old YMCA building in the heart of Honolulu. Called **The Hawai'i State Art Museum,** it displays works of art from the state's Art in Public Places collection. The building, itself, is a healing experience—quiet, dignified, set off from the street by an expanse of lawn and graced with an inner courtyard. This style reflects a time in Hawaiian history when life was more leisurely. Hours are 10:00 – 4:00 Tuesday through Saturday. Closed on state and federal holidays. (808.586.0900) (No Admission Fee)

In addition to these three extraordinary art museums, Honolulu has committed to bringing art into our everyday world. Many years ago, the legislature passed a bill providing funding for art to be purchased and placed in public places, showcasing the talents of our exceptional island artists. Two brochures have been published to guide you to this public art in the downtown Honolulu area. One is a walking tour of Chinatown and the other focuses on art in public and historic places. Contact the **State Foundation on Culture and the Arts** (808.586.0304) to have these brochures mailed to you or visit their office at 250 Hotel Street. In the process of viewing this art in public places, you will also discover Honolulu, which has one of the most beautiful downtown areas in the country. You'll find more fountains and trees per square foot than in any other similar city, and you can stand in the middle of most *mauka/makai* streets and see a mountain at one end and the ocean at the other

If your interest is *creating* art, there are several options. Three respected artists offer classes to individuals or small groups. **Sue Stagner**, a popular watercolorist who also has postcards displaying her art in shops around town, gives watercolor classes in her Mānoa Valley home. (808.988.3777) **Patrice Federspiel** also conducts classes or individual sessions and will meet you wherever you want. She is increasingly known as a muralist. Ask about her spirit-based greeting cards. (808.392.9104)

Every Saturday, **Mark Brown** takes a group to some site around the island for painting and instruction. He's a popular art instructor at one of the local universities and has a wealth of information about the art world. You'll need to bring your own materials. (808.843.0145)

If you aren't interested in instruction but want to just join local artists as they paint, you can show up with your own materials at **Foster Botanical Gardens** on Thursday from 9:00 a.m. to 12:00 p.m. Roger Whitlock is the informal leader of a group that meets and paints at this favorite botanical garden.

To explore buying art, we encourage you to start in Waikīkī at the **Zoo fence** (outside the Diamond Head side of the Zoo). You'll find an art show there every Saturday and Sunday with some of the best artists exhibiting. They hang their work on the fence and sit and chat with each other and visitors. You might even find Patrice Federspiel or Sue Stagner exhibiting there.

Cedar Street Gallery has one of the best collections of Hawaiian artists in the city. It carries about 150 artists and sells a wide variety of sculptures and paintings. The owners are personable, enthusiastic supporters of the talent in Hawai'i and are happy to just show you the art with no pressure to buy. (808.589.1580)

The historic town of Haleīwa on the north shore offers several art galleries including the gallery of the prolific marine life artist **Wyland**. His murals can be found on buildings at four locations around O'ahu, 12 in all of Hawai'i. Wyland's art is dedicated to promoting awareness and preservation of the world's oceans. (808.637.7498)

Nohea Gallery in Ward Warehouse Shopping Center on Ala Moana Boulevard is a gallery of more than 450 local artists whose creations include hand-made jewelry, bead necklaces, pottery, watercolors and oils, art glass, and Koa wood furniture, bowls, and boxes. It's definitely worth a visit. We prefer, when possible, buying directly from the artist or from their enthusiastic supporters. (808.596.0074)

In your exploration of art galleries, we urge you to find your way to the **Gallery & Gardens**, 47-754 Lama'ula Road in Kahalu'u, in windward O'ahu. This is a combination of a fine art gallery and botanical garden, open only on Saturdays, Sundays, and Mondays. Here, you find a wide variety of art works ranging from oils and watercolors to jewelry, wooden bowls, and art glass. We suggest you bring mosquito repellent because you will surely want to explore their extensive garden. (808.239.8146)

A unique opportunity to combine art with your inner pilgrimage is to have **Donna Segaran** paint your individualized astrology card. More than just your zodiac sign on cardboard, it includes the strengths and challenges of your life as revealed by your astrological chart. (808.946.8431)

Exploring, viewing, creating, and buying art can be an adventure on O'ahu. It will take you to places you wouldn't otherwise go, introduce you to people you will be glad you met, and hopefully open and expand your interest in art as a wellness experience.

5. Heal From Over Stimulation With A Silent Retreat

Unless we consciously choose otherwise, most of us go through our days over stimulated. Cell phones assure that we are only a phone call away—anywhere, anytime. The media bombards us with news of pain and suffering from all over the world. Family, friends, employers, and organizations all vie for our time. Vacation is a deliberate attempt to get away from it all. But, too often, vacations leave us exhausted.

A silent retreat returns us to ourselves, focusing our attention on the moment. If we take a silent retreat in nature, we have the natural elements to nurture and inform us. If you are in Waikīkī and decide to take just a few hours, we recommend Kapi'olani Park, at the Diamond Head end of Waikīkī. It is a large park with many picnic tables and areas where you can find seclusion. One option is a mini-park tucked up against Diamond Head crater. Or you may choose a picnic table looking out over the water, although there may be less solitude there. Any of the many gardens we recommend in this chapter would also be ideal for a retreat of less than a day.

For a silent retreat of more than a day, **St. Anthony's Retreat Center**, at the back of Kalihi Valley, has a tranquil, cool, and lushly tropical environment that encourages reflection. A half-mile trail wanders up the side of the valley with Stations of the Cross. The grounds include a small park with a grotto, a small chapel, and several meeting rooms. This is a favorite spot for groups on the weekend, so we recommend you take your silent retreat during the week. Single cottages with kitchen are available. (808.845.0065) (Budget)

6. Promote Family Harmony with Mindfulness and Intention

Relationships, especially in our family, are often our greatest challenge to balance and harmony. These relationships also offer our most profound learning opportunities. We often go on vacation with our family thinking that just being away from it all will have a magical effect, that we will be in perfect harmony while we're gone and will return home happier and more at peace with each other. Instead, we typically carry our conflicts and disharmony with us. A vacation offers a time to create healthy changes in family relationships. For families that already relate well, it can be an opportunity to become closer. If you came with children and want to pursue a wellness experience with your spouse or by yourself, **Aloha Nannies** provides quality childcare with a staff that speaks both Japanese and English. (808.394.5434)

Dr. Mitzi Gold at the **Venus and Mars Counseling Center** specializes in working with couples focusing on the different communication styles of men and women. In just one short session, you may be able to unravel the mysteries of male-female communication that caused unnecessary hurt and misunderstanding. This center focuses on John Grey's *Women are From Venus and Men are From Mars* bestselling series. He's a best-selling author because he struck a note with many of us. It's clear men and women often have different ways of viewing the world. Sometimes having that validated can dissolve personal hurts into laughter. (808.737.6277)

A hike and nature meditation offers an opportunity to gain clarity about relationships in the family. On a nature meditation, each family member can pose the question to themselves and to the environment "what can I do to make the family more balanced and harmonious?" or "what do I need to learn in my relationship with …?" After quieting the mind and asking nature to help you find the answer in its metaphorical wisdom, you might discover a bright yellow leaf in the middle of grass that tells you that its okay to be different. Or a little blue flower might signal to you "peace." If you are open to the answer and trust whatever first appears in your mind, you can discover great wisdom in the messages and metaphors of nature.

A picnic in paradise where each person contributes something to making the centerpiece a masterpiece from nature is a fun way to experience family closeness and cooperation.

Taste in music is often a source of conflict between generations in a family. In Hawaiian families, however, music traditionally has been a time of sharing as well as teaching. During family time at home, several generations gather around the guitarist or the person with the 'ukulele and sing together or dance the *hula*. Children learn to sing, dance, and play the 'ukulele at an early age. It is not that hard to learn the basics and it can be a fun instrument to entertain the family. As a family activity, consider taking a group lesson from **Roy Sakuma 'Ukulele Studio** located in Honolulu and also on the windward side of the island in Kāne'ohe. Call ahead if possible. Newspapers from Tokyo to New York City have done articles about him and visitors are increasingly finding their way to his studios for lessons. Learn a Hawaiian song or two, buy some reasonably priced instruments, and take your music home to continue the family activity and to renew the memories of your Hawaiian vacation. (808.732.3739)

7. Open To Your Lifelong Dreams: Explore a "Life Makeover"

A wellness vacation focusing on lifestyle modification takes you in search of the ways in which your life is out of balance. On such a vacation, you commit to investing the necessary time to ask the hard questions about your life. *What areas of your life are out of balance and harmony? What are you not finding time to do that you deeply care about? What do you need to do to honor and take care of your body? What type of work do you really want to do and how can you do it? Is there a better way to live your life?* On O'ahu there are several professional life coaches who will help you with both the questions and the answers.

Marilyn Nagel tells of a client who was highly successful in the real estate profession, but worked too many hours and felt burned out. After a few sessions with Marilyn, she was moved to pursue her passion. She discovered a particular effectiveness in helping people move through bereavement. That, plus her own personal loss, caused her to transform her career and her home into work she truly loved. This client is now successfully doing final stage home care.

Marilyn is a sensitive and supportive woman who makes it easy to discuss openly and honestly what's out of balance and creating disharmony. In addition to helping people with general life style modification goals, Marilyn specializes in helping entrepreneurs. If you are exploring the idea of starting your own business, she can help you consider personal strengths and weaknesses which can support or challenge you. (808.738.2001)

Lee Ann and Javier Del Carpio of **Inner Power International** are two recent transplants from New York City. They are a happy example of a couple who decided to abandon a highly stressful executive lifestyle and do the work they love. They're available to help you do the same thing or at least make your life less stressful. Because of their own experience, they are particularly effective in working with executive-level people who know something is out of balance but don't know what to do about it. If you want them to design your full vacation including finding accommodations as well as meeting with you throughout your stay, they're prepared to do that. (808.626.4680) *(See their article on Personal Life Coaching in Chapter Three.)*

Laura Crites, co-author of this book, is available to help you discover your life's purpose, that inner calling that perhaps was evident to you from childhood or is now experienced as an emptiness or even depression at a life not well spent. In her years as director of the Hawai'i Women's Business Center, Laura helped many women shape their dreams of entrepreneurship around the gift they most wanted to give the world. She tells of one middle-aged woman who came in deeply depressed over a divorce. In addition to the grief of the lost relationship, she was facing economic fears. Her limited employment experience offered little potential for supporting herself. During the interview they discovered that the client loved to house clean but it had never occurred to her that she could make a living doing it. After exploring the possibility of starting a house cleaning business, she left the counseling session feeling hopeful, even enthusiastic, for the first time in months. Within three months, she had her own cleaning business and was doing the work that she loved. (808.941.8253)

While life coaches and counselors can help you in planning desired changes, often there is an inner resistance or fear holding you back from implementing them. It is possible to uncover and effectively address these inner obstacles while on vacation in Hawai'i. A hypnotherapist can help identify the issue and shift the inner message to one of support. **Judy Koch** is a talented, popular, and respected hypnotherapist who is prepared to support your goal in reducing inner obstacles to making the shifts you want to make in your life. (808.526.4766)

Another approach is through holographic repatterning with **Lynn Morgan**. The underlying principle is that our body-mind system gives off frequencies or pulsating energy that reflect the issues or beliefs that are limiting us. Like a radio wave, they can be altered. The process focuses on muscle testing to bring our subconscious limiting beliefs and experiences to the conscious level. From there, self-healing modalities are used to complete the frequency shift. This means that you can start the process with Lynn and continue it after you return home. (808.722.3581)

A vacation, especially one to Hawai'i, typically causes us to wish for more balance and harmony in our lives—more of what Hawai'i seems to offer. You may be able to achieve that by focusing a few hours of your vacation time on examining the patterns, routines, and challenges of your lifestyle.

8. Let Nature Nourish and Replenish You: Have a Picnic in Paradise

We grew up with picnics as a form of celebration. As often as Mother could make it happen, we had them. While Dad considered them a bit of a bother with bugs, Mother never tired of picnics up until the final days of her life at age 87. This act of celebration involving each other, the food, and the environment, fed our souls as well as our bodies. We share her enthusiasm for this adventure in outdoor dining and have explored places all over the islands, which we're prepared to recommend. One of the aspects about picnics here that makes them truly an experience in paradise is that the trade winds support you in keeping bugs away. We're not promising your picnic will be insect free, but you aren't likely to be pestered by them as you often are elsewhere. Bugs with *aloha*!

We advocate picnics to celebrate sunrise, sunset, mid-day, and moonrise during full moon evenings. For it to be a true celebration, you'll want to pay attention to the aesthetics. We often use a *pareau* (the brightly colored beach cover up for women) as a tablecloth. You might want to pick up some matching Hawaiian decorator plastic plates at one of the shops at Ala Moana Shopping Center. They'll be a nice memory when you return home.

Sunrise and moonrise picnics are best on the windward side of the island. We recommend **Kailua Beach Park, Bellows Beach Park**, or **Waimānalo Beach Park**. Barbecue grills are available at each of these parks or there are ample places to pick up carry-out food in the area. Watching the full moon rise out of the water is a special cause for celebration. Any of these beach parks will give you an unobstructed view.

For a breakfast picnic near Waikīkī, we recommend **Kapi'olani Park**. You can pick up coffee at Starbucks at the corner of Kāpāhulu and Kalākaua and a breakfast carryout at any of the restaurants along the beachfront. There are oceanfront picnic tables as well as ones across the park tucked up under Diamond Head.

For sunset picnics, the Waikīkī side is best. From **Queens Beach**, the beautifully landscaped beach park on the Diamond Head side of Waikīkī, you can see the lights of Waikīkī come on as the night descends. **Magic Island**, another favorite spot, is a broad peninsula at the 'Ewa end of Waikīkī across from Ala Moana Shopping Center. Choices include tables on the 'Ewa side of the park to fully enjoy the sunset or ones that face the harbor where, between 5:00 and 6:30 on Friday evenings you can watch the sailboats leave and return to the harbor. From this location you'll also see the lights of Waikīkī come on, and on Friday nights, around 7:30 p.m. or 8:00 p.m., you'll have an ocean side seat for fireworks that are launched from the Hilton Hawaiian Village. For sunset picnics at Magic Island, we typically call ahead to California Pizza Kitchen at Ala Moana Shopping Center and order a pizza and salad to go. (808.941.7715)

Finally, we've had many a birthday celebration sunset picnic at the park at **Kewalo Basin** with a crowd as big as twenty. Our favorite table is right under the park light that allows us to linger after dusk. The area is somewhat protected from the trade winds and is close enough to the water to hear it lapping against the stone wall as you eat. The park at Kewalo Basin is a small park area sandwiched between the Kewalo Basin boat harbor and the ocean, 'Ewa of Ala Moana Beach Park.

There are many picnic spots for mid-day celebrations. As you drive around the island, if you have "picnic" in mind, you'll find beaches and look outs that continually invite you. Let your *pareau* be your picnic blanket if you don't find a table. ENJOY!!

9. Combine Fitness and Serenity: Hike The Many Tropical Trails of O'ahu

Hiking offers both an opportunity for fitness exercise and an experience of the healing power of nature. O'ahu has some of the best hiking trails in Hawai'i, and many of them are no more than 15 minutes from Waikīkī.

Tantalus, the mountain between Mānoa Valley and

Nu'uanu Valley has been called by some "Honolulu's backyard rainforest." Here you will find 17 trails that crisscross the mountain and intersect with each other. The two-lane drive up Tantalus is called Round Top Drive. It takes you under a canopy of kukui and banyan trees, introducing you along the way to the diverse foliage you will encounter on your walk.

The trailheads on Tantalus are clearly marked and parking areas are usually evident as well, although you may need to park along the side of the road depending on which trail you choose. Stop by the **Nature Center** (2131 Makiki Heights Drive, 808.955.0100) on the way up and get maps of the trails. There is a trail beginning at the Nature Center that goes up rather steeply though the return trip down is quite enjoyable. Our favorite trail, however, is the **Mānoa Cliffs Trail** that takes you past banana and coffee trees, through a bamboo forest to a lookout with a view of the ocean on the windward side. These trails are safe but it's good to hike with a companion or at least take a cell phone. At the end of this book we've listed hiking books that include trails on O'ahu as well as other islands.

If you don't want to venture out on your own, there are several opportunities to join others. Both the **Trail and Mountain Club** (808.488.0044) and the **Sierra Club** (808.538.6616) have weekly hikes on Sunday mornings. They normally carpool so you can catch a ride with one of the members. Call in advance, however. There is a nominal fee.

Roger Sorrell and David Frost are part of a Wednesday hiking group and they invite you to join them. Often there are as many as thirty people on the hike. Both Roger and David are committed nature lovers and their enthusiasm will win your heart. When you call, check with them about how strenuous the hike will be. The advantages of going with a group like theirs are that you'll meet local people, you'll go on trails that often aren't in the hiking books, and the price is right. (808.926.7208)

There are several hiking options designed just for visitors. With these, you have pick-up and drop-off transportation and guides who go out of their way to inform you about the natural world you'll be exploring. Guided hikes generally include snacks, mosquito repellent, water, and umbrellas. On the **Bike Hawai'i** hike, guests even have the option of wearing boots, provided by the company, to avoid the mud on the trail. **John**

Alfred, owner of Bike Hawai'i, (808.734.4214) combines a bike trip down Tantalus and a hike in the Mānoa Valley. He has access to private land that includes a 50-foot waterfall no other tour group will see. The combination of the early morning ride down the mountain and the exclusive hike into the rain forest has special appeal. **Hawaiian Islands Eco-Tours** (808.236.7766) and **O'ahu Nature Tours** (808.924.2473) are two other eco-tour companies that specialize in small groups and live their concern for the environment.

There are many options for hiking. Regardless of the option you choose, you'll discover something special about Hawai'i.

10. Transport Yourself to a World of Calm: Visit our Underwater Friends

Watching fish move silently and gracefully around an aquarium can mesmerize most of us. Perhaps they symbolize for us the silence, serenity, and peace that we long for. As a New York fire fighter here to heal from the trauma of 9/11 observed, "they seem to co-exist so peacefully. I wish we could do as well." For whatever reason, being around and watching ocean life is a healing experience. On O'ahu, you can get up close and personal with exotic fish at **Hanauma Bay**, one of the best snorkeling sites in the state. Note: it's closed on Tuesdays to give the fish a break from entertaining tourists. Please obey the rules that include not walking on the coral and not feeding the fish.

Sea Life Park, a dramatically beautiful drive along the windward coast from Hanauma Bay is another opportunity to observe sea life. Fish there seem to have fun, especially the performing porpoises. Having seen their playful antics in the wild, the porpoise show seems less forced and more natural than we thought before. The aquarium portion is extensive but less intimate than its sister in Waikīkī, the **Waikīkī Aquarium**. Having recently completed a renovation, the Waikīkī Aquarium is now world class. Here you can study at close range not only extraordinary fish but also an extensive assortment of exotic coral.

Perhaps the most popular and even mystical connection humans have with marine life is our relationship with dolphins. For centuries, humans have had an affinity for them. Greeks depicted dolphins on their vases. Stories abound of dolphins saving humans from drowning and dolphin therapy has been used successfully with a wide variety of developmentally challenged people including Down syndrome and autistic children. While there is no formal dolphin therapy available on O'ahu, there are many stories of people whose lives have been transformed by encounters with them on the Leeward coast of O'ahu.

Rich Holland, owner of **Dolphins and You**, has several such stories to tell including his own journey of awakening through dolphin contacts. Rich and his staff take small groups out on kayaks to minimize any negative environmental impact and maximize your exposure to these gentle, fun-loving creatures. He'll pick you up at your hotel, serve smoothies and muffins beachside, and do his best to assure that you have a good time. Even if the dolphins fail to show, which sometimes happens, you will have snorkel and fins to enjoy the underwater scenery. The view from off shore up into the Mākua Valley with its soft, emerald mountains is enough to make your trip worthwhile. You'll launch from one of the most sacred beaches on O'ahu, according to Hawaiian beliefs. The healing energy emitting from the Mākua Valley is also reputed to be some of the most powerful in Hawai'i. Rich suggests that this is why the dolphins are most likely to gather at the mouth of this extraordinarily beautiful valley. (808.696.4414)

Tori and Armin Cullins of **Wild Side Specialty Tours** also offer dolphin excursions. They operate from a catamaran that minimizes environmental damage and maximizes comfort. As with Rich, they will only take small groups. Tori is a marine biologist so your trip will include information you might not otherwise have. (808.306.7273)

Being on or near the water is one of the healing aspects of Hawai'i. When you add that to an experience of the beauty, grace, and fun of the wonderful animals that call Hawaiian waters *home*, you will have experienced the power of nature as healer.

11. Experience the Healing Energy of Gardens

Staying with the "nature as healer" theme, we encourage you to visit some of the remarkable gardens of O'ahu. These green oases offer anything from an hour to a full day experience in a different world. You may want to go there just to explore the exotic plants of Hawai'i or to nurture body and soul with a picnic in paradise. If your vacation is focused on the inner pilgrimage, you may seek out a nature meditation experience in this beautifully landscaped environment.

Beginning closest to Waikīkī, we guide you to **Lyon Arboretum**, a 194-acre botanical garden at the very back of Mānoa Valley. This garden provides trails that carry you up into the forest past more than 5,000 species of exotic plants. At the end of a 20-minute self-guided tour, you will find "inspiration point" with a clearing and bench inviting meditation and contemplation. You'll want to check in at the office, look through their gift shop and get mosquito repellent if you didn't bring any. (It's open from 9:00 a.m. to 3:00 p.m. everyday except Sunday.) (808.988.0464) (Donation Requested)

On your way through Mānoa Valley, to or from Lyon Arboretum, we suggest that you stop at the Japanese garden behind the **East-West Center** at the University of Hawai'i. Japanese gardens are designed to evoke quiet meditation with the elements of nature. The simplicity of these gardens invites you to free your mind from clutter and let it rest as you open yourself to a greater level of awareness. Often a Japanese garden will consist of carefully raked sand surrounding a large rock and perhaps one or two plants. Others have ponds, fountains or streams as their focal point. This garden represents the latter type. The manicured grass, flowing stream, strategically placed rocks and stepping stone path up to the top of a small waterfall suggest "engaged contemplation" rather than restful awareness. To get there turn Diamond Head off of University Boulevard on to Dole Street, then go *mauka* on East West Drive. You can ask the security person at the gate, where the garden and guest parking are. (Parking Fee Only)

Another garden in Honolulu, just 'Ewa of downtown, is the **Foster Botanical Garden**. This 14-acre tropical oasis is wedged between the freeway and Vineyard Boulevard, near Chinatown. Dr. William Hillebrand launched the garden with trees he planted in the 1850s. Among other things you'll find there are an orchid garden, a prehistoric glen, and a palm collection. (Open daily from 9:00 a.m. to 4:00 p.m. Guided tours at 1:00 p.m.) (808.522.7060) (Admission Fee)

A final favorite is the **Ho'omaluhia (peaceful place) Botanical Garden** tucked up against the base of the Ko'olau Mountains in windward O'ahu. Located at the end of Luluku

A Nature Meditation

The difference between a pleasant experience in a garden and a wellness experience that provides answers and insights is often "intention" and "focus." Take into the garden with you a specific issue or question for which you want answers. As you enter the garden pay attention to which plants call to you for closer inspection. Give yourself time and space to be pulled by a plant or scene that seems to invite your attention. Then focus on the larger issue you want addressed and ask what you need to be learning. Quiet your mind and open yourself to the metaphor in nature that might inform you or pay attention to the thoughts or words that come into your mind and how they respond to your search for answers.†

Road, this 400-acre garden features groupings of plants from major tropical regions around the world, emphasizing those that are native to Hawai'i. It is serenely quiet, as gardens should be, but its power and presence comes from the mountains towering above. You will feel it instantly when you arrive. Plan to walk around, feel, and explore. This is a favorite spot for a picnic in paradise. We have often gone with friends at sundown to celebrate, with wine and cheese, the end of the day and the mystical energy of nature. Overnight camping is available. Open from 9:00 a.m. to 4:00 p.m. except Christmas and New Year's Day. Guided nature hikes are offered at 10:00 a.m. on Saturdays and 1:00 p.m. on Sundays. Please call to register for the guided tours. (808.233.7323) (No Admission Fee)

12. Purchase Hawaiian Healing Products: Noni, Kukui, Macadamia Nut

Explore the healing power of nature, by experiencing the healing properties of the extraordinary plants of Hawai'i. There are three healing plants that find their home in Hawai'i—the *noni*, macadamia nut, and *kukui* nut plants. *Noni* and *kukui* nut were part of the pharmacopoeia of early Hawaiians. Macadamia nut is a modern introduction.

Noni is described as "the aspirin of the ancients" in a book by that name by Diana Fairechild. She labels it "the most widely used medicinal herb in Polynesia." The fruit is about the size of an apple, yellow in color and unpleasant in odor when ripe. This odor is its protection against insects and small animals. Fortunately, it doesn't taste the way it smells, although the taste of the green fruit is more pleasant, somewhat like apple juice. Hawaiians use many parts of the plant including its leaves, bark, flower, root, and both green and ripe fruit, depending on whether the need is topical or internal. It has been proven effective with such conditions as chronic fatigue, fever, heart disease, hypertension, depression, lung problems, obesity, menstrual problems and cancer. Hawaiians even used it as protection from evil spirits. One study administered *noni* to mice with lung cancer. The life span of treated vs. untreated mice was substantially increased. Diana Fairechild's book chronicles her healing experience using *noni.* As a stewardess she had become severely ill from the routine spraying of pesticides in the aircraft cabins. Her career was destroyed and life was threatened by this buildup of toxins in her body until she began taking *noni.* Her book is delightfully written with many testimonials. (www.flyana.com.)

Noni grown in Hawai'i is reputed to be the highest quality not only because of the fertile volcanic soil which seems to be especially important but also because of the way it is processed. Look for *noni* that has been hand picked and, if possible, freeze dried. **Maui Medicinal** follows this process and its products can only be found in stores in Hawai'i. (808.572.9331)

Another miracle plant is the *kukui* nut tree. Discovery of *kukui* pollen in ancient sites in Hawai'i suggests it is an indigenous tree. In 1959 it was made the state tree of Hawai'i.

As with *noni,* the **kukui nut tree** was used in many ways. Its wood was turned into canoes, the hard shells of the nuts were used as jewelry, the roots and bark could be made into dyes, the dried nuts could be burned and used as torches, the leaves helped reduce swelling and bruises, gum and resin was used in external sores and as glue and the charcoal from the shell was used for sore throats. The raw meet of the nut was used as a laxative.

The recently rediscovered healing power of its oils is truly exciting. **Oils of Aloha**, an O'ahu manufacturer, has begun producing *kukui* nut oil and the effects seem nearly miraculous. People from all over the world have provided written testimonials for its healing power with all manner of skin problems. *Psoriasis*—"It is fantastic! I've had psoriasis for 44 years and have never had a product that has helped as much." Canada; *Eczema*—"I am the lady who cannot thank you enough for the *kukui* oil. It has completely changed my life…I have a young friend who is 16, and has had the worst kind of eczema all over his body since he was born. His local dermatologist says it is the worst kind he's ever seen. So I went to see him and gave him a bottle of *kukui* nut oil with Vitamin E. Three weeks later his father came to see me to say he can't get over the relief his son has had since applying it. (England.) *Radiation relief*—"I was operated on October 13, 1998 for breast cancer. Then after I had radiation and chemotherapy…my skin was red, dry and burned. My boss gave me a sample of *Kukui* Nut Oil to treat my skin. It's fantastic! My skin is like before." (Belgium) *Burns*—"I used your cream on my arm which was severely burned and would not heal properly. It is now back to normal and I will continue to use your moisturizing cream and highly recommend it. Thank you…"(California)

Oils of Aloha is the only manufacturer of kukui nut oil that we've discovered. Their small factory is a converted country movie theater on the north shore of O'ahu. Their products are in most drug stores and health food stores but may not be available on the mainland yet. It works with mosquito bites, sunburns as well as those skin problems mentioned above. (www.oils-of-aloha.com.) (Toll Free 1.800.367.6010)

Exciting research on **Macadamia Nut Oil**, another tree that finds its home in Hawai'i, is also being done by Oils of Aloha. The world's first commercial macadamia nut plantation was on the Big Island and there are currently over 700 macadamia nut plantations on that island. Hawai'i supplies 70% of the world's consumption. Interest in macadamia nut oil has increased with our concern about the kinds of dietary fats and oils that contribute to heart disease and obesity. Research shows that macadamia nut oil is the healthiest of all oils, having the highest level of monounsaturated fat (healthy fat); higher even than Olive Oil. It has no cholesterol and no solvents are used in extracting the oil from the nut. As with the noni fruit, Hawai'i has been found to produce the highest quality of nuts and products made from the nuts

13. Nurture Mind, Body, and Spirit: Have a Spa Experience

Spas are an increasingly popular way of relaxing as well as pampering yourself—good for the body, mind, and spirit. O'ahu has a wide array of options beginning with hotel spas in Waikīkī. The **Hyatt Regency Waikīkī**, (808.921.6097) the **Outrigger Reef on**

the Beach, (808.988.0101) the **Hilton Hawaiian Village** (808.949.4321) and the **Royal Hawaiian Hotel**. (808.923.7311) Outside of Waikīkī, you will find the **Mālama Spa** on the third floor of Ala Moana Shopping Center in Honolulu. Mālama is run by a local couple committed to using natural products. (808.988.0101) There is also **Ampy's** a day spa (808.946.3838) adjacent to the Ala Moana Shopping Center. They offer facials and various body massages including prenatal massage and hand and foot care treatments.

Your most unforgettable spa experiences, however, may be those you seek out by visiting professionals at their locations around the island. For a fantastic facial, **Cheryl Nakachi** offers high tech facial and massage treatments that use ultrasonic massage, infrared rays and negative ions to bring out the natural beauty of your skin. An infrared blanket that seemed to induce sleep during the process covers the massage table—or perhaps it was just fatigue and deep relaxation. She is also a licensed massage therapist, Reiki master and does psychic readings and card readings. Her office is a short distance *mauka* of Waikīkī. (808.384.4464)

Susan Snyder, a licensed aesthetician, has partnered with a dermatologist at the Honolulu Medical Group office near downtown. Her treatment room and relaxing facials make for a very enjoyable spa experience. (808.537.2211)

Sabrina Stevens offers a sublime facial treatment in her studio in Honolulu. Her life commitment to supporting women in achieving facial balance and harmony from the inside out comes from a traumatic attack she experienced as a young career woman when she was knifed several times in the face by a burglar. After years of treatment, reconstructive surgery, and her own wellness work, she has fully healed with no signs of the attack. Her work and philosophy are so popular that aestheticians travel from all over the country to her teaching retreats on the Big Island. (808.923.6737)

In creating your own spa experience, your next step is the massage. On the Honolulu side of the mountain, there are several options. A short "trolley" ride from Waikīkī is the **Honolulu School of Massage** (808.733.0000) where economical student massages are available. **The Massage Specialists**, at the 'Ewa end of Waikīkī, also offer massage at student rates. You'll find them in the highrise across from Hard Rock Café. Massage Specialists have 70 therapists on staff and welcome drop-ins. (808.941.8101)

You might also consider having a massage amidst the beauty of nature. A short drive to the end of a valley behind Honolulu, **Morgan Blank** lives in a tree house that doubles as his massage studio. If you come with a partner who also wants a massage, one of you can relax on his deck with tea and fruit or go for a hike up the trail behind his house while the other has the massage. He also welcomes you to linger with refreshments, including fruit picked from his trees, read from his extensive library, and just enjoy the environment. (808.739.3866)

At the end of another valley, only 25 minutes from Waikīkī is the **Hawai'i Wellness Institute**, a retreat center, which offers an open-air massage next to a stream. **Sunny Massad**, the visionary and creative energy behind the Institute, offers a classy and comfortable environment to relax, enjoy, walk around, have tea, read books, and just relax. (808.848.5544)

On the windward side of the island, in Kailua, you have a beachside massage option that could potentially be your most unforgettable massage experience. **Jayme Newhouse** of **Aloha Body Therapy** plants her massage table on the beach by the water. As she covers your body with homemade natural products, you are caressed by the trade winds, warmed by the sun, and lulled into a deep relaxation by the sounds of the waves. If you and your partner want a tandem massage, she'll arrange that too. (808.255.4862)

For a hot stone massage visit **Rainbow Healing Arts Center. Kathy Edwards and Liza Delin** offer a combination of reiki, craniosacral work, and various types of massage at their home studio in the hills above Kailua. (808.262.3700) *(See the article by them on massage in Chapter Three.)*

Also in Kailua, the **Hawai'i Healing Arts Academy and School of Therapeutic Massage** provides discounted student massages in individual, attractively decorated massage treatment rooms. The teaching curriculum is more extensive than others in the state and their commitment to "beyond excellence" has them partnering with other bodywork professionals such as chiropractors. If, after a short interview session, your massage therapist believes that your condition might best be treated by a chiropractor first, he/she will help arrange an appointment. The student rate is very affordable but if you want to work with a fully licensed massage therapist, there are seven who call this their professional home. The Academy is located at the Kailua Medical Arts Building. (808.266.2462)

14. Find Out About Problems Before They Surface with Preventive Medical Screening

Many of us who view ourselves as generally healthy have experienced uneasiness as we see "healthy" friends succumb to cancer or heart disease. If this describes you, there are two very good opportunities on O'ahu to ease your mind. In many cases, preventive medical screening uses the most advanced technology to help identify potential physical problems before they manifest. This process can leave you feeling relieved and send you home with new peace of mind, or at least with greater clarity about challenges you face.

One option is the **Holistica Hawai'i Health Center** at the Hilton Hawaiian Village. Holistica is part of Hilton's commitment to making top quality wellness experiences available to visitors on O'ahu. It offers the most advanced Electron Beam Tomography scanning device available. This is a high tech, painless way of detecting potential problems that your doctor isn't able to discover. Several articles have appeared locally about people who discovered a critical heart problem with this screening just weeks after getting a clean bill of health from their doctor. It's a bit expensive but well worth the cost. (808.951.6546)

Also available on O'ahu is a thermal imaging screening process for early detection of breast cancer. If you are one of the millions of women who has deep reservations about the controversial mammograms, thermology could be a good alternative for you. Using a heat seeking technique, pre-cancerous cells, which radiate heat at a higher level than healthy cells, can be detected years before they become full blown cancer cells. This technology was not embraced by the American medical establishment because in early studies it showed signs of cancer that mammograms didn't pick up. It was, therefore, dismissed as inaccurate. A ten-year follow up study confirmed the accuracy of thermology, however. But, to date, the technology has not been accepted by doctors in the United States although it is used almost exclusively in Europe. **Dr. Linda Fickes** is the only wellness practitioner on O'ahu with a thermography machine. (808.377.1811) The internet has considerable information on thermology. Also, see an article by Dr. Fickes on thermology on our website at www.alohawellnesstravel.com.

15. Step Outside The Box With a Cutting Edge Therapy

The possibility exists that your vacation here can introduce you to a remedy for a debilitating condition that had seemed hopeless.

O'ahu has several complementary health providers who are doing cutting edge work in their specialty area. These highly trained professionals are committed to looking outside the box for solutions to problems which have eluded traditional approaches.

Dr. Jason Uchida, a naturopathic physician at the **Island Wellness Center**, has invested years in studying chronic immune deficiency diseases such as fibromyalgia, chronic fatigue, lupus, and rheumatoid arthritis. From his research he concluded that over 80 percent of these conditions are due to medications that are prescribed by thousands of doctors every day. The pharmaceutical culprits are antibiotics, estrogen, hormone replacement therapies, and steroids. Since women are most likely to take these medications, they are disproportionately the victims of these debilitating conditions. Dr. Uchida's treatment involves a strict dietary plan that corrects the digestive track where food sensitivities trigger the painful symptoms. In clear, understandable language, using the scientific textbooks of your primary care physician, he takes the time to explain the merits of his theory. His case is compelling and testimonials to his treatment are convincing. He is a man with a mission but doesn't push his remedy or philosophy on his patients. As one patient said, "I like Dr. Uchida because he doesn't send you out the door with a mass of supplements." Instead, he works with you in making the changes you need to make in your daily diet. If you suffer from any of the autoimmune diseases that he treats, a vacation devoted to working with Dr. Uchida could restore your health. (808.589.1955)

Both **Dr. Joni Kroll** (808.262.4550) and **Dr. Dennis Rhatigan**, (808.841.3456) may be the answer to your prayers if you suffer from allergies. Through their work, you are one session away from relief without medication and side effects. Their process is called Nambudripad's Allergy Elimination Techniques (NAET). The principle is that allergies result from energy blockages in the body caused by contact with the adverse energy of other substances. The two-step NAET process first identifies the allergens and then unblocks the energy. Rather than taking you through weeks of allergy tests, they use kinesiology, or muscle testing, to identify the substances you are allergic to. Then, as you hold a vial containing that substance, with a mechanical device, they first tap the energy meridians along your spine. Then, they further clear your energy with an acupuncture treatment. To support the process, you are asked to stay away from that substance for 25 hours since it takes two hours for energy to make its way through each of the body's twelve meridians. At the end of that time most clients become free of their allergic reaction to that substance. More than four hundred practitioners have been trained in this process. *Winning the War Against Asthma and Allergies*, a book by Dr. Cutler, describes the process and provides testimonials. Physicians using the process claim an 80% to 90% success rate and experiences with patients in Honolulu support that success rate.

At the **Integrated Health Care** center, you will discover **Dr. Teresa Denny**, whose open mind and voracious curiosity makes her especially valuable as a wellness resource. Her initiation into the healing profession began as a child who was always sick. Her mother, a nurse, sought out herbs and other remedies from local healers. Thirty years ago Dr. Denny almost died from a ruptured appendix. To solve her own health conditions she began the lifelong pursuit of knowledge about health, wellness, and prevention. After completing medical school, she has continued to pursue certificates and diplomas in many of the alternative treatments now available. Among other distinctions, Dr. Denny is a Member of the American Academy of Anti-Aging Medicine. Dr. Denny and her staff have created a center that offers truly integrated wellness opportunities. Along with traditional Western medicine, you will find cranial osteopathy, acupuncture, aromatherapy, herbal therapy, massage, nutrition and diet, shiatsu/trigger point therapy, and sound therapy. If you've wanted one source of expert advice on the various alternative approaches that might address your wellness challenges the Integrated Health Care center and Dr. Denny would be an excellent choice. (808.732.0888)

For those seeking the security of a medical environment as they venture into the alternative health care realm, the **Honolulu Medical Group, Inc.** has opened an **Integrative Health Care Department**. Here you will find chiropractic care, acupuncture, facials, and massage therapy. (808.537.2211)

Diane Poire, founder of **Touch of Life** in Honolulu, is an energy healer of remarkable skill. Her referrals come by word of mouth including several physicians who send patients they have been unsuccessful in treating. One testimonial to her abilities comes from a physician himself, who was referred by one of his colleagues for chronic, severe back pain. He writes that he rarely provides a written testimonial but the effect of her treatment on his painful condition was so profound that he made an exception. He further explains that he doesn't know how she did it but he left his treatment with her fully recovered after years of an inoperable condition. She also does gentle structural adjustments and advises on diet and herbs. While her results are impressive, she stresses that the pain is often a result of emotional, mental or spiritual issues and permanent freedom from a painful physical condition may require making changes in those areas. Diane is articulate, enthusiastic, and humble about her abilities. As with so many other talented healers, she began her work after extensive health issues of her own that did not respond to conventional treatment. (808.523.0878)

O'ahu offers many opportunities to explore advanced alternative healing possibilities. We invite you to come with an open mind, a curiosity about what is possible, and an awareness of the nurturing and healing environment of Hawai'i.

16. Explore The Power of Energy with an Energy Healing Session

Energy medicine is seen by some as the medicine of the 21st century. Its underlying concept is that everything consists of active, vital energy. Both ancient wisdom and modern physics support this theory.

Energy healing works under the premise that physical health is dependent on balanced, flowing and harmonious energy. Blocked energy leads to disease. Prevention, diagnosis and treatment focuses on energy flows and blockages. For those wellness providers who operate from this philosophy, the first thing to do when you arrive is examine your energy. *Acupuncturists* do it by taking your pulse in 12 different ways—6 pulses to assess 12 organs. For those of us who can barely find one pulse, their sensitivity in reading multiple pulses is astounding. An energy treatment may identify and relieve blockages you're not yet aware of and relieve conditions after they have become evident and uncomfortable.

Acupuncture is probably the best known and most researched form of energy healing. An estimated 5000 studies have documented its effectiveness. An acupuncture treatment could address an existing condition such as back pain or be a preventative measure, releasing blocks in your energy before they build up. **Lan Kao**, a Traditional Chinese Medicine practitioner and licensed acupuncturist will provide you with a highly professional acupuncture session but takes the time to explain the theory behind her work. She got her degree, with honors, in California and studied with some of the top acupuncture masters in China. Lan is highly professional, informative, gentle, and committed to working as a partner with her patients in achieving a maximum level of health. (808.262.7899)

Jane Starn provides another form of energy healing. She is a professor emeritus at the University of Hawai'i as well as a faculty member of the Barbara Brennan School of Healing. Her work involves sensing a person's energy field, identifying blocks and disharmony in that field and running energy through and around the client. Jane conducts her work in her hillside home above Honolulu. (808.737.8859)

The **Taorobics Center** specializes in Dahnhak, a Korean tradition of physical and mental exercises that seeks to use the energy of the body to attain a spiritual awakening. Their work includes a special form of yoga, tai chi, meditation, brain respiration, and Ki healing. The Center staff is particularly enthusiastic about the potential of brain respiration as a modality to enhance our mental capacities through manipulating the energy in the brain. (808.942.0003)

Healing Touch® is an increasingly popular form of energy healing with trained practitioners radiating their own energy onto the patient to relieve pain, reduce stress and promote healing. Queens Hospital in Honolulu is reputed to have more healing touch practitioners per patient than any other hospital in the country. While doctors were initially skeptical, most have accepted that something does in fact happen that benefits the patient. Many independent Healing Touch practitioners are available to meet with you. For a list of practitioners, call 808.432.8137.

Consider an energy healing session while you are on O'ahu with practitioners who are among the best in their profession.

Fitness and Sports

17. Combine Natural Beauty with Fitness: Do Tai Chi, Yoga, or Exercise in the Park

Because of the limitations of their climate back home, many visitors to Hawai'i view an exercise routine as extended periods on a treadmill in a gymnasium or other indoor environments. While in Hawai'i, allow the beauty of the land and the gentle climate to support you, at the beach or in the park, in launching a new commitment to your physical health.

Every morning about 9:00 a.m., a group of retired people gather for moderate exercise in the beach area between the Army museum at **Fort DeRussy** and the **Hale Koa Hotel**. They gear the level of exercise to those who want some exercise but not a strenuous workout. People seem to have fun and the view over the brilliant blue ocean is a great stimulus to fitness intentions. All are welcome.

Another option is learning yoga, tai chi or qigong in the park. **Donna Segaran** (808.946.8431) is prepared to meet you in the park near Waikīkī to give private or group yoga lessons. The **Taorobics Center** conducts yoga in the park every Saturday at 8:30 at Magic Island. This is across Ala Moana Blvd from the Ala Moana Shopping Center.

On the windward side of the island, **Charlotte Nuessle**, a very popular local yoga instructor, offers private lessons as well as regular early morning classes at Kailua Beach. Several people drive from Waikīkī to join her group. After starting your morning with yoga on the beach you might try breakfast at Cinnamon's in Kailua Square. Many locals rate it as the best breakfast place in town with several health conscious items. (808.230.8902)

K.C. Carlsberg, owner of **Try Fitness**, is a personal trainer with a commitment to helping women become and stay physically fit. K.C. partners with you in developing a fitness plan to take home and will continue her support long distance by phone. Many people are more motivated by fitness if it is a group activity. If that describes you, K.C. invites you to join a group of women she guides weekday evenings from 5:30-7:30 p.m. The locations vary but they are always outside in beautiful settings. K.C. is the force behind the Nike Wahine (women's) Triathlon. If you are a serious athlete, or at least feel you want to do a women's only triathlon, contact her for information. (808.531.8573)

Walking is the healthiest of all exercise and the gentle tradewinds and beauty of Hawai'i encourage you to walk. There are several convenient routes in the vicinity of Waikīkī to begin or continue a walking routine. These routes apply to joggers as well. The route around **Ala Wai Canal**, just five blocks *mauka* of Waikīkī, is 3.5 miles. The stretch between McCully and Kāpāhulu Avenues borders the canal on one side with views of the mountains and then takes you past a soccer field and along a golf course. Shaded areas and tradewinds keep you refreshed anytime of the day but this is an especially lovely walk at sunset.

Another option is around **Kapi'olani Park**, which is approximately 2.5 miles full circle. Kapi'olani Park is just a block from the ocean and part of Waikīkī. If that isn't enough for you, expand your route up the road to Diamond Head lookout. The walk up the hill to the lookout is lined much of the way with exquisite mansions. As you near the top, private homes give way to a public garden created and maintained by a committed group of locals who decided to transform a dumping area for trash into a celebration of beauty. The lookout parking lot at the top is a favorite place to watch the surfers below as well as just enjoy an unobstructed view of the ocean.

For free group runs, visit **Niketown**, located at the 'Ewa end of Waikīkī. Be at their store at King Kalākaua Plaza at 6:00 p.m. on Wednesday. They have three, five, and seven-mile options and meet afterward for socializing. (808.943.6453)

If you have a walking or running routine at home, or if you're thinking about starting one, we suggest taking advantage of the weather, scenery, and easily accessible routes while on vacation in Waikīkī.

18. Plan Your Vacation Around a Sporting Event

Hawai'i's year round warm climate means sporting events are scheduled twelve months of the year. Athletes who enjoy competing, or just want a unique fitness experience while on O'ahu can plan a vacation around a wide choice of participatory events. Imagine leaving behind the snowy weather of February to compete in a two-mile rough-water swim from one end of Waikīkī to the other. You may be a breast cancer survivor who came out of the trauma of that experience with a renewed commitment to being physically fit. **The Race for the Cure**, the nationwide fundraising event for breast cancer, is held in late September. (Call 808.754.1817 or check the Race Hawai'i website at www.racehawaii.com).

If you have a family commitment to fitness, you might be interested in the **Holokikī O 'Alele** race, which includes a 1-mile race and 100-yard relay for *keiki* (children) as well as a half-marathon, 5-kilometer race, or 20-kilometer relay for you. The Hawaiian emphasis on family is reflected in the many races that have a *keiki* component. Several of the athletic events have a health educational component as well. (Contact the Windward Marathon Association, P.O. Box 4528, Honolulu, HI 96812, or visit their website at www.active.com.)

Sporting events range from mountain biking, swimming, triathlons, 5-K races to marathons, walks, and amateur surfing. For information and a year-round event calendar, visit the Hawai'i Race website at www.hawaiirace.com. You can get on their mailing list by calling 808.538.0330, or writing Hawai'i Race, 9 N. Pauahi, #200, Honolulu, HI 96817.

Many of the activities are fundraisers so you are also contributing to a worthy cause while having a fitness vacation in Hawai'i. Some of the causes include the Global Environmental Fund, cancer research, AIDS awareness, Epilepsy Foundation of Hawai'i, and Alzheimer's Association.

Return home with a tee shirt commemorating your fitness/wellness experience on O'ahu.

19. Launch or Maintain a Strength Training Routine

Gyms and pilates opportunities are available to anyone who wants to use their wellness vacation to develop a strength training routine or stay in shape while they are here. Visitors can use the extensive set of machines at the **Central YMCA** for $10 a day. You'll find it on Atkinson Drive, across from the Ala Moana Shopping Center, easy walking distance from Waikīkī. In Hawaiian style, this YMCA has a casual open-air café and friendly staff. They have saunas, a nice sized swimming pool, and regular workout and aerobic classes.

The **Hawai'i Athletic Club** is a bit more upscale with air-conditioning and a greater variety of machines. It doesn't have a swimming pool, however. You'll find it an easy bus ride away, near downtown Honolulu. They also have a $10 day pass for visitors. The atmosphere here is a bit more "club-like" with monthly birthday celebrations for club members and a newsletter. (808.537.1131)

Pilates is an attractive alternative to weight lifting and an increasingly popular method of exercise. In his promotion of physical fitness, President Bush announced that he has pilates set up for the White House staff in their gym. This alternative to weight lifting has been around for about 80 years as a fitness program emphasizing strength training, flexibility, posture, and coordination. They promise to help you develop a healthier, more supple body without building bulk. In Honolulu, the **Body Balance Center** conducts pilates classes several times each day. They are located approximately a mile 'Ewa of Waikīkī in the vicinity of the Ward Warehouse shopping complex. (808.596.8663)

Finally, if you are staying at a B&B on the windward side of the island or just want to visit Kailua, we recommend the **Kailua Fitness Center**. They offer pilates classes, massage, and a newly popular form of exercise called the Rebound Exerciser. This mini-trampoline is fun and promises a variety of benefits including improved muscle tone, and enhanced circulation and immune function. It also provides a more complete workout with less strain on your body than running. The Kailua Fitness Center is small and personal with friendly people committed to supporting your fitness goals. (808.263.0101)

20. Volunteer Your Time to a Worthy Cause

One of the fastest growing types of tourism is volunteer tourism or travel for the purpose of serving others. People pay for the privilege of going all over the world to donate their time to the projects and needs of others. Volunteer opportunities range from working on a gorilla reservation in Africa, to an archeological dig in Egypt, to a blitz build with Habitat for Humanity in Mexico. People are doing this because it feeds the soul. They are looking for a more meaningful experience than they would otherwise get on vacation.

One of our most appealing volunteer opportunities on O'ahu is with **Habitat for Humanity**, which is now building homes all over the world with volunteer labor. On O'ahu, a very active group is building several houses simultaneously and would welcome your participation. Let them know if you don't have transportation and perhaps someone can pick you up. You're not expected to be a master builder. Just lending your time and energy to the overall effort is what is needed. A day building a house with the working poor will be an experience you won't forget and you may decide to become involved with the organization in your home area. (808.455.2355). *(See the article on Habitat for Humanity in Chapter Three)*

Both the **Sierra Club** (808.538.6616) and the **Trail and Mountain Club** (808.488.0044) on O'ahu devote one day a month to trail clearing. **The Nature Conservancy** (808.621.2008) also has nature-based volunteer opportunities the second and fourth Saturdays of the month. It's not hard labor, but you need work clothes. The feeling of camaraderie and accomplishment enhance the enjoyment of the trails on the trip back.

If caring for animals is your passion or you're just lonely for your pet back home, stop by the **Hawaiian Humane Society** and volunteer to be with and exercise the animals waiting for a home. Hours are noon to 8:00 p.m. weekdays and 10:00 a.m. to 4:00 p.m. weekends. (808.946.2187).

Healing Accommodations

Of the many hotels and resorts on O'ahu, we recommend the following as places offering tranquility, natural surroundings and beauty.

The **Royal Hawaiian Waikīkī Beach Hotel**, the grande dame of Waikīkī, was one of the first hotels in Waikīkī and holds that place with dignity. As hotels have risen skyward to mark their place above others, the Royal Hawaiian rests with confidence and elegance at sea level. It has maintained its natural surroundings with grand banyans trees in the mauka garden, separating it from the shopping center, and large trees at the circular entrance. The open-air hallways of the first floor assure that you feel the cool trade winds. When in the hotel, you feel as though this is the only place in Waikīkī. The Royal Hawaiian Hotel is superior in its ability to maintain balance and harmony in the middle of a fast-paced resort community. (800.782.9488) (Moderate to Luxury)

Outside of Waikīkī is the **Kahala Mandarin Oriental Hawai'i**, a luxury hotel popular with celebrities because of its isolation and serenity. At the end of a long road in Kahala, the most exclusive residential area of Honolulu, the quiet, gentle, elegant environment of this hotel encourages you to slow down and just *feel* and *be*. No one rushes. The cool breezes from the ocean find you wherever you are and nature is all around you. A golf course adjacent to the hotel offers both recreational possibilities and lush green views. (800.367.2525) (Luxury)

On the north shore, we recommend the **Turtle Bay Resort**. This recently remodeled resort is surrounded on two sides by the ocean. A lush golf course is right outside the door and mountains tower above. You have the choice of rooms in the hotel or cottages that front the beach. You'll find a luxury spa, short walks on property and forest trails a few minutes away by car. (800.203.3650) (Moderate to Deluxe)

Bed and Breakfasts are often the most successful in creating a healing environment partly because they usually offer the quiet of a residential neighborhood as well as private gardens. Our favorite on the Honolulu side of the island is the **Mānoa Valley Inn**, a short drive up Mānoa Valley near the university. This stately mansion was built in 1919 and is on the National Register of Historic Places. Seven rooms are available as well as a separate cottage perfect for honeymooners. A continental breakfast buffet is served on the wide verandah where wicker chairs and reading material encourage you to linger or just hang out watching the birds playing in the garden below. (808.947.6019) (Moderate)

ManuMele "bird song" B&B has two guest rooms, each with a private entrance. The beach is just a short walk down a sandy path. With its own swimming pool and garden, and a gracious hostess, **Carol Isaacs**, you've found the perfect accommodation for a wellness vacation. (808.262.0016) (Moderate)

Down the road a bit is **Beach Lane B&B** with a private studio and two lovely bedroom suites all with private entrance. All accommodations are attractively furnished in a tropical style. Owner **Tonic Bille**, is from Germany and very meticulous in her decorating and presentation of the rooms. Breakfast is part of the package for one of the rooms only. The others have limited cooking facilities. Your rooms are a short walk from the beach and, depending on the time of year, you can even watch the sunrise out of the ocean from one of the rooms. Tonic is president of the local B&B association and has a broad network of colleagues with B&Bs. If she is full, she will be happy to book you into the right B&B for you. (808.262.8286) (Moderate)

On the north shore at Sunset Beach is the **Sunset Beach Retreat** which has a charming one bedroom apartment with private patio and outdoor, bamboo-sheltered shower. This retreat is only a short block from one of the longest stretches of beach on the island. Sunset Beach is also where the biggest waves are to be found during the winter. Owner, **Sundari**, offers in-house spa treatments as well. (808.638.0708) (Moderate)

Verena Rainalter, of **Hawai'i Aloha Accommodations**, is also prepared to find the right healing accommodations for you. She has a large list of vacation rentals, especially in the windward O'ahu area. She describes herself as a picky Germany who won't settle for second best. (808.261.5446)

Perhaps your best resource of all is the website **www.lanikaibb.com**. Their listings of B&Bs and vacation rentals throughout O'ahu is extensive and includes superb photographs of each accommodation and its surroundings. (800.258.7895)

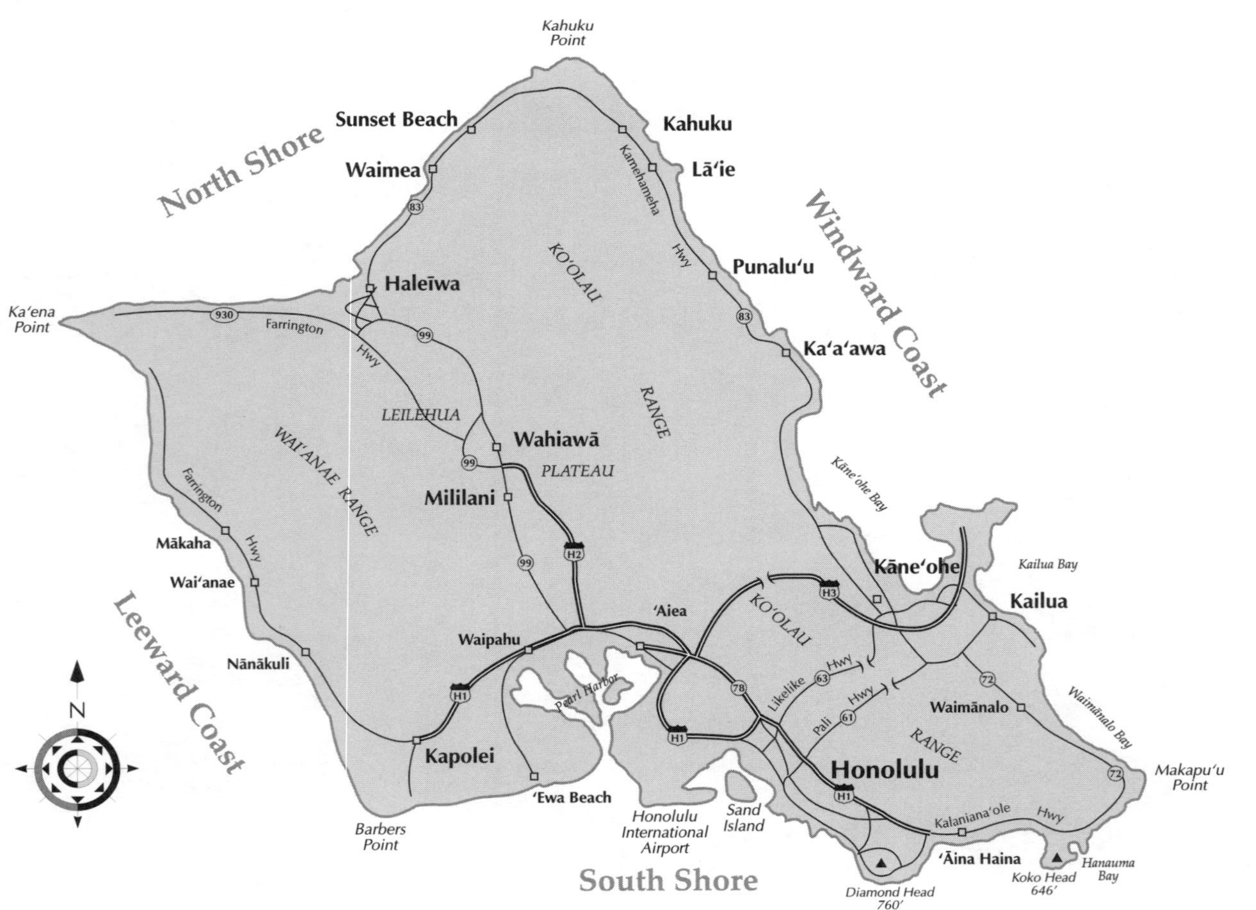

Kahuku Point
North Shore
Sunset Beach
Waimea
Kahuku
Lāʻie
Kamehameha Hwy
Windward Coast
Punaluʻu
Haleīwa
Ka'ena Point
Farrington Hwy
KO'OLAU RANGE
Kaʻaʻawa
LEILEHUA
WAI'ANAE RANGE
Wahiawā
PLATEAU
Mililani
Kāne'ohe Bay
Mākaha
Wai'anae
Kāneʻohe
Kailua Bay
Kailua
ʻAiea
Waipahu
Nānākuli
Leeward Coast
Pearl Harbor
Likelike Hwy
Pali Hwy
Waimānalo
Waimānalo Bay
RANGE
Kapolei
Honolulu
Makapu'u Point
ʻEwa Beach
Honolulu International Airport
Sand Island
Kalaniana'ole Hwy
Barbers Point
ʻĀina Haina
Koko Head 646'
Hanauma Bay
South Shore
Diamond Head 760'
N

Resources

The Island of O'ahu

O'AHU - WELLNESS DIRECTORY TABLE OF CONTENTS

Art and Art Therapy

CarolLynn • Whimsical Watercolors

CarolLynn is the creator of the watercolors on the "Oahu Wellness Tourism Provider" webpages. Her artwork has touched the hearts of many people worldwide. It is available not only as original watercolors and prints but also on tee shirts and baby clothes.

PO Box 61896 • Honolulu, HI 96839
contact: CarolLynn
808.739.2252
www.carollynn.com

Awakening Art

(personalized astrology cards)
2615 Date Street, #12
Honolulu, HI 96826
808.946.8431
donnasegaran@hotmail.com

Mark Brown

(group, plein aire lessons)
843.0145

Cedar Street Galleries

817 Cedar Street
Honolulu, HI 96814
808.589.1580
www.cedarstreetgalleries.com

Contemporary Museum

2411Makiki Heights Drive
Honolulu, HI 96822
808.526.1322 • Cafe: 523.3362
www.tcmhi.org

Haleiwa Art Gallery

66-252 Kamehameha Hwy
Haleiwa, HI 96712
contact: George Atkins
808.637.3366
haleiwaartgallery@hawaii.rr.com

Hawaii State Art Museum

250 South Hotel Street, 2nd floor
Honolulu, HI 96813
808.586.0300
www.state.hi.us/sfca

Art and Art Therapy

Honolulu Academy of Art

900 S. Beretania • Honolulu, HI 96814
808.532.8701 • Cafe **532.8734**
www.honoluluacademy.org

Roy Sakuma Ukulele Studios

(private & group lessons)
Honolulu, HI 96816
808.732.3739

State Foundation on Culture and the Arts

250 South Hotel Street, 2nd floor
Honolulu, HI 96813
808.586.0300
www.state.hi.us/sfca

Sue Stagner

(individual and group lessons)
808.988.3777

Watercolors by Patrice

(individual lessons)
PO Box 6170
Honolulu, HI 96839-1707
contact: Patrice Federspiel
808.392.9104
Heartrising@aol.com

Breath Therapy

Gwen Williams

Gwen is a psychotherapist with a part-time practice and an Associate Professor at the University of Hawai'i at Leeward Community College teaching counseling and self-exploration courses. Gwen specializes in trauma, depression, self-esteem, couples and meditation processes. She is a Grof Certified Transpersonal and Holotropic Breathwork facilitator and offers a unique nonordinary state process for inner exploration and transformation for individuals and groups.

PO Box 61532 • Honolulu, HI 96838
contact: Gwen Williams
808.375.1746
holotropical@hotmail.com

Hypnotherapy

Capstone Counseling and Training Center

Capstone is a counseling and training center specializing in medical hypnosis, sports performance and migraine and acute or chronic pain management. Judy Koch is one of Hawaii's leaders in hypnotherapy being one of the first to introduce it to doctors at Queen's hospital in Honolulu.

1270 Queen Emma Street #1104 * Honolulu, HI 96813
contact: Judy Koch
808.526.4766
capstone@gte.net • www.capstonecenter.com

Transformational Living Center

Advanced Transformational Therapies: Clear deep-seated, unresolved issues to reduce stress, depression, anxiety and trauma using hypnosis, guided imagery, VibraSound/ Music therapy, EMDR, Holodynamics, Inner Child Healing, Past Life Therapy, Quantum Transformational Healing(TM)

2851 East Manoa Road, Suite 1-203 • Honolulu, HI 96822
contact: Dr. Laura Sturgis, PhD
808.988.6168
tlc1@aloha.net • www.galaxymall.com/health/tlc

Personal Development/Psychology/Relationship Counseling

Awakening Aloha!

(Let your Heart, Soul & Spirit Soar!)

Experience the magnificent, healing power of love ~ the true Spirit of Aloha from within! Transform yourself, your life and relationships through regenerative, self-healing movement, breath, touch and energy of Lusana's compassionate wisdom. Learn of her own transformation through cancer and passionately celebrate your life through her extensive professional experience.

P.O. Box 22928 • Honolulu, HI 96823
contact: Lusana Hernández, MSW
(Psychotherapist, Dancer, Spiritual Coach, Reiki Master, BioTouch Healer)
Se Habla Español
808.942.LOVE (5683) cell: 808.386.LOVE
AwakeningAloha@msn.com

Silke Vogelmann-Sine, PhD

is a Hawaii licensed psychologist in private practice in Honolulu for over twenty years. She provides psychological services, conducts workshops and has developed a program of personal coaching to assist individuals in reaching deeply felt goals by trusting their spiritual connection. She incorporates energy therapies, EMDR and hypnosis to facilitate inner transformation.

700 Richards Street, #1502 • Honolulu, HI 96813
808.531.1232
silke@silke.com • www.drsilke.com

Transformational Living Center

Advanced Transformational Therapies: Clear deep-seated, unresolved issues to reduce stress, depression, anxiety and trauma using hypnosis, guided imagery, VibraSound/ Music therapy, EMDR, Holodynamics, Inner Child Healing, Past Life Therapy, Quantum Transformational Healing(TM).

2851 East Manoa Road, Suite 1-203 • Honolulu, HI 96822
contact: Dr. Laura Sturgis, PhD
808.988.6168
tlc1@aloha.net • www.galaxymall.com/health/tlc

Psychic

Real Dreams

(psychic readings, dream workshops, healing intensives)
53-086 Halai St. • Hauula, HI 96717
contact: Alice Anne Parker
808.293.5833
Parkerdreams@aol.com
www.aliceanneparker.com

Brian Samo Ross

3275A Pauma Place
Honolulu HI 96822
808.988.3305
rossb001@hawaii.rr.com

Retreats

Hawaii Wellness Institute

Ponds and a stream grace the Hawaii Wellness Sacred Retreat Center providing an ideal environment for rest and rejuvenation. Come to experience a wide range of classes relating to Hawaiian tradition, women's empowerment, and meditation. Or enjoy a hot rock or lomilomi massage or hypnotherapy session by the stream.

3670 Kalihi Ave. • Honolulu, HI 96819
contact: Valerie Finley
808.848.5544
insights@hawaii.rr.com

Spiritual Healing

Honolulu Church of Light, A Healing Sanctuary

The Honolulu Church of Light offers non-denominational, spiritualist services Sundays at 9:00 am and Wednesdays at 6:30 pm. Free healing sessions are available by appointment. Please see our online calendar of events.

1539 Kapiolani Blvd. • Honolulu, HI 96814
808.952.0880 or 1.800.390.1886
theshift@hulu.net • www.inward.com

Reverend Diana George

(wedding, commitment, vow renewal)
3969 Lurline Drive
Honolulu, HI 96816
808.739.9887 cell: **808.735.6092**
dianageorge@msn.com

Samaritan Counseling Center

1020 S. Beretania
Honolulu, HI 96825
808.545.2747

Lifestyle Modification

Fitness

Aloha Body Therapy

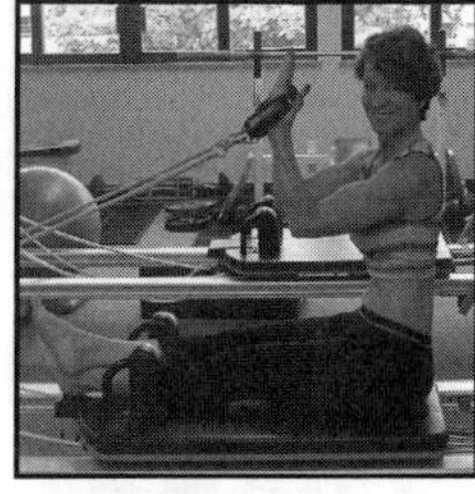

Jayme Newhouse has extensive training, education and practice in the fields of Massage Therapy, Pilates, Fitness and Nutrition. She is a licensed Massage Therapist, Certified Pilates instructor, Certified LaStone therapist, as well as a nutrition consultant. She also does massage and Pilates at the beach.

25 Maluniu Avenue • Kailua, HI 96734
contact: Jayme Newhouse
808.255.4862
jayme@bodytherapyhawaii.com
www.bodyTherapyhawaii.com

Try Fitness

1553 Pele St. #C • Honolulu, HI 96813
contact: KC Carlberg
808.531.8573
TryFitness@hawaii.rr.com

Retreats

Couples Retreats

(Couples Retreats and Therapy)
P.O. Box 628 • Kaneohe, HI 96744
contact: Jeff Wagner, M.A. or Helen Wagner
808.247.7962
helennjeff@hawaii.rr.com

Relationship Counseling

Silke Volgelmann-Sine, PhD

700 Richards St. #1502 • Honolulu, HI 96813
808.531.1232
silke@silke.com • www.drsilke.com

Success Coaching

Laura Crites, MS, MA

Discover Your Life's Purpose

There is a gift that we are each meant to give the world. Some people call it our soul's purpose. When we match that unique gift with a unique need, we have found our life's work and we have found joy. The "knowing" of that gift often pushes within us until we pay attention. Sometimes it takes an objective viewer to help us see what is so obvious in our lives. I offer my services to help you find your life's purpose.

2333 Kapiolani Blvd. #2108 • Honolulu, HI 96926
808.941.8253
crites@hawaii.rr.com

International Wellness Retreats in Hawaii

Half day, one day and 7 day life-transforming retreats. Custom designed to provide you with a meaningful, life-changing, mind body experience in a healing environment. Connect with your authentic self, and reclaim your deepest dreams with renewed passion and energy! Yoga, massage, Hawaiian healing & personal coaching.

contact: LeeAnn & Javier DelCarpio
info@innerpowerintl.com • www.innerpowerintl.com
808.626.4690

Awakening Aloha!

PO Box 22928 • Honolulu, HI 96823
contact: Lusana Hernández, MSW
Self-Healing Facilitator
808.942.LOVE (5683)
cell: 808.386.LOVE
AwakeningAloha@msn.com

Holographic Repatterning

contact: Lynn Morgan
Honolulu, HI
808.722.3581

Success Coaching

Marilyn Nagel

(personal & business coach)
3530 Sierra Drive • Honolulu, HI 96816
808.738.2001 • fax 808.738.2002
mrncoach@pixi.com • www.hawaiicoaches.com

Yoga

Sabrina Stevens Systems, Inc.

Consultation & Training
Maintaining our facelift. Recovery from laser/surgery/injuries. For anti-aging prevention, transformation & recovery. Sabrina has combined the ancient science of breath, slow tai chi like movement patterns, ELF current, massage, skincare to transform the face.
808.923.6737
www.starface.com

Bikram's Yoga College of India

808.773.5519
www.bikramyoga.com

Central YMCA

401 Atkinson Drive
Honolulu, HI 96814
808.951.1322

Living in Wellness

Kailua, HI
contact: Charlotte H. Nuessle
808.230.8902
livinginwellness@aol.com
www.livinginwellness.com

Taorobics Center

1640 S. King St.
Honolulu, HI 96826
contact: Karen "Lucky" Thornton or Anita Ahn
808.942.0003
Taomaster@hawaii.rr.com
www.rrhi.com/dahnhakhawaii

Yoga Chakra

675 Auahi St. • Honolulu, HI 96813
808.529.8889
yogachakra.net

NATURE AS HEALER

Ecotours

Annette's Adventures

Annette's Adventures plans itineraries and puts together packages using ecotourism principles for individuals and interest groups. Specializes in trip planning and tours for women 55 and older.
45-403 Koa Kahiko St. • Kaneohe, HI 96744
contact: Annette Kaohelaulii
808.235.5431
annettesadventures@juno.com
www.annettesadventures.com.

Ecotours

Mauka Makai Excursions

Mauka Makai Excursions provides all day trips on Oahu to visit cultural sites (heiau, ko'a, lo'I, fishponds), shoreline activities include fishing, thrownet, reef and tidepool exploration, and arts and crafts.
350 Ward Ave. # 106 • Honolulu, Hi 96814
contact: Dominic Aki
808.593.3525 • toll free: 1 800 ECO.OAHU
mauka-makai@oahu-ecotours.com

Bike Hawaii

877.682.7433
www.bikehawaii.com

Dolphins and You

PO Box 4277 • Waianae, HI 96792
contact: Rich Holland
808.696.4414
hawaii@dolphinsandyou.com
www.dolphinsandyou.com

Hawaiian Islands Eco-Tours

808.236.7766
Toll Free: 866.445.3624
info@hikeoahu.com
www.hikeoahu.com

Oahu Nature Tours

808.924.2473
www.oahunaturetours.com

Sea Life Park

41-202 Kalanianaole Hwy
Waimanalo, HI 96795
808.259.7933
www.sealifeparkhawaii.com

The Real Hawaii Eco-Cultural Excursions

808.524.4944 or
toll free 1.877.597.7325
www.therealhawaii.com

Waikiki Aquarium

2777 Kalakaua
Honolulu, HI 96795
808.923.9741
www.waquarium.org

Wild Side Specialty Tours

Waianae Small Boat Harbor,
Pier "A" - slip A1
Tori or Armin Cullins
808.306.7273 • fax 808.696.0103
wildside@sailhawaii.com
www.sailhawaii.com

Gardens

Foster Botanical Garden

50 North Vineyard Boulevard
Honolulu, HI 96817
808.522.7060
9:00–4:00 daily

Ho'omaluhia Botanical Garden

45-680 Luluku Road
Kane'ohe, HI 96744
808.233.7323
9:00–4:00 daily

Lyon Arboretum

3860 Manoa Road • Honolulu, HI 96822-1180
808.988.0456 • fax: 808.988.0462
lyonarb@hawaii.edu
9:00–3:00 Monday–Saturday

Health Products of Hawai'i

Oils of Aloha

Kukui Skin & Hair Care Collection For centuries Hawaiians have used the oil pressed from kernels of the kukui nut to relieve and protect skin from salt water, harsh sun and drying winds. Naturally provides relief and absorbs quickly. Available at fine stores and pharmacies in Hawaii.

toll free 1.800.367.6010

www.OilsOfAloha.com

Luscious Beauty Fragrance Oils, Inc.

203 South Vineyard St.
Honolulu, HI 96813
contact: Ramona J. Reyes-Akamine
808.536.4000
ramona@lusciousbeauty.com
www.lusciousbeauty.com

Nikken products

magnetic field energy
565 E Keolu Drive
Kailua, Hi 96734
contact: Jackie Paleologos
808.261.0801

Hikes

Hawaiian Trail and Mountain Club

PO Box 2238 • Honolulu, Hi 96804
808.488.0044
www.geocities.com/yosemite/trails/3660

Sierra Club

PO Box 2577 • Honolulu, Hi 96803
808. 538.6616
www.hi.sierraclub.org

The Hawaii Nature Center

2131 Makiki Heights Drive
Honolulu, HI 96824
808.955.0100

The Nature Center

2131 Makiki Heights Drive
Honolulu, HI 96822
808.955.0100
www.hawaiinaturecenter.org

The Nature Conservancy of Hawaii

808.537.4508

Massage and BodyWork

Essential Nurturance

A very gentle yet deeply nurturing Swedish-based full-body therapeutic massage, which incorporates energy healing (Japanese Reiki as well as Korean Dahn Hak) and aromatherapy. Other offerings include Pohaku (heated stone massage), Raindrop Aromatherapy and Bowen. Massage Instruction for Couples is also available. Inquire in English, Japanese, Spanish, French, or Czech.

1314 Pensacola St. #2 • Honolulu, HI 96814
808.348.3644
contact: yana svara
jana2810@aol.com

Massage and BodyWork

Ala Moana/Waikiki Clinical Massage Therapy

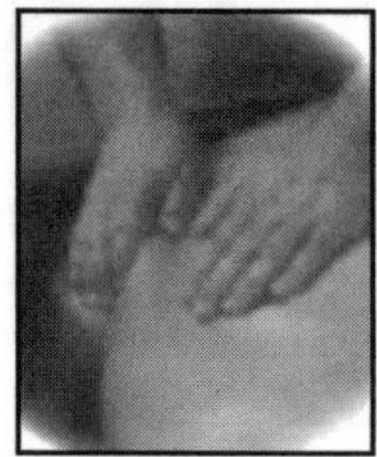

Clinical & Spa Massage therapy by a nationally certified therapist. Each Clinical Massage session includes: Gentle to Deep Tissue Massage; Foot Reflexology; Moist Heat Packs; Healing Hot Stones; and Shiatsu-Acupressure for problem areas. Cost effective benefits include a more rapid recovery, a decreased dependency on medications, and an improved return to work rate. Spa Massage includes new and ancient massage healing and relaxation techniques. Call for free consultation. Unwind & Relax for as little as $45 per hour!!

Stephen P. Lanzo, LMT
Ala Moana Hotel • 410 Atkinson Drive, Suite 442
Honolulu, HI 96814 (Honolulu/Waikiki Area)
808.955.2442
stevelanzo@hawaii.rr.com • www.stevelanzo.com

Asami Rainbows-Waves of Wellth

Asami Rainbows offers personalized therapies: Imperial Jade **Facial** (heavenly esteem booster!), **Reflexology, Lomilomi Massage,** IONFIRE **Sauna,** Soultones **Sound Therapy,** ISIS Rainbow Ancient Healing, ISISRAH Workshops, **Tarot-matherapy, Empowerment readings**. Waves of Wellth **products**: Lemurian Crystals, food supplements, Aranizer air purifiers, portable exercisers, Galvanic Spa, Richway's Biomat and Rejuvena Massager.

465 Kapahulu Ave. #2J • Honolulu, HI 96815
contact: Cheryl Nakachi
808.384.4466
lomirei5@yahoo.com • www.empower.paychecksforlife.com

Body of Bliss

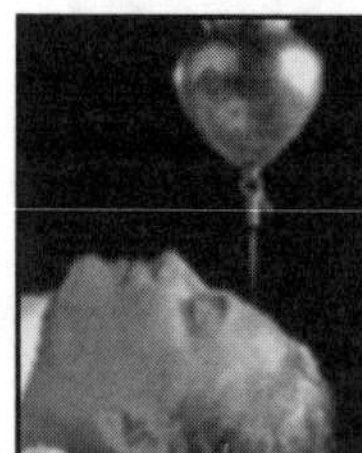

Spa Treatments to Transform the Body and Soul

Body of Bliss is a place of wellness and healing located on Oahu's North Shore, just steps from beautiful Sunset Beach. At Body of Bliss we incorporate ancient therapies with cutting edge techniques. For a sublime and deeply therapeutic experience come to Body of Bliss. Accommodations also available.

contact: Sundari
59-015 Hoa'lua St. • Hale'iwa, HI 96712
808.638.0780
shaktisundari@yahoo.com

Body Therapy By Akua

Embrace Healing! Comprehensive care by an experienced professional. Swedish-Esalen, Deep Tissue, Trigger Point, Connective Tissue and LaStone Therapy. In practice since 1986 in Manhattan and Windward Oahu, past clients include Alec Baldwin, Lauren Hutton, and Def Leppard. AMTA professional member.

toll free 877.258.2586 or 808.247.1106
akualum@hawaii.rr.com • www.akualum.com

Massage and BodyWork

Hawaiian Alchemy

Wonderfully restorative one-hour session includes a personalized therapeutic blend of essential oils massaged into the skin followed by energy work to soothe, balance, and repair the physical and subtle bodies. Other modalities include auricular, Acuscope/ Myopulse microcurrent, and lymphatic therapies; and polycontrast interference photography (Harry Oldfield) of the energy field.

contact: Lynn Hearl. LMT #3974, CHTP
Reiki Master, Certified Aromatherapist
925 Keala'olu Avenue • Honolulu, HI 96816
808.737.4443
lynninhi@lava.net

Hawaii Healing Arts College

is an outstanding school of massage therapy with a beautiful and relaxing clinic. Massage Professionals offer massage seven days a week by skilled intern therapists at a special rate, as well as by several licensed therapists with a wide variety of specialties.

Kailua Medical Arts Building
407 Uluniu St., Second Floor • Kailua, HI 96734
808.266.2468
blaze@hawaii.rr.com • www.hhacdirect.com

Massage Specialists

Massage Specialists is located at the corner of Kalakaua Ave. and Kapiolani Blvd across from the Hard Rock Cafe. We have over 70 therapists to serve you. We specialize in Swedish, Shiatsu, deep tissue, Hawaiian Lomi Lomi and Pohaku Hot Stones. Walk-ins welcomed. Open 7 days a week from 10 am to 11 pm.

1750 Kalakaua Ave., #512 • Honolulu, HI 96826
808.941.8101

Rainbow Healing Arts

Kathy Edwards and Liza Delin offer a full range of massage and body work including Reiki, Swedish Massage, CranioSacral Therapy, Essential Oils and Nutritional consultation. Their heaven and earth treatment includes simultaneous treatments by both Liza and Kathy. Their location is attractive, peaceful and inviting.

1132 Kina Street, Kailua, HI 96734
contact: Liza Delin or Kathy Edwards
808.262.3700
info@rainbowhealingarts.com •
www.rainbowhealingarts.com

TouchWorks

TouchWorks provides 10-20 minute seated massage sessions to groups working and visiting in Hawaii. Add a healthy break to your group's next meeting, conference or convention. Please visit our website: www.alohatouchworks.com. Member of Hawaii Visitors & Convention Bureau and American Massage Therapy Association.

contact: Johanna Chung
808.235.2075
info@alohatouchworks.com

Massage and BodyWork

Abby and Fraser's Massage Therapy
55-623 Kamehameha Hwy
Laie, HI 96762
contact: Abby Parker & Fraser Black
808.293.2656

"Everybody Needs To Be Kneaded"
contact: Morgan Blank
2464 Halelaau Pl
Honolulu, HI 96816
808.739.3866
morgan@hawaii.com

Haunani Kauka, LMT
(Swedish, deep tissue, lomilomi)
Kailua Fitness
25 Maluniu Ave., 2nd floor
Kailua, HI 96734
808.263.0101

Hawaiian Massage
(Pohaku-Hawaiian Stone Massage, Lomilomi & Japanese Massage)
808.949.3636

Honolulu School of Massage, Inc.
1136 12th Avenue, Suite 240
Honolulu, HI 96816
808.733.0033
fax: 808.733.0045

Life Healing Spa Therapies
contact: Sabino Manzulli, LMT
156D N. Kalaheo Ave.
Kailua, HI 96734
808.263.1955

Professional Lomilomi Bodywork
contact: Kapono Aluli Souza LMT
808.382.1559
808.596.8663
Nahenahe4u@hotmail.com

Sole Care
(reflexology and counseling)
contact: Linda Friedman
808.944.4588
cell: 787.7727
rainbows@att.net

Susan Snyder
(licensed aesthetician)
Integrative Health Department
The Honolulu Medical Group
550 S. Beretania Street
Honolulu, HI 96813
808.537.2211

Gayle Volger LMT
(massage and aromatherapy)
1136 12th Ave. #240
Honolulu, HI 96816
808.733.0003
gaylevlmt@yahoo.com

Meditation

Stephen P. Lanzo, LMT
Ala Moana Hotel
410 Atkinson Drive, Suite 442 • Honolulu, HI 96814
(Honolulu/Waikiki Area)
808.955.2442
stevelanzo@hawaii.rr.com

Spas

Abhasa Spa
Royal Hawaiian Hotel
808.923.7311
www.royal-hawaiian.com

Ampy's European Facials and Body Spa
1441 Kapiolani Blvd., Suite 377
Honolulu, HI 96814
808.946.3838
AmpysSpa@aol.com

JW Marriott Ihilani Resort & Spa
808.679.0079
www.ihilani.com

Mandara Spa and Holistica Hawaii
Hilton Hawaiian Village
808.949.4321
www.hilton.com

Malama Spa
Manoa and Ala Moana Shopping Centers
808.988.0101
www.avedahawaii.com

NaHo'ola Spa
Hyatt Regency Waikiki
808.921.6097
www.hyattwaikiki.com

Serenity Spa Hawaii
Outrigger Reef on the Beach
808.949.4321
www.outriggerreef.com

Complementary Treatment Therapies

Acupuncture

Acu-Power Clinic
615 Piikoi Street, Suite 1404
Honolulu, HI 96814
contact: Dr. Christiane W. Christ, D.Ac.
808.591.1404

Integrative Health Care Department
The Honolulu Medical Group
550 S. Beretania Street
Honolulu, HI 96813
808.537.2211

Ruby Jessop, L.Ac
Facial Rejuvenation and Nutritional Counseling
747 Wikiwiki Street, #1701
Honolulu, HI 96826
contact: Lan Kao
808.949.8966
hawaiihealthcntr@aol.com

Kailua Acupunture Clinic
320 Uluniu Street, #2
Kailua, HI 96734
contact: Joni Knoll, D.Ac
808.262.4550
knoll@pixi.com

Lan Kao, L.Ac
408 Uluniu St. • Kailua, HI 96734
contact: Lan Kao
808.262.7899
lankao@aol.com

Wendy Rhatigan L.Ac
(massage therapy)
2347 Makanani Drive
Honolulu, Hi 96817
808.841.3456

Chiropractic

Aloha Chiropractic
Network Spinal Analysis
2930 East Manoa Rd #C-5
808.988.5532
Chadsatodc@aol.com

Integrative Health Care Department
The Honolulu Medical Group
550 S. Beretania Street
Honolulu, HI 96813
808.537.2211

Energy Therapy

Ambassador of Love & Light
The **Melchisedek Method** is a remarkable spiritual science which is life changing for body and ascension. It has the ability to heal any illness as it is the living conscious holographic pattern of course vibration. Learn how to activate your lightbody and age reversal. Individual sessions and monthly workshops. (Ask about scholarships)

Deva Magdalena
808.947.4609
deva@worldnet.att.net • www.melchizedekmethod.com

Henri Furgiuele
Quantum-Touch energy healing is a powerful, new, breakthrough healing technique. It can help relieve pain, clear stress and enhance an overall sense of well being and clarity. Quantum-Touch has been featured in several magazines as an important new healing technique. Henri Furgiuele has twenty years experience in the healing arts and is one of only eight people nationwide, certified to provide instruction in quantum touch healing. She provides individual sessions, weekly lectures and monthly workshops.

PO Box 858 • Honolulu, HI 96808-0858
contact: Henri Furgiuele
808.221.1431
henri@quantumtouch.com

Jane Starn, DrPH, RN, HNC
is a nurse practitioner and Professor Emeritus, School of Nursing, University of Hawaii. She is both a graduate and a faculty member of the Barbara Brennan School of Healing and is also a Shakti yoga instructor. She practices healing from her peaceful hilltop setting above Honolulu.

3649 Nihipali Place • Honolulu, HI 96816
contact: Jane Starn
808.737.8859
Jane.starn@att.net

Energy Therapy

Taorobics Center

DAHN HAK teaches you to experience your own Ki Energy and balance the flow in your body. The main focus of the regular class is Asian form of Yoga, stretching, Energy Awareness, and Meditative Breathwork. Aura Photos, Private Healing Sessions, Brain Respiration, Organ Healing, Chakra Healing, Ki-Gong, and Outdoor Nature Meditations are also available.

1640 S. King St. • Honolulu, HI 96826
contact: Karen "Lucky" Thornton or Anita Ahn
808.942.0003 • cell: 808.429.5006 • 808.382.2079
fax: 808.943.0523
Taomaster@hawaii.rr.com • www.rrhi.com/dahnhakhawaii

Healing Touch

(island wide referrals)
808.432.8137

Reiki Hawaii

contact: Helen Sonobe
PO Box 963 • Aiea, HI 96701
808.485.0026
reikihawaii@hawaii.rr.com
www.reikiclasses.bigstep.com

Reiki Natural Healing

contact: Maureen Pua'ena O'Shaughnessy, Reiki Master
PMB 732, 150 Hamakua Dr. • Kailua, HI 96734
808.256.9620
www.reiki-hawaii.com • reiki@hawaii.rr.com

Hawaiian Healing Therapies

Reach Beyond

Lynn Kealohaleimahamae Eklund teaches and practices Ho'omana or Huna which is an Ancient Spiritual, Cultural, Physical and Healing way of being that was passed down in the family lineages of Hawaiians. Through her extensive network of Hawaiian healers, she also serves as a resource in connecting individuals with the Hawaiian Healing Arts Practitioner appropriate for them.

3398 Kalihi Street • Honolulu, HI 96819
contact: Lynn Eklund
808.847.7478
kealohalei@hotmail.com • www.winternet.com/~leklunk/mainlandws.htm

The Lomi Shop Va'a

The Lomi Shop Va'a is a unique experiential healing center which practices and shares traditional Polynesian culture, it's values, and the healing art of Hawaiian lomilomi massage. It also offers Polynesian medicinal herbs such as noni, awa, herbal teas, authentic crafts and other health products such as monoi (coconut) oils, soaps, and other body products.

The Windward Mall 808.234.5664
Hyatt Regency Waikiki 808.926.5664
kauhane@lava.net • www.lomi.com

Hawaiian Healing Therapies

Waimanalo Health Center Ai Kupele,

under the direction of Kawaikapuokalani K. Hewett, Kahuna Ho'ola and cultural health director, is a cultural healing center specializing in the following native healing practices: la'au lapa'au (medicinal plants), ho'oponopono (realignment of one's spirit, mind, body), and lomilomi (therapeutic massage). Scheduled appointments and site visits are welcome.

41-1347 Kalanianaole Highway • Waimanalo, HI 96795
contact: Kawena Mann
808.259.7948 • fax 808.259.5460
kawena@waimanalohc.org

Velma DelaPena

(herbal, spiritual, lomilomi healing)
41716 Kalanianiole Hwy
Waimanalo, HI 96795
808.259.6805

Kahuna Lā'au Lapa'au Mahi'ai

(herbal healing)
contact: Kaipo Kaneakua
47-626 Melekula Road
Kaneohe, HI 95744
808.239.9651

Lomi Lomi O Kawaianiani

Wesley Sen & Lehua McCandless-Sen
1529 Ala Amoamo Street
Honolulu, HI 96819
808 226.3114
www.skywebbiz.com/weslehua/hawaiianlomilomimassagetherapy
nakinikini@lycos.com •
lohelani2@hotmail.com

Professional Lomilomi Bodywork

contact: Kapono Aluli Souza LMT
808.382.1559
808.596.8663
Nahenahe4u@hotmail.com

Uncle Derek's Hawaiian Lomi Lomi Massage

Derek J. Ahsing
1650 Young St., Suite 402 • Honolulu, HI 96826
808.946.1040 • cell 808.381.4263
www.bodyhawaii.com

Holistic Health Practitioner

Fickes Holistic Care Corporation

In a loving, safe, low-tech environment, Dr. Linda Fickes uses "skilled detective work" to help the client identify and focus on the causes of their health issues. Her remedial responses address the mind, heart, body and spirit and include homeopathy, herbs, vitamins, minerals, soft tissue therapy, new decisions therapy, holodynamics and meditation training. She has the only thermography machine for breast cancer detection on Oahu.

4821 Kaimoku Way • Honolulu, Hi 96821
contact: Dr. Linda Fickes
808.377.1811
fickesl001@hawaii.rr.com

Holistic Health Practicioner

Integrative Health Department
The Honolulu Medical Group, Inc
550 S. Beretania Street
Honolulu, Hi 96813
808.537.2211

Life Healing Foundation
(breast cancer post surgery treatment and recovery)
156D N. Kalaheo Ave.,
Kailua, HI 96734
contact: Sabino Manzulli, LMT
808.263.1955

Dr. Dennis G. Rhatigan DC
2347 Makanani Drive
Honolulu, HI 96817
808.841.3456

Integrated Health Care
Dr. Teresa A. Denney, DO
4218 Waialae Avenue, Suite 106
Honolulu, HI 96816
808.732.0888
www.integratedhealthcarehawaii.com

MOA Hawaii
3510 Nuuanu Pali Drive
Honolulu, HI 96812
808.595.6344
moahawaii@lava.net

Touch Of Life
Century Square
1188 Bishop St., Suite 709
Honolulu, HI 96813
contact: Dianne Tomita Poire, LMT
808.523.0878

Hypnotherapy

Transformational Living Center
Advanced Transformational Therapies: Clear deep-seated, unresolved issues to reduce stress, depression, anxiety and trauma using hypnosis, guided imagery, VibraSound/Music therapy, EMDR, Holodynamics, Inner Child Healing, Past Life Therapy, Quantum Transformational Healing ™
2851 East Manoa Road, Suite 1-203 • Honolulu, HI 96822
contact: Dr. Laura Sturgis, PhD.
808.988.6168
tlc1@aloha.net • ww.galaxymall.com/health/tlc

Stephen P. Lanzo, LMT
Ala Moana Hotel
410 Atkinson Drive, Suite 442 • Honolulu, HI 96814
(Honolulu/Waikiki Area)
808. 955.2442
stevelanzo@hawaii.rr.com

Naturopathic Medicine

Dr. Kevin R. Gibson
Naturopathic Doctor
& Licensed Acupuncturist
808.372.5802
doctorkevin@hawaii.rr.com
www.pacificintegrativemedicine.com

Naturopathic Medicine

Island Wellness Center
Dr. Jason Uchida
615 Piikoi St., Suite 1114
Honolulu, HI 96814
808.589.1955

Dr. Diana Joy Ostroff
926 Noio St. • Honolulu, HI 96816
www.drdianajoyostroff.com
dianajoy@drdianajoyostroff.com

Pain Management

Capstone Counseling and Training Center
1270 Queen Emma Street #1104 • Honolulu, HI 96813
contact: Judy Koch
808.526.4766
capstone@gte.net • www.capstonecenter.com

Preventive Medical Screening

Holistica Hawaii Health Center
Holistica Hawaii is a medically based health center located at the exquisite Hilton Hawaiian Village hotel. It offers Electron Beam Tomography scanning and Vascular Ultrasound. They also offer executive retreats and residential programs that include a full medical evaluation and highly personalized activities including fitness, lifestyle modification, nutrition and spa activities.
2005 Kalia Road • Honolulu, HI 96815
contact: Holistica Hawaii Health Center
808.951.6546
robyn@lava.net • www.holistica.com

Fickes Holistic Care Corporation
(thermography)
4821 Kaimoku Way • Honolulu, HI 96821
contact: Dr. Linda Fickes
808.377.1811
fickesl001@hawaii.rr.com

Traditional Chinese Medicine

Lan Kao, L.Ac
130 Kailua Road, Suite 111 • Kailua, HI 96734
contact: Lan Kao
808.262.7899
lankao@aol.com

Fitness

Aloha Fitness Promotions

Our love of fitness, wellness and the Hawaiian lifestyle is our inspiration. We truly believe that utilizing the aloha spirit creates a more fulfilling, genuine and memorable experience. For corporate retreats, conventions, incentive groups and individual programs. Surf, hula, paddle & more! Malama pono.
contact: 808.661.5809 or m.napiliwahine@gte.net

Aloha Adrenaline Adventures, Inc.

PO Box 10575 • Honolulu, HI 96816
contact: Capt. Thomas R. Magee
808.271.8886
www.adrenalineadventures.com

Hawaii Athletic Club

432 Keawe Street
Honolulu, HI 95813
808.537.1131
fax 537.1732

Niketown Running Club

King Kalakaua Plaza
Honolulu
(Wednesdays 6:00 - 7:30 pm)
808.943.6453

Try Fitness

(fitness coach)
1553 Pele St. #C
Honolulu, HI 96813
contact: KC Carlberg
808.531.8573
TryFitness@hawaii.rr.com

Body Balance Centre

(pilates)
320 Ward Ave., # 201
Honolulu, HI 96814
808.596.8663
www.bodyhawaii.com
balance@lava.net

Kailua Fitness

(fitness facilities)
25 Maluniu Ave 2nd floor
Kailua, HI 96734
808.263.0101
kailuafit@aol.com

Glynis Ramiriz

(personal trainer)
PO Box 235355
Honolulu, HI 96823
808.225.7620

YMCA

(fitness facilities)
Ala Moana • 808.941.3344
Downtown • 808.536.3556
Kailua/Windward Oahu
808.261.0808
Mililani, West Oahu • 808.625.1040

Sports Hypnosis

Capstone Counseling and Training Center

1111 Bishop Street #513 • Honolulu, HI 96813
contact: Judy Koch
808.526.4766
capstone@gte.net • www.capstonecenter.com

Travel to Serve Others

Environmental Service Projects

Hawaii Nature Center
2131 Makiki Heights Drive
Honolulu, HI 96822
808.955.0100 ext.18
hawaiinaturecenter@hawaii.rr.com

Nature Conservancy
contact: Nat Pak, volunteer coordinator
808.621.2008
npak@pnc.org
www.nature.org/Hawaii

Serving People

Habitat for Humanity
contact: Alison Hunter, volunteer coordinator
808.384.7181
98-025 Hekaha St., Bldg 2 #201A • Aiea, HI 96701
ahunter42@hotmail.com
www.honhabitat.org

Serving Animals

Hawaiian Humane Society
contact: Eve Holt, Volunteer Coordinator
808.946.2187
2700 Waialae Avenue • Honolulu, HI 96826
www.hawaiianhumane.org
(hours: noon–8 pm weekdays, 10 am–4 pm weekends)

Healing Accommodations

BeachLane B&B
111 Hekili Street, #277
Kailua, HI 96734
contact: Tonic Bille
808.262.8286
info@beachlane.com
www.beachlane.com

Hawaii Aloha Accommodations
152 N. Kalaheo Ave.
Kailua, HI 96734
contact: Verena B. Rainalter
808.261.5446 • fax: 808.263.3301
verena@hawaii-aloha.net
www.hawaii-aloha.net

Hawaii's Hidden Hideaway
1369 Mokolea Drive
Kailua, HI 96734
808.262.6560
hhhideaway@yahoo.com
www.ahawaiibnb.com

Hawaiian Island Bed & Breakfast
Lanikai Beach, O'ahu, HI 96734
808.261.7895 • Toll free 800.258.7895
hi4rent@aloha.net
www.lanikaibb.com

Kahala Mandarin Oriental Hawaii
5000 Kahala Avenue
Honolulu, HI 96816
800.367.2525
www.mandarinoriental.com

Manu Mele Bed & Breakfast
153 Kailuana Place
Kailua, HI 96734
contact: Carol Isaacs
808.262.0016
manumele@pixi.com

Healing Accommodations

Manoa Valley Inn
2001 Vancouver Drive
Honolulu, HI 96822
808.947.6019
manoavalleyinn@aloha.net
www.aloha.net/!wery

Royal Hawaiian Waikiki Beach Hotel
2259 Kalakaua Avenue
Honolulu, HI 96815-2578
800.782.9488
www.royal-hawaiian.com

Sunset Beach Retreat
contact: Sundari
59-015 Hoa'lua Street
Hale'iwa, HI 96712
808.638.0780
shaktisundari@yahoo.com

Turtle Bay Resort
57-091 Kamehameha Hwy. • Kahuku, HI 96731
808.203.3650
www.TurtleBayResort.com

Other Resources

Aloha Nannies
Lori Chaffin, Owner
1400 Kapiolani Blvd. #C4S • Honolulu, HI 96814
808.394.5434
www.alohanannies.com

Notes

"The early ones believed there is one body of life of which we are all a part. We had our land and sea and sky, and they, too, are part of us."

Kaili'ohe Kame'ekua
Tales from the Night Rainbow

~ Chapter Seven ~

The Island of Kaua'i • Island of Discovery

When you begin your wellness vacation on Kaua'i you will undoubtedly bring your senses and perceptions to an understanding of what is unique about this healing island. Perhaps you knew before you even arrived. Maybe it was what you read and felt about Kaua'i that made you choose this island. You might have sensed the quiet, serenity and peacefulness or the natural beauty revealed in photographs. Because of this beauty, Kaua'i is the location for more movie productions than any other Hawaiian island. The mountains of Kaua'i often represent in our mind's eye the quintessence of the mystery and magic of the tropical paradise "Bali Hai". In fact, you'll see the Bali Hai mountain from the movie *South Pacific* on the north shore of Kaua'i.

Talking with people from Kaua'i, you'll discover that the promises offered by the tourism promotional materials are accurate but not complete. Most wellness providers on Kaua'i speak of the spiritual dimension of the island. Using the chakra system as the model as we have for the other islands, Kaua'i represents the third eye or spiritual aspect of energy. It is reputed to be the place where heaven and Earth truly meet, or at least where the veil between the two is thinner than anywhere else. It is the oldest of all the islands and according to legend the place where spirit first entered the Earth. Kaua'i's energy is also described as feminine. This means it has a *holding* rather than *projecting* energy. It is a place for remembering, realigning, and revitalizing to achieve well being. There is less about *doing* than about *being* on Kaua'i.

Until recently Kaua'i was identified as the garden island by the visitor's promotional materials. Because of its lush green landscape and mountains, the tropical forests and abundance of waterfalls, it seems like a garden of Eden. The Kaua'i Visitor's Bureau now calls it Hawai'i's Island of Discovery. That is especially appropriate for a wellness vacation. It's rural environment, laid-back lifestyle and welcoming population make it a perfect place to launch your personal voyage of rediscovery, your journey toward balance and harmony.

Twenty Ways to Pursue Balance and Harmony in Kaua'i

1. Pursue Balance and Harmony With a Silent Retreat

To reduce the likelihood of culture shock when arriving or leaving Kaua'i, we suggest a time of silence and solitude at the beginning and end of your wellness vacation. The quiet, beauty and spiritual energy of Kaua'i causes a dramatic shift from the overstimulation which is part of most of our lives. We suddenly slow down, begin to feel the air on our skin, notice the sounds of the birds and tune into the natural beauty. As you enter this other world which is Kaua'i, a silent retreat, even if for just a few hours, can ease you into your wellness vacation. This time provides an opportunity to deepen your intention about what you seek in the way of balance and harmony—your goals for your vacation. Having a period of silence and solitude before you return home allows you to reflect on what you have learned and prepare for the lasting changes you plan to make.

In Kaua'i, which is one of the most beautiful places on Earth, there can be no better way to gently go through this shift than spending time with nature. A few hours alone at the ocean, away from a crowded beach, begins the

> ***Island Orientation***
>
> *A note about the layout of Kaua'i before you begin. Princeville, Hanalei and Kīlauea dominate the north shore, which is the most lush and dramatically beautiful part of Kaua'i. It is also the rainiest area of the island. On the eastern coast, or the Coconut Coast, you will find Kapa'a, a sleepy two-story town, which mixes furniture and hardware stores with boutiques designed to attract tourists. Līhu'e, the county seat, is also on the east coast. This coastline has the greatest expanse of beaches and a number of hotels and condominiums, but the surf is often too rough for any but the strongest swimmer. Most of the tourist activity is on the south shore. This area has year round balmy weather, two major resort hotels and many condominiums. Here is where you will find the favorite beaches. Po'ipū and Kōloa are the names most often referred to in this area. The west side of Kaua'i is the least developed, driest and sunniest. Here you will find Waimea canyon, the Grand Canyon of the Pacific, as well as Waimea and Hanapēpē, two towns that time has nearly forgotten.*

process of returning you to your deepest inner knowing. Healing occurs simply as you watch the transparent curl of the waves, absorb the deep blue of the ocean, feel the wide expanse that seems to reach out forever and reflect on the peace and tranquility beneath the surface. This healing power of the ocean is a major contributor to making Hawai'i an ideal destination for those seeking greater balance and harmony in their lives. At the same time, the mountains and gardens of Kaua'i beckon you, offering their own invitation for reflection and deepening. Some of us resonate more with the energy of the ocean. Others of us find our soul in the mountains. You might want to choose one as your path to entering Kaua'i and the other as your meditative route before returning home.

Whichever you choose, this time of silence will surely enhance the power and lasting impact of your wellness vacation.

2. Take a Pilgrimage Into Your Center: Walk a Labyrinth

Just as nature offers many metaphors for your inner pilgrimage, so does a labyrinth walk. Thanks to the generosity of **Latifa Amdur**, one of the more talented wellness providers on Kaua'i, you have an opportunity to experience a labyrinth walk you're unlikely to forget. Latifa has created a hedged labyrinth just below her house on the Anahola hillside overlooking the ocean. The labyrinth, as a tool for self-reflection and inner pilgrimage, dates back thousands of years. The center represents the source or inner wisdom. Along the way we get diverted, lose focus and direction, and seem to arrive at dead ends or unyielding obstacles. Still, the center is there, unchanged by our struggles and frustrations, pulling us to continue the search. The journey to the center provides opportunity for practicing mindfulness. We can observe how our response to the process of walking the twists and turns reflects who we are and how we move through the world. On the way out we can integrate what we've learned or observed. We are then familiar with the route, see it more clearly, and understand that the dead ends were gifts rather than obstacles. To walk the labyrinth, call ahead to Latifa Amdur. (808.825.1155) Although there is no charge, a donation for maintenance is much appreciated. *(See article on Labyrinths in Chapter Three.)*

3. Discover Yourself and Your Creative Source Through Art

The beauty and power of nature is the focus of nearly all artists on Kaua'i. Art from Hawai'i can remind you not only of a place but also how you feel about that place.

There are many galleries in Kaua'i where you can purchase art. The **Waimea Gallery and Gifts** in the old renovated Waimea Theater is especially worth visiting. **Martin Wessler** is committed to showcasing top quality local artists at prices that are affordable to the customer and honor the talent of the artist. You'll find less of a mark up and will also have a chance to meet one of the artists. Either Martin or another artist will be there to talk with you about the art, the artists and their own work. (808.338.9033)

Creating a work of art is also an option during your wellness vacation on Kaua'i. Whether or not you consider yourself to be artistic, creating your image of the beauty of nature can open up new awareness in a number of ways. Painting can be an act of spirit more than of ego. Taking an art lesson and allowing your inner spirit to open is a way to communicate with nature through your painting. When **Helen Mehl** takes visitors and residents into nature to paint she gives them the four primary colors and instructs "don't focus on making a painting, let it happen with color." Just being open allows something to come through us. She has no set class schedule but will work at a time convenient to you. You'll find her art at the Waimea Gallery and Gifts. (808.742.6461)

Sarah Mangold, another local artist, will meet you at the Princeville Hotel to guide you in painting some of the most beautiful scenery on Earth. (808.651.0029) **Jean Bradley** offers art classes on Wednesday mornings in her home studio above Kalāheo, and on Thursday mornings in a private home in Kīlauea. Her favorite classes are those where students create a vision of their spirit guides. Jean will also do commissioned individualized paintings of your spirit guide. These paintings are extraordinary and have been very moving for those who receive them. (808.332.0515) **Annabel Spielman**, a professional artist with a master's degree, works with both beginners and accomplished painters. She provides painting instruction at the Kaua'i Marriott Resort on Wednesdays and Thursdays and at the Lāwa'i Beach Resort on Mondays from 1:30 to 4 pm. (808.332.5414) You'll also find her art at the Waimea Gallery and Gifts.

An option that we have discovered only on Kaua'i is the work of **Isa Maria** who will paint your portrait in nature. Not only will she capture the visual experience of you in a place that holds particular significance for you, but Isa has a way of bringing to the visual forefront the essence of her subjects. (808.635.2047)

A painting that you create or buy, or one that reflects the essence of who you are, will continue to keep alive the power and progress of your wellness vacation to Kaua'i.

4. Advance Your Inner Journey: Immerse Yourself in Hawaiian Culture

Many visitors to Hawai'i are fascinated by Hawaiian legends and traditions. The Hawaiian music is unlike any they have heard before. The hula speaks of exotic times and places. Stories of the *menehune* conjure up images of magical, miniature people. The healing power of Hawaiian plants shifts our thinking about our relationship with nature.

A Hawaiian healing experience takes you deeper into Hawaiian traditions providing you with a greater understanding of the Hawaiian people as well as yourself.

The hula can be a deeply spiritual experience for the dancer and audience alike. It involves story telling, learning the legends of the islands as well as sharing energy and *mana* through the hands. To be part of a true Hawaiian *hula halau* (school) if only for one night can be an unforgettable experience. On Tuesday and Thursday evenings at 4:00 *kumu hula*, **Puna Kalama Dawson**, provides hula instruction to a group of about thirty men and women at Anahola Beach Park (turn right at mile #13 and follow the road to the end of the beach park). Puna is the epitome of aloha—gentle, welcoming, encouraging regardless of how clumsy you feel, and happy to share what she knows with whomever arrives. She provides information about the deep inner meaning of each movement in the story you tell with your dance. An evening of dancing hula on the beach at sunset with a group of friendly people and a loving *kumu* will surely advance your pursuit of balance and harmony.

If you are lucky enough to be staying at the **Hale Ho'o Maha B&B**, hostess and owner, **Kirby**, will be happy to take you with her to the *hula hālau* she has been part of for many years. She will also share with you the story and spiritual meaning of hula. In fact, if you are genuinely interested in the culture, your stay with her can be a Hawaiian educational and cultural experience. (808.828.1341) **Sharon**, owner of **Rainbow Hale,** is also prepared to make Hawaiian activities and education part of your stay with her. (808.826.9386)

Set aside any night except Monday to go to **Café Coco** in Kapa'a and further immerse yourself in the local culture with music and dance. This garden café is a local favorite with a healthy, diverse but largely vegetarian menu. On Friday's, Antione plays and sings Hawaiian music in a deeply moving way and a local *hula hālau* performs just for the love of it. This may be a highlight of your visit to Kaua'i.

One of the gifts that is being rediscovered with the Hawaiian renaissance is herbal healing. **Dr. David Stoltz**, a recently transplanted mainlander, is apprenticing with Lavan Ohai, one of Hawai'i's foremost *la'au lapa'au*, (herbal healing masters). David conducts individualized tours of sacred places throughout the island weaving together the history and legends of the Hawaiian people with examples of how native plants can be used for healing. One of us arrived at her meeting with David with a fierce mosquito bite. At David's instruction she picked a leaf of an ocean side plant, chewed it briefly to release its juices, and rubbed it on the bite. The pain, itching and swelling disappeared almost immediately. (808.635.2963) A marvelous book about the secrets and practice of this newly revived art is *Hawaiian Herbal Medicine* by June Gutmanis.

For bodywork and massage, a must do is a half or full day experience at **Auntie Angeline's** day spa. This is unlike any spa you will visit. Don't expect sparkling, designer decor. This is your natural, Hawaiian style wellness center with a steam room where you will receive your salt scrub and a massage room where two body workers massage you simultaneously. The open air deck provides space to hangout and enjoy the mountain view. Be aware that this spa is co-ed and clothing optional, but people are discreet. (808.822.3235)

Many of the students of the Hawaiian healing arts are not Hawaiian, so don't be disappointed if your wellness experience is provided by a *haole* (Caucasian). The native Hawaiian masters are less available to visitors in part because they are committing their time to teaching. Non-Hawaiians are often their most ardent students. The masters recognize that and are willing to pass their wisdom to those who truly want to learn.

5. Enhance Family Harmony Through Greater Awareness of Self and Others

If your wellness vacation includes your family, many of the suggestions we offer throughout the book lend themselves well to the intention of enhancing family harmony.

Kayaking on Kaua'i is a favorite pastime in part because of the many navigable rivers. Taking your family on a kayaking trip where two of you share a kayak could be an opportunity for private conversation and sharing. Or turning a teenager lose in their own kayak can be equally therapeutic and supportive of family harmony. Kayaking companies are well-advertised all over Kaua'i.

Kay Snow-Davis, with 32 years of practice, offers specialized support for families based on her concept of the wheel of life cycle. Every 2.5 years each member in the family goes through a new life cycle, which changes the focus and direction of that member's attention. When you know what life cycle each of you is in, you can feel more relaxed and accepting of your own life changes as well as that of other members of your family. A session with Kay involves learning about this concept, which can be a powerful tool for achieving family harmony. Ask about her forthcoming book, *Wheel of Life Cycles*. (808.822.4332)

A nature meditation also could be adapted for family purposes. Nature gives us many metaphors for understanding each other and ourselves. During a family nature meditation one of you may discover a tree that seems to be overshadowing and smothering a smaller bush. Who in your family is the tree and the bush. Perhaps the flow of the stream will communicate to you that turbulence can pass if you just allow the flow rather than resist it. Later, under #8, we suggest people who can guide you in such a process. Just having quiet, individual time in nature can be healing by itself for family members who seldom interact with the natural world outside of a recreational activity. This experience may encourage you to create time when you return home, to allow nature to work its healing power on you individually and as a family.

As you read through the remainder of this chapter, think how each suggestion can lend itself to family harmony. Simply setting an intention to enhance balance and harmony in your family during your time on Kaua'i may create a lasting wellness experience.

6. Discover What is Missing in Your Life with Lifestyle Coaching

Vacations are a great time to take an objective look at which aspects of your life are keeping you off balance or causing disharmony. Perhaps it's the number of hours you work. It might be the job or career you have settled into by happenstance more than choice. As you age, you may discover an emptiness about life that wasn't there before—a feeling of lost opportunity. Whatever it is, your vacation in Kaua'i is a time to look more closely at changes that could enhance your life in a lasting way.

Petra Sundheim is a certified professional coach with many years experience working with people. She is a retired social work psychotherapist who is discovering the work she truly loves. Petra offers what she calls heart vision coaching, based on Carl Jung's idea that "Your vision will become clear only when you look into your heart. Who looks outside, dreams. Who looks inside, awakens." She defines coaching as providing sacred space for transformation and living life from the inside out—making choices from the heart. Petra's workshops include "Reinventing Your Life", "Awakening Attention", "Exploring Beliefs and Reality", and "Writing Your Own Mission Statement". Contact her to see when these workshops are scheduled or, if the topics interest you, ask if she can incorporate them into her individual counseling sessions. (808.332.0504)

You may decide that part of your lifestyle makeover should be a healthy diet. Perhaps you even have reason to believe that health problems are due to your diet. **Dr. Liz Lipski** is a great resource in looking at nutritional issues. Her doctorate in clinical nutrition and complementary medicine uniquely qualifies her to work with you in finding the right nutritional plan for your optimum health. (808.828.6401)

If you are a woman moving into the menopausal phase of your life, lifestyle issues may be surfacing for you regarding health, emotional, and spiritual challenges. A critical question many women are asking relates to alternatives to hormone replacement therapy. **Dr. Marilyn Roderick**, in Hanalei, is committed to looking at women's health issues from a holistic perspective. She is a Stanford Medical School graduate who became disillusioned with the limitations that insurance companies and HMOs put on the doctor-patient relationship. When she moved to Kaua'i she brought with her an unwillingness to let her values as a physician be compromised. She also became increasingly convinced that Western medicine did not have all of the answers. A visit to Dr. Roderick may open new doors for you and your health as you focus on the lifestyle you truly want to live. (808.826.9349)

Consult the other resources referenced at the end of this chapter to see which wellness professional could most support you in examining lifestyle changes you might want to make regarding your health, fitness, career, and relationships.

7. Create Peace and Compassion in Your Relationships

Without doubt, the biggest obstacle to balance and harmony in the lives of many people resides within intimate relationships. As we work through the inevitable tension and conflict of these important relationships, we can learn some of life's greatest lessons. In fact, these experiences can be our best teachers. Your vacation on Kaua'i gives you the necessary time and distance from everyday stress to step back and explore what is getting in the way of peace and harmony with the people you care the most about.

We mentioned **Kay Snow-Davis** earlier as an author of several books devoted to clarity and balanced living. A favorite is *Point of Power*, which offers a unique way of recognizing how we create disharmony and conflict by trying to force others and ourselves to disregard our natural way of being in and viewing the world. Kay uses the tree analogy—Root, Trunk, Branch, and Leaf—to help us recognize our individual style and creativity. For example, if you experience the world as a Leaf, it is natural for you to have many ideas and never be able to follow through and implement them all. The stability and consistency of a Trunk can be a great support for a Leaf or a Branch. A session with Kay can offer greater clarity, insight and tremendous relief knowing there is nothing wrong with either you or the person you love. You simply have different rhythms in life and these can be compatible if you understand them and choose to make them so. (808.822.4332)

Follow Kay's meeting with a session with **Joan Levy**, one of the most popular counselors on Kaua'i. She can help create new patterns of communication within your relationship. The "aha" you get from Kay will motivate you to work with Joan in letting go of expectations that are clearly unrealistic. Joan can also help you heal the pain of being pushed, or shoved to become something that you are not. Clients from all over the world come to Kaua'i to work with her. (808.822.5488)

In Kaua'i, nature offers its resources in healing relationship wounds and moving on. **Jane Winter** specializes in taking couples on a nature meditation to a stream and natural pool in the mountains behind her home. She has many years of experience as a counselor and workshop presenter. A hike and meditation in nature facilitated by Jane and focused on communication may be instrumental in salvaging a critically important relationship in your life. (808.822.2829)

Bring your communication issues with you and leave them here when you return home.

8. Learn From Nature's Wisdom with a Guided Nature Meditation

Because the people of Kaua'i believe that nature truly speaks to us, guided meditation opportunities will most often take you to nature to listen to its wisdom. Three women have designed guided meditation experiences, sharing with you their favorite places. Each is distinct so you might want to try them all.

Jeanne Rumen has found fairies and spirits in the **Limahuli Tropical Botanical Garden** at the far end of the north shore. This was a sacred valley for Hawaiians and she will guide you to experience why. It's important here to give credit to Chipper Wichman who is single handedly responsible for creating this extraordinary garden. His grandmother, a member of one of the oldest families of Kaua'i, lived down the road and devoted her life to holding onto this valley until someone came along who shared her passion and vision for what it was meant to be. It was a blessing to them both that this person was her grandson. Chipper's sensitivity to the history and meaning of the valley as he was landscaping it, and Jeanne's ability to communicate with its spirits assure you a memorable nature meditation. Ask about the book she has written on the spirits of Limahuli. (808.823.6451)

Kapua Gregory's nature meditation incorporates the spirit, legends, and history of the Hawaiian people and its culture. She opens her nature walk with a Hawaiian chant of greeting and closes it with a chant of gratitude. Throughout the nature meditation she introduces you to the significance of the natural world in Hawaiian culture. To fulfill your intentions, she guides you to connect with and hear the wisdom of that part of nature that most calls to you. (808.823.6451)

With the multi-sensory nature meditation of **Dawn Cantrell**, you will find yourself not only seeing and hearing nature but also tasting it. As you weave your way back up a stream she discovers tasty morsels—a flower, the head of a fern, a berry—for you to experience. Your destination is a particularly beautiful spot above the stream where you will tune into the sounds of the stream, experience the cool air of the forest, and really hear the bird songs. Let these support you in seeking answers to questions you offer up to nature's metaphorical wisdom. She supplements the private meditation experience with tools from her "awareness tool kit" including the *How 2 B Cards*, which she created. (808.822.0493)

It is our hope that you will continue to value the wisdom of nature and the many ways that it serves as a metaphor for the voyage of rediscovery—your journey toward balance and harmony.

9. Connect With Kaua'i's Healing Energy: Visit a Garden

Although Hawai'i offers many opportunities to connect with nature and its healing energy, gardens are always a recommended option. They are designed to deliver to you a variety of plants in an orderly, harmonious and attractive way. Gardens also provide benches at strategic places for the purpose of reflection. The three major gardens—Limahuli, McBryde, and Allerton—are part of the National Tropical Botanical Gardens. (NTBG) Standing above the entrance to **Limahuli Garden** is

Makana Peak, one of the most sacred mountains of the island. The terraced taro patches, paved trails that weave in and out of the forest, and spectacular views invite reflection and connection with the natural world at every step of the way. It is located in a narrow valley at the end of Hwy 56 on the north shore. (Closed on Saturdays. 808.826.1053) (Admission Fee)

Allerton and McBryde Gardens are on the south side of the island. Check into the visitor center above Spouting Horn on Po'ipū Beach and a trolley will take you to the gardens. McBryde is considered NTBG's garden of science with 252 acres of native and endangered species, only a portion of which is accessible to the visitor. You will be dropped off by the trolley and given unlimited time to tour on your own. The trolley returns every hour on the hour. The 100-acre Allerton garden is seen on a 2.5 hour guided tour. Here you will find landscape art including waterfalls and sculptures as well as tropical flowers. (Closed on Sundays. 808.742.2623) (Admission Fee for both gardens)

A hidden treasure of Kaua'i is **Na 'Āina Kai Garden** near Anahola. This 234-acre fairyland is the creation of **Joyce and Ed Doty**. The only way to see it is with a guided tour by trolley. The garden includes a hardwood plantation of recent vintage, a formal garden with paved path, a maze of mock orange hedges (smells like ginger), and a canyon that carries you down to the beach as part of your tour. You'll find yourself smiling at the beauty of nature and the infinite variety of plants and then you'll break out in laughter as you encounter one of the 63 sculptures. This is one of the most extensive sculpture gardens in the world and each one is designed to be whimsical and joyful. The little boy going face to face with a frog and the little girl having a tea party with her cat are two examples. You need to call ahead to reserve for one of the guided tours and they are only open Tuesday, Wednesday, and Thursday, so plan your schedule accordingly. (808.828.0525) (Admission Fee)

Another undiscovered garden without entrance fee, guide, or set days when it is closed, is the **Kukuiolina Japanese garden** at the Kukuiolina Park and Golf Course above Kalāheo. This is a place for both engaged contemplation and meditative awareness as you take the path around the perimeter and then sit on the lichen-covered wall to absorb the serenity of one of the two meditation circles. Lined with lava stones, the center of each circle holds a 6-8 foot dwarf pine tree surrounded by carefully raked sand. On either side of one of the circles are two stones resembling a serpent's head standing guard to encourage you to stay outside the circle and enjoy its order and serenity from a distance. (No Admission Fee)

While at the park, go up the hill a bit to see the Hawaiian stones from ancient times. Then walk along the paved path across the golf course to the pavilion lookout. The wide expanse of ocean view urges you to be present with the enormity of the natural world and is a pleasant contrast with the quiet meditation of your time at the Japanese garden.

The gardens of Kaua'i, though not numerous, are lovely and worth a visit. You'll see a wide variety of native tropical plants, many of which have been important to the Hawaiian culture.

10. Let Horses Guide You to Greater Balance and Harmony

Horseback riding as a tourist activity is more available on Kaua'i than on the other islands. Most of the opportunities are on the north shore and take you onto private land such as the Silver Cloud Ranch or the Princeville Ranch. **Dale Rosenfeld**, owner of **Esprit de Corp Riding Academy**, offers her services with the deep conviction and enthusiasm that comes from pouring yourself into a business that you truly believe in. Dale takes her rides on the Moalepe Trail, which is one of our favorites. Guides direct you to unusual flora and fauna and share Hawaiian legends. In addition to the five morning rides each week, Dale will put together a spiritual meditation ride by special request. She also conducts weekly horse instruction workshops that have been shown to help handicapped or troubled children develop self-esteem. Dale is one of the few practitioners of healing touch for animals in Hawai'i. She can share many stories of how she has used healing touch to save animals that were in danger of being put to sleep. Dale periodically offers classes or individual instructions on healing touch for animals. (808.822.4688)

For pet lovers, there could be no greater gift than to learn how to apply healing touch to your pet.

11. Connect With Spirit Through the Awe and Wonder of Nature

Simply sitting at the beach looking out over the ocean puts us face to face with the immensity of nature. Visiting a garden introduces us to the fascinating variety in the plant world as well as the natural order of change. We suggest that, while on Kaua'i, you take advantage of two additional, unforgettable opportunities to connect with nature: one is a boat trip up the Na Pali Coast and the other, a helicopter ride over the island.

The **Na Pali Coast** is an extraordinary coastline of deep velvet green valleys, sharp sea cliffs, waterfalls, and serenely blue coves for swimming and snorkeling. A boat trip along the Na Pali Coast has become a major attraction for tourists. There are two starting points for this tour: one from Hanalei, which is on the north shore, and the other from Waimea on the south shore. Not too many years ago all of the boats launched from Hanalei without sensitivity to their impact on the environment. Buses disgorged several hundred people onto the small beach park each day. Oily residue from the boats covered the water and the native birds and fishes were being crowded out, as were the native people who had once enjoyed this area as their park. Many of the boat owners were operating illegally which included not paying taxes. A concerted effort was launched to stop the environmental destruction, to exercise control over this very popular industry, and to return the community to its citizens. The governor at the time decided to close all the boat companies down. After a number of law suits, only the two or three companies that were legally licensed to operate were allowed to return to business there.

You will now find Hanalei a sleepy little town reflecting a bygone time rather than a mecca for tourists, big buses, and souvenir shops. This is a good place from which to take your boat tour because of its close proximity to the major cliffs along the Na Pali Coast State Park. **Captain Sundown** launches their boat, a forty-foot sailing catamaran from Hanalei Beach Park. The owner, **Bob Butler**, was born and raised in Hawai'i and has been sailing the coast for thirty years. He and his wife Stephanie are committed to sharing their enthusiasm and deep respect for the beauty and wonder of their world. Ask them about their other environmental efforts relating to monk seals. (808.826.5585)

On the south side of the island there are two recommended companies. The **Na Pali Explorer** is owned by two women who share their love of Kaua'i with visitors from all over the world. They have two rigid hull inflatables, which hold 16 or 35 people. These boats go at higher speeds and provide a bumpier ride than the catamarans. They can also take you further up the coast than the slower moving boats. The Na Pali Explorer launches from Kīkīaola Harbor in Waimea. (808.335.9909) The other boat company operating from this side of the island that we suggest you consider is **Na Pali Eco Adventures**. We respect their environmental policy of using vegetable based fuel rather than diesel for their boats. (808.826.6804)

A helicopter ride over the islands is a breathtaking, spiritual experience giving you a birds-eye view of the drama, beauty, and wonder of Kaua'i. This is truly a once-in-a-lifetime experience unless you decide to keep on doing it every time you return to Kaua'i. The Ultimate Kaua'i Guidebook writes, *"Going to Kaua'i without taking a helicopter flight is like going to see the Sistine Chapel and not looking up."* Because of its popularity, there are several well-advertised helicopter companies. We direct you to their ads and to the recommendations of the hotel staff or B&B hostess, but do strongly urge you to treat yourself to this extraordinary opportunity to soar over the most beautiful, awe inspiring scenery you are likely to encounter.

12. Pursue Wisdom and Wellness Through Massage Therapy

Ancient Hawaiians had great respect for the power of massage. Prior to important decision-making, the royalty would receive *lomilomi* massage nonstop for several days with the belief that it would result in greater wisdom. It is said that King Kamehameha's soldiers received *lomilomi* massage before going into battle as part of ancient psychological warfare. The massage left them feeling and looking stronger and more confident, thereby intimidating the opponent.

A massage is a great way to launch your wellness vacation, making you not only wiser and stronger but also defusing the stress you brought with you from home. We also recommend that you end your vacation with a massage assuring that your return home is as fully balanced as possible. On Kaua'i, the visitor has a wide variety of massage options. Hotel spas offer many forms.

While a spa massage is often the most convenient if you are staying at a nearby resort, you may want to go out into the community to discover places and people you wouldn't otherwise see. On the Po'ipū side of the island are three unique types of bodywork.

In Po'ipū, **Lida Martin** specializes in hot stone massage and also offers Swedish, *lomilomi*, LaStone therapy, deep tissue, and Shiatsu massage out of her private studio. Her unhurried, friendly, professional treatment combined with the personal, attractive, and homey studio make the experience especially relaxing and enjoyable. (808.742.2360)

A massage that you are unlikely to get elsewhere is the barefoot shiatsu massage **Alison Ebata** of Kōloa offers. As you lie face down on a mat on the floor Alison uses her barefeet to massage you from head to toe. No oils or need to undress with this massage. She began doing barefoot massage when people asked for more pressure than she could apply with her hands. A petite Japanese woman, Allison gently but firmly kneads your muscles with the balls of her feet. (808) 742-7226)

Trager Psychophysical Integration is a form of bodywork that has effects similar to those of massage, but is considered by many to be less intrusive. As with the barefoot massage, there is no need to disrobe. The therapist gently manipulates the body, stretching the arms and legs and moving them in circular motions. **Margee Faunce** provides trager therapy out of a studio at her home in the Po'ipū Beach area. (808.742.9387)

Moving to the north side of the island, near Kīlauea, **Sharron Norton** offers watsu, sometimes known as water shiatsu or wassertanz (water dance). Sharron's lovely house is in a rural area looking out over a pond and careful landscaping. Next to the house you'll receive your treatment in a redwood pool she designed. The pool deck is arrayed with plants while colorful streamers provide filtered light. Birds singing from nearby bushes accompany your treatment as Sharron slowly moves you about in body temperature water. Your limbs are gently pulled and stretched and your body becomes increasingly relaxed. The accumulated tension of months and years of stress melts away. (808.828.0928)

The massage unique to Hawai'i is the traditional *lomilomi*. **Lomi Kilohana** with **Paula Kressley and Toni Williams** (808.822.4619) offer *lomilomi* massage, as do several other providers (check the resources guide at the end of this chapter). This form of massage is typically done with clothes on and the body workers use their forearm rather than hands to press down and kneed your body. You may experience *lomilomi* in a variety of ways, however. As the training of this ancient style of body work has been passed down, massage therapists have adapted and revised it.

Massage therapists generally understand the power of nature to heal but **Kapua Gregory** has developed a massage procedure that honors and represents nature in all of its elements. Kapua begins the treatment with a gentle Hawaiian chant. This is followed by a whispering of fingers lightly touching your body representing air and the natural breezes. The hot stone portion of the massage represents the earth. Throughout the massage session, she plays a tape of nature sounds that she developed. This is a truly unique form of massage in a studio surrounded by nature. (808.821.9301)

Experience a massage as part of your commitment to wellness during your vacation on Kaua'i.

13. Restore Balance on All Levels: Have an Ayurvedic Treatment

Deepak Chopra, a physician who became an alternative health care advocate and best selling author, is responsible for making Ayurveda a household word. This 6000-year-old natural healing system from India identifies three body types called *doshas*. The goal of Ayurveda is to create a balance within these *doshas* and, in doing so, restore balance on all levels of our being. Massage and diet are two primary ways of achieving this balance. *(See the article on Ayurveda in Chapter Three)*

An Ayurveda massage is unlike any other you will experience. Medicated herbal oils are heated and applied by two massage therapists who work in synchronized movements on both sides of your body. The oils, selected especially for your body type, nourish your skin while the synchronized massage creates balance of the body and soothes the mind. Following the massage, you are encased from the neck down in an herbal steam bath. This process promotes circulation, opens pores, creates sweat to eliminate impurities and facilitates absorption of the herbal oil. If you chose, you can enhance this experience with what is called the Shirodhara. Here, warm medicated oil is continuously poured on your forehead and head. This further calms the mind and lifts the spirit.

All of this is available at **Tri Health Ayurveda Center**. Check into the office on Lighthouse Road where their ayurveda herbs are available for purchase and then be escorted to the massage center, a charming wooden house set off the road in a clump of trees. The natural wood and Persian carpets enhance the feeling that this is a place where all of your senses will be nurtured in a healthy, natural way. (808.828.2104 or www.oilbath.com)

Diet is the other primary means of balancing the *doshas* and **Darci Frankel**, owner of the **Ayurvedic Center**, offers both the ayurveda diet and ayurveda massage therapy in her 7 – 10 day retreats. If the above description of the massage and steam experience seems guaranteed to transport you to heaven, imagine having it every day for 7 days. Darci's individually designed Ayurveda Retreat experience includes this steam and massage experience each day, together with meals cooked specifically to meet your needs. She begins the retreat with a consultation to identify your particular condition, body type and wellness goals. She then develops the menu and works with you throughout the time you are there. Clients have experienced substantial weight loss, freedom of back pain, and relief from the symptoms of chronic fatigue syndrome and fibromyalgia. One client even attributes this experience to her success in stopping smoking. An overworked nurse released years of tension and left with her skin and face looking years younger. Although it isn't part of the package, Darci will arrange nearby accommodations for you. For the seven day retreats, she rents a luxurious home where participants stay and receive their treatments. The food is cooked onsite by a chef. (808.826.1811)

14. Get an Alternative Opinion: Visit a Complementary Health Provider

Conventional wisdom tells us that we should get a second opinion when receiving a challenging diagnosis. Medicine is an imprecise science with many opportunities for differing opinions. An increasing number of Americans are discovering that, not only do doctors not have all the answers, but the answers they do offer can sometimes cause more harm than good. While on your wellness vacation why not get an alternative opinion from a complementary health care provider.

Kaua'i has an expert on nutritional medicine who can suggest to you how your diet may be contributing to your health problems and how dietary change can help return you to health. **Dr. Liz Lipsky, PhD** has her doctorate in clinical nutrition and complementary medicine and has authored two important books on diet and chronic physical problems. Liz points out that the word "diet" means "manner of living" in Greek. A visit to her not only will help identify the role your diet is playing in your physical condition, but, consistent with the meaning of the word, she will also help you look at your lifestyle and suggest tools for making changes. This could include stress management and exercise plans, a behavior modification program as well as herbal supplements. (808.828.6402)

Latifa Amdur is a licensed acupuncturist who brings a highly tuned intuitive ability to her work. She combines this with kinesiology, acupuncture, and vibrational therapy to get to the core emotional issue that is affecting the body's natural ability to heal. During her thirty years of practice in complementary medicine, she has continued to upgrade her skills and training and has a high success rate in unblocking the stuck emotional energy that so often causes dis-ease. Latifa addresses issues of stress, allergies and pain on an acute as well as a chronic level. Your work with Latifa will likely uncover and help resolve emotional issues which are keeping you blocked. (808.828.6402)

Many people on Kaua'i who have found conventional medicine ineffective end up working with **Roger Deniscewicz**. His approach to finding the source of the problem as well as its solution is through listening to the wisdom of the body by means of muscle testing or kinesiology. We seldom recognize the body's willingness to communicate directly without pain and discomfort. Instead, we wait until it must shout at us to get our attention. Roger will allow you to communicate with your own body regarding what is missing and what is needed to achieve balance. (808.828.1946)

Your wellness vacation on Kaua'i could be a time to explore alternatives and to experience your mind, heart, body, and spirit in a different way. Complementary wellness providers can usher in a whole new realm of understanding about the causes of your physical distress and disharmony.

15. Advance Emotional and Physical Balance Through Energy Healing

Energy healing is increasingly recognized and accepted as a valid approach to pursuing health and healing. Most alternative therapists view the flow of energy in and around our bodies as a key indicator of our well-being. They work to manipulate that energy in order to maximize our health. Energy healing frequently involves belief in a spiritual presence or energy field that can be called on to support our goals and intentions. Sometimes this is referred to as the Higher Self. Energy healing can also be used to support larger life goals by clearing the energy blockages that might impede what we seek to achieve in life. On Kaua'i there are many wellness providers who specialize in working with energy to support you in achieving your intention.

Deborah Burnham works with a process called "integrated awareness" which involves setting an intention and then achieving deep relaxation in the water as Deborah guides energy to chakra areas that are blocked and that might impede achieving your intention. Deborah uses voice sound therapy, (a deeply relaxing experience), and craniosacral work, as well as therapeutic touch, all of which are energy approaches to achieving balance and harmony. (808.651.4534)

Holly Majestic uses her shamanic training to facilitate soul retrievals, open charkas and support integration in each individual. Holly is masterful in her approach to sound therapy using a beautiful crystal bowl that creates a strong resonance field as it is played. (808.821.0681)

Catherine Stovall is another advanced energy healer. She was a highly successful businesswoman before beginning her journey into alternative healing in 1980. Catherine's sensitive, gentle presence encourages immediate trust. She begins her session with a discussion of the principles and philosophy she works with, the process she will follow, and possible reactions you might experience. Catherine uses a Mayan hammock made of yucca fiber rather than a massage table. This allows her to work with energy centers surrounding the body. The use of her voice as sound therapy is particularly relaxing. Catherine is also available to work with you in creating a ceremony at sacred spots on Kaua'i. (808.246.8700)

16. Activate Your Inner Healer with an Alternative Treatment

If long-term relief for a painful physical condition has eluded you, your wellness vacation to Kaua'i offers an opportunity to begin an alternative treatment. Most alternative therapists believe that our body's natural healer can be activated and supported by each of us through self-care and a change in lifestyle. If follow-up treatments are necessary, you might find a similar practitioner within driving distance at home or return to Kaua'i. Some practitioners consult with you via phone to help you continue your treatment.

Naturopathic physicians are highly trained wellness practitioners who must attend four years of post-graduate medical training in naturopathic medicine in order to be licensed to practice. Many have gone on to add additional degrees to their vita. **Leia MeLead, ND** also has a degree in naturopathic medicine and a masters degree in oriental medicine and acupuncture. Her particular interests are hormonal balancing and women's holistic health. She uses acupuncture as an important tool to relieve discomfort and improve the flow of energy. A visit with Dr. MeLead can provide you with several alternative remedies. In one visit to her you can achieve what would normally require several visits to a variety of wellness providers. (808.822.2087)

Dr. David Stoltz, DC is much more than a licensed

chiropractor. In addition to the chiropractic adjustments and deep tissue work, he may also take you on a trip to an herb garden, or even the beach, to explore what herbs might respond to what you need. A recent example was a call from a patient to come to her house (he does house calls) because she was feeling pain in her neck, numbness in her hands, a pinched nerve and general malaise. After the chiropractic adjustment and neck work, he took her into her garden to explore what herbs could treat her condition. Together they selected herbs and berries to prepare a tea. It was an education for her of the pharmaceutical treasure in her backyard. Also, don't be surprised if he talks with you about lifestyle issues and recommends that you get a pet, deepen your spirituality, or take up dancing. His own life journey has led him to see the necessity of a larger worldview in living a full life. This means being attentive to matters of the mind, heart, body, and spirit. (808. 635.2963)

Risa Kaparo, PhD, is an internationally recognized psychologist whose success in helping people release chronic pain is nothing short of revolutionary. Physicians, therapists, chiropractors, and other health professionals are increasingly attracted to her work, which is based on thirty years of research. The basis of her therapy is teaching the client to move and become aware of their movement in a way that allows them to participate in restructuring and renewal. As she writes *"healing calls on each of us to become fully and consciously engaged in the process of how we live. In this way an injury or an illness becomes a learning environment, revealing the behaviors that create and sustain these life conditions. Through a 'self-sensing' awareness you learn to participate consciously in your own healing."* One on-going client describes Dr. Kaparo as one of the most profound healers she has ever met. Another client was so impressed with the results that he brought his wife and children to Dr. Kaparo on a wellness vacation to experience individual and family sessions. The John F. Kennedy Graduate School of Holistic Studies will be working with her to develop videos of her work. While on Kaua'i, if you are suffering from pain or physical discomfort, a session with Dr. Kaparo may open doors to a pain free existence and greater aliveness. (808.821.8884)

17. Heal Old Emotional Wounds on All Levels

There is increasing scientific evidence that emotional wounds become lodged in the body and must be cleared there as well as from the heart and mind. In fact, emotional wounds affect us on all levels—mind, heart, body, and spirit. If they are not cleared out, the body begins to respond with dis-ease. A wellness vacation to Kaua'i can begin, and perhaps complete, the process of letting go of old stuff on all levels.

Two wellness providers, in particular, can help with unblocking and dislodging the emotions at the physical level. **Virginia Beck, NP**, both a nurse practitioner and a Trager practitioner, describes emotions as energy in motion. Any blocked energy gets in the way of experiencing peace in the present moment. In the body, these feelings need to be released physically and she can work with you in doing so through Trager®. The desire for peace, for change, and for growth and renewal needs physical expression. Whether your embodied emotion is grief, or abuse, or self-esteem issues, fear or anger about death or illness, this gentle process of supported body movements, allows your body to release years of tension, and integrate the natural state of balance and peace. A wellness experience with Virginia is an excellent time to explore just how free and how peaceful your body and being can be. (808.332.7087)

Another physical approach to releasing blocked emotional energy is a combination of sound therapy and craniosacral therapy. **Manima Dacosse** offers both of these in her home above the Wailua River. Weather permitting, you will receive your treatment under a tree on the grassy point of her lawn looking down over the valley. She begins by guiding you to develop an intention for what you want your body to release, such as letting go of anger from a divorce, or grief from a lost loved one. With this intention at the conscious level, she works with tuning forks to entrain the intention at a deeper level. She explains that each part of our body has a natural frequency, which becomes altered by emotional chaos. The tuning forks help correct the frequency bringing it into a natural state. Craniosacral therapy works with the fluid which flows between the sacrum and the cranial area. Research by the Upledger Foundation has shown that this fluid has a pulse which can be altered in order to achieve healing on the physical level. Contact Manima for an extraordinary healing session in a beautiful environment. (808.822.4746) *(For more information on this process see the article in Chapter Three or the Upledger website at www.upledger.com.)*

Another approach to letting go and moving on is through psychological mask making with **Kathy Gaiser-Lichtenberg** of the **Kaua'i Institute of Imaginal Arts**. Kathy is a grief counselor by profession and describes her work as helping people recover from losses of any kind. The mask is an embodiment of the story of the loss and how it was experienced. It is experiential work that allows you to create a representation of what you were, what you want to be, or who you are now with wounds still present. Kathy works with either papier mache masks or a plaster gauze mask that is applied to your face and thereby accurately represents your physical image. She has had great success with this process with not only individuals but also families and with children seven years and older. (808.652.2680)

The variety and talent available to help you release yourself from old emotional wounds could make this a turning point in your life.

Fitness and Sports

18. Combine Fitness and Meditation With a Yoga Session

Yoga is becoming an increasingly popular form of exercise. Classes now exist for people ranging from Wall Street executives, professional athletes and Hollywood stars to those of us who find our way to the local "Y" fitness program. Yoga seems to promise everything from deeper spiritual meaning to a body free of pain and discomfort. There are 8 different schools of yoga. Some teachers remain loyal to what they were taught and others offer an eclectic form that has evolved out of their own practice.

Risa Kaparo, PhD has developed a yoga style that draws on her Somatic Learning process. One student described it as yoga from the inside out. Risa teaches how to develop an awareness of the movements of your bones, diaphragm, membranes, fluids, and organs. You learn how to participate consciously with the self-healing intelligence within. Risa offers one or more daylong classes each month. It is worth scheduling your vacation around one of these classes. Call her for a schedule. (808.821.8884)

Michaelle Edwards offers yoga classes and retreats as well as individual instruction. Her studio is in the Princeville area looking out over a valley to a spectacular mountain that has been a focus for many movie scenes. She calls her style of yoga, **YOGALIGN**, which is a combination of yoga, self massage, core alignment techniques, natural breathing, and movement meditation. The beauty of the environment plus Michaelle's attentiveness and commitment to supporting you in achieving your yoga goals can make this an especially attractive option. Michaelle holds public classes on Monday, Wednesday, and Friday mornings. (808.826.9230)

On the Po'ipū side of the island two yoga instructors offer private and public lessons in Kalāheo. **Margaret Kuffel**, teaches yoga several times a week either as group or individual sessions. (808.742.6363) **Sandra Leftwich** also offers yoga instruction in Kalāheo. (808.332.7681)

The Hyatt spa schedules yoga sessions twice a day, Monday through Friday, so if you are on the south shore it will be easy for you to participate in a yoga class. Call the Hyatt, 808.742.1234 ext 4949, for the class schedule. If you want to join an ocean side yoga class, contact **Joy Zepada.** She offers yoga for all levels Monday through Friday from 8:00 – 9:30 a.m. Upon arrival at the airport, pick up her rack card, which gives you directions to the class. Since the classes are outside, be aware that they may be cancelled because of weather. (808 639-9294)

> ***Health Tip***
>
> *When doing Yoga, be gentle with yourself If you are new at yoga, a caution about over stretching and trying to look like the instructor and the other participants who have been doing it for some time. Yoga is a gradual process of teaching our bodies to let go of the tension that comes from stress and other aspects of our lifestyle. The operative word here is "gradual". This is not meant to be painful. If it is, you have pushed yourself too hard.*

19. Experience a Nature-based Workout: Take a Hike

Nowhere else in Hawai'i will you find more diversity of hikes and breathtaking scenery than in Kaua'i. From dramatic coastline to inland forest to deep canyons, Kaua'i has it all. Your hikes on this island will surely stimulate feelings of joy, awe and deep gratitude for the natural wonder of this corner of the planet. They can also give you a challenging workout. Perhaps this is why the percentage of people coming to Kaua'i to hike is increasing each year.

A well-advertised favorite is the **Kalalau Trail** along the Na Pali Coast. On those occasions we've taken it, the conditions have been either muddy or hot and exposed, but the two-mile stretch to Hanakapi'ai Beach offers spectacular views. The 11-mile hike all the way into Kalalau Valley is for the most rugged and determined hikers. Don't set out to do it unless you're prepared to spend the night and have gotten a permit.

In the center of the island, behind Kapa'a is the **Moalepe Trail**. You'll walk for about a mile along a dirt road that becomes a path moving up toward the forest. Treasure the unobstructed view across the valley to the mountain with its summit—often laced in wisps of clouds. The hike will take you all to way to Keāhua Arboretum but we recommend that you turn this into two hikes. Begin the second, shorter hike, at the trailhead above the Arboretum.

One of our favorite coastline hikes is along the lithified cliffs of the south shore. There is no clearly marked trailhead but the walk along the coastline is familiar to most people in the area. Ask the hotel concierge for directions to Kawailoa Bay, which is a great starting point. As you work your way back along the coast your hike will weave in and out of isolated bays, up the cliffs to breathtaking views, alongside large fissures filled with rushing water, and around hissing blowholes where water spouts up into large fountains. There are endangered plant species and occasional petroglyphs along the way. Locals tell about finding bones from ancient wars when King Kamehameha tried unsuccessfully to conquer Kaua'i.

> **Health Tip**
>
> *Like any wilderness area, hiking in Hawai'i can be dangerous. Be sure to wear sunscreen, sturdy shoes, take water with you, and be prepared for sudden downpours, especially in lowlying canyon areas. The rangers at the park can give you up- to-date information on trail conditions and hazard advisories. One of the best ways for those unfamiliar with crumbling lava rock and the maze of trails and thick foliage is to use experienced trail guides.*

In Kōke'e, we recommend the **Kukui Trail**, **Alaka'i Swamp** and **Awa'awapuhi** hikes, for those interested in more strenuous hikes. Shorter hikes for the less adventurous are the **Pihea trail** at the Kalalau overlook at the end of the road, and the **Cliff trail** in Halemanu.

Excellent trail guides are available at the State Park Ranger's office or the Kōke'e Museum next to the Kōke'e Lodge. While getting out in nature can be an exhilarating and glorious adventure, this lush paradise can cause you to forget some common sense precautions.

Many hiking tour companies are prominently advertised. We introduce you to those that aren't because they offer individualized hikes. **Carl Berg's Hawai'i Wildlife Tours** offers customized tours for up to four people spotlighting areas of interest such as birds, endangered plants, and Hawaiian medicinal plants. With a PhD in botany, Carl has extensive knowledge about the plant world. (808.639.3968)

Kaua'i Nature Tours is owned by **Chuck Blay**. A prominent geological consultant, Chuck offers interactive specialized day hikes into canyons and other areas of geological interest. He also conducts six to eight day seminars for groups which include hikes and geological studies. Chuck's tours take you beyond the beauty of nature to a deeper understanding of its evolution, the natural order, and the complementary roles that plants and animals play in supporting each other. (808.742.8035)

A hidden gem of a hike is offered by **Na 'Āina Kai Botanical Garden and Sculpture Park**. The guided hike options are two hours or five hours, taking you along a meandering stream into their formal garden, through the Kuliha'ili Canyon and down to the beach. The longer hike explores the entire garden and includes a box lunch in a gazebo overlooking the ocean. The two-hour hike begins at 8 a.m. on Tuesdays, Wednesdays, and Thursdays and the five-hour hike is on Thursday beginning at 9:00. The latter requires advance reservations. (808.828.0525)

20. Get a Fitness Assessment and Launch a Workout Plan

Most big hotels which don't have a full-fledged spa at least have a fitness center as a nod to the growing number of guests who care about their bodies. You'll find fitness centers at the **Radisson Kaua'i Hotel** (808.245.1955), the **Sheraton Kaua'i Hotel** (808.742.1661) and the **Kaua'i Marriott Resort** (808.245.5050. In addition, for a nominal fee, you can use the facilities at the **Kaua'i Athletic Club** in the Kukui Grove Shopping Center. The fee covers use of the pool, racquetball court, exercise rooms as well as classes in aerobics and cardio kick boxing. (808.245.5381) Both the **Princeville Health Club & Spa** (808.826.5030) and the **ANARA Spa** at the Hyatt Regency Kaua'i Resort also have fitness rooms. (808.742.1234)

For those who want one-on-one training, **Murray Harris**, who works part-time as a trainer at the Kaua'i Athletic Club, is available to work with you on an individual basis. You will begin your sessions with a personal fitness assessment and development of goals. Then, Murray mixes fitness with an island experience such as hiking or kayaking. For example, if you decide that you would like to pursue fitness through kayaking, she will arrange kayaks and accompany you on a trip up the river discussing how kayaking addresses particular aspects of your body and enhances balance and harmony. (808.652.1236)

On either side of the island you can pursue fitness through pilates. **Mary Jane Kleiman**, of **Pilates in Paradise** is a personal trainer who will guide you in developing a personal fitness plan using pilates as her emphasis. (808.825.0342) **Sharon Agli** offers **Oceanfront Pilates in Paradise** as well as personal fitness training in the grassy area of the Sheraton in Po'ipū. Her work provides the pilates foundation that she believes should, ideally, precede work on the machines. It's nice for some of us to know that there is a machine alternative to this highly effective strength training approach. Her sessions are on Tuesdays, Thursdays, and Saturdays at 8:00 am. (808.651.8201)

The weather and beauty of Hawai'i invites you to launch or advance a fitness plan that will continue to be part of your quest for balance and harmony when you return home.

Healing Accommodations

Kaua'i North Shore

Sharron Norton's Manawai Guest Suite and Wellness Retreat offers guests a charming room with private bath and limited cooking facilities together with a healing environment and her own wellness services. Sharron's house is located off the main road connecting Kīlauea and Hanalei. It is only a short walk down the road for a morning swim at Kalihiwai Bay, one of our favorite beaches. Beautifully landscaped and quiet, the environment of Sharron's home and guest room invites a healing experience. Add to that Sharron's skills as a highly trained massage and sports therapist, kinesiologist and watsu practitioner and you have a truly healing accommodation. Vacationers can book for the guest room alone or can combine it with various treatments. (808.828.0928) (Moderate)

Just a short distance up the driveway from Sharron's is **Hale Ho'o Maha**, an old fashioned B&B—Hawaiian style. **Kirby Searles**, the owner and hostess, has offered her hospitality to visitors from around the world for 16 years. She is not only dynamic and friendly, but has immersed herself in Hawaiian legends and culture. Staying at Hale Ho'o Maha can be a cultural experience if you choose to take advantage of her offers to show you lei making, take you to her hula halau and otherwise learn about the true spirit of Hawai'i. There are four bedroom, three baths and a shared sitting room with fireplace, library, and many artifacts from Hawai'i and the South Pacific. Most of her visitors are repeat guests, which speaks for itself. (808.828.1341) (Moderate)

Another treasure on the north shore in the Hanalei Valley is **Taro Patch Hale**. This guest retreat is at the very end of the narrow dirt road that can be seen from the Princeville lookout. It threads its way between the Hanalei River and taro patches to a truly isolated, soothingly quiet area far from the experience of most tourists. **Mina Morita** (one of the most respected state senators in Hawai'i) and her husband **Lance Laney** are your hosts. The two cottages are separated from each other and the main house by a wide expanse of lawn. Both overlook a gentle flowing river. The cottages are a single room with covered deck for dining and an outside, attached bathroom. You can look out on wild ginger while you shower. (808.826.6612) (Moderate)

Moving toward the end of the Kūhiō Hwy on the north shore, you will find **Rainbow Hale and Gardens** located in a valley known to be one of the last places of the people of Mu. The people of this valley are quite protective of it because of its historical and sacred significance and its beauty. You'll get directions only when you've booked a stay. This is one of the reasons owner **"Mu"** has decided to devote her guesthouse to people interested in long term stays—for people who feel they are "drawn home." Rainbow Hale sits on land with powerful spiritual energy according to Hawaiian lore. The healing and awakening experience of some of her guests suggest this may be true. The main house has several rooms with a shared kitchen and sitting area. A wide lawn with tropical vegetation fronts the house and leads down to the rapidly flowing stream and natural swimming hole. There is also a sweat lodge on the property close to the stream. Mu is deeply involved with Hawaiian culture and will open you to authentic experiences you wouldn't otherwise have. (808.826.9386) (Budget to Moderate)

Moving toward the center of the island, in the valley and farm area behind Kapa'a, is **Rosewood B&B**. This former macadamia nut plantation house with adjoining cottages is a perfect site for those who love the rural area, mountain views and nearby hikes. Its charm is the rural environment as well as the architecture and landscaping. The yellow with white trim plantation house is fronted by a wide verandah with rocking chairs. Various cottages scattered around the property echo that theme with white walls, natural wood floors, tables, chairs, and rocking chairs. Sit outside to enjoy the view either of the mountain across the valley floor or the garden. Especially appealing are the outdoor showers housed in yellow and white trimmed stalls with friendly trees providing protection and ambience. For hikers, Rosewood is a short distance from the Moalepe Trail mentioned in #19. (808.822.5216)

Mahinas Guest House, in Kapa'a, caters exclusively to women. It is a relaxed environment designed specifically to help women connect with each other. Guests have an entire house to themselves, sharing the kitchen and common areas. In addition, there is a massage area for those who would like a local massage therapist to come to them. Owner **Sharon Gonsalves** has an extensive list of healing practitioners to share with her guests. The house is only a few steps from the beach and within easy walking distance from Kapa'a's shops and eating establishments. (808.823.9634)

We now shift to the western coast where most of the resorts are located. Po'ipū is a magnet for visitors in large part because of its climate. While the north shore is often rainy during the winter, the south shore is usually sunny and warm. **Gloria's B&B** is a dream place right on the water. It is booked several months in advance for good reason. **Bob and Gloria Merkle** are superb hosts who thoroughly enjoy meeting people and contributing to a memorable vacation. Rooms have private decks looking out over the ocean. Breakfasts are more than muffins and coffee. Don't be surprised if you're served eggs benedict with mango salsa or homemade bread. All of the key guidebooks have raved about it so if you find they are full, Bob and Gloria are prepared to book you into one of the other vacation rentals they manage---all with an ocean view. (808.742.6995) (Moderate)

Up the road about 15 minutes from Po'ipū Beach is **Victoria Place**, a frequent focus of rave reviews in guidebooks. Located in a quiet neighborhood, rooms look out on the swimming pool and have special touches such as the fresh flower arrangements. Breakfast is either poolside or on the deck overlooking the valley. As with the décor of each room, the breakfast is a visual work of art—carefully cut fruit colorfully arrayed around a platter, several types of jams, English and fruit muffins, aromatic teas and coffee. Three separate rooms have their own baths. A honeymoon suite downstairs has cooking facilities. Book ahead for this charming B&B as it is often filled. (808.322.9300) (Moderate)

Imagine yourself back in the plantation days of Hawai'i where the slow pace of life assures time for relationships, reading, sitting on the porch in a rocking chair, and just being. Owners and workers alike were free of distraction like TV, shopping malls and constant media demands to find meaning through buying. **Waimea Plantation Cottages** take you back to that time. Authentic cottages of the workers from olden days are now furnished in vintage wicker, rattan and mahogany furniture, all with porches. The cottages are set a comfortable distance from each other assuring privacy. Each is surrounded by plantings of hibiscus and palms. A wide expanse of lawn bordered by coconut palms takes the visitor from the verandah of the reception building down to their private cottage. You are ocean side so you can choose between a walk on the black sand beach or hanging out at the swimming pool. You'll also want to explore historic Waimea town, which is walking distance from the cottages. (1.800.922.7866) (Moderate to Deluxe)

Please visit our website for updated and new wellness resources and information.

www.alohawellnesstravel.com

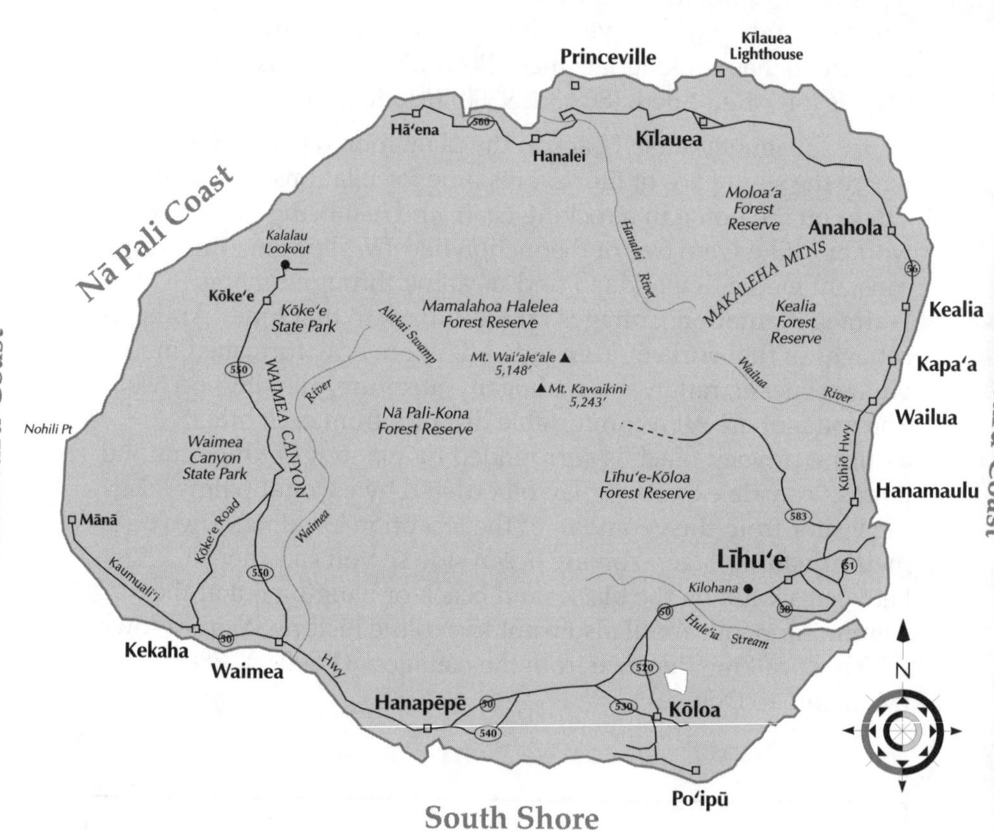
North Shore
Kīlauea Lighthouse
Princeville
Hā'ena
560
Hanalei
Kīlauea
Nā Pali Coast
Kalalau Lookout
Moloa'a Forest Reserve
Anahola
Hanalei River
MAKALEHA MTNS
56
Kōke'e
Kōke'e State Park
Alakai Swamp
Mamalahoa Halelea Forest Reserve
Kealia Forest Reserve
Kealia
Kapa'a
Leeward Coast
550
WAIMEA CANYON
River
Mt. Wai'ale'ale 5,148'
▲ Mt. Kawaikini 5,243'
Wailua River
Wailua
Nohili Pt
Waimea Canyon State Park
Nā Pali-Kona Forest Reserve
Kūhiō Hwy
Līhu'e-Kōloa Forest Reserve
Hanamaulu
Mānā
Kōke'e Road
Waimea
583
Kaumuali'i
550
Līhu'e
51
Kilohana
58
60
Hule'ia Stream
Kekaha
30
Waimea
Hwy
520
N
Hanapēpē
50
530
Kōloa
540
Po'ipū
South Shore

Resources

The Island of Kauaʻi

KAUA'I - WELLNESS DIRECTORY TABLE OF CONTENTS

Art and Art Therapy

Jean Bradley

is a prolific and talented artist and instructor. She offers private instruction as well as two group classes a week—one in Kilauea and one in Kalaheo. Her special interest is art as meditation, guiding the student to paint their inner vision. Jean will work with groups in creating an art/nature experience upon request.

PO Box 432 • Kalaheo, HI 96741
contact: Jean Bradley
808.332.0515
artsoul@hawaiian.net

Helen Mehl

Makanui Studios
1675-2 Makanui Road
Koloa, HI 96756-9539
808.742.6461
helenmehlart@hotmail.com
www.helenmehlgallery.com

Images, Kauai's Art Gallery

contact: Ray Charron
808.821.1382
www.alohaimages.com

Art and Art Therapy

Isa Maria
PO Box 1218
Kilauea, HI 96754
808.635.2047
www.isamaria.f2s.com

Kaua'i Spirit
(art workshops)
contact: Sarah Mangold, owner
PO Box 1332 • Kilauea, HI 96754
808.651.0029 cell
sarzac@aloha.net

Annabel Spielman
PO Box 479
Waimea, HI 96796
808.332.5415
whiski@aloha.net

Waimea Gallery & Gifts
PO Box 1089
Waimea-Kauai, HI 96796
808.338.9033
www.wesslerfineart.com
eternalimages@yahoo.com

Crystal Healing

The Crystal Academy of Advanced Healing Arts
PO Box 1334 • Kapaa, HI 96746 USA
Open Tuesday, Thursday & Saturday 11 - 3 (Hawaii time zone)
808.823.6959 • fax: 808.821.1165

Dance, Movement and Sound

Deborah Burnham

Our body is the magnificent gateway to optimum health and expanding our life's journey. In sea float or table session, Deborah will utilize sound, touch, and movement while supporting you to harmonize all levels of consciousness. Therapeutic Touch, CranioSacral Therapy®, Integrated Awareness®, and Physical Therapy ground and enrich Deborah's work.

5609 Honua Road • Kapa'a, HI 96746
808.651.4534
freebeing@juno.com • www.inawareness.com

Heartherapy
6437 Kahuna Road
Kapa'a, HI 96746
contact: Kimba Arem
808.823.6238
Kimbadoo@gte.net

Inquiry
(somatic learning for transformational healing and self renewal)
contact: Risa Kaparo, Ph.D
PO Box 609 • Anahola, HI 96703
808.821.8884
risa@somaticlearning.com

Mana Massage
(sound therapy combined with cranial sacral therapy)
P.O. Box 3228 • Lihue, HI 96766
contact: Manima Dancosse
808.822.4746
leslee@wwdb.org • www.manamassage.com

Intuitive/Spiritual Guidance

"Being Who You Really Are"

provides counseling in perceiving people and situations as What They Really Are; helping clients free themselves from expectations, judgments and fears that distort the present moment. Gaby intuitively assists you in recognizing and transforming beliefs, attitudes, patterns and behaviors that keep you from living an authentic, happy and fulfilled life.

1491 C Wanaao Road • Kapa'a, HI 96746
contact: Gaby Kornmann
808.823.8217
gabjoyiam@hotmail.com

HOLOGRAM OF WELLNESS

is a lifelong journey. Balance is the key to wellness. Without a personal reference for what balance is for you, you cannot focus and direct your energy for change. These are some of the tools I use to specialize and create your support system for balanced living SOUL PURPOSE ASTROLOGY, POINT OF POWER, WHEEL OF LIFE CYCLES and EMOTIONAL FREEDOM TECHNIQUE. I am available to support individuals, couples, families, teens, corporations, organizations and communities:

Box 60 • Kapa'a, Hawaii 96746
contact: Kay Snow-Davis
808.822.7244
ksd@aloha.net • www.soulpurposeacademy.com

Francesca Azuremare

(intuitive readings)
P.O. Box 120
Anahola HI 96703
808. 826.4574

I AM

(soul integration, healing hands)
contact: Johnny Dickerson
PO Box 601• Kilauea, HI 96754
808.639.8435
johnny.dickerson@verizon.net

"Iseum of Isis"

(Spiritually orientated; retreats, ceremonies, self empowerment classes, and private sacred healing sessions)
PO Box 280 • Kapa'a, HI 96746
contact: Catherine Stovall, Priestess
808.246.8700
info@soulinitiation.com
www.soulinitiation.com

Angela Kahealani

(clairvoyant healer)
c/o 6510 Olohena Rd.
Kapa'a, Kaua'I, HI 96746
808.635.6688
angela@kahealani.com
www.kahealani.com

Kauai Zen Satsang

(guided meditation & intensives retreats)
contact: Stephan Bodian
PO Box 762 • Kapaa, HI 96746
808.821.9689
www.stephanbodian.org
Stephan@midpac.net

Krystal Flores

(psychic)
6745 Kawaihau Rd. • Kapaa, HI 96746
808.821.0763
krystalguidance@hotmail.com
www.krystalguidance.com

Intuitive/Spiritual Guidance

Reality Crafting

(sacred union process through intensives)
PO Box 970 • Kilauea, HI 96754
contact: Suzanna Kennedy
808.828.6327
sacredunion@realitycrafting.com

Siri Shabad

808.937.5446
waipua@hawaiian.net

Sukyu Mahikari

Donna D'Alessio
808.822.11510
sonen@pixi.com

Tanya V. Zychlinsky

(energy healing and intuitive readings)
PO Box 2108 • Kapa'a, HI 96746
808.823.0399 • cell 635.931

Trance Channel Team

(channeling the Masters/Spirits)
contact: Katherine and Rod Russell
PO Box 962 • Kapa'a, HI 96746
808.821.9606
www.allowlove.com • rod@hawaiian.net

Personal Development & Psychology

Body Mind & Breath Center:

A holistic, transformational work for individuals & couples to heal your heart and evolve your consciousness. Uproot dysfunctional patterns of thinking, feeling & behaving. Reichian-assisted release of body armoring, buried emotions & memories. Inner-Child. Spiritual Purpose. 1-4 Session Intensives. "One evening with Joan went deeper & further than my past two years of therapy." –B.H.
PO Box 160 • Kapaa, Hi 96746
contact: Joan Levy, MSW, ACSW, LCSW, QCSW
808.822.5488
joan@joanlevy.com • www.lauhala.com/joan

Diana Fairechild

Author/ speaker/ expert witness Diana Fairechild offers consultations based on her books (NONI, Office Yoga, Jet Smart, Jet Smarter) and her vast experiences —flying 10 million miles, publishing 10 years, detoxifying, pursuing wellness. Consultations on "publishing," "fear of flying," "healthy flying," "noni." Smart Money: "Take the advice of Diana Fairechild."
PO Box 248 • Anahola, HI 96703
808.828.1919
diana@flyana.com • www.flyana.com

Personal Development & Psychology

Holly Majestic

Integrative Healing Facilitation that inspires, empowers and energizes you to re-invent, re-vitalize and re-enchant your life. Shamanic, Qi Gong, CranioSacral Therapy tools and Nature nurture and nourish group vacationers and individuals in creating a magnificent life. "The best thing you could ever do for yourself."

PO Box 1102 • Kapa'a, HI 96746

808.821.0681

info@hollymajestic.com • www.hollymajestic.com

Island Blessings

Island Blessings offers rituals of healing, love and empowerment. These rituals include counseling for individuals, couples and families. Training in Huna practices of harmony and healing are integral to their process.

PO Box 603 • Kilauea, HI 96754

contact: Fern Merle-Jones

808.828.1342 or 1.800.988.1548

bless2u@aloha.net • www.islandblessings.com

Dennis Mendonca, MA, Psychotherapist

(Education & Empowerment for Change)

PO Box 3956 • Lihue, HI 96766

808.822.4155

starbird@aloha.net

Healing Vacations

7100 A Kahuna Rd.

Kapaa, HI 96746

contact: Jane Winter

808.822.2829

janew@hawaiian.net

Kauai Institute of Imaginal Arts

(mask making and psychology)

PMB 145 • PO Box 223300

Princeville, HI 96722

contact: Kathy Gaiser-Lichtenberg

808.652.2680 (cell)

kglmasks@hawaiian.net

Gayle Newhouse

(Intuitive Readings, EMF Balancing, Tibetan Feng Shui & Blessings)

PO Box 1195 • Kilauea, HI 96754

808.828.0182

moonlighting80@hotmail.com

Jet Star Video/TV Productions

Judith Thomson, M.S. Counseling Psychology, Video/TV Producer |

PO Box 1891 • Koloa, HI 96756

808.245.7944

jet@aloha.net

Miki Kaipaka

(Fibromyalgia/Chronic Fatigue Reversal Support)

808.245.9202 or 808.635.7383

kaipaka@aloha.net

Lifestyle Modification

Fitness

One-on-One Fitness Training
PO Box 1163 • Kapa'a, HI 96746
contact: Murray Harris, ACSM
808.652.1236
jewelofwilson@hotmail.com

Nutrition

Liz Lipski, PhD, CCN

is a board certified clinical nutritionist and author of two highly acclaimed books on nutrition Digestive Wellness and Leaky Gut Syndrome. She is a frequent guest on radio shows nationwide and has worked with many visitors to Kauai. Individualized programs may include: diet, nutritional and herbal supplements, exercise, detoxification programs, and testing.
4166 Momi Street • Kilauea, HI 96754
contact: Dr. Liz Lipski
808.828.6402

Success Coaching

Heart Vision Coaching

As a Certified Professional Coach, "I am a dream catcher. You, the dreamer, can change the dream anytime. Nightmares become lessons, breakdowns become breakthroughs" A coaching partnership provides sacred space for transformation, making choices from the heart, living your vision.
2363 Pu'u Rd. #5C • Kalaheo, HI 96741
contact: Petra Sundheim, MSW, CPC
808.332.0504 • fax 332.0944
coachpetra@myexcel.com • www.pathwaysoflight.org

Jet Star Video/TV Productions

expressing, educating and empowering via media.
A video company documenting life: celebrations, events, and individual projects. Celebration Workshops include "Lighten Up with Laughter" and "The Reel You" in which you rediscover the joy of life through your bubbling expression. "Take Two" polishes your on-camera skills for interviews and life!
contact: Judith Thomson, M.S.
Counseling Psychology, Video/TV Producer
PO Box 1891 • Koloa, HI 96756
808.245.7944
jet@aloha.net

Frieda Freitas
(Professional Business & Life Coach)
PO Box 31 • Lawai, Hawaii 96765
808.742.7999
frieda@aloha.net
www.thevsi.com/coaching.htm

Heart to Heart
(Life coach and Hypnotherapy)
contact: Patti Valentine
PO Box 194 • Kapa'a, HI 96746
808.652.0433
pattiv1@juno.com

Yoga

Body Resonance

Margaret has many services to offer the visitor in search of relaxation, rejuvenation and lifestyle modification. She teaches yoga several times a week as well as offers individual and group yoga sessions. In addition, her body work includes sound therapy, therapeutic massage, hot stone massage, polarity therapy and ortho-bionomy.

PO Box 1120 • Kalaheo, HI 96740
contact: Margaret Kuffel
808.742.6363
bodyresonance@hawaiian.net

ManaYoga Center

Located in a beautiful, serene site near Hanalei, Mana Yoga owner and instructor Michaelle Edwards has been practicing yoga 30+ years and teaching for ten years. She has developed a yoga style called YOGALIGN which is a combination of yoga, self massage, core alignment techniques, natural breathing, and movement meditation. Michaelle offers public and private yoga sessions, week-long yoga retreats, YOGALIGN teacher trainings, massage and vacation accommodations. Public yoga classes are held Monday 9:15-10:45am, Wednesday and Friday 8:30-10:15am.

PO Box 681 • Hanalei, Hi 96714
contact: Michaelle Edwards
808.826.9230
manayoga@yahoo.net • www.manayoga.com

Oceanfront Yoga

Poipu area
contact: Joy Zapeda
808.639.9294

Yoga in Kalaheo

3513 Waha Rd • Kalaheo, HI 96714S
contact: Sandra Leftwich
808.332.7681
sandyoga@hotmail.com

Nature as Healer

Animal Therapy

Esprit de Corp Riding Academy

Small Group horseback trail rides with trotting and cantering in a lush forest reserve. English and Western lessons in the arena for ages 2 and up. Specialties include Spiritual Exploration Rides, Weddings on Horseback, and Day Camps. See our website at www.KauaiHorses.com for more information, photos and guest comments.

contact: Dale Rosenfeld
808.822.4688
riding@kauaihorses.com • www.kauaihorses.com

Ecotours

Captain Sundown

Captain Sundown is a small family business and the only sailing catamaran departing from Hanalei on the North Shore. That means you see the entire Na Pali coast. "Captain Bob" –Captain Sundown– was born & raised in Hawaii and has been sailing the Na Pali for 30 years. As he says himself "I get to do what I love every day." Sailing along the Na Pali with no noisy motor is relaxing and inspiring. The magnificence of the coast is mystical & touches people deeply. We limit our passengers to 15 on our beautiful 40ft Catamaran. Come sail & listen to Captain Bob talk story about the coast, its people, its marine life. Reservations recommended early.

808.826.5585
sundown@aloha.net

Journey Into Nature

Join Jeannie Ruman on an adventure through the natural wonders of Kaua'i. Jeannie will take you into the home of the forest dwellers where you will encounter Hawaii's nature spirits. Imagine walking into the woods, your footsteps matching the rhythm of a heartbeat; yours or the Earth's? Make them one and the same Journey with Jeanne and discover the hidden wisdom of the woods.

PO Box 143 • Kapa'a, Hawaii 96746
contact: Jeannie Ruman
808.635.5576 or 808.823.6451
merlynj@webtv.net

Let Nature's Wonders

touch you –body, mind, and spirit– bringing renewal, rejuvenation, and serenity. Options include gentle excursions into wild and wondrous places, bodywork drawing upon the energies of nature's elements: Hot Stone, Elemental Energies, Kahi Loa. Instruction, Temple Style Lomilomi, Shamanic techniques of Huna, guided visualization, ritual, and movement. • Serene Touch •

1711 Ahiahi Rd • Kapaa, HI 96746
contact: Kapua at **808.821.9301**
kapua@lava.net

NaPali Explorer

The boat adventure of a lifetime leaves from the harbor just south of Waimea. Five hour or three and one-half hour snorkeling or scenic tours up the Na Pali Coast in your choice of two different boats. Make this a must do on your vacation in Kauai.

808.338.9999 • toll free 877.335.9909
www.napali-explorer.com.

Siri Shabad

Experience the playful spontaneity of Siri as your Nature Guide to the freedom of spirit within you by opening to your divine child of one heart. Explore the Big Island of Hawaii and the Garden Island of Kaua'i's magical gifts of the volcanoes, hot water pools, dolphins in the wild, rain forests, waterfalls, rainbows and the gifts of the spirits of this sacred "aina" Catch the Aloha spirit.

Call Siri at **808.937.5446**
waipua@hawaiian.net

Ecotours

Catherine Stovall
(Eco tours, retreats & nature adventures)
PO Box 280 • Kapa'a, Hawaii 96746
808.246.8700
stovallstar5555@yahoo.com

Hawaiian Wildlife Tours
contact: Dr. Carl Berg, PhD
cberg@pixi.com
808.639.2968

Holistic Nature Walks
6141 Alapaki Rd. • Kapaa, Hi 96746
contact: Dawn Cantrell
808.822.0493
sam.dawn@gte.net

Kauai Nature Tours
contact: Dr. Chuck Blay, PhD
808.742.8305
www.teok.com

Main Artery
(Art Therapy in Nature for Healing)
contact: Leonora Orr
PO Box 603 • Hanalei, HI 96714
808.821.1521

Flower Essences

Starmen Unlimited • Kauai Healing Energies
PO Box 698 • Kilauea, HI 96754
contact: Ken Carlson
808.828.2166
starman@aloha.net • www.starmen.com

Gardens

Allerton Garden
(closed Sundays)
4425 Lawai Road (visitor's center)
Koloa, HI 96756
808.742.2623
tours@ntbg.org • www.ntbg.org

Limahuli Gardens
(closed Saturdays)
PO Box 808 • Hanalei, HI 96714
808.826.1053
lghaena@ntgb.org
www.ntbg.org

McBryde Garden
(closed Sundays)
4425 Lawai Road (visitor's center)
Koloa, HI 96756
808.742.2623
tours@ntbg.org • www.ntbg.org

Na 'Aina Kai
(open Tues, Wed, Thurs)
4101 Wallapa Rd • Kilauea, HI 96754
808.828.0525
NaAinaKai@msn.com

Herbal Therapy

W. David Stoltz, D.C.
PO Box 1964 • Kapa'a, HI 96746
808.821.0086 or 808.635.2963
david.stoltz@verizon.net

Massage and BodyWork

Island Blessings

Fern Merle-Jones has been teaching and practicing massage and healing for twenty years. She specializes in the Hawaiian lomilomi form of massage. She is available to provide lessons in lomilomi as well as do individual massages for visitors to Kauai.

PO Box 603 • Kilauea, HI 96754
contact: Fern Merle-Jones
808.828.1342 or 1.800.988.1548
bless2u@aloha.net • www.islandblessings.com

Kimberly M. Cates, LMT,

Watsu® & Waterdance® practitioner Kimberly brings nine years of professional healing experience to the table, mat and water. Crafted from years of personal exploration and travel adventures, her style is an oceanic dance fusing the modalities of East and West. She nurtures the body with an intuitive blend of Zen Shiatsu, Deep Tissue, Lomi-Lomi and Warm Water Body Integration Therapies.

PO Box 1898 • Kapa'a, HI 96745
808.651.8289
kimberly@midpac.net

Lomi Kilohana

Lomi Kilohana therapists, Paula Kressley and Toni Williams offer a wide variety of wellness opportunities including Swedish and sports massage, shiatsu, myofascial release work, deep tissue and polarity work, reiki and educational workshops.

4-1558 Kuhio • Kapaa, HI 96746
contact: Paula Kressley or Toni Williams
808.822.4619
paula@hawaiian.net • toni@aloha.net

Manawai • Aquatic Bodywork

Experience Thermal Aquatic Intergration at Manawai. Once resting in the pool's warm embrace, relax in the Zen concept of movement and stillness, float in a three-dimensional field of precise support, allowing limitless ways for your body to be safely moved, stretched, masssaged and healed. Sharron is guided by intuitive wisdom, extensive education, and fifteen years professional massage experience.

Sharron Norton LMT, Watsu Therapist, Jahara Specialist, Healing Dance Practioner & Water Dance
808.828.0928
www.watsukauai.com • allies@manawai.com

Massage and BodyWork

Massage Therapist

A Profound Way to Honor Your Being: Therapeutic Massage, with nurturing, connective awareness focus and structural integration specialty. Clients respond: "deeply intuitive," "very present, caring and aware," "after first session, I woke with no pain for the first time in months."

P.O. Box 247 • Kilauea, HI 96754
contact: Shakira Freeman
808.828.1007
earthmatters@hawaiian.net

Support your Health Massage Therapy

Nursing Care Support your Health offers therapeutic massage enhanced by 25 years of professional nursing care. Each table session creates a safe haven for the awakening of your body's wise journey toward health. In the comfort of your home or vacation getaway massage techniques are individualized for your special health goals.

contact: Ken Jopling, RN, BSN, LMT
609 Honua Road • Kapaa, HI 96746
808.635.5988
kenden@aloha.net

Trager©

Psychophysical Integration: A way of being which is lighter and freer. Through a combination of movements called Mentastics® and table bodywork, the Trager practitioner utilizes light, gentle, non-intrusive movements to facilitate deep, effective release. To schedule a Trager Bodywork session or for training information

PO Box 429 • Koloa, HI 96756
contact: Margee Faunce, MAT-2407
808.742.9387
margee@aloha.net

Allison Ebata

(barefoot shiatsu massage)
Koloa, Kauai
808.742.7226
reikiwater@hotmail.com

A Touch In Paradise Massage

1435 Kuhio Hawaii, Suite 205
Kapaa, HI 96746
contact: Paula O'Very
808.821.0444
flo@aloha.net

Alo La'a (sacred space)

(Ashtanga Yoga, Massage, Sacred Dance)
Toi Pua La'a
PO Box 1663 • Hanalei, Kauai, HI 96714
808.652.YOGA (9642)
toipualaa108@yahoo.com

Body Resonance

PO Box 1120 • Kalaheo, HI 96740
contact: Margaret Kuffel
808.742.6363
bodyresonance@hawaiian.net

Massage and BodyWork

Jin Shin Jyutsu on Kauai
6675 Iliki Street
Kapaa, Kauai, HI 96746
contact: Jim Allbrandt
808.822.2721
jallbrandt@hawaiian.net

Lida Martin
(specializes in Swedish, LomiLomi, LaStone Therapy, Deep Tissue, Shiatsu, Reiki)
Koloa, Kauai
808.742.2360

Lomi Mai Ka Na'au
(lomi massage training)
PO Box 655 • Anahola, HI 96703
contact: Penny Prior
808.822.0919

Mana Massage
PO Box 3228 • Lihue, HI 96766
contact: Manima Dancosse
808.822.4746
leslee@wwdb.org
www.manamassage.com

Mucolaulani
(Traditional Hawaiian Lomi Lomi Massage and Steam)
contact: Auntie Angeline
Kamalomalo'o St.
Anahola, HI 96703
808.822.3235

Toni's Skin & Body Care
1736 Kaehulua Place #1
Kapaa, HI 96746
contact: Toni Liljengren
(formerly Toni Rames)
808.821.0135
toniskin@hawaiian.net

Tri Health Ayurveda Center
4270 Lighthouse Road
Kilauea, HI 96754
contact: Pamela Phillips
808.828.2104
oilbath@aloha.net • www.oilbath.com

Virginia Beck, CNP
Women's Health and Wellness
West Kaua'i Clinic
4469 Waialo Road
'Ele'ele, HI 96705
808.335.0579

Complementary Treatment Therapies

Acupuncture

Classical Acupuncture
Customized health/wellness trainings enhanced by 5 element classical acupuncture treatment. Learning and practicing routinely a body of knowledge that clarifies consciousness, the unifying link of body/mind/spirit—in the spirit of aloha on beloved Kauai. Inquire for detailed description.
3265 B Kalihiwai Rd. • Kilauea, HI 96754
contact: Alton Kanter
808.828.1139
kanter@aloha.net

Ayurvedic Practice

The Ayurvedic Center
PO Box 127 • Hanalei, HI 96714
contact: Darci Frankl
808.826.1811
darciayur@aol.com
www.panchkarma.net

Tri Health Ayurveda Center
4270 Lighthouse Road
Kilauea, HI 96754
contact: Pamela Phillips
808.828.2104
oilbath@aloha.net
www.oilbath.com

Colon Hydrotherapy

Kauai Colonics

(colon hydrotherapy/massage/energy healing)
contact: Annalia
4938 B Kuhio Hwy • Kapa'a, HI 96746
808.822.2686
annaliaomm@earthlink.net

Energy Therapies

Lomi Kilohana

Lomi Kilohana therapists, Paula Kressley and Toni Williams offer a wide variety of wellness opportunities including Swedish and sports massage, shiatsu, myofascial release work, deep tissue and polarity work, reiki and educational workshops.
4-1558 Kuhio Hawaii • Kapaa, HI 96746
contact: Paula Kressley or Toni Williams
808.822.4619
paula@hawaiian.net • toni@aloha.net

Siglinde Schwenzl

Experience Siglinde's deep healing touch, feel the tension melt away and reconnect with the unlimited multi-dimensional being that you are! Ten years client-based practice integrating light touch (CranioSacral, Lymphdrainage, Reiki) with deep tissue releasing (Neuromuscular, Myofascial) brings alignment and free flow of energy. Enjoy the wild beauty of Kauai and discover the "islands within."
siglindes@earthlink.net
808.651.3992

Deborah Burnham

(land and sea-based sound, touch and movement practice)
5609 Honua Road
Kapa'a, HI 96746
808.651.4534
freebeing@juno.com
www.inawareness.com

Inquiry

(somatic learning for transformational healing and self renewal)
PO Box 609 • Anahola, HI 96703
contact: Risa Kaparo, Ph.D.
808.821.8884
risa@somaticlearning.com

Dr. Liz Lipski

(body alignment technique)
4166 Momi Street
Kilauea, HI 96754
808.828.6402
dr.lipski@innovativehealing.com
www.innovativehealing.com

Tanya V. Zychlinsky

(energy healing and intuitive readings)
PO Box 2108
Kapa'a, HI 96746
808.823.0399 cell 635.1931

Holistic Health Practitioner

Acupuncture and Natural Healing Center

Latifa's work is a combination of thirty years of intensive and continual study and practice of complimentary medicine with a goal of facilitating transformation at a core level to release symptoms and the beliefs which accompany them. This is accomplished by a combination of Acupuncture Natural and Vibrational modalities. She addresses issues of stress, illness, allergies, pain relief on an acute as well as chronic level.

4620 Kapuna Road • Kilauea, HI 96754
contact: Latifa Amdur **808.828.1155**
iam@aloha.net

Body Talk

Roger uses kinesiology, i.e. muscle testing to access the innate wisdom of the body facilitating a conscious expansion of your ability to heal on a physical, emotional, mental and spiritual level. By tapping into the wisdom of the body he uses a variety of techniques to guide the process of addressing and healing from whatever issue arises.

Roger Denisewicz
808.828.1946 • toll free 1.800.431.5360
Oahu: 808.521.8593
bodytalk@gte.net • www.soulpurposeacademy.com

W. David Stoltz, D.C. Chiropractor

Medicine Maker • Herbal instructor • Emergency and outcalls. David's personal approach to health is a blend of manual Chiropractic, nutrition, Western and Hawaiian Herbalism. He treats most acute and chronic conditions. Eighteen years experience, flexible scheduling, gentle yet dynamic care. Herbal Hikes and instruction available on Kauai.

PO Box 1964 • Kapa'a, HI 96746
808.635.2063 or 808.635.2963
david.stoltz@verizon.net

Kauai Center for Holistic Medicine

(Vega Testing, Live Blood Analysis, Nutritional Practitioner)

4504 Kukui St. #13 • Kapa'a, HI 96746
contact: Joe Holt
808.823.0994

Dr. Marilyn Roderick

P.O.Box 216 • Hanalei, HI 96714
808.826.9349

Kinesiology

Allies in Love & Healing • Specialized Kinesiology

Combines muscle testing with principles of Chinese Medicine to assess energy & system function, which uncovers the cause & symptom of imbalance. Your body's healing response is enable with reflex & acupressure points, specific movements, massage, Bach Flower Remedies, color/sound therapy, nutritional guidance. This brings harmony to all aspects of the Being-mental, emotional, physical, and spiritual bodies become cooperative, to support affirming life choice.

PO Box 1269 • Kilauea, HI 96754
contact: Sharron Norton **808.828.0928**
allies@manawai.com • www.manawai.com

Naturopathic Medicine

Natural Health & Pain Relief Clinic

Miles Greenberg, ND
Naturopathic Physician
3093 Akahi Street • Lihue, HI 96766
and
4270 B Kilauea Rd. • Kilauea, HI 96754
808.245.2277
miles@hawaiian.net

Dr. Leia Melead

Naturopathic Physician, Licensed Acupuncturist
1435 Kuhio Highway, Suite 206
Kapaa, HI 96746
808.822.2087
Dr.Leia@medscape.com

Fitness

ANARA Spa

Hyatt Regency Kauai Resort
808.742.1234 ext 4848

Captain Don's Wind Venture

(Custom catamaran adventures, rides, lessons and rentals)
Captain Don Bogowitz
Kalapaki Bay, HI
808.245.8550
captdon1111@yahoo.com

Kauai Athletic Club

Kukui Grove Shopping Center
808.245.5381

Oceanfront Pilates in Paradise

PO Box 281 • Koloa, HI 96756
contact: Sharon Agli
808.651.8201
fitforlifesja@hotmail.com

One-on-One Fitness Training

PO Box 1163 • Kapa'a, HI 96746
contact: Murray Harris, ACSM Certified
808.652.1236
jewelofwilson@hotmail.com

Pilates in Paradise

(Personal Trainer, Pilates, Gyrotonics)
Ching Young Village Suite B6
Hanalei, HI 96714
contact: Mary Jane Kleiman
808.825.0342
maryjane@aloha.ne

Princeville Health Club & Spa

Princeville Resort
808.826.5030

The Fitness Center

Kauai Marriott
808.245.5050 ext 5110

The Fitness Center

Sheraton Kauai
808.742.1661

The Earth Team Works

PO Box 280 • Kapa'a, HI 96746
808.246.8700
Eco tours, retreats, and
nature adventures
www.theearthteamworks.com
info@theearthteamworks.com

Kauai Humane Society Volunteer Program

"Dog Buddy or Cat Cuddler"
PO Box 3330
3-825 Kaumualii Highway
Lihue, HI 96766
808.632.0610
khs@pixi.com
www.kauaihumanesociety.org

Mahina's Women's Guest House on Kauai

Mahina's Women's Guest House provides clean, quiet, comfortable, attractive and affordable beachfront accommodations to women travelers. The wellness vacationer can experience sunrise beach walks outside our door, massage on site by appointment, and yoga classes daily at a nearby yoga studio. Alternative healers, communal women-only space is conducive to healing
4333 Panihi Rd • Kapa'a, HI 96746
contact: Sharon Gonsalves
808.823.9364
mahinas@hawaiian.net • www.mahinas.com

Manawai Guest Suite & Wellness Retreat

Nestled in a serene valley with pond and adjacent waterfall, a short walk to Secret Beach and Kalihiwai Bay. From the mediation garden and Aquatic Therapy pool,
enter into a large, light, and airy suite; a futon couch, and table for two at the garden window.
808.828.0928
allies@manawai.com • vrbo.com/vvrbo/13360.htm

Gloria's Bed and Breakfast

4464 Lawai Beach Road
Koloa, HI 96756
contact: Gloria & Bob Merkle
808.742.6995

Grantham Vacation Rentals

3176 Poipu Rd.
Koloa, HI 96756
1.800.325.5701
www.grantham-resorts.com
info@grantham-resorts.com

Hale Ho'o Maha (House of Rest)
PO Box 422 • Kilauea, HI 96754
1.800.828.2046 toll free
or 808.828.1341
hoomaha@aloha.net
www.aloha.net/~hoomaha

Hale Kua
Box 949 • 4896 E. Kua Rd.
Lawai, HI 96765
contact: Kathy Cowran
800.440.4353
halekua@aloha.net
planet-hawaii.com/halekua/

Poipu Oceanview Bed and Breakfast
1675-2 Makanui Road
Poipu, Kauai, HI 96756-9539
www.poipuoceanview.com
808.742.6461
or cell 808.651.5975

Taro Patch Hale
(the back of Hanalei Valley)
contact: Lance Laney or Mina Morita
808.826.6612
lklaney@aloha.net

The Rainbow Hale Guesthouse
(Haena area)
808.826.9386
info@rainbowguesthouse.com
www.rainbowguesthouse.com

Rosewood B&B and Vacation Rental
Kaua'i, HI
808.822.5216
rosewood@aloha.net
www.rosewoodkauai.com

Victoria Place
P.O. Box 930 • Lawai, HIi 96765
contact: Edee Seymour
808.332.9300

Waimea Plantation Cottages
9400 Kaumualii Highway #367 •
Waimea, HI 96796
808.338.1625
www.aston-hotels.com

BOOKS • RELATED TO A WELLNESS EXPERIENCE IN HAWAI'I.

PUBLICATIONS AND BOOKSTORES that we identify here are those with a particular interest in and commitment to promoting balance and harmony. Books provide the reader with information about Hawai'i as it relates to achieving wellness on all levels of our being.

ESPECIALLY FOR CHILDREN

The Hawaiian Monk Seal, by Patrick Ching, University of Hawai'i Press

Sea Turtles of Hawai'i, by Patrick Ching, University of Hawai'i Press

Flowing to the Sea, by Maura O'Connor, Moanalua Gardens Foundaton

Maui and His Magical Deeds, by Kats Kajiyama, Barnaby Books

HAWAI'I'S PLANT AND AMIMAL WORLD

Hawai'i's Sea Creatures, by John Hoover, Mutual Publishing

Hawai'i Fishes, A Guide for Snorklers, Divers & Aquartists, by John Hoover, Mutual Publishing

COOKBOOKS

Ethnic Foods of Hawai'i, by Ann Kondo Corum, Bess Press

Hawai'i Cooks from the Garden, by Maili Gardley, Mutual Publishing

The Food of Paradise, by Rachel Laudan, University of Hawai'i Press

HEALING PLANTS AND PRACTICES

Aloe Vera: Nature's Soothing Healer, by Diane Gage, Healing Arts Press

Aloe Vera: Nature's Soothing Healer, by Diane Gage, Healing Arts Press, Rochester, Vt.

Hawaiian Magic & Spirituality, by Scott Cunningham, Lewellyn Publications

Hawaiian Herbal Medicine, by June Gutmanis, Island Heritage

Ka Lama Kukui: Hawaiian Psychology, by William Rezentes, III, Phd, Aali'i Books

Kahuna Healing, by Serge King, A Quest Book

Noni: Aspirin of the Ancients, by Diana Fairechild, Flyana Rhyme Publishing, www.flyana.com

Plants in Hawaiian Medicine, by Beatrice Krauss, Bess Press

Practical Folk Medicine of Hawai i, by Likeke McBride, Petroglyph Press

HAWAIIAN HISTORY AND CULTURE

Exploring Lost Hawai'i: Places of Power, History, Mystery & Magic, by Ellie and William Crowe, Island Heritage Publishers

Ku Kanaka: A Search for Hawaiian Values, by George Kanahele, University of Hawai'i Press

Nana I Ke Kumu: Look to the Source, by Pukui, Haertig, Lee, McDermott, and Hui Hanai, Queen Liliuokalani Children's Center, 1300 Halona Street, Honolulu, HI 96817

Tales from the Night Rainbow, by Koko Willis and Pali Jae Lee, Night Rainbow Publishing Co, c/o Native Books, Inc. nativebk@lava.net, www.nativebookshawaii.com

Voices of Wisdom: Hawaiian Elders Speak, by MJ Harden, Aka Press, 103 Johnson Road, Kula, HI 96790, mjh@maui.net

HIKING & BIKING

Hiking Kaua'i, by Robert Smith, AHOA Publications

Hiking Maui, by Robert Smith, AHOA Publications

Hiking Hawai'i, by Robert Smith AHOA Publications

Kaua'i Trails, by Kathy Morey, Wilderness Press

Hawai'i Trails, by Kathy Morey, Wilderness Press

The Backpackers Guide to Hawai'i, by Stuart Ball, University of Hawai'i Press

Exploring Hawai'i Parklands, by Marnie Hagman, Falcon Press

Paddling Hawai'i, by Audrey Sutherland, University of Hawai'i Press

Hikers Guide to the Hawaiian Islands, by Stuart Ball, Jr., University of Hawai'i Press

Mountain Biking the Hawaiian Islands, by John Alford, 'Ohana Publishing

MUSIC • HEALING FAVORITES

Pure Hawaiian, Music & Images of Hawai'i, (vocal, mellow)

Hawaiian From the Heart

Memories of Hawai'i, (part of a series) Henry Allen, steel guitar (mellow)

Kika Kila Meets Ki hi alu, Cyril Pahinui & Bob Brozman (instrumental, steel & slack key guitar duets)

Chants of Hawai'i, George Naope

Humpback Whales, Songs Across the Pacific, Pacific Whale Foundation

Whale Cry and the Ocean, Lisa Lering & Pierre Grill

Hawaiian Slack Key Guitar Masters Collection, Dancing Cat label

Kolonahe from the Gentle Wind, Keola Beamer, Dancing Cat label (vocal & instrumental)

Pekelo Day, (chanting, traditional instruments, natures sounds)

Lineage, Sam Kapu III

Boat Days in Hawai'i, Moana Chang

Ho'okupu "The Gift", Moses Kahumoku

Alone in the World and **E Ala E,** Israel Kamakawiwio'ole

PUBLICATIONS • (PRINT AND ONLINE)

SPORTS

Hawai'i Golf News and Travel (lists tournaments)
PO Box 6107 • Honolulu, HI 96818 • 808.625.9860

Hawai'i Race Magazine
9 N. Pauahi, #200 • Honolulu, HI 96817 • 808.538.0330 • www.hawaiirace.com

Ke Kukui: A Healing Island Resource Guide (Big Island of Hawai'i)
P.O. Box 437200 • Kamuela, HI 96743 • 808.887.1280 • fminfo@fivemtn.org

HEALTH MAGAZINES & WEB BASED RESOURCES

Zento (Your Guide to Transformational Travel)
5966 Heamoi Place • Kapa'a, HI 96746 • 808.821.2880
info@zentomag.com • www.zentomag.com

Maui Health Online Magazine - Lead By Example!
Maui and surrounding areas. • Jeff Parham, DC - Editor • www.mauihealth.org

Hawai'i Health Guide
PO Box 562 • Haleiwa, Hawai'i 96712 • 808.638.0888
info@hawaiihealthguide.com • http://www.HawaiiHealthGuide.com

Hawaiian Lomilomi Association
www.lomilomi.org

Holomana 'O Hawai'i • Hawai'i Healing Arts Network
Sharman O'Shea, Executive Director • 808.887.0044
holomana@turquoise.net • www. hawaii-healing.com

Glossary

Acupuncture • Acupuncture has a long history in Traditional Oriental Medicine. Very fine sterilized needles are inserted into specific points along the body's vital energy pathways, or meridians. This stimulates, disperses and regulates the flow of vital energy in the body. Acupuncture treats chronic acute conditions, offers pain relief, prevents illness and enhances the body's inner healing abilities.

Ag-Tourism • Ag-tourism, one of the fastest growing areas of the tourist industry, is about getting back to nature. People who want to "return to the land" and take a learning vacation that gives them hands-on experience with a plethora of farming and ranching activities in a picturesque rural environment, can experience what has been traditionally called "farm stay."

Animal Therapy • Animal therapy involves using an animal's innate compassion and ability to connect emotionally with humans in a way that brings forth the inner healer of the client and soothes emotional and mental distress.

Aromatherapy • Aromatherapy is the holistic application of essential oils to improve physical, mental, emotional and spiritual well being. Each essential oil possesses distinct therapeutic properties that can promote health and prevent disease. By supporting and harmonizing both body and mind, they have been found to increase vitality, alleviate tension, and fight infection.

Art and Art Therapy • Art and art therapy recognizes the creative medium of art and artistic expression as a means for uplifting and shifting each of us to our authentic self. Art therapy emphasizes the healing, integrating and ultimately joyful experience of contacting one's own inner sources of creativity.

Astrology and Numerology • Astrology is the study of the influences of celestial bodies upon living and non-living things. It is an art that uses the position and influence of the planets in our solar system to enable us to better understand ourselves emotionally, mentally, physically and spiritually. Like astrology, numerology draws on ancient wisdom using numbers derived from an individual's birth, name, etc. to better understand oneself and one's life pattern.

Body Work and Massage • Many types and styles of massage therapy and bodywork offer both therapeutic and relaxing effects. Through the touch and manipulation of a person's soft tissue and muscles, physical and emotional stress and blockages are relieved, circulation is increased and pain and discomfort are diminished or eliminated.

Breath Therapy • Breath therapy uses the breath to reach and release physical, emotional and psychological blocks. This approach bypasses the unconscious defensive structure, allowing the individual to heal old wounds, break dysfunctional relational patterns and live more fully and authentically in the present moment in ways that conventional "talk" therapy often cannot address.

Chiropractic • Chiropractic is an increasingly accepted form of treatment for a variety of physical conditions. It specializes in detecting, locating and correcting spinal displacements which may block or alter the flow of nerve energy. The chiropractor seeks to analyze and correct these displacements through spinal manipulation or adjustments, resulting in enhanced health, balance and energy.

Colon Hydrotherapy • Colon Hydrotherapy is a gentle and thorough intestinal cleansing treatment using purified water and herbs which bathes away debris and toxins in the colon and cells. It leads to vibrant energy, healthy elimination, and assists many other health practices in being more effective.

CranioSacral Therapy • This diagnostic and healing approach uses corrective pressure to the cranium and spine to regulate the cranial rhythms impulse which affects every cell in the body.

Crystal Healing • Crystal Healing is an advanced modality that works directly with the light, color, beauty and perfect geometric forms that the mineral kingdom provides to assist us in balancing all aspects of our being (mental, spiritual, emotional and physical).

Dance, Movement and Sound Therapy • This approach to therapy uses movements, body awareness exercises and/or breathing exercises to improve health. Dancing opens the way to the inner self. Physical and emotional tensions loosen and slowly dissolve. New vitality returns with a fresh view to life, uncovering hidden blockages and healing emotional wounds.

Ecotourism • Ecotourism is nature and culture-based tourism that is ecologically sustainable and supports the well-being of local communities.

Energy Therapy • Energy therapy is based on the principle that our body emotes energy which can be seen and felt by those trained to do so. Energy therapists work with a person's energy field in identifying and treating inner emotional and physical distress

Flower Essences • Each flower has its own unique energy signature. Flower essences activate and release energy patterns by balancing, repairing and rebuilding imbalances on the physical, emotional, mental and spiritual levels. A flower essence practitioner can facilitate the choice of the appropriate essences for an individual's condition.

Fitness • Fitness promotes overall wellness by strengthening muscles, enhancing lung capacity and improving blood circulation.

Hawaiian Healing Therapies • Hawaiian healing therapies draw on the ancient wisdom of the Hawaiian people. These therapies are based on the belief that pursuit of wellness must address the Higher Self, the conscious mind, the subconscious and the body. Hawaiian healers use plants and herbs, massage, prayer and hypnotic suggestion to identify and address conditions that are distressed within their patient. Being "right with spirit" is a requirement for the healer and is the ultimate goal of the treatment.

Herbal Therapy • Herbal therapies are frequently used by Traditional Chinese Medicine practitioners as well as indigenous peoples such as Hawaiian healers. They draw on ancient wisdom to identify and prepare natural herbs in treating a variety of conditions. Herbs must be grown, picked and prepared in a particular way in order to maximize their effectiveness.

Healing Products of Hawaii • Healing products of Hawaii are either created from the herbs of Hawaii or are manufactured in Hawaii

Holistic Health Practitioner • The holistic health practitioner recognizes that mind, heart, body and spirit are all connected to the state of a person's health. These practitioners work with a variety of modalities to assess and address all four levels of our wisdom to activate the inner healer and return the body to it's natural state of balance.

Homeopathy • Homeopathy recognizes that every living organism possesses an intelligent, self healing capacity that seeks to restore and maintain a state of optimum health. Homeopathy is based on the idea that very diluted doses of medicines that produce symptoms of a disease in healthy people will cure that disease in afflicted patients by activating the inner healer.

Healing Vacations • Experiencing healing activities in a healing place away from the distractions and responsibilities of daily life brings new meaning and possibility to the time spent on vacation.

Hiking • Hiking is a wellness experience involving planned exercise in nature offered either by organizations and companies or local groups open to or catering to visitors

Hypnotherapy • Hypnotherapy is a relaxed, yet highly focused, natural state of mind. Hypnosis empowers you to discover and clear the underlying causes of unwanted attitudes, behaviors and emotional responses.

Intuitive Guidance • Intuitive guidance is used by those with advanced intuitive abilities to tap into their deepest wisdom and guides as well as access the deepest knowing of the client in order to address life issues and resolve problems

Iridology • Iridology uses the appearance of the eye, in particular the iris to determine the overall health of the client. Its focus is on pinpointing weaknesses as a preventative measure. Iridology is sometimes used as an adjunct to diagnostic tools by naturopathic and homeopathic physicians.

Kinesiology • Kinesiology is a muscle testing technique which accesses the innate intelligence of the body, revealing subconscious information regarding physical, mental, emotional and spiritual states.

Life Coaching • Life coaching uses a variety of techniques to help clarify values and set goals in order to live a more balanced, harmonious and fulfilling life.

Lymph Drainage Therapy sm • LDT is an original hands-on method of lymphatic drainage developed by Bruno Chikly, MD, of France. Using exacting anatomical science and distinctive manual processes, LDT enables practitioners to detect the specific rhythm, direction, depth and quality of the lymphatic flow. LDT benefits the immune system, relieves chronic pain, edema, scars, wrinkles, stretch marks, etc.

Massage and Body Work • Many types and styles of massage therapy and bodywork offer both therapeutic and relaxing effects. Through the touch and manipulation of a person's soft tissue and muscles, physical and emotional stress and blockages are relieved, circulation is increased and pain and discomfort are diminished or eliminated.

Meditation • Meditation includes a wide range of practices that involve training one's awareness or attention to bring the body and mind into greater harmony.

Naturopathic Medicine • Naturopathic medicine treats symptoms and disease without the use of surgery or synthetic drugs. It uses interventions like fasting, special diets, massage, and herbal remedies which support the body's inherent ability to heal itself.

Nutrition • Nutrition involves the combination, preparation and assimilation of foods and supplements to support health and immunity for various constitutions and conditions in the human body.

Neurofeedback • This is an advanced form of biofeedback that works directly with the brain and the central nervous system.

Pain Management • Pain management work is based on the belief that, while a painful condition may exist, suffering is not necessary. Pain management techniques can range from high powered drugs to meditation, biofeedback, hypnosis and herbs.

Personal Development/Psychology/Relationship Therapy • There are many therapies and philosophies that fall under this category. Generally, they are based on the premise that we can live life more fully and with greater inner peace when we become aware of and consciously seek to resolve beliefs and heal emotional wounds that are limiting us.

Preventive Medical Screening • Preventive medical screening uses the most advanced technology to help clients identify physical problem areas before they manifest.

Pilates • Pilates is fitness-training program that combines muscle strengthening and increasing flexibility. It can be modified for the frail and injured as well as highly conditioned athletes

Psychic • Psychic therapy involves someone whose sensitivity to non-physical or supernatural forces and influences is developed beyond the experience of the average person.

Reflexology • Reflexology is the application to specific points on the feet, hands or ears which correspond with organs and tissues throughout the body. Reflexology addresses a wide range of illnesses, ailments and pain relief.

Reiki/Healing Touch • A powerful system using hand placements to channel energy to the recipient. It promotes greater wholeness on all levels by balancing and aligning the physical, mental, emotional and spiritual bodies.

Relationship Therapy • Relationship counseling works with individuals, couples or families to promote greater harmony and balance between individuals.

Retreats • Retreats are experiences focused on bringing like-minded people together for wellness experiences addressing the well-being of mind, heart, body and spirit.

Retreat Centers • Retreat centers are designed for groups of people to share space and personal growth in a peaceful, natural environment.

Rolfing • Rolfing works with fascia, the thin, elastic connective tissue enveloping muscles, to diminish the negative effect of emotional and physical stress.

Sacred Healing • Sacred healing uses rituals, symbols and ceremonies to achieve healing and harmony at the highest levels of our being.

Spas • Spas are specially designed centers that provide individualized treatment addressing most often the physical well being of the client through stress reducing procedures such as massage, aromatherapy, mud baths, etc. Increasingly, spas are opening up to the interconnectedness of mind, heart, body and spirit as it relates to an individuals health and well being.

Spiritual Healing • This focuses primarily on working with the spiritual aspects of ourselves and our connection with Spirit to promote healing, harmony and balance

Sports Medicine • This is a specialized form of medical intervention addressing the goals, physical hazards and capacity for achievement of athletes and those engaged in sports.

Sports Hypnotherapy • Hypnotherapy is a relaxed, yet highly focused, natural state of mind. When used with sports, it guides a focused awareness to create maximum performance.

Tai Chi • Tai chi combines movement, breathing and life energy awareness and focuses on quieting the mind and restoring balance in the body

Tantra • Tantra is both a science and a discipline. It teaches improved communication, breath exercises and a practice to open up critical energy centers.

Traditional Chinese Medicine • This is a comprehensive 3000 year old process of preventing and, if necessary, treating physical ailments. The underlying principle is that health is achieved through a balance of "chi" or energy in the body. Foods, herbs, acupuncture and other forms of treatment are used to achieve that balance.

Trager • Through a combination of movements called Mentastics® and table bodywork, the Trager practitioner utilizes light, gentle, non-intrusive movements to facilitate deep, effective release.

Watsu • A Watsu session ideally takes place in a pool of chest-high water, warmed to 94-97* F, and lasts 45-90 minutes. It is a form of water massage which promotes deep relaxation and relief of physical tension and pain.

Yoga • There are many forms of yoga, all of which seek to help access a deeper consciousness and encourage physical, mental, emotional and spiritual well-being. Some of the more well known forms are hatha, bhakti and kriya.

Eighty Ways to Have a Wellness Experience in Hawai'i

THE ISLAND OF O'AHU

The Island of Kaua'i

Index

A

I

N

O

P

Q

R

Y

Z

~ About the Authors ~

Betsy and Laura Crites are sisters who are committing their energies to sharing with the world information about the resources Hawai'i offers to find wellness on all levels—mind, heart, body and spirit. This commitment grows out of their own healing journeys in Hawai'i.

My first encounter with the Big Island was on a wellness vacation in February 2000. I was weak from years of fatigue, muscle, joint, and nerve pain and unsure about my vocation and life purpose. My hope was simply to return to my life on the mainland with renewed energy. My journey was not to be so simple.

In those three weeks in North Kohala, I received regular treatments, meditated, ate well, and walked for exercise. Perhaps more powerful were the meaningful coincidences that became part of my healing experience... upon entering a sacred site and resolving to reactivate my prayer life, a praying mantis appeared on a tree. A plea for guidance before falling asleep resulted in an unequivocal word planted in my mind upon awakening: "courage", as if to say "there will be rough seas ahead, but you must face them if you truly wish to heal". The treatment I received turned out to be only the beginning of my recovery. Perhaps more important, my relationship with the Big Island launched me into a healing journey, expanding my understanding of myself and my health and leading to major life changes.

Betsy Crites

The healing powers of Hawai'i have worked their way with me, off and on, for over 20 years. I recognized their potential in the late 60's as I flew as a stewardess transporting troops back and forth to Vietnam. It was an R&R destination for military stationed there—a place to recover sufficiently to return to battle.

I moved to Hawai'i in the early 80's engrossed in the domestic violence movement. My Waikīkī office, as director of a domestic violence counseling agency, was two blocks from the beach. Often, I escaped the stories of violence that were part of our daily fare by sitting on the sea wall. The clear blue water, gentle curl of the waves and limitless horizon soothed my soul. Walks in the mountains were equally cleansing.

For the last three years I have shifted my focus from wounding to healing, from violence to peace. In doing so, my joy in life and hope for the planet have returned.

Laura Crites

Order Form

Telephone orders: **808.223-2533**
toll free: **866.223.6941**
fax: **808.955.4233**
Aloha Wellness Publishers
2333 Kapiolani Blvd., #2108
Honolulu, HI 96826-4444
Online: www.alohawellnesstravel.com

Please send _______ copies of The Call to Hawai'i

$15/ea *(tax incl.)* $ __________
S/H: $3.50 *(U.S. destinations)*
$1.50 each add'l copy $ __________

Total $ __________

USPS shipping to United States destinations.
Call for information on express shipping, international rates and bulk orders.

Name ______________________________
Business ______________________________
Address ______________________________
____
City ____________ *State* ______ *Zip* _____ - ____
Tele ____________ *Fax* ______________
email ______________________________

Ship to : (if different from above)
Name ______________________________
Address ______________________________
____
City ____________ *State* ______ *Zip* _____ - ____

Payment:
☐ Check or Money Order (Payable to Aloha Wellness Travel)
☐ MasterCard ☐ Visa

Card# ______________ *Exp. date* ____ / ____
Name on card ______________________
signature __________________________

visit our website
www.alohawellnesstravel.com.